MAKING
SENSE
OF
BURGUNDY

Also by Matt Kramer:

Making Sense of Wine (1989)

MAKING
SENSE
OF
BURGUNDY

Matt Kramer

WILLIAM MORROW
AND COMPANY, INC.
New York

Recognizing the importance of preserving what has been written, it is the policy of William Morrow and Company, Inc., and its imprints and affiliates to have the books it publishes printed on acid-free paper, and we exert our best effort to that end.

Library of Congress Cataloging-in-Publication Data

Kramer, Matt.
    Making sense of burgundy / Matt Kramer.
       p.   cm.
    Includes bibliographical references and index.
    ISBN 0-688-08667-5
    1. Wine and wine making—France—Burgundy. I. Title.
TP553K63 1990
641.2'2'09444—dc20   90-38036
                                  CIP

Printed in the United States of America

BOOK DESIGN BY PAUL CHEVANNES

For Lalou Bize-Leroy

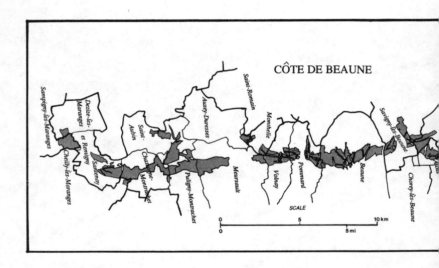

CÔTE DE BEAUNE

Sampigny-lès-Maranges
Dezize-lès-Maranges
et Remigny
Cheilly-lès-Maranges
Santenay
Saint-Aubin
Chassagne-Montrachet
Puligny-Montrachet
Auxey-Duresses
Saint-Romain
Meursault
Monthelie
Volnay
Pommard
Beaune
Savigny-lès-Beaune
Aloxe
Chorey-lès-Beaune

SCALE

0   5   10 km

0   5 mi

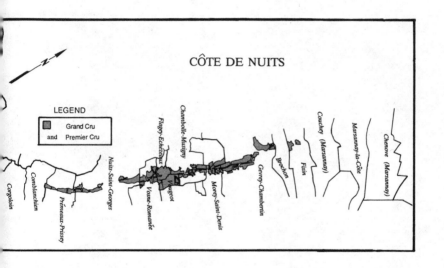

CÔTE DE NUITS

LEGEND

Grand Cru
and   Premier Cru

Preface

The vineyard and wine are great mysteries. Alone in the vegetable kingdom, the vine gives us a true understanding of the savor of the earth. And how faithfully it is translated! Through it we realize that even flint can be living, yielding, nourishing. Even the unemotional chalk weeps in wine, golden tears.

—COLETTE, *Prisons et Paradis*

omething about Burgundy excites spirituality. Where Napa Valley restores hope that beauty has a future in the modern era and Bordeaux simply makes one want to live, so as to continue to sample its extraordinary array, Burgundy elicits a different emotion. Even the most skeptical are willing, after savoring a genuinely great Burgundy, to concede that there may well be—dare one say it?— a Presence in the universe beyond our own.

One thing is clear: The Earth speaks in Burgundy as it does nowhere else. And the grapevine is its interpreter. "The vine gives us a true understanding of the savor of the Earth," observes Colette with admirable concision. Nowhere else has so much effort been expended in defining the nuances of its message.

The wine of Burgundy can be said to be five wines, as there are five distinct subregions that make up the whole of what is today called "Burgundy." Historically, it is one of the oldest winegrowing regions, with a viticultural history that dates back well over a thousand years. Politically, it was once the grandest and richest duchy in France, and remained outside the thrall of the French monarchy until the fifteenth century. What constituted Burgundy then would today encompass present-day Burgundy, Franche-Comté, Lorraine, Holland, and Belgium.

It is partly because of this historical context and partly because of a common employment of a same few grape varieties that the five distinct districts of Chablis, Côte d'Or, Côte Chalonnaise, Mâconnais, and Beaujolais are collectively referred to as "Burgundy."

In practice, a reference to Burgundy today almost invariably refers to the wines of the Côte d'Or, a thirty-one-mile-long escarpment that, by virtue of the beauty of the wines it creates and the prices they fetch, deserves its title of the "Slope of Gold." The Côte d'Or *is* Burgundy, and hereafter the term *Burgundy* will refer to the Côte d'Or only.

The casual observer of wine could be forgiven for wondering why people pay the prices they do for Burgundy. It's easy to conclude that it's a matter of fashion and snobbery. Some of it surely is that. But it is more complicated than a bunch of wine-bibbers apparently being fleeced by wily old Burgundians. Fashion explains little about Burgundy. It's more a matter of passion. A world-spanning tribe of Burgundy lovers is transfixed by a vision of beauty that only this one spot of land can offer. To understand why, it is necessary to comprehend the force behind the wine passion.

As with any other passion, only a certain number of those touched by wine are transformed by it. Millions of people drive cars and wear clothes, yet only a relative few find a particular joy or meaning in automobiles or clothing. When they do, they delve ever deeper into the complications of the subject. Usually there is an informing element. With clothes it's fabric; with cars it's engineering.

With wine, it's a search for "somewhere-ness." You taste a wine, knowing nothing about its origins or status. A truly great wine, no matter what the grape variety or country of origin, enables you to say, "I don't know anything about this wine, but I know one thing: This wine didn't come from just anywhere." This is the Burgundy passion.

No wine anywhere gives a greater sensation of "somewhereness" than Burgundy. One sip of a Chevalier-Montrachet and its particularity is so great that its source could only be so small. This grips Burgundy lovers. This is what makes them so willing to pay such high prices and, more than that, so willing to devote so much exacting attention to what is, after all, seemingly just a wine.

"Somewhere-ness" in a wine is more than just an expression of a grape. To be a good Cabernet Sauvignon or Chardonnay is a modest calling. The proof of that is the enormous number of good Cabernets and Chardonnays we now can find from California, Australia, Washington, Italy, and elsewhere. Many, if not most, are interchangeable, blurred by the Esperanto of varietalness. As Gertrude Stein said in another context, "There isn't any there there."

Memorable wine is as much a map as a taste. It is why wine lovers in general, and Burgundy lovers more than anyone else, spend so much pleasurable effort exploring the distinctions between one vineyard and another. It is why, upon tasting a blurred, muddied bottling of a wine known for being nearly a homing device of "somewhere-ness," a Burgundy drinker can become so offended. It's not the money—although that hurts. It's the loss of place. This is why a thirty-one-mile slip of land, the Côte d'Or, has captivated wine drinkers for a millennium. Through its wines, one has the sensation of having found a terrestrial crossroads, a place where man and plant and planet meet.

A
Cautionary
Foreword

I t is impossible to examine the wines of Burgundy without acknowledging at the outset a contradiction that cannot easily, if at all, be reconciled: Red and white Burgundies today are at once better than they have been in decades and yet perilously close to betraying the voice of the land that is uniquely theirs to express.

Virtually everything that follows serves to try to unravel the reasons for this contradiction that Burgundies are simultaneously improving and declining, but this declaration deserves at least a brief explanation from the outset.

The variability in the quality of red and white Burgundies is hardly unique to our time, nor is it a calculated malevolence. Winemakers and shippers have been engaged in creating poor-quality Burgundy as well as good since the first casks were made available to a thirsty market centuries ago. One can no more blame the contemporary erosion in quality on a single generation of growers and shippers than one can finger the last wave of a storm as the sole cause of the erosion of a shoreline. What is happening in Burgundy today cannot be separated from what transpired twenty-five years ago, or even three hundred years ago.

But there is a distinction to the current situation that renders it different from anything in Burgundy's long, convoluted history as a fine-wine region. Now, the erosion of quality is taking place at a moment when the degree of control in ensuring quality in red and white Burgundies has never been greater. Control of the vineyards has never been greater on the part of the state, courtesy of the Appellation Contrôlée system; control in the winemaking process has never before been available to such a degree to the winemaker.

Yet sometimes when this control has been exercised, it has served to create more Burgundy of lower quality to sell at an increasingly higher price. The French government threw in the regulatory towel years ago, when it relinquished any real control in limiting yields. Some winemakers have employed the latest technology less to enhance wine than to ease their labor, such as using filters or centrifuges to clean up wines in one harsh swoop rather than nurse them carefully over time. This is the peculiar indignity of our time. Those who look only at the formidable prices see near-criminality, or at least a measure of venality, and they despair. Those who look at the near-heroic efforts of strong-willed winegrowers today will discover, I believe, reason for considerable hope—even joy.

There are now more winemakers, many of them in their twenties and early thirties, who are resolved to create the most authentic expressions of site and grape possible. They are equipped with excellent technical educations in winemaking, as well as modern equipment that can help translate their thoughts into controlled action in the cellar. These producers already are giving us the most authentic and purest wines issued from Burgundy in generations. They are cited and lauded in this book wherever possible.

Yet these same producers, as well as their less-committed colleagues, are subject to commercial pressures that are more intense today than ever in the thousand-year-old history of Burgundy. The pressure is easily understood. It comes down to the fact that any Burgundy sporting a famous name—Chambertin, Clos de Vougeot, Puligny-Montrachet, and so on—commands a high price regardless of quality.

What is galling—and endlessly tempting—to the producer committed to the highest quality is that his or her wine rarely fetches much of a premium relative to the same wine offered by a greedier grower. With few exceptions, buyers will pay only so much for a certain appellation and no more. Where one plot in a famous vineyard is pruned severely and yields just thirty hectoliters per hectare (about 2.2 tons of grapes per acre), a neighboring plot might gush twice that amount. Because the demand is so intense, both wines sell easily, yet one grower reaps twice as much money as the other.

Burgundian winegrowers and shippers are neither collectively cynics nor saints. They are, however, more than amply paid for their efforts, and thus that much more deserving of critical attention. They are also a remarkable people, the more so for being astonishingly humble in the face of centuries of praise and patronage. But if the outside world doesn't care, they surely can be forgiven for not being self-abnegating saints. The market for shoddy Burgundy, like the poor, will always be with us. The role of the Burgundy lover is to care—and to know what to care about.

Acknowledgments

The acknowledgments page is likely the most boring for the reader, yet the most meaningful for the author. It is a public thank-you note, and no less sincere for being so. When a writer attempts to anatomize a region and its wines, he must pilot between affection and remove. One hopes that this book offers both. This page, however, is reserved exclusively for affection.

I am indebted to Lalou Bize-Leroy, to whom this book is dedicated. My wife and I first met Lalou in 1980. Jancis Robinson, in her section on the Domaine de la Romanée-Conti in *The Great Wine Book*, noted the difficulty of gaining entrée to this most famous of Burgundian estates. But, she added, "They are not *that* exclusive—there was the young couple from Oregon who arrived by bicycle, with no appointment, and with nowhere to stay, but showed such an intense love of her wines that Madame invited them back to stay with her."

We were that young couple. In fact, we *did* have an appointment, which I had pulled a lot of strings to get. And we did have a place to stay, of sorts. Our tent was pitched at the excellent municipal campground in Beaune. My wife and I like to bicycle and we were on our honeymoon, having just been married a few days earlier in Alsace, with Hubert Trimbach as our best man. But that's another story and another book. We did bicycle to our appointment at the Domaine de la Romanée-Conti, which, Lalou tells me, was a first. After tasting the wines and walking through the vineyards, she turned to us and inquired, "What are you doing for lunch?" We had no plans. "You will have lunch with me and my family," she declared. "And what are you doing for dinner?" Again, we had no plans. "You will have dinner with us," she commanded. Finally, she asked, "Where are you staying?" The mention of the municipal campground in Beaune brought forth a shout of delight. "You will stay with us," she decreed. And we did. It was the beginning of a beautiful, if argumentative, friendship. Whatever understanding I might have about the wine of Burgundy I credit to Lalou. She is not to blame, though, for whatever I have failed to grasp.

Many others have contributed to this book, sometimes by practical assistance and advice, sometimes simply by their example. I am most indebted to Armand Cottin and Louis Cottin, who made an insider's Burgundy available to an outsider. Without them, this book would not have been possible.

Other debts are owed to Jacques d'Angerville, Jean-François Bazin, Michel Bettane, Bertrand Devillard, André Gagey, Pierre-Henry Gagey, Stephen Gilbertson, Jim Gordon, Maria Guarnaschelli, Greg Lemma, Mike Lynch, Richard Olney, Philippe Senard, Jacques Seysses, Jan Steubing, John Tomsich, Peter Vezan, Aubert de Villaine, and Rebecca Wasserman. Their advice, insight, or support made a difference.

The final acknowledgment also is the most heartfelt: To my wife, Karen, who has withstood Burgundy—and me—by bicycle, barrel, bottle, and, most trying of all, by manuscript.

Contents

THINKING
BURGUNDY

The
Vineyard
Ownerships

*But in every corner where the earth is deep enough and mellow
enough, the vine has been planted. It has been done in strips and
bits and pieces. . . . That is why Burgundy, whose riches and
glory are known to the whole world, looks as though it were
clothed in a secondhand garment; patched, darned, and bor-
rowed: a beggar's coat on a millionaire's shoulders.*

—Paul de Cassagnac, *French Wines* (1930)

One of the fascinations of Burgundy is the fractionalization of
its vineyard holdings. Virtually every book on Burgundy has informed readers of this fact, always exclaiming over the extreme
subdivision of the ownerships. But until now, it has been impossible
for Burgundy followers to see, at least on paper, for themselves.

The vineyard-ownership listings in *Making Sense of Burgundy*
mark the first time that the ownerships of nearly all of the best
vineyards in the Côte d'Or have been revealed. It may also be the
last time. This is because this previously undisclosed data has been
removed from the public record. The French government has declared it off-limits.

The ownership listings in this book represent a methodical sift-
ing through the public record of each communal *cadastre*, what we
call the town hall bureau of records. In each *cadastre* used to be found

large ledgers in which were recorded, parcel by parcel, the ownerships of every vineyard in that commune or district.

The listings in this book were compiled in 1986. This was when research began for *Making Sense of Burgundy*. Between then and now, record-keeping was modernized, changing from handwritten entries in dusty ledgers to computerized magnetic disks. When I subsequently sought to update and expand the ownership listings compiled in 1986, I was thwarted. Now, the only information publicly available at each *cadastre* is a computer record of the amount of vineyard land owned by an individual, but without any detail of which vineyards are owned or how much in each one.

Yet I discovered that these details do exist. In fact, they are available in computerized form. The Office National Interprofessional des Vins de Table (ONIVIN), a governmental agency, has listings of every vineyard ownership in Burgundy. The agency will not release these listings, citing French computer-privacy laws. What was once public record no longer is.

Representations were made on my behalf, all the way up to the national board of the Institut National des Appellations d'Origine des Vins (INAO), the governing body of French wine. It was to no avail. Short of a challenge in the law courts, what appears in this book will probably be the only public record of vineyard ownerships as recorded in the communal *cadastres*.

Since being collected in 1986, some of the information, inevitably, is out of date. Still, the ownerships in Burgundy change grudgingly, if at all. Some of the data here, interestingly enough, may have been inaccurate at the time. Although the *cadastre* documents were then, and still are, the official records, it appears that they were not always updated as accurately or thoroughly as might be expected. What appears here, apart from any typographical error, is what was recorded. It should be noted that the listings are rarely 100 percent complete in terms of the ownership of every last row of vines. For reasons of space (sanity even), I directed the researcher I engaged to perform the work to record only the significant vineyard ownerships. In most cases, however, at least 90 percent of the ownerships in a vineyard are accounted for.

Another reason why vineyard ownerships and the vineyard size do not always tally precisely is that it was only in 1985 that INAO completed redefining the boundaries of Burgundy vineyards. The size of a vineyard, according to the *cadastre*, does not always jibe with that cited by INAO. For example, in Montrachet, INAO has it at 7.9980 hectares or 19.76 acres. But the local *cadastre* has Montrachet at 8.0751 hectares or 19.95 acres. Such minor discrepancies are found throughout the Côte d'Or. The vineyard acreage figures cited in this book are those of INAO.

Why is this knowledge of vineyard ownerships important? For the Burgundy enthusiast, it is a first-time-ever treasure map to locating the source of grapes. For example, it has long been known that the vineyard of Rugiens in Pommard is divided into Rugiens *bas* (lower) and Rugiens *haut* (upper). *Bas* is better, because of a superior subsoil. But the labels never draw the distinction, even though the local Pommard growers privately do. If you look in the Pommard chapter, you will see, for the first time, who owns parcels of Rugiens *bas* and how much they own.

Other insights are available. Look at the listings to see how *little* is owned. Then look at the number of cases of wine such a holding can produce. And then marvel over finding that wine from that producer in New York or San Francisco or Sydney, Australia. It's one thing to be told that it's amazing; it's another to see how astonishing it is for yourself. The listings leave an indelible impression.

You can also see the material effects of the Napoleonic Code of inheritance, with its provision that a parent divide an estate equally among all the offspring. Also to be seen is the effect of local marriages, with many prominent Burgundian names being allied to others in the ownership of inherited vineyards.

Above all, the tiny parcels make clear what a task it is simply to assemble enough wine for a commercial offering. It becomes obvious how and why the *négociant* system evolved. Equally evident is the task for a domaine to vinify tiny holdings—and how tempting it must be to combine them under one (fraudulent) vineyard name. It is a testament to the Burgundian love of *terroir* (site) that more of that sort of thing doesn't go on than already happens.

The listings are divided by vineyard; owner; the amount of land owned in hectares, ares, and centiares; the conversion of hectares into acres; and finally, a generalized conversion of how much wine that plot could create based upon the *rendement de base* for that vineyard plus 20 percent (see the section Yields in the chapter The Burgundian Sensibility—in the Vineyard). The case figure is only an indication; in reality the figure could be lower or higher. But it's a pretty good notion, all the same.

It should be noted that some of the names officially recorded in the *cadastre* records, and reproduced in this book, do not always reflect the current status of the owner. For example, some women listed as unmarried (*mademoiselle*) now are married (*madame*). Other listed owners may now be dead, or even dead for years. As long as the taxes are paid on the vineyard plot, the local *cadastre* probably doesn't care excessively about maintaining up-to-date ownership listings.

What the listings *don't* show is whether the owners actually make their own wines, i.e., estate-bottle. Nor do they show whether a holding is sharecropped (called *métayage*), where a grower tends someone else's vines—and even makes his wines—in exchange for a percentage of the crop, usually one third or one half. Not least is the absence of knowledge of who is related to whom, especially by marriage. It would be a mistake to conclude that the 89 cases of Monsieur X from his 0.4-acre plot is all he makes from that vineyard. He could be sharecropping someone else's vines in the same vineyard. Or he could be making wine from his sister's, brother's, father's, mother's, or any of his in-laws' holdings. The grapes from all of these could be added to his own, and the wine he makes from them legally entitled to the designation "estate-bottled" (*mise en bouteille à la propriété* or *mise au domaine*). On the other hand, just because two owners obviously are related, do not automatically conclude that they go in together under one label—or even make wine together. The Burgundians are ferociously individual.

Burgundy is a matter of detail. This has been its frustration and always will be, no matter how much well-meaning wine writers or wine shippers try to simplify it. The ownership listings in this book tell you why at mere glance.

The
Burgundian
Landscape

*What single cloudless day, what soft late rainfall decide that a
vintage shall be great among the others? Human care can do
almost nothing towards it; It is all celestial wizardry, the orbits
of planets, sunspots.*

—COLETTE, *Prisons et Paradis*

I t is tempting to view the great winegrowing regions everywhere
in the world as somehow preordained; an expression of the earth
unmistakably designed for the sole purpose of creating a certain
superb wine. The temptation toward this view is strong because it
is always after the fact. It now seems so obvious that the Piedmont
district of northern Italy should be the birthing place of so many
fine red wines from the Nebbiolo grape variety. Or that Bordeaux
was unmistakably slated to be a treasure trove of vineyards. Even
the precipitous hillsides of the Mosel might conceivably be viewed
as existing only for the revealed purpose of fostering impeccable
sweet Rieslings.

But the truth of winegrowing is far from this pleasant retro-
spective fancy. The Mosel is hardly obvious as a winegrowing region
at all, let alone one of the world's greatest. The Piedmont fosters

other lesser red wine grapes than the quirky Nebbiolo. As for Bordeaux, its most glorious stretch, the peninsula called the Médoc, was simply marshland until the Dutch helped drain it in the late 1600s. The adage that a grapevine must struggle in order for a wine to achieve greatness is a truism. But its corollary is less often noted: The struggle is no less hard for the grape grower.

The "landscape of Burgundy" refers not only to the lay of the land but, as in an expansive garden, to the choice of plantings; the selection of the best sites for the grandest arrangements; and the never-ending pruning by which order is maintained and beauty revealed. It is the creation of man. The Earth remained mute in this most eloquent of all vineyard sites until it was given voice through centuries of remarkable labor and insight.

The modern Burgundian winegrower is, at this point in the long history of the landscape, a guardian, a caretaker. This is no small charge, as the landscape he is called upon to nurture is of a profoundly complex design planted to particularly sensitive vegetation. As a garden must be constantly renewed in order to remain true to its overall design, so too must the vineyard landscape be maintained. Every generation of Burgundian winegrowers proves the truth of Wordsworth's observation that the child is father of the man.

In order to understand the challenge faced today by winegrowers in Burgundy, and the betrayal that occurs when they carelessly or willfully abandon the finely evolved distinctions of site that make Burgundy unique, one must have at least a sense of what occurred in Burgundy prior to the French Revolution. For it was then that the landscape of Burgundy was conceived and shaped. Who owned what, prior to 1789, and what they did with what they owned, determined the destiny of Burgundy—and continues to determine it today.

THE BURGUNDIAN LANDSCAPE PRIOR TO 1789

Prior to the Revolution of 1789, all of the best vineyard sites were in the hands of the nobility and the Church. The Church played the more critical role, as it not only was present at the very start of shaping the Burgundian landscape (which began as long ago as A.D. 600) but it also was a continuous and powerful presence as well as having the highest viticultural ambition. It set a standard, maintained it, and sought constantly to improve upon it without interruption for twelve hundred years. As a result, the landscape of Burgundy was shaped with a rare constancy of purpose.

The Church-owned wines were considered the finest, not only because of the estimable quality of their vineyard sites, but also because of the long-term involvement of generations of monks and nuns in vineyard practices and winemaking techniques. They had the time, lived on the property, had the financial resources, and, perhaps most critical of all during the Middle Ages, retained the necessary attitude of analysis and method. They sought to improve their wines at every turn. Eventually, they had more than was needed for the sacrament, and these wines were sold.

The preeminence of the Church gave rise to two fundamental and enduring legacies: the cultivation of Pinot Noir and Chardonnay as the informing grapes of Burgundy and the elaborate delineation of the qualities of one plot of land from another. If one were called upon today to differentiate Burgundy from any other winegrowing district, these two features still would be the distinguishing elements.

Pinot Noir, and to a lesser degree, Chardonnay, are inherently limited grape varieties. They are subject to an impressive number of grapevine diseases, making them delicate as grapevines go. Compared to other grape varieties, they are low-yielding, proffering few clusters per vine. Moreover, to create a distinctive wine from either variety, one must prune them severely, thus limiting the number of clusters that much more. The resulting wines, however, are of unmatchable quality.

A striking aspect of this unmatchable quality is the exceptional sensitivity of Chardonnay and, especially, Pinot Noir to the soil and subsoil in which they are rooted, to the slope of the land, its drainage of water and absorption of sun, and all of the many pieces of the jigsaw puzzle that today is called a "microclimate." These pieces are constantly varying in number and influence from one plot to another. Because Pinot Noir and Chardonnay are such expressive vehicles, it becomes that much more reasonable that the Burgundians, alone in France, use the word *climat* to refer to an individual vineyard or, more often, just a section of one.

Given this exquisite sensitivity and delicacy, it is not surprising that the upper stratum of pre-Revolutionary Burgundian society should have identified with the frail, delicate, prima donna-ish attributes of these varieties, especially that of Pinot Noir, the more fickle and frailer of the two. Although a portion of the harvest from the noble and Church vineyards found their way into commerce, the wines created from the Middle Ages up to the Revolution were largely for private use, or at least personal prestige. Their quality was a reflection of the status and glory of the landowner. (When the prince de Conti purchased the Romanée vineyard in 1760, he promptly reserved its entire production for his private use.) The highest quality was the only goal as the vineyards served one compelling purpose: to add to the social and political luster of the owner. Owning a fine vineyard was truly a hallmark of nobility.

At first, commerce played only a minor role and had little influence on the winemaking or grape growing. The nobility emulated the Church practices as best they could. The landscape of Burgundy had come into being under the most chaste of circumstances. It was the most acclaimed and sought-after wine in all of Europe. This was not to last.

A new tension in the vineyards arose from an unlikely source: the arrival of the Plague in Burgundy in 1349. As it promptly struck down a good many of the clergy (who tended the sick) as well as much of the Burgundian work force, the vineyards were neglected. For fourteen vintages little was harvested. Left unpruned, unweeded, and generally unattended for as little as one season, Pinot Noir and Chardonnay vines will produce only poor-quality grapes and will likely contract any of a number of diseases to which they are prone, thereby limiting future quality. Neglect over a span of fourteen vintages is catastrophic. Pinot Noir suffered incalculably, being the more sensitive vine.

But during this period it was observed that another red grape variety, growing in the Côte d'Or village of Gamay, was flourishing compared to Pinot Noir. It was naturally more resistant to disease, yielded three times as much as Pinot Noir, and the red wine it created wasn't half-bad. In an era when wine was not only wealth and glory but caloric sustenance, the discovery of what has since come to be called the Gamay grape variety during the beleaguered Plague period must have seemed like the biblical manna from heaven.

Gamay was enthusiastically planted in a variety of vineyards along the Côte d'Or, especially in the many lesser plots owned or rented by the peasants. Some of the finest vineyards were planted to Gamay in hopes that it would prove to be as fine in quality as Pinot Noir even while three or four times as fecund. It was not.

Thus emerged the oft-quoted edict of Duke Philippe le Hardi (the Bold) in 1395. His noble sensibilities repulsed by the coarseness of the Gamay wine (to this day it does far better in the Beaujolais region, where it is virtually the sole grape variety, than in the Côte d'Or), the ruler instructed his subjects to uproot "the very nasty and very disloyal plant named Gaamez," which, he went on to declare, gave wine in abundance but of a very great and horrible harshness. Moreover, it was "most harmful to every human creature; to such a point that many who have used it in the past have suffered from serious illnesses."

The decree was all but ignored, as proved by the fact that a similar edict was issued only forty-six years later, in 1441, to a similar effect. So much for the absolute power of feudalism. The reason for the lack of effectiveness was not due to its lack of veracity, but rather, to a ducal inability to enforce it. No doubt part of the problem was a lack of support for the measure from wine merchants, who had much to gain from a supply of cheap Gamay. During the 1400s, according to William Younger in *Gods, Men and Wine*:

> The deceit of merchants in Burgundy was less subtle. They dealt in wine from heavily productive vineyards of Gamay grapes, wine which was of a "great and horrible bitterness." It had, however, at one stage in its making, a certain amount of softness and this the merchants prolonged or resurrected at the time of its sale by putting hot water into the barrels. When the doctoring wore off, the wine became "stinking." . . .

The renowned and envied quality of the red wines of Burgundy was under a pall of public suspicion and disapproval, the first instance of a pattern of praise and damnation that has haunted the region and its wine merchants in particular ever since. Philippe le Hardi was not unaware that his dukedom's greatest glory had slipped in both quality and esteem. One of his less frequently noted decrees was a prohibition against the use of manure in the vineyards of the Côte d'Or. Then, as now, excessive fertilization resulted in larger yields but dramatically lower quality. The duke, anxious to restore the wines of Burgundy to their pre-Plague renown, knew full well that quantity could not coexist with quality in either Pinot Noir or Chardonnay.

The chaste and noble goal of the highest quality to the greatest glory of Burgundy was even at this early date being nibbled away at by the temptations of excessive yields, the fecundity of the Gamay grape, and the lure of easy profits gained by disreputable wine merchants at the expense of an unknowing audience.

By the end of the 1600s, Saint-Evremond, the witty courtier and litterateur, would write that Burgundies have almost all lost "their old Reputation with the Citizens." Sloppy or greedy winemaking coupled with a reliance on the "disloyal Gamaaz" brought about the downfall.

Although feudal and seignorial rule prior to 1789 exercised a goodly degree of power over the land and people of Burgundy, its control was not as absolute as it might seem to the modern imagination. Peasants did own vineyard land, as did a growing merchant class.

The real triumph of Gamay came with the newfound habit of wine drinking among the peasants and urban workers of France, in other words the great majority of its inhabitants. It seems astonishing that a country as steeped in wine as France could have come to universal wine drinking only in the 1700s. Nevertheless, it is so. Prior to the 1700s, wine drinking among the peasantry and workers was not a widespread practice, even in winegrowing districts. What little was drunk among wine laborers themselves was not what could be called proper wine. Rather, it was a beverage called *piquette*, a suitably derisive name for a colored liquid created by adding water to the *marc* or pressed-grape skins. Sometimes a bit of sugar was also thrown in to help provide some flavor. (Cellar workers were famous, even into the mid-twentieth century, for taking care that not too much juice was pressed from the skins, so as to ensure that their *piquette* had some flavor.)

But in the 1700s the rural peasantry and urban workers grew more demanding. Gamay was the high-production, quality-be-damned ticket. Those who produced it found themselves prosperous enough to actually purchase fractions of the coveted Pinot Noir properties of the upper classes. This ability made such growers no doubt that much more resentful of the holdings of the aristocracy.

The Gamay/Pinot Noir tension, and all it symbolized, was tautened yet another notch because of the increasingly heavy taxes imposed on commercial wines in the form of a duty or tariff to be paid when a shipment of wine entered a city or town. Theodore Zeldin, in *France 1848–1945*, summarizes the effects of the tariffs:

> Cheap wine sometimes had to pay twice its value in tax by the end of the ancien régime. This became a burning issue between the masses

and the government. . . . Of course, different regions produced different situations: the Beaujolais region for example could afford to expand its production of cheap wine because it had the right to send its wines to Lyon cheaply; Mâcon by contrast had to pay tariffs four times higher and so found it necessary to specialize in fine wines.

The result of this heavy taxation was that cheap wine did not cost very much less than good wine: the peasants who produced it therefore concentrated on quantity rather than quality, often harvesting three times as many grapes from their land, and selling these at half the price of the high-class vineyards.

Upper-class vineyard owners and the Church did not pay any taxes at all, because the wine for their own use never entered commercial channels. Privilege begat privilege.

THE BURGUNDIAN LANDSCAPE AFTER 1789

The effects of the French Revolution upon the Burgundian landscape were felt not so much upon its design as its ownership. By then, Pinot Noir and Chardonnay had been established as the true voice of the land and were the unquestioned pinnacle of Burgundian winemaking. While Gamay was encroaching at every turn, impelled by economics, there was little question that Pinot Noir fetched a higher price on the export markets and certainly rewarded its producer with far greater social cachet. This remained a legacy of pre-Revolutionary Burgundy and is still in effect today.

The differentiation of vineyards along the length of the Côte d'Or was similarly untouched. The millennium of thought that accrued to the Burgundian landscape from the monks, nuns, and noble owners remained. The vineyard distinctions of the Côte d'Or were not melted down like the silver and gold accoutrements of the aristocracy. In fact, vineyard distinctions were to increase over the next century, as the vineyard ownerships splintered into ever-smaller holdings.

The cause of this increase lay in the great upheaval that did affect the Burgundian landscape: the change of ownership of it. This in turn was to affect not only the grape varieties planted (an increase of Gamay and Aligoté, a lesser white wine variety), but also the overall quality of the winemaking itself.

With the confiscation of all the properties of the nobility and the Church, the ownership of the finest holdings of Burgundy were loosened and dislodged from what must have once seemed an eternal grip. Like large ice floes, the previously frozen properties of the Church and the aristocracy floated into the stream of commerce. With them went a singular commitment to quality at any price, although a legacy of high standards remained.

These vineyards were put up at auction and bid upon by the newly wealthy merchant class, bankers, and other members of the bourgeoisie. At first, all that really occurred immediately after the Revolution was the transference of the finest vineyards from the hands of aristocracy and Church into the hands of the new upper class. One of the reasons for this, apart from the obvious fact that such vineyards were inherently expensive, was that only the wealthiest could afford to participate. The rural peasantry, which by then already owned small parcels of land, were excluded from even attempting to enter the bidding.

This was the irony of the French Revolution: The peasants in whose name it was initiated were shouldered aside at the trough. In the Beaujolais region, for example, where Gamay, the peasant's grape, was and still is king, independent small landowners did not possess even 10 percent of the land in upper Beaujolais, where the best vineyards are located. Even in lower Beaujolais, the small landowners held only 30 percent of the vineyards after the dust of the Revolution settled.

The Côte d'Or peasants and small landowners fared only a little better. They managed to secure about 25 percent of the vineyards on the slope of the Côte d'Or, the sliver of land where all of the truly fine vineyards are sited. But the bulk of their opportunity—which had great consequences for the future ownership of the choice plots—lay in the lesser vineyards on the plateau lands above and behind the slope and the flat plains in front of the slope. In time, the ownership of the fine vineyards of the slope itself would be ambushed, as it were, from behind and in front, courtesy of the new Gamay-created wealth of these lesser properties. Small landowners secured more than 60 percent of these less estimable vineyards. By 1855, Gamay was strangling the Côte d'Or: 87 percent of its then 65,480 acres of vineyard (today it is 19,000 acres) was planted to Gamay.

The striking question that emerges when examining this reordering of ownerships is: Why didn't the peasants simply take over the land of the nobility and the Church and divide it up among themselves? The most convincing explanation is Theodore Zeldin's in *France 1848–1945*:

The answer is that on this point their interests varied and they were not united. Already in 1789 about 30 to 40 percent of France was owned by peasants, so there was a first division between those peasants who owned land and those who did not. Equal partition was not so attractive to those who already enjoyed a privileged position. Moreover, most of the land owned by the wealthier classes was rented out, under various forms of tenure, to peasants. These [tenant farmers and share-croppers] were fighting their way up the social scale by acquiring these tenancies. They would lose if all the land was divided equally between all peasants, including the vast multitude of landless labourers.

Nevertheless, the vineyards of Burgundy were certainly scat-tered among a greater number of owners than ever before. Also, for the first time Burgundy was subject to a commercial consciousness more penetrating than ever before, as few of the new owners could afford to remove a choice wine entirely from the marketplace, as the ancien régime prince de Conti did with his renamed Romanée-Conti vineyard. With the breakdown of the old social order came a new, tenuous fluidity. Standards of quality, winemaking styles, fluctuat-ing fortunes and ownerships, all began to influence the received message of the landscape.

It was not long before the Revolutionary Era gave way to the Napoleonic. And with the ascendance of Napoleon Bonaparte came a provision of the *Code Napoléon* (Article 745, Book Three) that ac-celerated the multiplicity of ownerships in Burgundy.

A provision of the Code stipulated that a father must divide most of his property equally among all of his children, male and female. This precluded the traditional practice of primogeniture, the eldest son getting the whole wad, usually of land, and the rest of the brood left to fend for themselves. Common in pre-Revolutionary France (and still operative in Great Britain), it does have the one salutary effect of allowing a landed estate to remain intact.

The effect of this provision of the Code upon the landholdings of all of France is a matter of dispute among historians, as equal division of land was already in practice in some regions at the time of its promulgation. The provision is thought to have differed in its impact from region to region.

But in Burgundy the impact of equal division of the land among heirs could not be more apparent. The new fluidity of the Revo-lutionary period brought about an initial parceling-out of vineyards. Some land speculators purchased the large parcels offered at auction and subsequently subdivided them, selling sections of one small vineyard to several different purchasers. Other land speculators, or simply the overreaching nouveaux riches, found themselves cash-poor as a result of their social climbing or speculation, and sold their purchases not long afterward. Thus, properties that were once offered only to the few in prohibitively expensive chunks eventually reached the many in a more financially digestible form. The peasant owners of the Gamay-planted vineyards, which were lucrative, found themselves in a position to buy at least part of a choicer Pinot Noir vineyard.

Add this to the pressure of the Napoleonic Code of inheritance, which still exists in France today, and you need little imagination to envision how the already multiple ownerships of a quite small vineyard area can proliferate like aphids on a rose. Ever-smaller segments of vineyards were dispersed into the hands of an ever-larger number of landowners. The effect of this upon the quality and consistency of Burgundies made today cannot be overestimated, as multiple ownerships virtually guarantee corresponding multiple standards of quality and ability.

It is important to note that the reason the numerous owners have not lived up to the past performance—and still-present promise—of the land is not due to uneconomically small holdings. Many owners create magnificent, authentic Burgundies, and labor under the same constraint. Small holdings are not an obstacle to quality, only an irritation to efficiency. The price of a bottle of Burgundy renders all but the most minuscule slice of the Côte d'Or more profitable than any other piece of agricultural land anywhere.

But what the owners do with the land, and the grapes and wine it nurtures, is something else again. The bane of Burgundy has always been its rampant inconsistency. The greater the number of proprietors in a vineyard, the greater the likelihood of dramatically different standards in viticulture and winemaking.

A glance at the fractionalized holdings provides an insight into why Burgundies are so wildly inconsistent from one producer to the next, no matter how great the property. Only a handful of people are afforded the opportunity to compare multiple examples of wines from the same vineyard and vintage. Those who do are invariably rocked by the differences, especially when one realizes that they all fetch more or less the same stratospheric price. These differences, one hastens to add, are not a matter of taste and personal preference. Even in matters of subjective taste, which is certainly intrinsic to wine or food, there still are standards. As one of Burgundy's finest (and most outspoken) producers, Lalou Bize-Leroy, puts it, "We have in Burgundy a lot of bad wine. Wine that is simply not well made. It's like cooking. We also have a lot of restaurants whose chefs cannot cook. It's exactly the same. We shouldn't have bad Burgundy. It's people who make bad wine." Many bottles from many illustrious vineyards are little more than mere ventriloquism, impersonations of the authentic voice of the land.

There is now a growing awareness of the need to reassert old standards. Partly this is due to the increasing number of commercially successful Chardonnays and Pinot Noirs produced in the New World modeled on the Burgundian originals. But partly it is a shouldering of a moral burden. Caretakers of an original, be it a painting or a vineyard, have obligations different from those who seek only to copy. A wine known for its exquisite and unique expression that turns out to be something more laryngitic than full-voiced, is a disappointment that goes beyond the pocketbook. A new generation of Burgundian winegrowers acknowledges this obligation.

The Notion
of
Terroir

Always the beautiful answer who asks a more beautiful question

—e. e. cummings, *New Poems*

The "more beautiful question" of wine is *terroir*. To the English speaker *terroir* is an alien word, difficult to pronounce ("tair-wahr"). More frustrating yet, it is a foreign idea. The usual capsule definition is "site" or "vineyard plot." Closer to its truth, it holds—like William Blake's grain of sand that contains a world—an evolution of thought about wine and the Earth. One cannot make sense of Burgundy without investigating the notion of *terroir*.

Although derived from soil or land (*terre*), *terroir* is not just an investigation of soil and subsoil. It is everything that contributes to the distinction of a vineyard plot. As such, it also embraces "microclimate": precipitation, air and water drainage, elevation, sunlight, and temperature.

But *terroir* holds yet another dimension: It sanctions what cannot be measured, yet still located and savored. *Terroir* prospects for differences. In this it is at odds with science, which demands proof by replication rather than in a shining uniqueness.

Understanding *terroir* requires a recalibration of the modern mind. The original impulse has long since disappeared, buried by commerce and the scorn of science. It calls for a susceptibility to the natural world to a degree almost unfathomable today, as the French historian Marc Bloch evokes in his landmark work, *Feudal Society*:

> The men of the two feudal ages were close to nature—much closer than we are; and nature as they knew it was much less tamed and softened than as we see it today. . . . People continued to pick wild fruit and to gather honey as in the first ages of mankind. In the construction of implements and tools, wood played a predominant part. The nights, owing to wretched lighting, were darker; the cold, even in the living quarters of the castles, was more intense. In short, behind all social life there was a background of the primitive, of submission to uncontrollable forces, of unrelieved physical contrasts.

This world extended beyond the feudal ages, as rural life in Europe changed little for centuries afterward. Only the barest vestiges remain today, with the raw, preternatural sensitivity wiped clean. The viticultural needlepoint of the Côte d'Or, its thousands of named vineyards, is as much a relic of a bygone civilization as Stonehenge. We can decipher why and how they did it, but the impulse, the fervor, is beyond us now.

The glory of Burgundy is its exquisite delineation of sites, its preoccupation with *terroir*: What does this site have to say? Is it different from its neighbor? It is the source of Burgundian greatness, the informing ingredient. This is easily demonstrated. You need only imagine an ancient Burgundy planted to Pinot Noir and Chardonnay for the glory of producing—to use the modern jargon—a varietal wine. The thought is depressing, an anemic vision of wine hardly capable of inspiring the devotion of generations of wine lovers, let alone the discovery of such natural wonders as Montrachet or La Tâche. *Terroir* is as much a part of Burgundy wines as Pinot Noir or Chardonnay; the grape is as much vehicle as voice.

The mentality of *terroir* is not uniquely Burgundian, although it reaches its fullest expression there. It more rightly could be considered distinctively French, although not exclusively so. Other countries, notably Germany and Italy, can point to similar insights.

But France, more than any other, viewed its landscape from the perspective of *terroir*. It charted its vineyard distinctions—often called *cru* or growth—with calligraphic care. Indeed, calligraphy and *cru* are sympathetic, both the result of emotional, yet disciplined, attentions to detail. Both flourished under monastic tutelage.

Italy, for all of its ancient winegrowing tradition, never developed a mentality of *terroir* to the same or even similar extent as France. It lacked, ironically, the monastic underpinning of the Benedictine and Cistercian orders, which were represented to a far greater degree in France and Germany. An ecclesiastical map of Western Europe during the Middle Ages (*Historical Atlas* by William R. Shepherd) shows hundreds of major monasteries in France and Germany, nearly all of them Benedictine or Cistercian. In comparison, Italy had less than a dozen.

The phrase "mentality of *terroir*" is pertinent. The articulation of the Burgundian landscape increased steadily long after the decline of the feudal ages. Ever-finer distinctions of site mounted along the Côte d'Or through to the Revolution of 1789, when the Church lands were confiscated and publicly auctioned. The monks and nuns, whose wines and vineyards remained the standard for nearly a millennium, never wavered in their devotion to *terroir*. If only by sheer longevity, their vision of the land became everyone else's.

But in France there exists, to this day, a devotion to *terroir* that is not explained solely by this legacy of the Church. Instead, it is fueled by two forces in French life: a long-standing delight in differences and an acceptance of ambiguity.

The greatness of French wines in general—and Burgundy in particular—can be traced to the fact that the French do not ask of one site that it replicate the qualities of another site. They prize distinction. This leads not to discord—as it might in a country gripped by a marketing mentality—but consonance with what the French call *la France profonde*, elemental France.

This is the glory of France. It is not that France is the only spot on the planet with remarkable soils or that its climate is superior to all others for winegrowing. It is a matter of the values that are applied to the land. In this, *terroir* and its discoveries remind one of Chinese acupuncture. Centuries ago, Chinese practitioners chose to view the body from a perspective utterly different from that of the dissective, anatomical approach of Western medicine. Because of this different perspective, they discovered something about the body that Western practitioners, to this day, are unable to see independently for themselves: what the Chinese call "channels" and "collaterals," or more recently, "meridians." The terminology is unimportant. What is important is that these "meridians" cannot be found by dissection. Yet they exist; acupuncture works. Its effects, if not its causes, are demonstrable.

In the same way, seeking to divine the greatness of Burgundy only by dissecting its intricacies of climate, grape, soil, and winemaking is no more enlightening than learning how to knit by unraveling a sweater. Those who believe that great wines are made, rather than found, will deliver such wines only by the flimsiest chance, much in the same way that an alchemist, after exacting effort, produces gold simply by virtue of having worked with gold-bearing material all along.

Today, a surprising number of winegrowers and wine drinkers—at least in the United States—flatly deny the existence of *terroir*, like weekend sailors who reject as preposterous that Polynesians could have crossed the Pacific navigating only by sun, stars, wind, smell, and taste. *Terroir* is held to be little more than viticultural voodoo.

The inadmissibility of *terroir* to the high court of reason is due to ambiguity. *Terroir* can be presented, but it cannot be proven—except by the senses. Like Polynesian seafaring, it is too subjective to be reproducible and therefore credible. Yet any reasonably experienced wine drinker knows upon tasting a mature Corton-Charlemagne, or Chablis "Vaudésir," or Volnay "Caillerets," that something is present that cannot be accounted for by winemaking technique. Infused in the wine is a *goût de terroir*, the savor of the site. It cannot be traced to the grape, if only because other wines made the same way from the same grape lack this certain something. If only by process of elimination, the source must be ascribed to *terroir*. But to acknowledge this requires a belief that the ambiguous—the unprovable and unmeasurable—can be real. Doubters are blocked by their own credulity in science and its confining definition of reality.

The supreme concern of Burgundy is—or should be—making *terroir* manifest. In outline, this is easily accomplished: small-berried clones; low yields; selective sorting of the grapes; and, trickiest of all, fermenting and cellaring the wine in such a way as to allow the *terroir* to come through with no distracting stylistic flourishes. This is where *terroir* comes smack up against ego, the modern demand for self-expression at any cost, which, too often, has come at the expense of *terroir*.

It is easier to see the old Burgundian enemies of greed and inept winemaking. The problem of greed, expressed in overcropped grapevines resulting in thin, diluted wines, has been chronic in Burgundy, as are complaints about it. It is no less so today, but the resolution is easily at hand: Lower the yields.

But the matter of ego and *terroir* is new and peculiar to our time. It stems from two sources: the technology of modern winemaking and the psychology of its use. Technical control in winemaking is recent, dating only to the late 1960s. Never before have winemakers been able to control wine to such an extent as they can today. Through the use of temperature-controlled stainless-steel tanks, computer-controlled winepresses, heat exchangers, inert gases, centrifuges, all manner of filters, oak barrels from woods of different forests, and so forth, the modern winemaker can insert himself between the *terroir* and its wine to a degree never before achieved.

The psychology of its use is the more important feature. Self-expression is now considered the inalienable right of our time. It thus is no surprise that the desire for self-expression should make itself felt in winemaking. That winemakers have always sought to express themselves in their wines is indisputable. The difference is that today technology actually allows them to do so, to an extent unimagined by their grandparents.

Submerged in this is a force that, however abstract, has changed much of twentieth-century thinking: the transition from the literal to the subjective in how we perceive what is "real." Until recently, whatever was considered "real" was expressed in straightforward mechanical or linear linkages, such as a groove in a phonograph record or a lifelike painting of a vase of flowers. Accuracy was defined by exacting, literal representation.

But we now have come to believe that the subjective can be more "real" than the representational. One of the earliest, and most famous, examples of this was Expressionism in art. Where prior to the advent of Expressionism in the early twentieth-century, the depiction of reality on a canvas was achieved through the creation of the most lifelike forms, Expressionists said otherwise. They maintained that the reality of a vase of flowers could be better expressed by breaking down its form and color into more symbolic representations of its reality than by straightforward depiction.

How this relates to wine is found in the issue of *terroir* versus ego. The Burgundian world that discovered *terroir* centuries ago drew no distinction between what they discovered and called Chambertin and the *idea* of a representation of Chambertin. Previously there were only two parties involved: Chambertin itself and its self-effacing discoverer, the winegrower. In this deferential view of the natural world, Chambertin was Chambertin if for no other reason than it consistently did not taste like its neighbor Latricières. One is beefier and more resonantly flavorful (Chambertin) while the other offers a similar savor but somehow always is lacier in texture and less full-blown. It was a reality no more subject to doubt than was a nightingale's song from the screech of an owl. They knew what they tasted, just as they knew what they heard. These were natural forces, no more subject to alteration or challenge than a river.

All of which brings us back to Burgundian winemaking. In an age where the subjective has been accepted as being more "real" than the representational, the idea of an immutable *terroir* becomes troublesome. It complicates ego-driven individualism, the need to express a personal vision. In an era of relativism and right of self-expression, Chambertin as *terroir* has given way to Chambertin as emblem. The notion of *terroir* as an absolute is rejected. All Chambertins therefore become equally legitimate. We have come to accept that a grower's Chambertin is really only his or her idea of Chambertin. The vineyard name on the label is merely as a general indication of intent.

How, then, does one know what is the true voice of the land? How does one know when the winemaker has interposed himself or herself between the *terroir* and the final wine? Discovering the authentic voice of a particular *terroir* requires study. The only way is to assemble multiple examples of a wine from a particular plot and taste them side by side. Ideally they should all be from the same vintage. This eliminates at least one distracting variable.

In seeking to establish the voice of a *terroir*, one has to concentrate—at least for the moment—not on determining which wines are best, but in finding the thread of distinction that runs through them. It could be a matter of structure: delicate or muscular; consistently lean or generous in fruit. It could be a distinctive *goût de terroir*, something minerally or stony; chalky or earthy. Almost always, it will be hard to determine at first, because the range of styles within the wines will be distracting. And if the choices available are mostly second-rate, where the *terroir* is lost through over-cropped vines or heavy-handed winemaking, the exercise will be frustrating and without reward. *Terroir* usually is discovered only after repeated attempts over a number of vintages. This is why such insight is largely the province only of Burgundians and a few obsessed outsiders.

Nevertheless, hearing the voice of the land is sweet, and you will not easily forget it. Sometimes it only becomes apparent by contrast. You taste a number of Meursault "Perrières," for example, and in the good ones you find a pronounced mineraliness coupled with an invigorating, strong fruitiness. You don't realize how stony or fruity, how forceful, until you compare Perrières with, say, Charmes, which is contiguous. Then the distinction of Perrières clicks into place in your mind. It's never so exact or pronounced that you will spot it unerringly in a blind tasting of various Meursault *premiers crus*. That's not the point. The point is that there is no doubt that Perrières exists, that it is an entity unto itself, distinct from any other plot.

Such investigation—which is more rewarding than it might sound—has a built-in protocol. When faced with a lineup of wines, the immediate impact is of stylistic differences, a clamor of producer's voices. Once screened out, the lesser versions—the ones that clearly lack concentration and definition of flavor—are easily eliminated. Some are so insipid as to make them fraudulent in everything but the legal niceties. Then you are left with the wines that have something to say. At this moment you confront the issue of ego.

The ideal is to amplify *terroir* without distorting it. *Terroir* should be transmitted as free as possible of extraneous elements of style or taste. Ideally, one should not be able to find the hand of the winemaker. That said, it must be acknowledged that some signature always can be detected, although it can be very faint indeed when you reach the level of Robert Chevillon in Nuits-Saint-Georges; Bernard Serveau in Morey-Saint-Denis; or the marquis d'Angerville and Gérard Potel, both in Volnay, to name a few. The self-effacement of these producers in their wines is very nearly Zenlike: their "signature" is an absence of signature.

Such paragons aside, the presence of a signature is not intrinsically bad, as long as it is not too expensively at the cost of *terroir*. A good example of this is the winemaking of the Domaine de la Romanée-Conti. The red wines of this fabled property—Echézeaux,

Grands Echézeaux, Romanée-Saint-Vivant, Richebourg, La Tâche, and Romanée-Conti—all share a stylistic signature that becomes immediately apparent when the wines are compared with other bottlings from the same vineyards. (Only two of the properties are exclusively owned or *monopoles*, La Tâche and Romanée-Conti.) All of the wines display a distinctive silkiness, almost an unctuosity, as well as a pronounced oakiness.

Nevertheless, the wines of the Domaine de la Romanée-Conti do overcome this stylistic signature to display a full measure of their particular *terroirs*. This is confirmed when tasting other good examples of Richebourg or Grands Echézeaux or the other properties. The reason is that the yields are admirably low; the clonal selection is astute; the harvesting punctilious in discarding rotted or unhealthy grapes; and the winemaking—stylistic signature aside—devoted to expressing the different *terroirs* to the fullest degree. The wines could be improved if the signature were less pronounced, in the same way that a beautiful dress could be improved if the designer's initials were eliminated.

This matter of signature only becomes apparent when tasting multiple examples of the same *terroir*. Although the ideal is what stereo buffs call a "straight wire," where the signal goes through the amplifier without any coloration, this simply is impossible given the intervention of both grape and grower. In this, winemaking in Burgundy really is translation. The poet W. S. Merwin maps out the challenge:

> The quality that is conveyed to represent the original is bound to differ with different translators, which is both a hazard and an opportunity. In the ideal sense in which one wants only the original, one wants the translator not to exist at all. In the practical sense in which the demand takes into account the nature of translation, the gifts—such as they are—of the translator are inescapably important.*

A good example of this would be the various Meursaults of the Domaine des Comtes Lafon and those of Jean-François Coche-Dury. Stylistically the Lafon wines are more voluptuous, more apparently oaky when young, but impeccable in their definition and separation of flavors. There is no mistaking one *terroir* for another when tasting their wines. The same may be said of Coche-Dury, except that his

---

Selected Translations 1968–1978 (New York: Atheneum, 1979), p. xi

style is more austere and somehow leaner, with distinctions of *terroir* that are almost painfully precise. The depth and concentration are the equal of Lafon, yet the delivery is slightly different. In both cases, the distinctions of site are preserved at all costs. Both accomplish what W. S. Merwin intends when translating someone else's poetry: "I have not set out to make translations that distorted the meaning of the originals on pretext of some other overriding originality."

Awareness of the existence of signature in a Burgundy is critical, if only because it is easy to be seduced by style at the expense of *terroir*. A surprising number of Burgundies, especially the white Burgundies, do just that. Character in a white wine is much more hard-won than in a red, if only because white wine grapes usually have less intrinsic flavor than red wine grapes. This is very much the case with Chardonnay compared to Pinot Noir.

Moreover, much of the flavor in a wine is extracted from the skins during fermentation. Where many red wines, and certainly Pinot Noir, are made with extended skin contact, most white wines see little or no skin contact. This is true for Chardonnay as it is produced in Burgundy, although there are exceptions. At most, a white Burgundy will see no more than twenty-four hours of its Chardonnay juice fermenting or simply macerating in contact with its skins; most Pinot Noirs are given anywhere from seven days to three weeks on the skins.

Because of this, the temptation is strong for the winemaker to infuse flavor into white wines by means of various winemaking techniques in lieu of winning it in the vineyard. The most common of these is the use of brand-new oak barrels, which provide an immediately recognizable scent of vanilla and toastiness. Another approach is to leave the young but fully fermented wine on its lees or sediment while aging in the barrel and stir up this sediment from time to time. Here, the winemaker is seeking to capitalize on the subtle flavorings of autolyzing or decomposing yeasts. Sometimes, though, the result is a wine with "off" flavors from microbial deterioration.

Too often, signature substitutes for insufficient depth. It is easier, and more ego-gratifying, to fiddle with new oak barrels and winemaking techniques than to toil in the vineyard nursing old vines and pruning severely in order to keep yields low. Character in a white Burgundy, even in the most vocal of sites, does not come automatically. One need only taste an overcropped Montrachet—it is all too common—to realize how fragile is the voice of the land when transmitted by Chardonnay. As a grape, it is surprisingly neutral in flavor, which makes it an ideal vehicle for *terroir*—or for signature.

Character in a red Burgundy is just as hard-won as in a white, but its absence is not as immediately recognizable because of the greater intrinsic flavor of Pinot Noir. That said, it should be pointed out that flavor is not character, any more than a cough drop compares with a real wild cherry.

Where Chardonnay is manipulated to provide an illusion of depth and flavor, the pursuit with Pinot Noir is to make it more immediately accessible and easy down the gullet. An increasing number of red Burgundies are now seductively drinkable virtually upon release only two years after the vintage. Such wines can be misleading. Rather than improving with age, their bright, flashy fruitiness soon fades, like an enthusiasm that cools. The wine drinker is left stranded, stood up by a wine that offered cosmetics rather than character.

All of which underscores why *terroir* is the "more beautiful question" of wine. When the object is to reveal, amplify, and transmit *terroir* with clarity and resonance, there is no more "beautiful answer" than Burgundy. When it is ignored, wine may as well be grown hydroponically, rooted not in an unfathomable Earth that offers flashes of insight we call Richebourg or Corton, but in a manipulated medium of water and nutrients with no more meaning than an intravenous hookup. Happily, the more beautiful question is being asked with renewed urgency by both growers and drinkers. A new care is being exercised. After all, without *terroir*—why Burgundy?

The Burgundian Sensibility—in the Vineyard

Truth is not that which can be demonstrated by the aid of logic. If orange trees are hardy and rich in fruit by this bit of soil and not that, then this bit of soil is what is truth for orange trees. . . . Logic, you say? Let logic wrangle its own explanation of life.

—ANTOINE DE SAINT-EXUPÉRY, *Wind, Sand and Stars*

Applying "truth" to Burgundy is as unwise as combining certain innocent ingredients that, together, become explosive. However tempting it is to seek truths in Burgundy, it is a treacherous exercise. Nevertheless, there are Burgundian "sensibilities," delicacies of perception. They are found in both the vineyard and the winery. The finest Burgundies are the result of the application of these perceptions. A sensibility coarsened by greed, apathy, or plain bad judgment results in a wine that does not fulfill the promise of its origins, like a racehorse of lineage that fails to show.

This chapter focuses on the sensibilities of the vineyard. The most profound vineyard sensibility, *terroir*, already has been examined at length. This is because all other sensibilities in the Burgundian vineyard and winery follow from it. Without *terroir*, there is little reason for a winegrower to concern himself or herself with clonal selection, rootstocks, soil types, and yields. Grapes could be planted willy-nilly, without a care for the exactitude of the resulting expression.

THE SENSIBILITY OF THE SOIL—No perception about the Burgundian vineyard is more complicated, less clear, and yet more compelling than that of soil. Here, we are not talking about *terroir*, which too often is (wrongly) defined as soil and subsoil. As already noted, *terroir* is the ecology of a vineyard site, of which soil is only one element.

The degree to which soil is the informing ingredient of a wine is an issue that is argued more today than ever before. It extends beyond Burgundy, but nowhere is soil seen—at least by the locals —as more authoritative in the shaping the character of a wine. For Burgundians, it is very nearly Freudian: Soil is destiny. Others are not so sure, especially once past the matter of soil structure—pebbly, clayey; well or poorly drained—into the influence of trace elements such as magnesium, nitrogen, and the like.

Burgundians devote an extraordinary amount of attention— some say obsessively so—to just the soil. The reason is that all other variables being equal, such as elevation, exposure, and slope (they rarely are, which complicates things), soil, like genes, can influence the fate of an embryonic wine.

It helps determine whether the wine will be red or white: Pinot Noir performs on clayey soils; Chardonnay thrives on chalky soil. It will determine the physique of the wine: Pinot Noir grown on soils with noticeable amounts of chalk or limestone, such as the upper slopes of Volnay (chalk) or throughout Chambolle-Musigny (limestone), will be more lightly built than if grown on soils gripped by clay, such as Chambertin, where the resulting wine is thickly muscled.

The precise degree of importance of soil in red and white Burgundies is not going to be established here—or probably anywhere else. But one thing is certain: Without the multitude of soils and subsoils found along the Côte d'Or, the wines indisputably would not taste as they do. Moreover, they would not repeatedly convey the same distinction that has allowed dozens of generations of Burgundy drinkers to agree on the particular quality of certain wines. It is not soil alone that achieves this. But without a certain soil, more than a few of the most eminent Burgundies would be stripped of their rank.

A good example is Volnay "Clos des Ducs," a six-acre vineyard owned exclusively by Marquis Jacques d'Angerville. An ancient vineyard, of noble origins as the name suggests, it is situated high up on the slope of Volnay. Its distinction derives not only from d'Angerville's subtle, signature-free winemaking and careful clonal selection, but ultimately from the chalky subsoil of the vineyard.

Volnay has three lateral bands of subsoils that cummerbund the commune. At the base of the slope the subsoil is plumped with a rich, clayey earth. The middle band, where most of the *premiers crus* are found, has a subsoil with some chalk, never more than 25 percent according to the Dutch writer Hubrecht Duijker in *The Great Wines of Burgundy*. The topmost band, where Clos des Ducs is found, is chalkiest of all; the subsoil of Clos des Ducs is at least 50 percent chalk. No matter how the wine is made, Pinot Noir grown in such aggressively chalky soil will always reveal an intrinsic delicacy compared to, say, Volnay "Champans," smack in the middle of the central band. Champans is always a beefier wine, with a noticeably different *goût de terroir*. Jacques d'Angerville owns a piece of Champans too. Taste his Clos des Ducs alongside his Champans from the same vintage, and you will find what "truth" of the soil there is in Burgundy right in your glass.

THE SENSIBILITY OF CLONES—Any discussion of Chardonnay and Pinot Noir will eventually come to the subject of clones. A clone is a vegetatively reproduced plant. Although she didn't know it, my grandmother was constantly cloning her African violets by rifling a leaf stem from a thriving specimen and inserting it in fertilized potting soil to take root.

The virtue of cloning, as all science-fiction buffs know, is that a cloned specimen will exactly reproduce all of the characteristics of the parent. Although the word itself is of fairly recent usage (the *Oxford English Dictionary* cites the first instance only in 1903), the technique of cloning has been practiced since the Romans. Its etymology is apt: *Clone* is derived from the Greek *klon*, a slip or twig.

Virtually all grape varieties, and many other fruits as well, are genetically unstable when grown from seed: What you sow isn't necessarily what you reap. As a result, grape growers have for centuries reproduced grapevines with desirable characteristics by means of vegetative reproduction, either by burying a shoot from a vine into a trench dug nearby or simply by cutting off a shoot and grafting it onto a new rootstock. Today, the techniques of cloning are more sophisticated, but no different in either principle or result.

In modern usage, the term *clone* actually refers to a particular strain of a variety that is isolated, cataloged, and identified by a variety of characteristics such as disease resistance, vigor, yield, adapatability to various grafted rootstocks and wine quality. When a vine is growing in a vineyard, it will proffer several "buds," each of which will create a small shoot upon which leaves and clusters of grapes will form. For still-inexplicable reasons, one bud on a vine might mutate, creating a shoot that offers greater disease resistance to a leaf virus, or more clusters of grapes than the rest of the vine, or any of a number of subtle or dramatic qualities of flavor, color, or robustness. Grape growers are forever on the lookout for such mutations.

Mutations can arise for a variety of reasons. It may be a vine's adaptation to the soil (high limestone or iron content), to the amount of moisture available to it, to its exposure to sunlight, or to a baffling interaction of these and many other factors. A fickle species such as Pinot Noir is that much more willing to change its stripes. As a result, over the millennium of Pinot Noir and Chardonnay cultivation in Burgundy, practically every vineyard developed mutations of these grapevines, some of which the vine tenders chose to reproduce. Each vineyard developed its own peculiar clonal mix over a span of multiple generations of winegrowers, as the luck of the mutations draw came up and as each grower took advantage of his opportunities.

This great clonal assemblage in the many vineyards of Burgundy was easily perpetuated by the once-common method of renewing a vineyard known as *provignage* or "layering." It is now defunct, but prior to the late 1800s was universal in Burgundy and lent itself perfectly to the perpetuation of different strains within the same vineyard.

Vineyards then looked utterly different from today. There were no rows, no wires upon which the vines were trained. Instead, the vineyards began in the same way as they are now: A hole was dug and a vine shoot inserted. Eventually, it was staked. But several years later it would be pruned in such a way as to create a long shoot. This shoot would be buried in a small trench dug nearby and covered with earth and manure. Eventually, the shoot would form its own roots and would itself develop into a proper grapevine. After five or six years, it would itself engender a shoot to be layered.

Over time, trenches had to be dug in every direction, and eventually a vineyard would appear as unruly as a school playground at recess. But just as violinists in an orchestra don't all have to bow in the same direction to create the same sound, neither does a vineyard have to be planted in rows.

The "layered" vineyard was not only inefficient and untidy, but cramped and stunted. A modern vineyard in Burgundy has 8,000 to 10,000 grapevines per hectare (2.47 acres), where the old layered vineyards had 20,000 to 30,000 grapevines in the same space. Because of this crowding, each vine produced a minuscule quantity of grapes, typically with very small berries. This explains how the Corton vineyard described by Cyrus Redding in 1833 (see Corton) produced just 10 or 12 liters of wine per hectare compared to the 300 or so liters per hectare today. Redding's figures are probably a typographical error. It generally is thought that the yields of the mid-1800s were between 10 and 15 *hecto*liters per hectare (hl/ha).

The opportunity of identifying a mutant shoot and cloning it by layering was ever-present. Or one could maintain the original strain selected when the vineyard was first established (although one's bundle of purchased shoots was unlikely to be of a single strain; even today many growers find themselves with volunteers from another regiment). Most likely, clonal mixes arose inadvertently, as shoots were layered willy-nilly.

The doom of the layered vineyard was the American root louse called phylloxera. It invaded Burgundy in 1878, performing the same rite as it had everywhere else in Europe: sucking the life from the native roots of the *Vitis vinifera* grapevine. Only certain American grapevines had roots with an inborn resistance to the bug. Then, as now, there was only one resort: grafting a *vinifera* shoot onto a resistant American rootstock.

With this new reality, the *provignage* system came to an end. But the clonal mix of each vineyard did not necessarily cease as well, for growers could, if they wished, use shoots of their existing grapevines as the material for a new vineyard. After all, it was the soil that was diseased, and only the roots were affected. The shoots needed only to be grafted onto resistant rootstocks.

At the time, growers feared that American rootstocks coupled to their vines would result in altogether new grape varieties lacking the flavor and character of the old vines. That didn't happen. The shoot, rather than the root, is the "DNA" of a vine. The last ungrafted patch in Burgundy, the great Romanée-Conti vineyard, finally gave up the fight against phylloxera in 1945. The clonal mix of the modern Romanée-Conti vineyard is virtually identical to its pre-phylloxera ancestors. No difference in character can be discerned, according to the few who have tasted 1945 or older Romanée-Conti bottlings against those of 1953 or later, that year being the first bottling from the new, grafted vines.

Now, one of the fiercest debates in Burgundy is between those who advocate what is called *sélection clonale*, where a vineyard is replanted to only a few identified, selected clones and *sélection massale* (literally, from a crowd), which seeks to replicate the old mix when replanting a vineyard. The clonal selection advocates, most notably Raymond Bernard, the longtime director of the Office National Interprofessionel des Vins de Table (ONIVIN), contend that the best clones are but a few. That they are more disease-resistant; give fuller-flavored wine with yields that are commercially viable. And that they have adapted well to specified rootstocks.

The essence of *sélection massale* is the theme of a sum being greater than its parts. Its adherents maintain that many of the old strains do not show well in clonal trials because their yields are thought uneconomic and susceptible to disease, and individual wines from the different grapes are considered deficient in strong varietal characteristics. Like the runt of a litter, such strains therefore are culled. Supporters maintain that this is narrow thinking, that the transmission of *terroir* in a vineyard is sometimes muted, or overwhelmed, by the plantation of just a few clones with vibrant, even intrusive varietal characteristics. This argument is most vehement with Pinot Noir.

Is there a clear conclusion? No. Some clonal selection clearly is necessary, especially with Chardonnay, if only for increased disease-resistance. Too many Chardonnay vines in Burgundy are diseased, leading to fewer grapes of lower quality. Also, some of the new Chardonnay vines are excessively Muscatlike in their flavors, which is the result of inappropriately chosen clones. Clonal selection can cut both ways. It is true that clonally selected vines tend to produce more. Although it is estimated that only 15 percent or so of the Pinot Noir in the Côte d'Or is now planted to just a few clonally selected vines, a significantly higher amount of Chardonnay vineyards are clonally selected. And there's no question that white Burgundy yields have increased substantially. Effect following cause, the regulations on maximum yields have been revised upward to reflect this.

The argument for *sélection massale* is especially persuasive with Pinot Noir. Its flavor is the proverbial moving target, and is rarely able to be fixed in the gunsights of even the most acute tasters. Unlike Cabernet Sauvignon, which is almost belligerently forceful in its flavor definition, Pinot Noir is a matter of shadings. A few strains, no matter how well selected, probably cannot accomplish what a sampling of twenty or thirty clones can do. In this regard, Burgundy continues to frustrate the demands of science: to eliminate variables so as to achieve predictability. Pinot Noir coupled with *terroir* refuses to oblige. Still, the scientists continue to try, as well they should.

THE SENSIBILITY OF YIELD—Here, "sensibility" is stretched to its breaking point. What sensibility exists in Burgundy today on the subject of yields is not found in the law, but rather, is the private preserve of individual growers who choose to pursue what everyone knows: Low yields in the vineyard are a prerequisite to greatness in a wine. At issue is just what constitutes a low yield?

As the section on clones demonstrates, what used to be considered a low yield before phylloxera would today be considered absurd, and rightly so. The argument today is that with advances in disease control, fertilizers, anti-rot sprays, clonal selection, more suitable rootstocks, and so forth, a "reasonable" yield is significantly higher at no loss in quality from what used to be extracted from the vineyards in the 1950s and 1960s, when yields were no more than 30 hl/ha and often less.

How much has changed? For one thing, the size of the vineyard in the Côte d'Or itself has changed. In 1961 the Côte d'Or had 13,300 acres under vines. By 1986 the figure grew to 19,520 acres under vines, a 47 percent increase. Most of this has occurred in the Hautes Côtes and in areas entitled only to the appellation "Bourgogne". Because wines from these districts are lower-priced, the pressure for high yields is great. And when the time comes to figure out the average yield in the Côte d'Or, these vineyards are necessarily included in the calculation.

All of which is to suggest that any assertion about increased yields in the Côte d'Or have to be viewed carefully. One thing is certain: Yields have gone up significantly in many of the best vineyards. The aggregate figures tell us this: In 1951, the average yield in the Côte d'Or, red and white wines combined, was 29 hectoliters per hectare (hl/ha) or 129 cases of wine per acre. By 1979, the figure rose 41 percent, to almost 41 hl/ha or 182 cases of wine per acre. Part of this surely is accounted for in the expansion of outlying vineyards technically considered part of the Côte d'Or.

But the revealing point about yields in the best vineyards is found in the law. Here, you see that control of wine quality by the government through limiting vineyard yields is all pretense and posturing, a case of the inmates having taken over the asylum if ever there was one. The system was once ostensibly strict, the authorities at least pretending that low yields and quality are intimately linked. It was flouted by the growers and shippers so flagrantly that the regulatory authority, INAO, had but two choices: Attempt to actually enforce the regulations and risk the real possibility of failing miserably (and publicly), or change them to make legal what the growers already were doing—namely, increasing the yields well beyond the original mandated limits.

The old system was known as the "cascade." Then, as now, the government set a maximum-yield limitation for each vineyard. Chambertin, for example had a maximum yield of 30 hl/ha, which is a reasonably low yield. Someone who owned one hectare of Chambertin could not sell more than 30 hectoliters or 330 cases of wine labeled Chambertin. But there was a gaping loophole. Greedy growers would prune the vines for a larger yield, say, 45 hl/ha. The law allowed them to sell off 30 hectoliters as Chambertin and—here comes the "cascade"—sell the balance at an authorized lower classification, such as Gevrey-Chambertin. The two wines were identical, of course. But the person buying the wine labeled as Chambertin was really not getting what he or she paid for, except in the legal niceties. It was a system that encouraged overcropping.

In 1974, the authorities instituted a new approach, to be phased in over five years. Now, you still have purported maximum yields. They are called the *rendement de base*. But that's just the starting point. Every year a committee of government authorities, growers, and shippers convenes in late August or early September to establish for each appellation an annual maximum yield known as the *rendement annuel*. Previously, growers complained that the old system was inflexible, failing to take into account that some vintages are inherently abundant. The *rendement annuel* was installed to address this.

So far, so flexible. But no sooner is the *rendement annuel* set than the authorities bestow an additional benefit: the *plafond limite de classement* or PLC. This allows a grower to produce an additional percentage of wine over the *rendement annuel*—usually it's 20 percent—subject to an obligatory tasting by an authorized panel. It's a bit of a "sudden death" playoff in that if the tasting panel refuses to acknowledge that the wine tastes like a Vosne-Romanée or Meursault or whatever the requested appellation, all of the wine made must be distilled. The "cascade" thrill is gone. Rarely, however, are the wines rejected. The tasting panels are necessarily composed mostly of other growers in the commune—along with shippers and representatives of the Ministry of Agriculture—and it's tough to look your neighbor in the eye and tell him that all of his wine has to be distilled, along with his income.

Still, the PLC is not the problem. It's the *rendement annuel*. Rarely is it less than a 20 percent increase over the *rendement de base*. And that foundation itself was jacked up in 1983, when the *rendement de base* for many appellations was revised upward. Where the *rendement de base* for Chambertin previously was 30 hl/ha, now it's 35 hl/ha. The same increase applied for all of the *grands crus* in Vosne-Romanée such as La Tâche or Richebourg. Montrachet soared from 30 hl/ha to 40 hl/ha. Add a 20 percent boost to that, and you wind up with an authorized yield of 48 hl/ha, no questions asked.

A realistic depiction of the typical yield in a decent vintage in the Côte d'Or today is 20 percent over the *rendement de base*, which is pretty much what the usual *rendement annuel* works out to be. Because of that, the case quantities in the grower listings are calculated on each appellation's *rendement de base* plus 20 percent.

The Burgundian Sensibility—in the Winery

I t would not be too far-fetched to consider the Côte d'Or a nine-teen-thousand-acre preserve of the rare, the unusual, the outdated, as well as the most advanced in winemaking techniques. The views of the eighteenth century coexist, not always congenially, with those of the late twentieth-century. Burgundy is the Walden Pond of winegrowing. In it one can view the whole world of science, art, history, fact, fallacy, and fancy in winemaking technique.

The Burgundian winemaker, if such stubborn individualists can ever be so characterized, is an amalgam of high tech and low labor. One winemaker will insist with no little fervor that great Pinot Noir can only be created if the grapes are crushed by foot and the floating "cap" of skins in the fermentation vat is regularly submerged through the (sapping) efforts of a naked man lunging his body into this cap. Pinot Noir was made that way two hundred years ago.

Yet not a quarter of a kilometer down the road, another wine-maker will report with equal assurance that greatness is aided through the use of an expensive "must cooler," a cylindrical sausage of stain-less-steel refrigeration pipes that can lower the temperature of the just-crushed grapes to achieve a better fermentation. A third wine-maker will tell yet a different tale, and so on down the road, all thirty-one miles of it along the Côte d'Or.

It is difficult to know whom, or even what, to believe. The temptation is strong to conclude that there is only one "right" way to make Pinot Noir or Chardonnay. But winemaking is not a cook-book recipe, however formulaic it may seem when put down on the printed page. The finest winemakers are always adaptable. Every winemaker goes into the cellar with his or her approach, only to discover that the weather, like a surprise witness in a courtroom trial, forces a complete rethinking of the case. Last year he may have added a high proportion of stems to the fermenting grapes so as to add tannin; this year the grapes are more tannic than usual, so no stems. This in turn invites a reconsideration about barrels: tannic new barrels or tannin-free old ones? Or perhaps a mix of the two? A bottle of wine is a summation of a winemaker's thoughts.

WHEN TO PICK?

The first critical step in winemaking occurs outside of the cellar. Deciding when a grape is picked can greatly determine the course of winemaking events to follow. If picked too soon, a grape will lack sugar and the panoply of flavors that characterize ripeness or, really, maturity. Too often, ripeness is discussed merely in terms of sugar content, which is too crude a measure. The re-sulting wine may taste "green," too tart, and will need to have sugar added during the fermentation in order to achieve a re-spectable alcohol level. (This procedure is known as "chaptali-zation," about which more further on.)

In Burgundy, the question of when to pick is an especially risky one, as the region is harried by autumn rains. The decision to allow the grapes to remain on the vines for an additional week or ten days in order to gain greater depth of flavor and higher sugar content can be an expensive gamble.

The 1986 vintage offers a good example. It began to rain just at the moment of harvest. Local weather forecasters predicted more rains to follow. Some growers pulled in their grapes, figuring that things would only get worse. The resulting wines were thin, "hollow," and watery. More committed (and courageous) growers decided to wait, recognizing that if any sort of real quality was to be achieved, the grapes simply would have to have more time on the vine. They risked the real chance of losing everything in the gamble for quality. These growers won. The rains stopped. The grapes picked late made the finest wines, worthy of the highest accolades. But the reputation of the vintage was marred by too many watery wines. As is often the case, the best growers had to struggle for reputation against their own colleagues.

Historically, the preference of peasant growers was to haul in their grapes as early as possible to preclude any chance of damage from the rain. Prior to the Revolution, the aristocracy sought to contain this "quality be damned" attitude through the use of the *ban de vendage*—an authorized beginning of the harvest. In Burgundy, growers weren't even allowed, in theory anyway, to enter their vineyards as the harvest dates approached.

Each Burgundian commune had a different beginning day, so as to allow an adequate supply of pickers for everyone. Also, different vineyard areas or at least sections on the slope tended to ripen earlier or later than others. There was one exemption to the *ban de vendage*: Vineyards surrounded by walls, the *clos* created by religous orders, could be harvested at any moment church authorities pleased.

The *ban de vendage* lapsed, predictably, during the Revolution, but was reinstated shortly afterward. Gradually, it fell from use, and by 1848, when universal male suffrage was instituted, the authoritarian *ban de vendage* was completely abandoned.

Today, growers of the Côte d'Or are advised by the Station Oenologique at Beaune as to ideal picking dates for Pinot Noir and Chardonnay. The beginning dates of the harvest vary from year to year. Chardonnay is typically harvested before Pinot Noir, although in some years they can mature almost at the same moment, which can strain winemaking facilities to overflowing. The majority of harvest dates in the Côte d'Or in the past twenty years have occurred in the last week of September or the first week of October. The date of the harvest reveals very little. A superb vintage such as 1978 began on October 5, yet the poor 1977 harvest also commenced on that same date. It is only upon learning that picking for the 1976 vintage began around September 5 that one can infer that 1976 must have been a very hot year indeed to allow such early harvesting. The hot 1989 vintage began similarly early.

Although harvest dates have changed little from those of earlier times, a contemporary problem echoes an ancient one: Too many of today's Burgundies are made from grapes harvested too soon. Since we will get our price anyway, goes the grower's reasoning, why risk losing all or part to the potential rains? We'll pull the grapes in and make up for any sugar deficiency with some added cane sugar during fermentation. Hence the local slang for chaptalization: "sun in sacks."

But ripeness is not just a matter of sugar content, although it is a critical measure. When a grape is approaching the stage described as "ripe," its skin has changed color, typically from green to either a deep purple for a red wine grape or a yellowish-green for a white wine grape. Within the grape there is also a shifting balance of power. Acidity is decreasing and is being cut into by the increasing quantity of sugar. The grape is getting less tart and sweeter. The flavors are concentrating in the skin. The winemaker's objective is to harvest the grape when it teeter-totters between not sugar-rich enough and too rich; between mouth-puckering tartness from the acidity and a "flabbiness" from too little acidity.

Since the Burgundian climate is very cool, both Pinot Noir and Chardonnay are only just beginning to reach this ideal balance as the cool, rainy weather of autumn encroaches. Once the grape leaves change color, no more sugar is being sent to the grapes, as photosynthesis has stopped. As they remain on the vines, the grapes slowly lose moisture—which can increase the amount of sugar in relation to the juice as the water in the grape evaporates. Also, acidity will decrease, as sunlight on the grape skin ripens it, perhaps too much so. In theory, the flavors of the grape will be intensified the longer it remains on the vine, providing it does not rot under a steady play of rain or freeze from an early winter.

Some of the finest growers in Burgundy are convinced of the importance of late harvesting, especially for Pinot Noir. The most dramatic example is the Domaine de la Romanée-Conti, which habitually is the last to pick in Vosne-Romanée and probably the whole of Burgundy. They seek the most intense Pinot Noir flavor possible and are willing (and financially able) to gamble on autumn rains. If part of the crop does rot, the rotted grapes will be painstakingly removed, and only ripe, healthy ones will go into the fermenting vat. And we will pay dearly for this risk and care. In exchange, the reward can be some of the most opulent of Burgundies. Very late picking is a technique that appears to work best in the lesser vintages. Where other growers in the commune turned out equally fine wines in a glorious year such as 1978, few properties managed to create palatable, let alone fine, wines in such soggy situations as 1980, where the wines of the Domaine de la Romanée-Conti and others like them emerged as genuinely fine and much to be sought after.

TO STEM OR NOT TO STEM?

As soon as the grapes are harvested, the Burgundian winegrower faces the next question of the season: Include the stems from the Pinot Noir or Chardonnay grapes or exclude them during fermentation? It is a minor question that engenders major emotions. The stems or stalks contain a great deal of tannin, something that the skin of Chardonnay is almost devoid of and that even the skin of Pinot Noir may occasionally lack. (Red wine grapes are more tannic than white wine grapes.) It is tannin that makes young red wines so puckery and astringent to taste. But it also acts as an effective bacteria fighter and antioxidant.

There are many types of tannin, which explains why it is sometimes referred to in the plural as *tannins*. Grape juice itself is almost devoid of any tannins, less than half of 1 percent. The pips are very tannic, from 5 percent to 6 percent of their composition; the skins range from 0.5 percent to 1.5 percent. The stems are about 3 percent tannin.

Proponents of the use of stems point to the fact that stems help loosen the texture of the grape mass during crushing, allowing more juice to flow easily into the vat. They also note the addition of tannin from the stems as necessary for the creation of long-lived Pinot Noir and Chardonnay; it gives a wine "backbone."

Opponents deride these arguments, contending that the tannins from the stems are excessively bitter and unnecessary. The stems are also known to absorb both color and alcohol during the fermentation.

The winemaker has complete control in the matter, courtesy of a device known as a stemmer/crusher, which strips the grapes from the stalks with admirable thoroughness and then lightly crushes the destemmed grapes. One can, therefore, include any percentage of stems in the fermenting vat one likes.

The inclusion of most or all of the stems in the fermentation of Pinot Noir is a facet of the so-called *méthode ancienne*, which is not so ancient as the phrase implies. Burgundies up to the Revolution, red and white alike, were extremely light, meant to be drunk between one harvest and the next. Although stems were typically included with the crushed grapes, the fermenting period was so brief that there was little time for the tannins to be leached.

The *méthode ancienne* dates only from the latter half of the 1800s, when the call came for richer, deeper, very long-lived Burgundies. Tannins were essential as a preservative, and stems are the most abundant source. The pendulum swung sharply the other way in the 1970s, when consumers sought wines that could be drunk sooner. After that, a reaction set in. At that moment, the phrase *méthode ancienne* became a catchword for traditional, old-style Burgundies. Whether a producer included stems in his Pinot Noir was seized upon as a key to his commitment to recreating the glories of the past.

If one reviews the winemaking techniques of some of the finest producers in the Côte d'Or today, it becomes readily apparent that no clear-cut proof exists that stems are absolutely vital to the creation of great Pinot Noir or Chardonnay, or even for reasonably long-lived wines. Many fine producers will change their approach dramatically in this matter based upon their assessment of the grapes at the time of the harvest. The issue of stems or no stems is a hollow symbol, a catchy way to identify who is in the vanguard of *vin de garde*.

PINOT NOIR—HOW TO FERMENT?

Apart from the matter of yield, there is no more critical factor in achieving greatness with Pinot Noir than the method of fermentation. Fermentation is a deceptively simple activity, a matter of doing what comes naturally for a grape. A grape is broken open; the wild yeasts mired in the waxy "bloom" of the skin of the ripe grape are awash in sugar-rich juice, and they immediately proceed to feed, exhale carbon dioxide, and do what also comes naturally to yeasts: reproduce. If all of this occurs inside a vat, the mixture begins to bubble furiously, (a phase the French descriptively call *embouillage* or "boiling"). This remarkable activity, which can sound like an angry swarm of bees, is due to the carbon dioxide exhaled by the yeasts. It is powerful enough to push a dense cap of grape skins and stems a foot or more thick to the top of the vat.

Technically, the process of fermentation is caused not by the yeasts, but by the enzymes they secrete. But the yeasts are critical, as they must constantly be reproducing and secreting enzymes if fermentation is to continue. There is, however, a limit. As the sugar in the juice is consumed, the alcohol level of the soon-to-be-wine begins to increase. In this regard, one might view yeasts in a Freudian manner: They are self-destructive. Alcohol paralyzes yeasts, and as it increases in the vat, the yeasts progressively weaken.

In this oversimplified depiction, the winemaker seemingly does little more than assemble the grapes, crush them to get the juice flowing, offer a home for it in the form of a vat or barrel, and then stand back and let nature take its course. However, winemaking is not this pleasant reverie of man in tune with the forces of the universe. Rather, it was probably winemaking that Murphy had in mind when he postulated his famous law to the effect that anything that can go wrong will go wrong.

What can go wrong during the course of a fermentation is what some drinkers call "a three-bottle story." In Burgundy, one of the initial difficulties is that by the time of the harvest, the weather is cool. The grapes are downright cold, and yeasts find their ardor suppressed by the cold. Fermentation occurs most readily between about 60 degrees Fahrenheit and 70 degrees Fahrenheit. Too often the grape juice is significantly cooler, and if wine is going to be made, the winemaker will have to step into the picture.

This is literally what occurred in Burgundy until quite recently: Naked men would lower themselves into a large vat of sluggishly fermenting must (which is the term for the mélange of grape juice and skins before the juice turns into wine). A description of such a scene was accurately reported by Agoston Haraszthy in 1862 in *Grape Culture, Wines, and Wine-Making*, the title of his report to the California state legislature.

> According to the size of the tank, from four to ten men, stripped of all their clothes, step into the vessel, and begin to tread down the

floating mass, working it also with their hands. This operation is repeated several times if the wine does not ferment rapidly enough. The reason given for this, in my eyes, rather dirty work, is that the bodily heat of the men aids the wine in its fermentation; but this object might be gained by throwing in heated stones, or using pipes filled with steam or hot water.

Haraszthy's suggestion about using pipes has since been taken up, although I am assured by a Burgundian friend that he knows at least one winemaker in Burgundy today who still employs what Haraszthy calls the *"costume à l'Adam"* to heat his must.

Nowadays, there are several alternatives, such as the creation of a *pied de cuve* or the use of a radiatorlike device called a *drapeau*. A *pied de cuve* (literally, "base of the vat") is a small amount of must that is heated gently until a fermentation is really under way. It is typically begun shortly before the bulk of the grapes are to be harvested. This small vat becomes, in effect, a starter. The batch is added to the first vats of wine to get them going. It is an odd feature of winemaking that the first vats of wine are always reluctant to "catch," but once one vat gets going, the others are seemingly ignited from the profusion of yeasts in the air. This is particularly true in French and Italian winemaking, where the wild yeasts on the grape skins are employed, rather than inoculated yeast cultures that are universal in Germany and the United States.

But if the must is simply too cold, the winemaker plunges a *drapeau* into the vat. This radiatorlike device is hooked up to a tube that sends hot water coursing through its intestinal piping. Fermentation usually begins forthwith.

A third variation is the simple measure of heating part of the must in each vat in a small cauldron. The ones I've seen are double-jacketed copper steam kettles, identical to the big soup kettles one finds in institutional kitchens. The warmed must is pumped into the vat until it warms the whole sufficiently, and fermentation then ensues.

Once the must is warmed and fermentation is under way, the Burgundian winemaker confronts a different fret: keeping the must from getting too hot. The fermentation process produces considerable heat, and yeasts will become increasingly sluggish as the temperature reaches 95 degrees Fahrenheit. When it exceeds 104 degrees, they will die. Such peril is known as a "stuck" fermentation. There will usually be a good deal of sugar remaining in the half-fermenting wine, but it is difficult to restart a fermentation once it becomes "stuck." It can be done, but the results are rarely very good, as the high heat also bakes away some of the acidity, making the resulting wine a bit flabby. Also, acetic-acid bacteria can build up rapidly, which can result in a vaguely vinegary wine.

One means of addressing this problem is by reversing the technique of heating the must. One can cool it, by running cold water through the *drapeau* or by means of an expensive device known as a "must cooler." A feverish must is pumped out of the vat and run through this heat exchanger at an impressively rapid rate, and is returned to the vat cool as a cat burglar. One might alternatively ferment the wine in stainless-steel tanks equipped with "jackets" on the outside of the tank that contain glycol or cold water. Although expensive, these are increasingly common throughout the world, and even the Burgundians, a hidebound bunch if ever there was one, have come round to this marvel of control. Nevertheless, a goodly number of diehards still prefer the old-style, elegant wooden vats. The wood, it is true, will retain heat, which is useful during cold autumns. Conversely, the same insulating qualities allow it to retain the coolness of the air in which it is situated, which can be beneficial if the must becomes too warm.

Excessive heat is of particular concern to Pinot Noir producers because they skirt closer to the danger line than most other winemakers. It is generally conceded that Pinot Noir offers greater depth of flavor, and color, when it is fermented at what might be considered a dangerously high temperature: 30 degrees centigrade or about 86 degrees Fahrenheit. This doesn't leave the winemaker much of a margin for error in that although it is not easy to get the temperature that high, once it gets there it's not easy to keep it from going higher yet. Fortunately, the high heat is most desirable at the beginning of the fermentation, where most of the color extraction occurs, and also when the greatest quantity of grape sugar is available and the yeasts are really randy. The complication to this high-heat fermentation is that the whole business is over too quickly; fermentation can be complete in a matter of four or five days. The finest producers seek a long, leisurely process, dribbling out as much as fourteen to twenty-one days. To achieve this, some add whole clusters of uncrushed Pinot Noir. The juice inside the berries is cool and is released slowly, and the fermentation is prolonged. Others employ the addition of sugar, called "chaptalization."

CHAPTALIZATION

It is during the fermentation, particularly the first few days, that the Burgundian winemaker must make yet another critical decision that affects the quality and style of his Pinot Noir. The decision hinges upon the practice of adding sugar to the must, what is known in both French and English as "chaptalization" (in French *chaptalisation*). The procedure couldn't be easier: Granulated sugar is simply poured into the vat. The total quantity is not added at one time, but is spaced out over a period of days. This prevents a runaway fermentation. The issue of whether to chaptalize or not is of less concern with Chardonnay, as it is inherently richer in sugar and therefore less likely to be in want of an added dose. Nevertheless, many if not most white Burgundies are chaptalized, something that too rarely is pointed out.

The term *chaptalization* is derived from the name of a notable figure in French history, Comte Jean-Antoine Chaptal de Chanteloup (aka the comte de Chanteloup) who was a chemist, a minister of agriculture under Napoleon Bonaparte, and president of the French Academy of Science. Chaptal believed in the virtues of science and pragmatism, and his endorsement of the addition of sugar to the fermenting must proves the point. He did not, however, invent the technique. The French chemist Maquer investigated and described the process as early as 1776, twenty-five years before Chaptal weighed in.

One of Chaptal's chores under Napoleon Bonaparte's regime was the promotion of the sugar-beet industry. Until the mid-1700s, sugar was a luxury confined to the upper classes. Whatever sweetening was done was accomplished with honey. But by the late 1700s the importation of sugar from sugar cane growing in the West Indies and Brazil made sugar much more widespread. The only problem was that the British controlled the trade and, because all of it was seaborne, they could effectively block its arrival on the European continent if they wished. Which is precisely what occurred during the Napoleonic Wars.

However, half a century earlier, in 1747, a Prussian chemist discovered sugar in beet juice; by 1793 a Frenchman living in Berlin perfected a process to extract this sugar on a commercial scale. Napoleon consequently saw beet sugar as his salvation and ordered vast tracts of land in northern France to be planted to the beet. It was a successful ploy.

Chaptal, the pragmatic man of science and politics, saw at least one potential use, which would provide a substantial market for the soon-to-emerge sugar-beet industry. Too often grapes would not ripen adequately, leaving them sugar-deficient, with the resulting wine deficient in alcohol. Why not brace up the wine with a tonic dose of sugar? It was and is a sound idea, chemically, aesthetically, and commercially. The yeasts, after all, make no distinction whatever between natural grape sugar and any other form of sucrose. (There is absolutely no chemical difference between sugar from cane and sugar from beets, nor is there a difference in appearance or taste after processing.)

From the first, Chaptal cautioned against excess. This was in his landmark book in 1801, *Traité théoretique et practique sur la Culture de la vigne et l'Art de faire le vigne, les eaux de vie, esprit de vin, vinaigres simple et composés* (*A Theoretical and Practical Work on the Cultivation of the Vine and the Art of Making Wine, Fruit Brandies, Wine Brandy, and Simple and Blended Vinegars*). Too much sugar added to fermenting wine creates an imbalance. The wine does not necessarily taste sweeter, as the yeasts will consume every last granule of sugar, but it will seem "spirity," overly alcoholic, "hot." There will be a burning sensation in the aftertaste.

Regrettably, too many Burgundian winegrowers blithely ignore this yawning pitfall of an otherwise laudable practice. Although Chaptal only legitimized what was no doubt going on anyway (probably with honey rather than sugar), the advent of cheap sugar from beets and an official sanction from one of the great scientific minds of the day made the practice of adding sugar to the must a normal procedure in winemaking, and excessive sugaring an inevitability.

It is well established that adding enough sugar to raise the alcohol content to the extent of one degree is a beneficial practice. Virtually no one, no matter how acute his or her palate, is likely to be able to detect any effect at this minimal level. French law generously allows for a maximum of two degrees, but any level of chaptalization supposedly can be performed only after petitioning the authorities just before harvest. The law requires each producer to file a declaration of intent and wait for permission. Permission is granted without fail every year in Burgundy (and in Bordeaux as well), even in such ultraripe vintages as 1976 and 1989. The law also forbids them from adding the sugar a little at a time. Winemakers are supposed to add all of the requested sugar at one time, but they almost never do. Instead, it gets dribbled in, often to extend the fermentation so as to allow for greater extraction of color and flavor.

Excessive chaptalization is nothing new in Burgundy. It probably was worse in past times. Agoston Haraszthy informs us that in 1862 as much as thirty pounds of sugar was "often" added to each sixty gallons of fermenting wine, which works out to about three degrees of added alcohol. To raise the alcohol by only one degree, ten pounds of sugar is needed for every sixty gallons of wine. There weren't even any regulations limiting the use of sugar until the introduction of the Appellation Contrôlée system.

It cannot be emphasized too strongly that the practice of chaptalization is highly desirable when held to a maximum of 1 to 1.5 degrees of alcohol. The additional degree or so can raise a perfectly mature, fully ripe Pinot Noir grape naturally offering eleven degrees of alcohol to a more secure twelve degrees, which will help it endure, as well as ship better. It is also an essential practice when Pinot Noir is fermented in open wood vats, which is traditional in the Côte d'Or, although beginning to give way to the closed, stainless-steel versions. Roughly one degree of alcohol evaporates from the open vats, along with a slight amount absorbed into the wood itself. This must be restored, and chaptalization, within limits, is the ideal recompense.

Nevertheless, judicious chaptalization has yet to become universal in Burgundy. A large part of this is due to too-early picking; part of it is also due to a perceived public demand for big, beefy Burgundies. Too many Burgundy drinkers have come to believe that Burgundies are heady, heavy, powerful wines. The real thing rarely, if ever, fits this description. Even the most profound and powerful red Burgundies, such as Chambertin or Richebourg, reveal an intrinsic delicacy. Such wines will never leave one with a headache, a common malady among many Burgundy drinkers. Excessive chaptalization is a likely culprit—assuming of course that excessive drinking is not.

SKIN CONTACT

Perhaps the key issue in the fermentation of Pinot Noir is how long the fermenting grape juice is allowed to remain "on the skins," i.e., in contact with the flavor-infusing, tannin-rich grape skins.

Leaving the fermenting grape juice on the skins is known as the technique of *cuvaison*. The word is logically derived from *cuve*, a tank or vat.

To a historian, one of the striking features of tapestries depicting harvest scenes in the 1400s is the absence of large fermenting vats capable of holding the mass of skins and juice. These appeared by the 1600s, but not for the purpose of *cuvaison*. The wine was fermented as briefly as before, but only in larger quantities. The lightness of all red wines of this era is best revealed by a contemporary observer, Olivier de Serres, who was secretary of state under Henry IV. In his 1615 work *Le Théâtre de l'Agriculture et la Nouvelle Maison Rustique*, he described what passed for *cuvaison* in the early 1600s:

> As soon as the vat was filled with crushed grapes, a man stood guard with his ear against the outside until he heard it start to "boil." This took anywhere from two to three hours, after which an excellent *clairet* wine could be taken out, the most delicate and flavorful coming first.

The fermentation style of red Burgundies remained resolutely committed to this ideal of lightness and delicacy, long after other red wines, notably those of Bordeaux, had pursued the possibilities of lengthier vatting periods. As late as 1807, Jean-Antoine Chaptal would describe the still-traditional method of fermenting Pinot Noir in Burgundy as follows:

> The sweeter the must, the longer it should be left in the vat. Lighter wines of Burgundy can't take more than six to 12 hours of *cuvaison*. The most famous of these is that of Volnay. This wine, so fine, so delicate, so agreeable, can't stand a *cuvaison* of more than 18 hours, and doesn't last from one harvest to the next. Pommard is the second quality of light wine of Burgundy. It lasts longer than that of Volnay, but if kept for more than a year, it gets oily, stale, and takes on an onion skin color.

The duration of the *cuvaison* kept increasing during the nineteenth century. By 1862, Haraszthy was reporting that in Burgundy, "Five days is generally sufficient for the fermenting of wine." It was not until the late 1800s that the length of the *cuvaison* increased to the multiweek span that today some claim is necessary for great Pinot Noir. There is no definitive length of time that fermenting wine needs to spend on the skins in order to extract all of the flavor and tannins desirable. A vintage such as 1976, which was so warm that the grapes had comparatively little juice encased within extremely deeply colored and exceptionally tannic skins, was not well served by a lengthy *cuvaison*. Such wines came out like overbrewed tea, too tannic to be bearable, with a sluggish, stewed, raisiny taste.

It does appear that the finest Pinot Noirs in Burgundy are the product of reasonably extended *cuvaison*, typically between fifteen to twenty days long. The usual fermentation time in Burgundy today is between eight and fifteen days. Although the skins can be removed while a wine is still fermenting, this is usually not done in Burgundy until very near the completion of the fermentation.

To seek an extended *cuvaison*, and thus a long fermentation as well, is to invite fatigue. The cap of grape skins and stems is pushed to the top of the vat by the rising carbon dioxide. Since it is the intermingling of the wine with the flavor-rich skins that makes extended *cuvaison* worth the trouble, one must redistribute the floating skins back into the wine. This can be achieved mechanically by pumping the wine over the cap; by laboriously pushing this surprisingly thick cap back down into the wine with a plunger; or most traditionally, by climbing into the vat, holding both sides, and jumping up and down. The fact that a hefty Burgundian (they do seem a little meatier than other Frenchmen) can almost stand on top of the cap without sinking, gives one an idea of just how solid the cap can get.

Whatever the technique—of course there are fervent proponents of each—it is tiresome, as the cap must be pushed down or pumped over at least twice a day throughout the fermentation. Otherwise, the yeasts will be deprived of oxygen (the carbon dioxide pushes up the cap, which then seals the top of the open vat, imprisoning the layer of carbon dioxide beneath it). The temperature can also rise precipitously, especially in the middle of the vat, as the cap is a terrific insulator. During harvest time, it is not at all unusual for the winemaker to simply move a cot and a hot plate into the fermentation room and call it a life for two or three weeks.

COLD MACERATION

Without question, the greatest uproar in Burgundy today is over the practice of cold maceration. Simply put, it is a matter of taking lightly crushed or whole grapes (usually a combination of the two), placing them in a refrigerated sealed vat, adding a sizable dose of sulfur to ward off bacteria, and then allowing the grape juice to macerate with the skins without fermenting. The juice is then slowly warmed and allowed to ferment. The resulting wine, at minimum, is very deeply colored.

Cold maceration is not a new process. Indeed, many growers allow wine to macerate with the skins for a varied number of days before drawing off the juice and then pressing the skins. But that occurs with new wine rather than unfermented juice, because it is much trickier to keep juice from fermenting than wine from spoiling—although that sometimes happens anyway. Usually, the result is dark, extremely tannic wine, often coarse and rough.

Cold maceration is something else again. Its most famous practitioner, who employed it in a modified fashion, is Henri Jayer, a recently retired winegrower in Vosne-Romanée whose dark, rich wines commanded some of the highest prices in Burgundy. Jayer used to cold-macerate his Pinot Noir grapes for four to six days before commencing an otherwise conventional fermentation.

But the Jayer approach is small stuff indeed compared to that advocated by a Lebanese oenologist named Guy Accad, who has become the first consulting oenologist of any note in Burgundy. Although common in Bordeaux and Tuscany, consulting oenologists were unknown in Burgundy until Accad arrived in Nuits-Saint-Georges in the mid-1970s. What he advocates is nothing short of revolutionary for Burgundy, and has caused controversy in the region itself and prompted the French regulatory authorities to deny one grower using Accad techniques (Jacky Confuron-Cotetidot) to sell some of his wine with an appellation label. So far, little has reached the public about Accad, largely because his influence is only now taking hold. He consults to fifteen Burgundian winegrowers, some of them possessors of some of the greatest red Burgundy vineyards, such as Richebourg and Corton. A few of these, such as Maison Joseph Faiveley, employ Accad only as a consultant for vineyard, rather than winemaking, matters.

This is not to say that Accad has operated in secret, although it is alleged that he keeps little tricks confidential, such as the addition of certain enzymes to help kick-start the fermentation. He does have his public supporters, notably the French wine writer Michel Bettane, who is Accad's leading propagandist and whose public support and influence in the French wine world is formidable. In America, Accad has the enthusiastic support of Robert M. Parker, Jr., whose newsletter *The Wine Advocate* is the most influential of its kind anywhere.

The Accad approach takes cold maceration to extremes, calling for a cold maceration of unfermented grape juice for fifteen to twenty-five days. He also is deeply interested in the soil in which the grapes are grown, contending that many Burgundian vineyards are deficient in magnesium and overendowed with potassium, courtesy of excessive use of chemical fertilizers. Accad's original training, in fact, was as an agronomist.

In November 1989, I went to Burgundy to investigate more closely the effects of the Accad approach on red Burgundies (he shows no interest in the white wines). I arranged to visit Accad's oldest client, Jacky Confuron-Cotetidot in Vosne-Romanée. I asked Michel Bettane, who stays with Jacky Confuron when in Burgundy, to accompany me during the visit, which he gladly did. Bettane considers Confuron's wines to be the finest expression of the Accad school, although Confuron takes pains to point out that he doesn't do *everything* Accad tells him to do, citing that Accad wants his clients to exclude all the stems from the vat before macerating. Confuron can't let go of the old habits, so in go the stems—some of them, anyway.

The Confuron wines were indeed the essence of what the Accad approach is all about. All of the wines, regardless of the stature of the vineyard, were equally deep, bright blackish-garnet in color, semi-opaque. All of them displayed an exuberant fruitiness. Tannins were evident in the young wines, but softly so. The wines seemed pumped up, Pinot Noir on steroids. The real question is: How much detail do the wines show? Does the Accad method of extended maceration blur the distinctions of *terroir*? Or can it heighten them?

After hours of tasting and talking, it became apparent with Confuron's wines, and others, that although the wines display an appealing "weightlessness" about them—Bettane's most persuasive point is that the Accad style creates red Burgundies that are *sans maquillage*, "free of makeup"—the vineyard distinctions are submerged under a flamboyant winemaking signature.

But perhaps time in the bottle would allow a wine of known distinction to emerge in detailed glory? I asked Confuron if he would be kind enough to allow me to taste the oldest example of an Accad-influenced wine in his possession. He obliged, hauling out a Vosne-

Romanée "Les Suchots" 1978, a *premier cru*. We had already tasted a 1988 Suchots from the barrel, as well as a 1985 Suchots. With these, one could get a sense of the transformations that might occur, all three being outstanding vintages.

Here, finally, was the telling point: The 1978 Suchots had a deep, mature color with a noticeable orange cast. But it looked good, nevertheless. It had a scent of coffee and orange peel, in an attractive way. But it lacked what a mature *premier cru* Vosne-Romanée should have—namely, that exciting sense of layers being uncovered, of discovering new subtleties and details with every sip. This wine was one-dimensional. It certainly was pleasant. It was supple and had that pumped-up "weightlessness" about it. But it was dull. It had not transformed, only endured.

Subsequent visits to other Accad clients such as Domaine Daniel Senard in Aloxe-Corton; Château de la Tour in Clos de Vougeot; and Domaine Jean Grivot in Vosne-Romanée, all of whom have gone over to the Dark Side, confirmed this impression. Commentaries on each of these properties can be found in chapters on their respective communes. Suffice it to say that in every instance the wines lacked detail, nuance, and subtlety. *Terroir* was suffocated by the cold-maceration signature.

Oddly, even an enthusiast of the Accad approach, in the course of praising an Accad wine, inadvertently reveals the degree of the distortion rendered by the style. In writing about the 1987 wines of Domaine Jean Grivot (which domaine reportedly adheres to the Accad directives more unswervingly than any other), Robert M. Parker, Jr., in his newsletter *The Wine Advocate* (Number 65) reports, "The Echézeaux was superb in 1987, but I could not help noticing [that] it smelled like Syrah rather than Pinot Noir. Skeptics of the Guy Accad style of winemaking will no doubt say [that] the wine does not taste like Echézeaux. However, it is great wine, impressively colored, rich and full. But is it really typical of what Pinot Noir renders? In any event, this is a wine to drink by 1996–1997, and appreciate for its wonderfully pure, hedonistic, seductive fruit and voluptuous texture."

That's it in a nutshell. If one doesn't care whether a red Burgundy tastes more like Syrah than Pinot Noir; if the presence of a defining *terroir*, let alone in a *grand cru* such as Echézeaux, is of no consequence; if all one seeks in a Burgundy is a "pure, hedonistic, seductive fruit and voluptuous texture"—never mind where it's from or even what grape it's made of—then the Accad wines are for you.

They represent what might be called a "Cabernet-zation" of Pinot Noir, a pursuit of uniform, deep color and almost pornographic fruitiness in lieu of "somewhere-ness." Cold maceration seems to lend itself to easy abuse. But because of its flashy, accessible qualities, it seems likely that we shall see more Burgundies being made this way, at least until the novelty wears off or the maturing wines demonstrate their shallowness compared to more traditionally made versions.

PRESSING THE GRAPES

Contrary to a general misconception, it is only after the grape juice has finished fermenting and graduated to the status of wine that the grape mass is pressed. Pressing the wine-soaked cap is different from the original crushing at the start of the process. Crushing the grapes is merely a matter of liberating the juice. Pressing the skins and stems after the wine has been drained is a more persuasive exercise. One of the reasons for confusion in this matter, apart from the confusing terminology, is that white wine grapes are simultaneously crushed and pressed before the fermentation begins. This is because there is no *cuvaison* for white wines; even the most traditional treatments allow the juice to macerate with the skins for hours rather than days.

Burgundy is a trove of old winepresses, many of them dating to the 1400s and 1500s. One gets a glimpse of the reluctance of Burgundians to leave off their traditional ways upon discovering that some of these antiques were still in use only fifty years ago. The *vieux pressoir* ("old press") of Clos de Tart, thought to have been built around 1570, was last used for the 1924 vintage. Now, however, nearly everyone employs the latest models.

Despite the number of old presses left, they were still rarities, due to the great expense involved. Presses capable of handling sizable lots of grape skins were enormously expensive, as well as physically enormous. This was yet another reason why so much Burgundy wine was channeled through *négociants* or shippers, as only they (and the Church) could afford winepresses of any size. Domaine-bottling was an impossibility prior to the arrival of inexpensive, small winepresses, along with prices high enough to justify the cost and an ability to sell small lots of wine, typically to passersby from the improved roads of the post–World War II period. For example, only a generation or two ago, the entire harvest of the Chablis region was processed by twenty-six winepresses owned by only twenty-two families.

In order to perform the pressing operation, one must remove the wine from the mass of skins and grapes. This wine is known as the "free run" or the *vin de goutte*—literally, "drip wine." It is universally acknowledged that the free-run wine is the finest, although it can sometimes be deficient in tannin content. The free-run wine is placed in small barrels and set aside.

After the free-run wine is drawn off, the laborious job of shoveling the skins and stems out of the vat and into the press is performed. A goodly amount of wine is still clinging to or saturated in the skins and stems; only 85 percent of the wine is able to be effectively segregated during the free-run process.

The wine pressed from the "cake" of skins and stems is given several names, depending upon the number of times the cake is squeezed. The first pressing is usually very gentle; the wine that emerges is considered on a par with the free run and is usually mixed in with it. Wine emerging from successive pressings is known as the *vin de presse*, and it too is usually stored in separate barrels. Although flavorful, it can also be extremely tannic, as the skins and stems are really getting put to the screws at this stage. However, many fine winemakers will add at least a portion of the *vin de presse* to the free run in order to incorporate some of this tannin. The balance may or may not be used for topping up the barrels during the barrel-aging period, where evaporation reduces the contents by as much as 10 percent. What finally remains is a somewhat desiccated "cake," which is also known as the *marc*. This is either spread on the vineyards for fertilizer, or more often, sold to distillers to create a brandy known as *marc de Bourgogne*.

CHARDONNAY—HOW TO FERMENT

In comparison to Pinot Noir, the fermentation of Chardonnay in Burgundy is a simple procedure. Having said that, one feels compelled to retract it: Nothing is simple in winemaking, especially when it comes to Burgundian winemaking.

The simplicity of making white Burgundy lies in the lack of a *cuvaison*. The grapes are harvested, immediately crushed, and then pressed to extract as much juice as possible without extracting unwanted bitterness from the pips. The gentleness of the pressing is therefore a paramount concern. Immediately after the juice is extracted, it usually undergoes the practice known as *débourbage*—a "cleaning out."

When grapes are crushed and pressed, the juice retains a considerable amount of solids: bits of skin, stems, any material clinging to the grapes. The practice of *débourbage* allows these gross lees, as they are called, to settle out, leaving a reasonably clear juice behind, ready to be fermented.

The trick is to prevent the juice from starting to ferment before this coarse sediment has settled. *Débourbage* can take anywhere from twelve hours to three days, depending on the winemaker. The alternative is the use of a centrifuge. By whipping off the sediment by centrifugal force, the centrifuge clears the juice in minutes and it is ready to begin fermentation. But centrifuges are very expensive, and the traditional settling-out method is still the favored technique. Not least, centrifuges are considered harsh treatment and, in unskilled hands, capable of stripping the juice of flavor.

If the challenge of Pinot Noir fermentation is the extraction of flavor, that of Chardonnay is the exclusion of oxidation. White wines of any variety are typically more delicate and susceptible not only to the effects of oxygen, but also to bacterial infection. The lack of tannins makes it vulnerable. Because of this, one of the leading treatments throughout the winemaking process is the use of sulfur dioxide, commonly referred to as SO_2. It is also employed for red wines, but typically not in as large a quantity or to as dramatic an effect. This is one of the sulfites in the phrase now seen on all wine labels in America: "Contains Sulfites."

Sulfur may be fairly described as the miracle drug of wine: Grapevines are sprayed with it to ward off disease; barrels are sterilized with its fumes; and both fermenting wine and bottled wine are protected and preserved by it. It has been in constant use in wineries since at least the late 1600s. (Its powers had been known long before that moment, but there is little evidence in either ancient Greek or Roman writings that sulfur was regularly employed in their winemaking or winegrowing.)

For winemaking purposes, the form of sulfur employed is sulfur dioxide. In the old days, sulfur dioxide was created by burning a sulfur candle or match (the "burnt match" smell is the smell of sulfur dioxide). This was held inside of a barrel that needed to be sterilized. The burning sulfur combined with oxygen to form the gas sulfur dioxide, which annihilated any microorganisms inside a wooden barrel or cask. Today, the most common form of sulfur dioxide in commercial winemaking is liquefied SO_2 gas, although many small wineries use a powdered form of sodium or potassium metabisulfate. Whatever the means of introducing sulfur dioxide into a must or wine, the effect is the same: It is a germicide and antioxidant.

CELLARING

After the tension and controlled frenzy of the harvest and its winemaking, the Burgundian winegrower settles into the more leisurely, but no less critical, practice of cellaring the wine. Cellaring refers to the aging of wine, red or white, in barrels, and the bottling of it. To the outside observer, nothing could be simpler. Wine is allowed to remain in a small barrel, is topped up occasionally to compensate for losses due to evaporation, and after a while the wine is drawn from the barrel, bottled, corked, and put on the market. There is nothing dramatic about cellaring, and its measured pace is lulling. What evil could befall an innocent young wine in such a situation?

The purpose of cellaring is to expose a wine gradually and in a controlled manner to its most rapacious opponent: oxygen. One might view cellaring as a system by which a young wine is made to be sterner stuff by selectively exposing it to its nemesis.

Barrels of varying size have proved to be an ideal means of exposing the wine to oxygen in a controlled but limited manner. The Burgundian *pièce* or barrel is 228 liters or 60 U.S. gallons. The wine will oxidize, but minimally enough that the effect is thought beneficial rather than destructive. In the meantime, the wine is extracting whatever flavors the wood might offer (although the flavor diminishes greatly after two years' use), hence the current fascination in California, Australia, and Italy with various sources of oak from forests in America, Yugoslavia, and, especially, France. Each imparts a distinctive flavor, some of which marry especially well with certain grape varieties.

FILTERING

One of the most publicized concerns of Burgundy lovers, especially in America, concerns the practice of filtering both red and white Burgundies. Several importers are vehement in their insistence that the Burgundies they import not be filtered. It is a persuasive argument, although rarely, if ever, are absolutes useful in wine-making.

The antagonism to filtering Burgundies is simply that Pinot Noir, especially, is readily "bruised." It oxidizes easily. Filtering does indeed remove some body and flavor from a Pinot Noir, although the degree of the loss varies greatly depending upon the way the wine was made, its concentration, and, of course, the nature of the vintage.

Growers are reluctant to release unfiltered Burgundies for fear of micoorganisms being retained in the bottled wine, with the possible result of a wine spoiling or somehow going "off." Wines made in clean wineries using clean barrels are unlikely to be afflicted, but many winemakers want to take no chances. Yet other winemakers point out, rightly, that wines sometimes need to be filtered because they are not as bright and clear as they should be. Usually, a wine will "fall bright" in a barrel. But sometimes a light haze remains. Often this can be addressed through the practice of "fining" the wine, which is the incorporation of an ingredient that attracts the suspended particles that cause the haze to fall to the bottom, carried along by the fining agent. Traditionally and to this day, the gentlest fining ingredient is egg whites. Also used is a very fine clay called bentonite. Unlike egg whites, bentonite can strip a wine of some flavor if used excessively. These and other fining agents work by molecular electrostatic attraction, the haze particles being of a different charge than that of the fining agent.

Filtering is a more forceful, aggressive process, usually a matter of pushing the wine through "micropore" filter pads. The smaller the pores—or the greater the number of filter pads used—the more heavily filtered the wine. Strong wines such as Cabernet Sauvignon can withstand filtering far better than Pinot Noir.

White Burgundies also are filtered, often excessively so. A bright, clear wine is vital with white wine, and filtering is the fastest and most efficient process of ridding a wine of any particles. It seems that Chardonnay is less susceptible to filtering damage than Pinot Noir, but only to a degree. In both cases, gentle filtration likely does little damage to a Burgundy, but only when it is of the gentlest sort. Ideally, a Burgundy, red or white, is best off when it is least manipulated.

The Realities of Buying Burgundy

In the universe of supply and demand, Burgundy is a black hole: Conventional economics do not apply. Short of a world fiscal collapse, Burgundy is immune to market forces in the classic sense. For example, there's the economic law that if a producer doesn't give the market what it wants, it will lose that market. Yet what Burgundy drinkers have always wanted they've never received: wines of consistency and unvarying high quality. They never will get it. As the grower listings in this book so vividly reveal, the ownership of the land is so fractionalized as to prohibit consistency. It is structurally impossible.

This is no news; Burgundy drinkers have lamented this for centuries. In 1789, Thomas Jefferson wrote to his "wine man" in Burgundy complaining, "The shipment I just received from you was not as perfect. I would have thought it was a year other than 1784, if you hadn't told me it was that year."

How does the Burgundy buyer protect himself or herself? The first step is to recognize that there never will be a guarantee of great Burgundies all the time, no matter who the producer, how reputed the vintage, or how much you pay. Growers are fallible; winemakers make mistakes; wine writers can mislead. Sometimes promising vintages turn out to be more of a lie—1983 is a good example. Sometimes vintages turn out better than the early press reports would have them be—1972 and 1982 for examples.

Buying Burgundy is not for those who are not prepared to accept risks. And it's not for those who don't enjoy doing a bit of homework. You're just going to have to learn a few good names in each of the communes. This book—and others, along with wine newsletters and specialist wine magazines—attempts to clue in buyers as best as possible.

PRICE

It is essential for the American buyer of Burgundies to understand how they get priced, if only to comprehend why there isn't much variation in price between a great vintage, such as 1985, and a poor one, such as 1984. The reasons are not entirely "reasonable."

The first element in the pricing equation is the mentality of the Burgundian winegrower. Making such a generalization is risky, and too often it collapses into caricature. Nevertheless, Burgundy is an ancient region, with deeply ingrained ways. However sentimental it may seem, many Burgundian winegrowers are profoundly dedicated to their vines. Burgundian growers tend not to view their vines simply as a viticultural cash cow. They may not take care of them as well as outsiders would like. And they may not make wines with the care or insight that can and should be applied. But they are devoted in their way. Some of them are peasants; some are worldly sophisticates. Essentially, they are farmers who enjoy their lot, enjoy the attention of the outside world and visit parts of it occasionally, but wouldn't trade places with anybody—except someone who owns more or better Burgundy vineyards.

Above all, it is a seller's market. Who owns the grapes has his choice. He can sell everything immediately after the vintage at an officially established (although not binding) price to *négociants*. *Négociants* used to buy weeks-old wines. Now, an increasing number of quality-minded *négociants* want the grapes instead, the better to give them control over the winemaking and create better wines. Initially, growers resisted this, fearing that they would not receive as much money for grapes as they did for wine. Slowly, this concern is diminishing. To induce them to change, *négociants* will sometimes pay more for grapes than for wine.

A grower can also sell his finished and bottled wines directly to a coterie of private buyers. This is widely practiced, with clients clamoring for wines in France, Germany, Switzerland, Belgium, the Netherlands, and Great Britain. French clients buy through the mail or through wine clubs. The very best growers can, if they want, sell virtually everything they make only to two- and three-star restaurants.

Then there are the importers. They are major figures in a Burgundian grower's life, if only because they buy larger quantities of wines at the same cellar-door retail price as private clients. This business of importers paying the retail price is the key. It is why American consumers pay so much more for Burgundies than do the French, who buy direct. Sometimes importers can achieve a slightly lower price if the importer is willing to advance a grower part of the purchase price months or years before delivery. But mostly the importers pay the same price as the grower sells the wine for retail at the cellar door, what's called *vente directe*.

The good growers know that they can sell everything they make right at the cellar door. So why should they sell the wine for less simply because someone wants to ship it 3,000 miles or 6,000 miles away? They say, "You want my wines, you pay what I could sell them for anyway."

But it doesn't end there. Demand is so great that there is yet another advantage. Foreign buyers, especially Americans, want only the best vintages. But the lesser vintages have to be sold too. So the grower allows an importer to buy, but with the following proviso: "You can only have as much of my '85s as you took of the '84s." If the importer finds that indigestible, he loses his place in line.

The odd part of this process is that the price demanded by the grower usually does not sharply reflect the quality of a vintage. In Burgundy, prices reach a certain threshold and then remain near or at that level for years afterward, until a new threshold is reached. Off vintages are not much less expensive than great vintages. This is part of the Burgundian's farmer mentality. The growers say, "We have our costs. And besides, this is what the vintage is like. We make wine every year, and it comes from the same vineyards. You were willing to pay so much last year, so why not this year?" Since the demand is so intense for good-vintage Burgundies, importers swallow the lesser years and try to make it up by taking a larger markup on the great vintages when they appear.

One of the few growers who does change his prices in accordance with vintage quality is Jacques Seysses of Domaine Dujac. But then, he is a Parisian who was trained as a banker, and only later became a devoted winegrower. "Where I have a big difference with my colleagues is in pricing methods," he says. "I believe in the quality of the vintage being reflected in the price. My prices go up and down, reflecting the vintage." Dujac's 1983 Morey-St.-Denis was 75 francs. His 1984 was only 40 francs. But his 1985 was 110 francs. In comparison, Seysses's neighbor Bernard Serveau sold his 1983 Morey-Saint-Denis for 60 francs; his 1984 for 60 francs, and his 1985 for 69 francs.

So what happens to the price of the wine when it arrives in the States? First the importer paid the Burgundian retail price. Let's say that it was 120 francs a bottle, which is what many red *premiers crus* fetch. At six francs to the dollar, that's twenty dollars a bottle. Most wines reach the American consumer through a three-tier system: importer, wholesaler, retailer. Each takes between a 33 percent and 50 percent markup. Shipping and taxes account for very little: about seventy-five cents a bottle.

If the wine goes through all three tiers, the price on the shelf of the retailer will be about $47, assuming each party worked on a 33 percent markup. The importer buys at $20 and sells for $26.60. The wholesaler buys at $26.60 and sells for $35. The retailer buys at $35 and sells for $47.

Sometimes retailers engage in what's known as direct importing, where the wine is purchased directly from the producer, bypassing the middlemen. The retailer can then pocket the profits of two of the three tiers (importer and wholesaler) and sell the wine for forty-seven dollars. More often, a direct importer will pocket only part of it and sell the wine at a lower price, say, thirty-five dollars. If the demand for the wine is unusually strong and the importer has an exclusive, he might choose to make a killing, padding the price well above the usual markups. It's rare, but it happens.

Where does the Burgundy buyer find the best deals? Usually,

from two sources: retailers in highly competitive major markets such as New York, San Francisco, Washington, D.C., and Los Angeles, or from retailers who are direct importers. Although the laws about shipping wines across state borders are either vague or outright prohibitory, the fact is that nearly all merchants now ship wines across the country. You have to be careful in shipping wines during very hot or cold seasons, especially if the wine is to travel a long distance. Reputable merchants will hold the wine for you until the weather or season is favorable.

No one gives away Burgundies, but some of the best sources of high-quality Burgundies at good prices include such San Francisco–area merchants as Draper & Esquin; Premier Cru; Pacific Wine Company; Marin Wine Merchants; and Kermit Lynch. In Washington, D.C., there are Mayflower Wines and Pearson's. In New York, Zachy's in Scarsdale is a major conduit for Burgundies imported by Seagram Chateau & Estate. The real specialist merchant in New York is the Burgundy Wine Company in Greenwich Village, which is run by an exceptionally serious fellow who is committed to finding top-drawer Burgundies and storing them in good condition.

A monthly publication called *The New York Wine Cellar* (P.O. Box 392, Prince Station, New York, N.Y. 10012) offers a listing of hundreds of Burgundies available in that city, showing the best prices from a variety of merchants. It shows you immediately the range of prices for a particular Burgundy from a particular producer in a particular vintage. For the serious Burgundy buyer, it is an invaluable resource. Not least are the advertisements in *The Wine Spectator*, which frequently show sources for well-priced Burgundies.

Not to be dismissed are local merchants. Sometimes merchants in smaller cities are allotted small quantities of sought-after Burgundies that disappear quickly in more avid markets. I've seen surprising selections in New Orleans, Atlanta, Seattle, and Portland, Oregon, among other places. The biggest cities aren't always the best sources, especially once the word gets out.

THE BEST-PRICED BURGUNDIES

The problem with Burgundy is that, too often, only the rarest and most expensive wines get the write-ups. Sure, it's tough to deny that a great-vintage La Tâche or Chevalier-Montrachet isn't a joy to behold. But below that exalted level lies a pool of terrific red and white Burgundies that should constitute the great majority of a Burgundy lover's cellar, no matter how rich the buyer.

The Burgundies that are currently the best deals are the following: red and white Savigny-lès-Beaune; Volnay; red and white Pernand-Vergelesses; red Chassagne-Montrachet; red and white Auxey-Duresses; white Saint-Romain; red Ladoix-Serrigny; Santenay, Fixin, and Côte de Nuits-Villages.

Some of the best deals come from the Haute Côte de Nuits and Haute Côte de Beaune appellations. In great years, these appellations can create surprisingly fine wines that reward several years' cellaring. The same may be said of the humble Bourgogne *rouge* and *blanc* categories. Let the reputation of the producer be your guide. Many top-notch domaines issue such wines, often at surprisingly low prices.

AVAILABILITY

This is one of the trickiest elements in buying Burgundies. The problem is hype. In the last ten years, we have seen a dramatic increase in wine newsletters devoting enormous amounts of energy, diligence, and enthusiasm to tasting Burgundies. This is wonderful and should be applauded. The problem is that many of these tastings are performed in the cellars of the Burgundy producers, often long before the wines are bottled.

Barrel-tasting, as the practice is called, is a tentative thing at best. Some barrels are better than others. A visiting journalist (or buyer) never can know whether you're being led to the best barrel, from which you'll draw your conclusions. This is not to suggest that Burgundy producers are duplicitous, but to point out that it happens—inadvertently or otherwise.

An example of just how different barrels of the same wine can be is seen in the practices of the Domaine de la Romanée-Conti. For decades, the Domaine de la Romanée-Conti insisted on bottling directly from the barrel, despite an ever-increasing stream of complaints about bottle variation. Finally, with the 1985 vintage, it conceded the point, and from that vintage on, has blended six barrels of the same wine before bottling. Complaints about bottle variation in their wines seem to have subsided.

The most pernicious effect of these journalistic barrel-tastings is the hype that emerges from them. Wines are raved about and urgently recommended before they are even bottled. Yet no one denies that much can go wrong between when somebody last tasted a wine from the barrel and when it was bottled. A grower gets sick, and because of the illness leaves his wines in the barrel longer than is advisable. Another grower decides to filter his wines heavily, figuring that the wines will be shipped long distances and he doesn't want any complaints about the condition of the wine. Yet another grower decides to use one of the local companies that have bottling-line machinery mounted on the back of a truck. They roll in and run the wines through, often in the most careless, even abusive fashion. The list of possibilities of what can go wrong in cellaring and bottling is enormous. Ask any importer. All of this can occur, and frequently does, after the wine writer has prowled through Burgundy tasting wines from the barrel. Granted, the best producers, the ones with fine track records of cellaring and bottling wines responsibly, allow the writer a reasonable likelihood that what he or she tasted will, indeed, emerge from the bottle when you buy it. But Burgundy is too much of a sweepstakes for those odds to be anything but passable, at best.

Nevertheless, the fix is in long before the wines reach these shores. Burgundy buyers clamor for the wines. Retailers are happy to oblige them in the form of what are euphemistically called "futures."

The business of buying wines on futures is hardly new, but until recently it was confined exclusively to Bordeaux. And let's face it, buying Bordeaux today is no more chancy than pulling a lever on a vending machine. You find your brand, put in your money, pull the lever, and out it comes. Rarely do you get a surprise, and then only that of the vintage, rather than of the winemaking. When Château Phélan-Ségur recalled its entire release of 1983 from the market, the astonishment caused by that unprecedented move was as much due to the idea that a reputable Bordeaux property could have bungled the job that badly as by the loss of face and money incurred.

But when was the last time you can recall a Burgundy domaine or *négociant* recalling its wines because of poor quality? The only instance that I can recall is that of Domaine Dujac's 1977 Morey-Saint-Denis, when Jacques Seysses recalled fifteen thousand bottles from the market because the wine was, in his words, "really bad."

The idea of a future is premised on the notion that by buying early not only can you "lock in" the best price, but that subsequent offerings will be higher in price. Implicit also is a confidence about the quality of the wine.

The notion of early buying guaranteeing the best price comes from Bordeaux practice of feeding the market in *tranches*, or slices. Typically, the first *tranche* is 50 percent of a château's production. A few offer their entire output, such as Château Lynch-Bages, but that is rare. They are playing the market, hoping that the value of their remaining inventory will increase as the demand exceeds the supply. It usually does these days.

None of this applies to Burgundy. Unlike the name-brand châteaux and the very real consistency of quality and uniformity, you never can be sure about Burgundies. The wines are too handcrafted, especially (and ironically) at the highest-quality levels. Pinot Noir and Chardonnay are far more subject to mishandling and sensitive to even minor weather disturbances than Cabernet Sauvignon and Merlot. Name your favorite domaine or *négociant* and a knowledgeable Burgundy connoisseur can reel off particular bottlings or even whole vintages where they bungled the job or just were dealt a joker in the form of an isolated hailstorm.

But this lack of assured and consistent quality is not due only to unpredictable weather and quirky grape varieties. It also comes from the quantity of the supply. In Bordeaux, the great properties routinely sell off lesser barrels or even whole vats of wine. This is a major reason why the standard can remain so consistently high at the best estates. They can discard wine and still have plenty left to sell.

Why is Bordeaux so different? Look at how much is produced. The average offering of *each* of the five First Growths (Lafite, Latour, Mouton, Margaux, and Haut-Brion) is 20,000 cases a year or 100,000 cases annually for all five combined. That's the minimum.

Compare that with, say, Chambolle-Musigny, which is neither the largest nor the smallest of the great communes of the Côte d'Or. The annual average production for the entire commune is no more than 60,000 cases a year. And of that, its two *grands crus*, Musigny and Bonne Mares, account for just 3,000 cases and 4,500 cases respectively.

Look at the ownership listings of Chambolle-Musigny. You'll discover that among the twenty-four *premiers crus*, the largest single holding in any one vineyard is just four acres. Given the minuscule amount of wine that each grower can claim and today's Burgundy prices, who's going to cull out the lesser barrels? Believe it or not, it gets done. You know who gets those wines? *Négociants.*

Rich as the Burgundians are, few can afford to forego an entire crop or even a part of one. And unlike with Bordeaux, the quantities are so small that few can retain reserves of wines from previous vintages as an income hedge. There's not enough wine and, since most growers make wine literally in the basements of their homes, not enough room.

All of which is to point out that Burgundy futures really aren't futures at all. They are reservations. Many, if not most, merchants who sell Burgundy futures sell the wines for the same price as they would when the wines actually arrive—with you paying half or all of the price for as long as a year in advance. This trend toward Burgundy futures, so-called, is simply a passing off to the consumer of retailers' financial and professional responsibilities—at no saving to the consumer.

The newsletter writers, however admirable and conscientious —and they are—have become agents of change in how Burgundies get sold. As long as they insist on reporting about individual wines within months of the harvest, they are asking their readers to invest in them—in every sense—a degree of knowledge about a wine that no one, not even the winegrower, can pretend to possess. For example, one newsletter writer offered detailed notes on the 1988 white Burgundies in June 1989, just seven months after the grapes were picked. And even he had to concede that "the malo-lactic fermentations having taken a long time to complete, these 1988s are somewhat difficult to pass judgment on." Are you prepared to bet four hundred dollars a case on that?

The difficulty is that these advance reports whip up a buying frenzy among Burgundy lovers who, knowing the small quantities available, are afraid that they are going to miss out. The only reasonable advice is: Resist it. Talk to your merchant. If you buy a future, get a guarantee that if you don't like the wine, you'll get your money back. Ultimately, it'll only be his or her word, but with reputable merchants, that's enough.

Better yet, wait for the wine to come in. Keep in mind the 1983 red Burgundies, where the newsletter writers went wild, tasting dark, richly fruity, tannic red Burgundies out of the barrel, completely missing—because it was hard to detect at so early a stage—

the enormous rot and hail taste that so disfigured the wines not long after release. Often just before bottling, the winegrowers filtered the '83s severely, to rid them of the rot or hail tastes, in the process stripping them of flavor and color. All of that was reported too late—if at all—for futures buyers. Today, you can find 1983s at fire-sale prices. Many of the '86s were disappointing, as were the '87s. Futures were offered on both. The 1988s look to be good, but not all of them. And there're going to be some rude shocks about the quality of some of the wildly hyped '89s, which probably will sell for some of the highest prices ever. The best advice I ever got came from an old importer who had seen it all: "Remember, there's always another vintage."

DRINKING

BURGUNDY

Côte de Nuits

Côte
de
Nuits-Villages

The name Côte de Nuits-Villages would lead one to believe that any wine in the Côte de Nuits could be sold under this banner. But it's not so. The only communes with the right to sell their wines as Côte de Nuits-Villages are Brochon, Comblanchien, Corgoloin, Fixin, and Prémeaux-Prissey. And of these, only Fixin has the right to use its own name on a label.

Of all the "generic" wines of Burgundy, Côte de Nuits-Villages is likely the best deal of all. The overall standard is high, which is to say that I often find myself pleased with a Côte de Nuits-Villages from a previously unknown producer. You can't ask for more than that as a Burgundy buyer.

Good Côte de Nuits-Village should reflect the name. The wine should be fairly dark, with some tannin and a vaguely earthy fruiti-ness. Sometimes they can be finer than this, taking on such wines as commune-level Fixin or Gevrey-Chambertin or even (lesser) Nuits-Saint-Georges.

Some of the best producers include domaines Jayer-Gilles and Daniel Rion. An exceptional bottling of Côte de Nuits-Villages comes from Domaine Michel Sirugue (bottled and distributed by the *negociant* Labouré-Roi) called Clos de la Belle Marguerite. Located on the southern edge of Brochon in the Queue de Hareng vineyard, it is a *monopole* of Domaine Michel Sirugue.

Marsannay

At the northernmost tip of the Côte de Nuits lies the commune of Marsannay-la-Côte, a name that only now is beginning to be revived as a source of good-quality Pinot Noir. Because of its proximity to Dijon, which lies only a few miles to the north of it, Marsannay seemed to identify more with Dijon than the Côte d'Or. It supplied the everyday red wine of Dijon. That wine, not surprisingly, was always Gamay. Until the early part of the 1900s, no Pinot Noir was planted in Marsannay.

The arrival of Pinot Noir came from the brainstorm of Joseph Clair (of the former Clair-Daü estate), who planted Pinot Noir with the intent of creating a *rosé*, a type of wine virtually unknown (at least by design) in Burgundy. But *rosés* were the rage of the age, and Clair found himself a local hero—at least to his bankers. Marsannay began cranking out volumes of *rosé*, and its fame, if not its stature, was ensured.

Inevitably, economic security gave over to a craving for respectability. The Marsannois, who also produced straight red wine from their Pinot Noir, wanted their own *appellation contrôlée*. They obtained one, of a sort, in 1956. They were authorized to create a wine labeled Bourgogne Marsannay or Bourgogne Rosé de Marsannay.

This was unsatisfying. Their sights were now directed squarely toward the Côte d'Or. We make a good Bourgogne, the growers argued. We should be able to sell our wine under the Côtes de Nuits-Villages *appellation*. They lobbied for this status for years with no success. The other members of that club, the communes of Brochon, Comblanchien, Corgoloin, Fixin, and Prémeaux-Prissey, wanted no part of it.

Finally, on May 19, 1987, the growers of Marsannay received a curious consolation prize. They *still* couldn't sell their wines as Côte de Nuits-Villages. Instead, the Appellation Contrôlée authorities granted them the right to label their wines simply as "Marsannay," making Marsannay a full-fledged *appellation contrôlée*, coequal with Gevrey-Chambertin or Aloxe-Corton or Volnay rather than being merely an anonymous contributor to a wine labeled Côte de Nuits-Villages. They asked only to be allowed to sweep the walk of the local lords, and instead were granted a title of their own!

The decree granted this viticultural seigneurial right to the commune of Marsannay-la-Côte as well as the neighboring communes of Couchey and Chenôve. They still can—and will—make *rosé* under the name "Marsannay Rosé." Moreover, the name can also apply to white wine, even though relatively few white wine grapes are grown there. They will probably be planted now, though, given the demand for white Burgundies.

Now, we are beginning to see a trickle of red Burgundies sporting the name "Marsannay." The wines are richly fruity in a simple, grapey fashion. They are best drunk young and cool, the better to enhance these qualities. One of the best producers at the moment is Domaine Marc Brocot, which offers a juicy red Marsannay from 7.4 acres of thirty-year-old Pinot Noir vines and 2.5 acres of unspecified white wine grapes.

Other producers to look for include Domaine Bart, Domaine Bruno Clair, Domaine Jean-Pierre Guyard, and Domaine Huguenot Père et Fils. The *négociant* Joseph Faiveley also offers a Marsannay, one of the few major houses to do so.

Fixin

One of the oddities of Burgundy is why Fixin remains one of the least-appreciated red wines of Burgundy. The name isn't hard to pronounce, although the local pronounciation has it as "Fees-an," the Burgundians hissing like snakes whenever confronted with a word with x in it. (Aloxe-Corton and Auxey-Duresses are two other examples.) And the wine isn't hard to enjoy, either. Granted, a good Fixin is not something that can be enjoyed immediately upon release. Fixins are too tannic and dense for that. But after a few years they become much more accessible. In this, they are no different than Gevrey-Chambertin, which is snapped up instantly.

Comparing Fixin to Gevrey-Chambertin is inevitable. Not only are the two communes nearly adjacent (technically, Brochon separates Gevrey-Chambertin proper from Fixin), but the two wines are similar in character and structure. Fixin at its best is robust, long-lived, and earthy. So, too, is Gevrey-Chambertin. Where they part company is a matter of finesse and refinement: The best Fixins simply cannot deliver these attributes to anywhere near the degree of the best Gevreys. The wine of Fixin is decidedly earthy, with the best bottlings having a minerally quality due to the presence of limestone, which is rare in the Côte de Nuits.

One of the reasons that the Fixin light remains so well hidden under a bushel is that the *appellation* of Fixin is also entitled to sell its wines under the lesser name of Côte de Nuits-Villages. The *appellation contrôlée* of Fixin applies only to 265 acres within the commune of Fixin as a whole. These wines can be sold *either* as Fixin or Côte de Nuits-Villages.

But the commune of Fixin has considerably more vineyard acreage: 488 acres. These wines are not Fixin. They can be sold *only* as Côte de Nuits-Villages. The result is that some wine legally entitled to be labeled Fixin winds up incorporated into a shipper's Côte de Nuits-Village for reasons of easier sale, augmenting quantities or improving the quality of the blend. That Fixin can really boost the flavor wattage of a blend was made clear to me when tasting a wine labeled Bourgogne—the humblest designation available—from Domaine Modot in Chambolle-Musigny. It was a 1986 no less, a vintage not noted for muscularity. Yet this mere Bourgogne was bulging with firm, rich fruit. I freely declared that it was one of the best Bourgognes I'd ever tasted. I was then told that it was mostly, but not entirely, Fixin.

THE VINEYARD

There are 107.3494 ha/265 acres of AOC Fixin, of which 55.3 acres are ranked *premier cru*. There are no *grands crus*.

THE PREMIERS CRUS

LES ARVELETS—3.3571 ha/8.3 acres. This vineyard can also be sold as Les Hervelets.

CLOS DU CHAPITRE—4.7880 ha/11.8 acres

CLOS NAPOLÉON—1.8312 ha/4.5 acres divided between two *climats*: Aux Cheusots (4.3 acres) and Le Village (0.2 acre)

CLOS DE LA PERRIÈRE—6.7006 ha/16.5 acres divided among three *climats*: La Perrière (12.1 acres); a portion of Queue de Hareng (4 acres); and En Suchot (0.4 acre)

LES HERVELETS—4.3203 ha/10.7 acres divided into two *climats*: Les Hervelets (9.5 acres) and a section of Le Meix Bas (1.2 acres) that also can be sold as Le Meix Bas

LE MEIX BAS—1.3804 ha/3.4 acres

PRODUCERS WORTH SEEKING OUT

DOMAINE BERTHAUT—Less well-known than the two power-house landowners, domaines Gelin and Joliet, Domaine Berthaut is among the best in the district. This sixth-generation Fixin grower makes Fixin as it is meant to be: concentrated, tannic, rustic yet characterful. The label used to read "Guy Berthaut" (father); Now it's "Vincent et Denis Berthaut" (the sons). Wines include 2.5 acres of Les Arvelets, which is the signature bottling. Also commune-level Les Clos (2.5 acres) and Les Crais (2.5 acres).

DOMAINE BRUNO CLAIR—One of the younger generation from the former Clair-Daü estate who started off on his own. He is widely considered an up-and-coming producer, creating wines from remnants of the old family holdings. An excellent Fixin comes from a 2.5-acre holding in the commune-level La Croix-Blanche vineyard. Also, there is a rare white Fixin made from from Pinot Blanc, which I have not tasted. Worth watching.

DOMAINE CLÉMANCEY FRÈRES—A producer of deeply colored but curiously lackluster wine from the *premier cru* Les Hervelets.

DOMAINE PIERRE GELIN/DOMAINE GELIN ET MOLIN—Perhaps the leading name in Fixin. Gelin is in the enviable position of working with two of the best *premiers crus*: Clos du Chapitre and Clos Napoléon, which is a *monopole* of Domaine (Pierre) Gelin and (André) Molin. The Clos Napoléon is more perfumy, lighter-weight and more delicate. It matures sooner than Clos du Chapitre, which is chunkier, more tannic, and longer-lived. Both are superb, especially in top vintages. Also there's an excellent Les Hervelets from a 1.5-acre holding as well as commune-level Fixin.

DOMAINE PHILIPPE JOLIET—By common consensus, the Clos de la Perrière is the finest vineyard in Fixin. The 16.5-acre vineyard is a *monopole* of Philippe Joliet. In recent years, Joliet has improved the wine, which previously was of spotty quality. Now, it offers the breed and depth that once gave it acclaim. It used to sell for the same price as Chambertin, according to Dr. Jules Lavalle in his 1855 *Histoire et Statistique de la Vigne et des Grands Vins de la Côte d'Or*. Back then, though, the vineyard yielded just 14 hl/ha according to Lavalle.

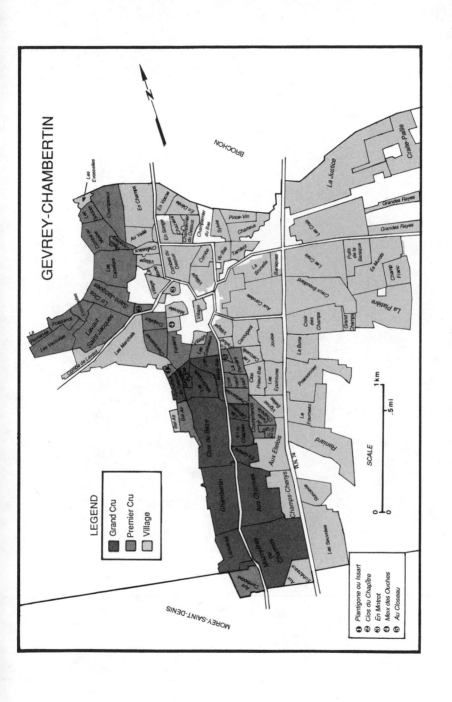

GEVREY-CHAMBERTIN

LEGEND
- Grand Cru
- Premier Cru
- Village

① Plantigone ou Issart
② Clos du Chapître
③ En Motrot
④ Meix des Ouches
⑤ Au Closeau

SCALE

0 — 1 km
0 — .5 mi

MOREY-SAINT-DENIS

BROCHON

Les Evocelles

Les Goulots
Les Jouises
Poissenot
Champeaux
En Champs
En Vosne
En Songe
Au Valé
Craipillot
Les Cazetiers
Le Clos Saint-Jacques
Lavaux Saint-Jacques
Combe du Dessus
Estournelles St-Jacques
Château
La Romanée
Les Verroilles
Combe au Moine
Village
Clos Prieur
Village
Combe du Dessus
Village
Marchais
Charmoise du Dessus
Charmoise du Bas
Charmier du Bas
En Derée
Sylvie
Pince-Vin
Charreux
Tamisot
La Bossière
Baraque
Aux Combes
Croix des Champs
La Burie
Le Fourneau
Renard
Champeaux

Les Marchais
Bel-Air
Clos du Beze
Chambertin
Aux Charmes
Mazoyères ou Charmes
Aux Combottes
Échézeaux
Champs-Chenys
Les Seuvrées
Raviotte

Clos St-Jacques
Clos Tamisot
La Perrière
Clos Prieur-Haut
Clos Prieur-Bas
Les Épointures
Le Pissonnier
La Platière
Grand Champs
En Murots
Champ Franc
Puits de la Baraque
Les Crais
Grandes Rayes
Grandes Rayes
La Justice
Craie-Paille

Les Corvées
Clos St-Jacques
En la Chapelle
En Pallud
Carougeot
Jouise
Vignes Basses
Creux Brouillard
Aux Etelois
RN 74

Gevrey-Chambertin

It is not hard to acquire a taste for less than the best. A soft-headed acceptance of the perfectly O.K. and the routinely blameless usually comes first. From there it is a slippery slope: a grudging tolerance for mediocrity and, when the bottom is reached, an unembarrassed affection for whatever is. In especially mystical cases, discrimination withers away and the purest trash can be cheerfully countenanced, appreciated as the manifestation of a folkish oversoul.

—DONAL HENAHAN, *The New York Times* (1988)

With the possible exception of commune-level Vosne-Romanée, no red Burgundy is less reliable than commune-level Gevrey-Chambertin. The reason in both cases is the same: The fame of the name is so great that anything legally entitled to it is gold in the marketplace. Commune-level Gevrey-Chambertin has become a "slippery slope" of mediocrity. Through no fault of their own, wine buyers have come to cheerfully countenance just about anything that comes their way, so long as it says "Gevrey-Chambertin."

How did this come about? Apart from the obvious reasons of laxity and greed among the Gibriacois, as they call themselves, a leading factor that contributes to the dismal standard of commune-level Gevrey-Chambertin is the sheer size of the *appellation*. It is the largest, by far, in the Côte d'Or, with a total of 1,354 acres. Commune-level Gevrey-Chambertin alone accounts for 889 acres of this, or two thirds of the total.

Too many of these commune-level vineyards are located in less estimable sites. In the Côte de Nuits, only Gevrey-Chambertin has *appellation* vineyards located across the N74 highway, on the flat plain in front of the slope. In fact, 39 percent of all the commune-level AOC Gevrey-Chambertin vineyards are found there. It is as close to an agricultural *zone industriel* as Burgundy gets.

Commune-level Gevrey-Chambertin at its best can be immensely satisfying wine, almost a miniature of the *premiers* and *grands crus*, without the same depth or breed. All Gevrey, regardless of status, should be substantial wine, dark in hue and infused with a strong, assertive fruit. It should be a bit unyielding in youth, but scented all the same. There should be a pronounced earthiness, the degree of which is amplified as you go up the ladder from commune-level to *premier cru* to *grand cru*.

What one should *not* expect of, or seek from, commune-level Gevrey-Chambertin is great weight. All good Gevreys are substantial wines, but the old vision of beefy, iron-building-in-the-blood Burgundy was spawned from fraudulent wines that were blended with Syrah or Grenache from the Rhône. Too often, such wines were labeled Gevrey-Chambertin (as well as Nuits-Saint-Georges and Pommard). While the *grands crus* certainly have muscle, even they should not be lumbering. At the commune level, the best wines have pronounced flavor impact but rarely textural thickness.

PRODUCERS WORTH SEEKING OUT

The best producers of commune-level Gevrey-Chambertin almost invariably are those who issue the best *premiers* and *grands crus*. The reason is simple: They lavish on their lower-ranked vineyards the same care and standards that make their top-ranked wines so good. See the producer comments in the following chapter, Gevrey-Chambertin Premiers Crus.

Gevrey-Chambertin Premiers Crus

The distinction of Gevrey-Chambertin is apparent only when one reaches the *premiers crus*. Here, it can be discovered just how massively endowed is this commune, going from strength to strength from Cazetiers to Clos Saint-Jacques to Combe au Moine. All told, Gevrey-Chambertin counts twenty-six *premiers crus* sprawled across 211 acres. Several of them are good enough to be *grand cru*, if only there weren't so much holy ground already.

For the Burgundy lover, the *premiers crus* provide a grasp of the essential qualities of Gevrey-Chambertin. Here, you find the muscularity and structure that distinguishes Gevrey-Chambertin from any other *appellation*. Inevitably, not all of the *premiers crus* are equal. Some are lighter-weight, such as Combottes, which adjoins Morey-Saint-Denis. Others are scaled to proportions few *premiers crus* anywhere else even approach, such as Clos Saint-Jacques and Combe au Moine.

THE PREMIER CRU VINEYARDS

Gevrey-Chambertin has 85.5255 ha/211 acres in 26 vineyards.

Bel-Air—2.6523 ha/6.6 acres

	Hectares	Acres	Cases*
Mme. Jean-Claude Boisset	0.4582	1.1	242
M. Jean-Claude Boisset	0.1563	0.4	83
M. et Mme. Jean-Claude Bourtourault	0.1548	0.4	82
M. Pierre Guyot	0.2450	0.6	129
Mme. Veuve Joseph Clair and M. Bernard Clair	0.0367	0.1	19
M. et Mme. Edouard Mortet	0.0807	0.2	43
GFA Quillard et Fils	0.1463	0.4	77
M. et Mme. André Seguin	0.1745	0.4	92
M. et Mme. Gilles Seguin	0.0113	0.03	6
M. et Mme. Jean Taupenot	0.3546	0.9	187

La Bossière—0.4490 ha/1.1 acres

	Hectares	Acres	Cases*
M. Lucien Geoffroy	0.4490	1.1	237

Les Cazetiers—9.1190 ha/22.5 acres

	Hectares	Acres	Cases*
Mme. Veuve Denis Bizot and Mme. Jacques Coudray	0.1760	0.4	93
Consortium Viticole et Vinicole de Bourgogne	1.7735	4.4	936
GFA du Domaine des Chezeaux	0.0545	0.1	29
Mme. Veuve Joseph Clair Mme. Jacques Vernet	0.0461	0.1	24
M. Michel Clair (et Copropriétaires)	0.8743	2.2	462
M. et Mme. Bernard Dupont	0.8722	2.2	461
M. et Mme. Gilles Duroche	0.0715	0.2	38
Commune de Gevrey-Chambertin	0.0708	0.2	37
M. et Mme. Albert Grandvoinnet	0.8872	2.2	468
M. Louis Grenier	0.0351	0.1	19
M. Alain Langlais Mme. Veuve Henri Langlais	0.1590	0.4	84
M. et Mme. Philippe Leclerc	0.3093	0.8	163
M. et Mme. André Lucot	0.4077	1.0	215
M. et Mme. Henri Magnien	0.3280	0.8	173

*Cases calculated on the *rendement de base* of 40 hl/ha plus 20 percent

	Hectares	Acres	Cases*
Mlle. Anne-Marie Magnien	1.0357	2.6	547
M. et Mme. Michel Magnien	0.1798	0.4	95
M. Charles Rousseau	0.5960	1.5	315
M. Jacques Vernet	0.0700	0.2	37

Champeaux—6.6785 ha/16.5 acres

Mme. Alize Bizot and Mme. Veuve Denis Bizot	0.4230	1.0	233
Mme. Fernand Bouvier and Mme. Veuve Fernand Bouvier	0.3568	0.9	188
M. et Mme. Paul Champy	0.4116	1.0	217
Mme. Pierre Charchaude and Mme. Veuve Pierre Charchaude	0.2905	0.7	153
M. Pierre Charmillet	0.1462	0.4	77
Mme. Veuve Auguste Chevillard	0.1298	0.3	69
M. et Mme. Michel Cluny	0.0792	0.2	42
M. et Mme. Jacques Coudray	0.2937	0.7	155
M. et Mme. Pierre Dugat	0.3247	0.8	171
M. et Mme. Gilles Duroche	0.1340	0.3	71
M. et Mme. Jean-Claude Fourrier	0.2093	0.5	111
M. Joseph Geoffroy	0.1008	0.2	53
M. Lucien Geoffroy	0.1140	0.3	60
M. Marcel Guyard	0.4367	1.1	231
M. et Mme. Philippe Leclerc	0.3834	0.9	202
M. et Mme. René Leclerc	0.4315	1.1	228
M. et Mme. Henri Magnien	0.2545	0.6	134
M. Bernard Maume and M. Jacques Maume	0.2727	0.7	144
M. Edmond Mortet and Mme. Veuve Edmond Mortet	0.2097	0.5	111
GFA en Recilles	0.2720	0.7	144
Mme. Veuve Georges Souillard	0.0034	0.008	2
M. et Mme. Gabriel Tortochot	0.7484	1.8	395
M. Guy Wendehende	0.1683	0.4	89

Champitenois or Petite Chapelle—4.0034 ha/9.9 acres

M. Felicien Caillet	0.1708	0.4	90
M. et Mme. Paul Chanceaux	0.0549	0.1	29
Mme. Veuve Auguste Chevillard	0.0308	0.1	16

---

*Cases calculated on the *rendement de base* of 40 hl/ha plus 20 percent

	Hectares	Acres	Cases*
Mlle. Marie Derangère and Mme. Veuve Roger Derangère	0.1161	0.3	61
M. et Mme. Gilbert Desserey	0.3777	0.9	199
SCI Domaine Drouhin-Laroze	0.0591	0.1	31
M. et Mme. Hubert Grillot	0.3709	0.9	196
Mme. Jean Groc and M. Georges Grosperrin	0.0525	0.1	28
M. et Mme. Joseph Guenin	0.0506	0.1	27
M. Gaston Livera	0.0468	0.1	25
M. et Mme. Pierre Mantillet	0.0186	0.04	10
M. et Mme. Michel Marchand	0.4031	1.0	213
Mme. Louis Noblet	0.2813	0.7	149
SC les Perrières	0.6454	1.6	341
M. et Mme. André Seguin	0.1550	0.4	82
Mme. René Thibaut	0.1860	0.5	98
M. et Mme. Gabriel Tortochot	0.0879	0.2	46
M. Louis Trapet	0.0010	0.002	1
M. Louis Trapet and Mme. Jacques Rossignol	0.5202	1.3	275
M. Jean Trapet and M. Louis Trapet	0.3747	0.9	198

Champonnet—3.3177 ha/8.2 acres

	Hectares	Acres	Cases*
M. Lucien Boillot	0.1914	0.5	101
Mme. Jeannine Galland M. René Galland	0.2462	0.6	130
M. René Galland and Mme. Pascal Seurre	0.1289	0.3	68
M. Marcel Grandchamp and Mme. Veuve Marcel Grandchamp	0.0466	0.1	25
M. Marcel Grandchamp	0.1266	0.3	67
M. Michel Guillard	0.1224	0.3	65
M. et Mme. René Jacqueson	0.0568	0.1	30
M. et Mme. Philippe Leclerc	0.1308	0.3	69
M. et Mme. André Lucot	0.1093	0.3	58
M. et Mme. Edouard Mortet	0.1135	0.3	60
M. et Mme. André Seguin	0.0520	0.1	27
M. Stephane Sordkaty	0.1195	0.3	63
M. Georges Thomas	0.2158	0.5	114
SC du Domaine des Varoilles	0.6957	1.7	367

*Cases calculated on the *rendement de base* of 40 hl/ha plus 20 percent

	Hectares	Acres	Cases*
Cherbaudes—2.1870 ha/5.4 acres			
M. Étienne Beaumont and M. Marcel Beaumont	0.3062	0.8	162
M. et Mme. Marcel Beaumont	0.1126	0.3	59
M. Lucien Boillot	0.3397	0.8	179
M. Félicien Caillet	0.2232	0.6	118
M. et Mme. Jean-Claude Fourrier	0.6682	1.7	353
Mme. Bernard Guyot	0.0485	0.1	26
M. et Mme. André Lucot	0.0925	0.2	49
Mme. Jean-Pierre Martin	0.0673	0.2	36
M. Jacques Maume and M. Jean-Louis Maume	0.0446	0.1	24
M. René Poullot and	0.1198	0.3	63
M. et Mme. Jean-Louis Sirugue	0.0508	0.1	27
M. Louis Trapet and Mme. Jacques Rossignol	0.1136	0.3	60
Clos du Chapitre—0.9820 ha/2.4 acres			
Coop. Viticole Union des Propriétaires de Vins	0.9820	2.4	518
Au Closeau—0.5285 ha/1.3 acres			
SCI Domaine Drouhin-Laroze	0.4435	1.1	234
SC les Perrières	0.0850	0.2	45
Combe au Moine—4.7686 ha/11.8 acres			
Mme. Alice Bizot and Mme. Veuve Denis Bizot	0.0333	0.1	18
Consortium Viticole et Vinicole de Bourgogne	1.0838	2.7	572
Mme. Veuve Joseph Clair and Mme. Jacques Vernet	0.1697	0.4	90
M. et Mme. Robert Dupont	0.3002	0.7	159
M. Jean-Claude Fourrier and Mme. Veuve Louis Fourrier	0.6288	1.6	332
M. René Gallois	0.4045	1.0	214
M. et Mme. Philippe Leclerc	0.3988	1.0	211
M. et Mme. René Leclerc	0.6594	1.6	348

---

*Cases calculated on the *rendement de base* of 40 hl/ha plus 20 percent

	Hectares	Acres	Cases*
Aux Combottes—4.5720 ha/11.3 acres			
M. Pierre Amiot	0.6185	1.5	327
GFA Domaine Arlaud Père et Fils	0.4501	1.1	238
M. Etienne Beaumont	0.2365	0.6	125
M. Marcel Beaumont			
Mme. Veuve Charles Chanut	0.2843	0.7	150
M. André Coquard	0.4262	1.1	225
M. Maurice Ducherpozat	0.1376	0.3	73
SC d'Exploitation du Domaine Dujac	1.1584	2.9	612
M. et Mme. Georges Lignier	0.0550	0.1	29
GFA Domaine Georges Lignier Père et Fils	0.3598	0.9	190
M. et Mme. Claude Marchand	0.0523	0.1	28
M. et Mme. Jean Raphet	0.1737	0.4	92
M. Marie-Philippe Remy	0.4603	1.1	243
M. et Mme. Jacky Truchot	0.1593	0.4	84
Les Corbeaux—3.2100 ha/7.9 acres			
M. Bernard Bachelet	0.2775	0.7	147
M. Lucien Boillot	0.2892	0.7	153
M. Félicien Caillet	0.1441	0.4	76
M. Jean-Marie Thomas Collignon	0.2559	0.6	135
M. Jean-Marie Thomas Collignon and Mlle. Suzanne Thomas	1.0578	2.6	559
M. Marcel Garnier	0.0621	0.2	33
M. Michel Guillard	0.1215	0.3	64
M. Bernard Heresztyn	0.1907	0.5	101
Mme. Luciano Ianelli	0.0896	0.2	47
M. et Mme. René Leclerc	0.1062	0.3	56
M. René Leclerc and M. Roger Leclerc	0.1215	0.3	64
M. et Mme. André Lucot	0.0684	0.2	36
SA Rotisserie du Chambertin	0.2397	0.6	127
M. et Mme. André Seguin	0.0810	0.2	43
Craipillot—2.7594 ha/6.8 acres			
Consortium Viticole et Vinicole de Bourgogne	0.1351	0.3	71
Mme. Veuve Eugène Chouiller	0.1613	0.4	85

*Cases calculated on the *rendement de base* of 40 hl/ha plus 20 percent

	Hectares	Acres	Cases*
SCI Domaine Drouhin-Laroze	0.1372	0.3	72
M. et Mme. Roger Humbert	0.0296	0.1	16
M. Edmond Mortet and Mme. Veuve Edmond Mortet	0.0496	0.1	26
Mme. Louis Noblet	0.4871	1.2	257
M. et Mme. André Seguin	0.2178	0.5	115
M. et Mme. Hippolyte Seguin	0.0432	0.1	23
M. et Mme. Pierre Seguin	0.3107	0.8	164
M. et Mme. Arthur Sermet	0.0519	0.1	27

En Ergot—1.1667 ha/2.9 acres

	Hectares	Acres	Cases*
SC les Perrières	0.3942	1.0	208
M. Auguste Simeon	0.0225	0.1	12
Mlle. Chantal Tortochot	0.1124	0.3	59
M. Félix Tortochot	0.1383	0.3	73
M. et Mme. Gabriel Tortochot	0.1805	0.4	95
M. Jean Trapet and M. Louis Trapet	0.3188	0.8	168

Étournelles—5.9735 ha/14.8 acres

	Hectares	Acres	Cases*
M. Bernard Clair	0.0860	0.2	45
Mme. Veuve Joseph Clair and Mme. Jacques Vernet	0.2920	0.7	154
M. et Mme. Philippe Duroche	0.1277	0.3	67
M. André Esmonin	0.3577	0.9	189
M. André Esmonin and M. Henri Esmonin	0.4072	1.0	215
M. Roger Humbert and Mme. Veuve Roger Humbert	0.1002	0.2	53
M. et Mme. Roger Humbert	0.0470	0.1	25
M. et Mme. Henri Magnien	0.3437	0.8	181
M. Charles Rousseau	0.1260	0.3	67

Fonteny—3.7335 ha/9.2 acres

	Hectares	Acres	Cases*
SCI du Domaine Clair-Daü Bartet	0.6750	1.7	356
Duchesse de Bourgogne	0.0287	0.1	15
Mme. Veuve Joseph Clair Mme. Jacques Vernet	0.0877	0.2	46

---

*Cases calculated on the *rendement de base* of 40 hl/ha plus 20 percent

	Hectares	Acres	Cases*
M. Pierre Naigeon and Mme. Veuve Pierre Naigeon	0.0766	0.2	40
M. Charles Poulain	0.0420	0.1	22
M. et Mme. Joseph Roty	0.4519	1.1	239
M. Stanislaw Serafin	0.2373	0.6	125
M. Guy Wendehende	0.2228	0.6	118

Les Goulots—1.8109 ha/4.5 acres

Mme. Jean-Claude Boisset	0.1575	0.4	83
M. Jean-Claude Fourrier and Mme. Veuve Louis Fourrier	0.3408	0.8	180
M. René Gallois	0.1682	0.4	89
M. et Mme. Stanislas Heresztyn	0.2092	0.5	110

Lavaut or Lavaut Saint-Jacques—9.5303 ha/23.5 acres

M. Albert Boichard	0.0405	0.1	21
M. Gustave Bourgeot and Mme. Veuve Gustave Bourgeot	0.1257	0.3	66
Mme. Veuve Gustave Bourgeot and M. Henri Bourgeot	0.1237	0.3	65
M. et Mme. Yvon Burguet	0.0921	0.2	49
M. et Mme. Claude Charles	0.5410	1.3	286
Mme. Veuve Auguste Chevillard	0.0363	0.1	19
GFA du Domaine des Chezeaux	0.1373	0.3	72
SCI Domaine Drouhin-Laroze	0.4537	1.1	240
Mlle. Marguérite Dugat and M. Maurice Dugat	0.2898	0.7	153
M. et Mme. Gilles Duroche	0.2896	0.7	153
M. et Mme. Philippe Duroche	0.9129	2.3	482
M. André Esmonin and M. Henri Esmonin	0.0943	0.2	50
M. François Fichot	0.3665	0.9	194
Mlle. Marie-Louise Gaulard	0.4046	1.0	214
M. Albert Grandvoinnet	0.2953	0.7	156
Mme. Bernard Guyot	0.3604	0.9	190
M. et Mme. Roger Humbert	0.0610	0.2	32
M. et Mme. Émile Lambert	0.0620	0.2	33
M. et Mme. René Leclerc	0.5200	1.3	275

*Cases calculated on the *rendement de base* of 40 hl/ha plus 20 percent

	Hectares	Acres	Cases*
M. et Mme. Henri Magnien	0.2610	0.6	138
M. et Mme. Pierre Marchand	0.0809	0.2	43
M. René Masson	0.2973	0.7	157
M. Bernard Maume	0.2882	0.7	152
Mme. Louis Noblet	0.2974	0.7	157
M. Bernard Poullot	0.0895	0.2	47
M. et Mme. Jean Raphet	0.2223	0.5	117
M. Charles Rousseau	0.4672	1.2	247
M. et Mme. André Seguin	0.4147	1.0	219
M. et Mme. Pierre Seguin	0.0992	0.2	52
M. Georges Thomas	0.0824	0.2	44
Mme. Veuve Ernest Tisserandot and M. Ernest Tisserandot	0.1503	0.4	79
M. Félix Tortochot	0.1259	0.3	66
M. et Mme. Gabriel Tortochot	0.4884	1.2	258
M. et Mme. Georges Vachet	0.0684	0.2	36
M. et Mme. Gérard Vachet	0.4645	1.1	245
Mme. Jacques Vernet and Mme. Veuve Joseph Clair	0.2205	0.5	116

La Perrière—2.4706 ha/6.1 acres

	Hectares	Acres	Cases*
M. et Mme. Henri Bourgeot	0.2452	0.6	129
M. Henri Bourgeot and Mme. Veuve Gustave Bourgeot	0.1571	0.4	83
M. Auguste Chevillard and Mme. Veuve Auguste Chevillard	0.0902	0.2	48
M. Alexandre Doré	0.0053	0.0	3
Mlle. Marguérite Dugat and M. Maurice Dugat	0.1376	0.3	73
M. René Galland and Mme. Jean-Louis Sirugue	0.1820	0.4	96
M. Lucien Geoffroy	0.2000	0.5	106
M. Marcel Grandchamp and Mme. Veuve Marcel Grandchamp	0.0973	0.2	51
M. et Mme. Hubert Grillot	0.2112	0.5	112
Mlle. Regina Heresztyn	0.3457	0.9	183
M. et Mme. Jacques Maume	0.2734	0.7	144
M. Émile Rebourseau	0.1320	0.3	70

*Cases calculated on the *rendement de base* of 40 hl/ha plus 20 percent

	Hectares	Acres	Cases*
Mme. Jean-Pierre Sirugue	0.1158	0.3	61
Mme. René Thibaut	0.0840	0.2	44
M. Ernest Tisserandot and Mme. Veuve Ernest Tisserandot	0.1050	0.3	55
M. et Mme. Georges Vachet	0.0888	0.2	47

Petits Cazetiers—0.9487 ha/2.3 acres

Mme. Alize Bizot and Mme. Veuve Denis Bizot	0.2950	0.7	156
Consortium Viticole et Vinicole de Bourgogne	0.2745	0.7	145
M. René Gallois	0.2137	0.5	113
Commune de Gevrey-Chambertin	0.0425	0.1	22
M. et Mme. Philippe Leclerc	0.1443	0.4	76

Plantigone or Issart—0.6237 ha/1.5 acres

M. Bernard Dufour	0.6095	1.5	322

Poissenot—2.2017 ha/5.4 acres. The La Romanée vineyard can also be sold as Poissenot.

M. et Mme. Edouard Geantet	0.6213	1.5	328
Mlle. Odette Guillard	0.0917	0.2	48
M. et Mme. Frédéric Humbert	0.1676	0.4	88
M. et Mme. Roger Humbert	0.1886	0.5	100
Mme. Veuve Joseph Clair and Mme. Jacques Vernet	0.1867	0.5	99
M. et Mme. André Lucot	0.1891	0.5	100

Clos Prieur or Clos Prieur-Haut—1.9786 ha/4.9 acres

SCI Domaine Drouhin-Laroze	0.2930	0.7	155
M. Bernard Dupont	0.0824	0.2	44
M. Michel Gaite	0.1890	0.5	100
M. René Galland and Mme. Jean Louis Sirugue	0.0513	0.1	27
M. Stéphen Gelin	0.2300	0.6	121
M. Lucien Geoffroy	0.1207	0.3	64
M. Marcel Grandchamp	0.0497	0.1	26
M. et Mme. André Lucot	0.0378	0.1	20
M. et Mme. Edouard Mortet	0.1382	0.3	73

*Cases calculated on the *rendement de base* of 40 hl/ha plus 20 percent

	Hectares	Acres	Cases*
M. Pierre Naigeon and Mme. Veuve Pierre Naigeon	0.1470	0.4	78
M. Charles Rousseau	0.0703	0.2	37
M. et Mme. Arthur Sermet	0.0969	0.2	51
M. Jean Trapet and M. Louis Trapet	0.2072	0.5	109
M. Louis Trapet and Mme. Jacques Rossignol	0.2651	0.7	140

La Romanée—1.0630 ha/2.6 acres

	Hectares	Acres	Cases*
SC du Domaine des Varoilles	1.0630	2.6	561

Le Clos Saint-Jacques—6.7049 ha/16.6 acres

	Hectares	Acres	Cases*
Mme. Genevrière Bartet and M. Bernard Clair	1.0001	2.5	528
M. Henri Esmonin and M. Michel Esmonin	1.6017	4.0	846
M. et Mme. Jean-Claude Fourrier	0.8887	2.2	469
M. Charles Rousseau	2.2143	5.5	1169
M. Jacques Vernet	1.0001	2.5	528

Les Verroilles or Clos des Varoilles—6.0303 ha/14.9 acres divided into two *climats*: Les Verroilles (14.8 acres) and a section of Etournelles (0.14 acre)

Clos des Varoilles

	Hectares	Acres	Cases*
SC du Domaine des Varoilles	0.0568	0.1	30

Les Verroilles

	Hectares	Acres	Cases*
SC du Domaine des Varoilles	5.9733	14.8	3154

PRODUCERS WORTH SEEKING OUT (AND SOME NOT)

BOUCHARD PÈRE ET FILS—This producer issues both a Chambertin—under its Domaines du Château de Beaune label, signifying its estate-bottled wines—as well as a Chambertin-Clos de Bèze purchased from others. The Bouchard style is present regard-

---

*Cases calculated on the *rendement de base* of 40 hl/ha plus 20 percent

less: good wine but well short of great. The wines lack concentration and depth, relative to what Chambertin can offer.

DOMAINE ALAIN BURGUET—The source of some of the best commune-level Gevrey-Chambertin around. Burguet offers two bottlings: a regular and a *vieilles vignes* ("old vines") from fifty-year-old vines. Not surprisingly, the *vieilles vignes* is superior, but both are what commune-level Gevrey-Chambertin should be about: well-structured, with good concentration and, above all, real flavor definition and breed.

JOSEPH DROUHIN—If I had to choose just one Drouhin wine, I would reach for this shipper's magnificent Griotte-Chambertin, which surely is reference-standard. There's also good Cazetiers that holds its own against the better estate-bottlings of this *premier cru*. Commune-level Gevrey-Chambertins have been (inevitably) less satisfying, usually too soft and less characterful than one would like. But don't miss that Griotte if you can find it. Also good, if a little diffused, Chambertin, certainly one of the better ones.

DOMAINE DUJAC—The famed Morey-Saint-Denis producer creates a delectable Gevrey-Chambertin *premier cru* from Aux Combottes. The intrinsic lighter weight of this vineyard seems tailor-made for the silky Dujac style. Dujac also offers an excellent Charmes-Chambertin, again a vineyard that seems to respond to the Dujac style, courtesy of its characteristic soft fruitiness.

DOMAINE MICHEL ESMONIN—A newly emerging domaine that previously sold everything to *négociants*. No doubt the *négociants* mourned when Esmonin decided to estate-bottle, starting with the 1987 vintage, because this producer is one of the few owners of Clos Saint-Jacques and a substantial one at that: four acres, the second-largest holding after that of Domaine Armand Rousseau. The vines are now hitting their stride at twenty years old. The prospects look good indeed. Also there are 10.3 acres of commune-level Gevrey-Chambertin from thirty-year-old vines. To watch.

JOSEPH FAIVELEY—The wines from this *négociant* leave me baffled, if only because it is so evident that they seek to do the right thing. Some 80 percent of their total production is made from grapes they own. Their yields in the *grands crus* are very low, well below the average. Yet too often, the Faiveley wines are lackluster: vegetal, stemmy (despite never using more than 50 percent stems in the vinification), and prone to oxidation. The wines strike this taster as coarse, uneven, and too often dried-out and tired. They lack freshness after only just a few years. The Chambertin-Clos de Bèze is no exception, more's the pity given Faiveley's impressive 3.2-acre holding (listed under the corporate name of Consortium Viticole et Vinicole de Bourgogne).

DOMAINE PIERRE GELIN—Famous for their Fixin wines, Gelin also owns parcels in Mazi-Chambertin and Chambertin-Clos de Bèze. Although I admire the Fixins, I confess to not being overly impressed with these *grands crus*. They seem to be either muddy and clumsy in rich vintages such as 1985 or a bit thin, as in 1986. This doesn't make sense, considering the more consistent quality of the Fixin wines, but there it is.

DOMAINE HERESZTYN—One of the up-and-coming producers in Gevrey-Chambertin with parcels in the *premiers crus* Les Corbeaux; Les Champonnets; Les Goulots; and Les Perrières. Many of the vines are older, between twenty years and fifty years of age. Long fermentations lasting up to three weeks create intense, beefy wines. Worth watching.

HOSPICES DE BEAUNE—The Hospices owns just one property in the Côte de Nuits, in Mazi-Chambertin. A 3.9-acre parcel in Les Mazi-Hauts was donated by Thomas Collignon in memory of his mother, Madeleine Collignon. The first vintage auctioned was 1977. The wine typically is the best red wine at the auction, although the 1989 vintage left much to be desired. The 1985, however, was a wonderment.

Cuvée Madeleine Collignon—1.5862 ha/3.9 acres in Mazi-Chambertin

LOUIS JADOT—With their purchase of part of the old Clair-Daü estate in 1985, this *négociant* has vaulted to the top rank in Gevrey-Chambertin. Long the source of good commune-level Gevrey-Chambertin, Jadot now creates what may be the most compelling Chambertin-Clos de Bèze available, courtesy of Clair-Daü's old vines. Right behind it is the shadow *grand cru* of Gevrey-Chambertin, the great Clos Saint-Jacques. The Jadot rendition, again from Clair-Daü vines, now rivals the previous reference standard, Domaine Armand Rousseau's Clos Saint-Jacques. It is *grand cru* in everything but name. Also fine is the Chapelle-Chambertin, which is about as good as that vineyard gets: a combination of chocolate and cassis. Jadot now shares with Leroy the mantle of being the leading *négociant* for reference-standard Gevrey-Chambertin.

DOMAINE PHILIPPE LECLERC—Perhaps the newest superstar in Gevrey-Chambertin (his first domaine-bottled wine appeared in the 1979 vintage), Philippe Leclerc, along with his brother René, who has his own domaine, creates magnificent wines: concentrated, tannic, muscular, and destined for long life. If Philippe Lerclerc wines have a drawback, it's that they can be excessively oaky, as he prefers to use 100 percent new oak barrels. (His brother René uses new barrels more sparingly.) But the quality of the fruit is incontestable. Leclerc's Combe au Moine is better than most *grand crus*, coming as it does from fifty-year-old vines. The Cazetiers, always lighter, is filled with character and depth, courtesy of sixty-year-old vines. And, miracle of miracles, Philippe Leclerc issues a commune-level Gevrey-Chambertin from the flat plain across N74 from the Les Platières vineyard that actually shows what can be done in that area by a producer of exacting standards. He also produces a superb Bourgogne Rouge, the 1985 vintage of which still is maturing in my cellar and does not yet seem to have traveled its full transit as a wine. This is one of the top producers in Gevrey-Chambertin.

DOMAINE RENÉ LECLERC—When the family domaine was divided (not equally) in 1975 between Philippe and René Leclerc, each went his own way. Philippe preferred all new oak, and René, until the 1986 vintage, eschewed new oak altogether. Since then he has been adding new barrels; reportedly about 25 percent new oak now is employed. Certainly, René's wines are less marked by oak than Philippe's. The quality of the fruit is equally intense, rich, and concentrated. The two brothers' wines are not identical, making comparisons a fascinating exercise in ascertaining a winemaker's signature. As with Philippe, the standout René Leclerc wine is the Combe au Moine, which is massive and concentrated. After all, the vines are over fifty years old. The Cazetiers and Lavaux Saint-Jacques are similarly outstanding. There's also a Clos Prieur that I have not tasted. Unlike his brother's, René Leclerc's style still seems to be evolving. But the raw material already puts him in the top rank.

LEROY—This is the source of the greatest Gevrey-Chambertins I know. This is doubly amazing when one recalls that until 1988, when the newly founded Domaine Leroy was established (built on the foundation of the former Domaine Charles Noëllat in Vosne-Romanée), Leroy owned a mere particle of Chambertin, just one-quarter acre. All of the many Leroy bottlings from Gevrey-Chambertin came from purchased grapes or wines. So somebody, somewhere, is making the real thing, and clearly Lalou Bize-Leroy knew who they were.

For example, there's Leroy's Mazi-Chambertin which is the reference standard: implacably intense, concentrated, and truly *sauvage*. The consistency was achieved because the grapes came from just one owner. Then there are the Chambertins, which demonstrate as few others do why Chambertin is indeed majestic. The list expands with Lavaux Saint-Jacques; Étournelles Saint-Jacques; a magnificent Ruchottes-Chambertin; and about as good a Charmes-Chambertin as can be found.

In 1989 Domaine Leroy purchased Domaine Remy, acquiring parcels in Chambertin, Latricières-Chambertin, and Aux Combottes. These wines will be released under the Domaine Leroy label, and judging from wines tasted out of the barrel, they promise to be of the same exceptional standard as the Leroy *négociant* label.

DOMAINE HENRI MAGNIEN—A noted producer of the *premier cru* Cazetiers, the Magnien wines have not shown well in recent years. They seem a bit thin and weedy, lacking depth and concentration.

DOMAINE MARCHAND-GRILLOT—A middle-of-the-road producer, the wines of which can seem a bit hollow at times. Still, the domaine offers a good Petite Chapelle *premier cru* and a decent commune-level Gevrey-Chambertin, among other wines. Not in the top rank, however.

DOMAINE MAUME—The source of some of the richest, most concentrated Mazi-Chambertin available. Bernard Maume likes intensely colored wines of sumptuous texture, occasionally employing carbonic-maceration techniques. The problem is that sometimes they can seem a little soupy or overworked. Nevertheless, there's quality here, and Maume's *premier cru* Lavaux-Saint-Jacques and, especially, the Mazi-Chambertin, are worth seeking out.

DOMAINE GEORGES MUGNERET—The late Dr. Mugneret of Vosne-Romanée (he died in November 1988) created extraordinary Ruchottes-Chambertin from a 1.6-acre holding. His only rivals were the Ruchottes of Domaine Armand Rousseau and that from Domaine Georges Roumier. Usually, I wound up giving the nod to the Mugneret version, although not by much. His daughter, Marie-Andrée, has taken over the estate, although I have not tasted any wines made under her command. Robert M. Parker, Jr., of *The Wine Advocate*, who is also a great fan of this domaine, reports that the standard has been maintained. That's good enough for me.

DOMAINE NEWMAN—This tiny property has one singular distinction: Domaine Newman was until 1985 the only American owner of *grand cru* vineyards in Burgundy. (This distinction was lost when Kobrand Corporation, owned by three sisters, all American, purchased Maison Louis Jadot in 1985. Through that vehicle, they subsequently purchased *grand cru* vineyards.) Robert Newman, who is in his eighties, lives in Metairie, Louisiana, a suburb of New Orleans. I was so curious about this remarkable situation that I visited him to inquire how it came about that an American owned pieces of Mazi-Chambertin (0.5 acres), Latricières-Chambertin (0.4 acres), and Bonnes Mares (0.8 acres).

He explained how he started collecting wine in 1942, having

traveled to Europe almost yearly since his early twenties. Born into an investment-banking family, he was one of the late Alexis Lichine's original syndicate to purchase Château Lascombes in Bordeaux in 1952. (Other investors included David Rockefeller and John Ringling North.) "I told Alexis that I was very much interested in wine. I wasn't content just to be in a syndicate of twenty-odd people who visited the château for two or three days and could say that they had an ownership. I mean, I was really interested in doing something," explained Newman.

"So it happened that a piece of property in Burgundy, these parts of Bonnes Mares and Latricières-Chambertin and Mazi-Chambertin, became available in 1955. Alexis didn't have any money. And so I bought it. But my deal with Alexis was that I would make him a half-owner when he paid off his half-share of the cost. He was to manage it and sell the wines. And he would make his usual commission for that, as well. I was willing to carry him. Lichine managed it for a few years, but he hadn't paid for it yet. We had a man who was a full-time employee who took care of the property, and he hanged himself. When I went to inspect the property, I found that it had gone all to hell. And I was very unhappy with Alexis, because he was supposed to manage it and he should have seen what was happening. So I told Alexis that I was keeping it all."

The property now is overseen by one of Robert Newman's two sons, Christopher, who was educated in Switzerland before returning to New Orleans as an investor. The Newman vines are tended on a sharecropping basis. A few cases trickle into the States from time to time.

DOMAINE JEAN-MARIE PONSOT/DOMAINE DES CHEZEAUX— This is an extraordinarily inconsistent producer. The Ponsot style emphasizes a luxurious silkiness, almost a flashy fruitiness that can be enchanting. Not to be ignored is the fact that the wines seem most impressive when young and, too often, decline in quality as the years go by. In a world where judgments are rendered on months-old wines tasted out of the barrel, this is an alluring and commercially viable style indeed.

Nevertheless, in the very best vintages the Ponsot wines can be memorable, including their tiny quantity of Chambertin from a one-third-acre plot in Chambertin (listed under the Ponsot corporate name of GFA du Domaine de Chezeaux). Ponsot's most compelling wine is his Griotte-Chambertin, which seems to lend itself to the Ponsot suppleness. You can find all the wild cherries you want in this version. Lesser vintages should make one wary. There's a lot of hype about Ponsot at present, which, given the wide quality swings of this producer, should make the careful buyer all the more reluctant to buy first (on futures) and then taste later. Still, Ponsot wines are worthy of investigation.

DOMAINE JOSEPH ROTY—A very fashionable estate that has been embraced by Burgundy buffs in Paris and San Francisco, the two strongholds of Burgundy connoisseurship. The Roty style emphasizes delicacy with penetrating flavor, which is an attractive combination. The best Roty wine surely is the Charmes-Chambertin, which is as finely drawn an example of this vineyard as can be found. The reason surely can be traced to vines reported to be eighty-five years old. Also excellent Mazi-Chambertin and really fine Griotte-Chambertin. Any Roty wine is worth pursuing. They are very pure, very fine: A real standard is being upheld.

DOMAINE GEORGES ROUMIER—One of the consistently best producers in Burgundy, Roumier issues a Ruchottes-Chambertin from a recently acquired parcel that rivals those from domaines Georges Mugneret and Armand Rousseau. The problem is finding it. Also, there's a Charmes-Chambertin from the same purchase, but I have never seen or tasted it. However, Roumier doesn't miss these days, so if you spot it . . .

DOMAINE ARMAND ROUSSEAU—Long since run by the son Charles Rousseau, this is the most renowned domaine in Gevrey-Chambertin, and for a long time one of the best. Sadly, it went through a slump in the late seventies and early eighties, for inexplicable reasons. Charles Rousseau was known to have been distraught over what seemed to be a deterioration in the wines.

With the glorious 1985 vintage, the standard has improved considerably, although longtime devotees still concede that the wines never have returned to the standard achieved in the fifties and sixties.

Some suggest, perhaps with justification, that Rousseau's insistence on filtering—which he performs now and, prior to the mysterious decline, did not insist upon—may be keeping the Rousseau wines from reaching the pinnacle that is rightly theirs. Nevertheless, the wines now are very good to near-great. Chambertin-Clos de Bèze is one of the reference standards. The Clos Saint-Jacques is a marvel, a true *grand cru* in all but regulatory name; the Clos des Ruchottes is equally fine, with an intense *goût de terroir*. Any Rousseau wine is worth sampling. One only hopes that Rousseau claws its way back to the pinnacle.

DOMAINE LOUIS TRAPET—One of the most famous, and well-endowed, domaines in Gevrey-Chambertin. I never have understood the hoopla. Trapet intentionally creates light wines, so light that they can make you wonder exactly which commune they come from. I recall a blind tasting of Trapet's acclaimed Chambertin 1985 "Vieilles Vignes" with a Leroy Chambertin 1985. The degree of difference bordered on the absurd. There was breed to the Trapet wine, but in a shriveled sort of way. It lacked depth, concentration, and the well-bred muscle that one has a right to expect from Chambertin. The winemaking signature in all of the Trapet wines is as intrusive as any in Burgundy. They also are extremely uneven from vintage to vintage, even by Burgundy standards.

Chambertin and Chambertin-Clos de Bèze

> *The history of maize does not appear in cornflakes, nor of wheat in bread, but it is the history of the grape's year, especially its last few sugar-generating weeks, that appears in the wine. When you drink a glass of Burgundy you experience the year's sun and rainfall and the quality of the earth. . . . The wine becomes a kind of liquid geography.*
>
> —ADAM NICOLSON, *Long Walks in France* (1983)

No wine is more symbolic of Burgundy than Chambertin. It connotes capillary-bursting pleasure, *the* red wine of red wines. It has the unequivocal imprimatur of Napoleon Bonaparte, who somehow has since acquired the aura of having been a wine connoisseur. He was nothing of the sort. But he did drink Chambertin, which accompanied him on all his campaigns. He also watered the wine considerably. In certain circles, to this day, this exaltation of Chambertin by Napoleon is approbation like no other.

Napoleon's abilities as a taster aside, the fact is that Chambertin is the longest-running hit in Burgundy. In this, one includes Chambertin-Clos de Bèze. Technically, the vineyard assigned the name "Chambertin" is a parvenu compared to that called "Clos de Bèze." Clos de Bèze is said to have been established in 630, after Duke Amalgaire gave the site to the Abbey of Bèze. It was only in the

1200s, so the story goes, that a local peasant called Bertin who owned a strip of land that is, in effect, an extension of Clos de Bèze, decided to plant it to vines. Thus was born Le Champ de Bertin, or Chambertin. This is the hoary tale, and so far nobody has effectively debunked it.

French wine law, ever respectful of past usage, distinguishes between Clos de Bèze and Chambertin. Clos de Bèze may be sold simply as "Chambertin," but wine from the Chambertin vineyard proper may not append the name "Clos de Bèze."

Chambertin at its best is Burgundy's strongest statement. Unlike the common misconception, it is not a heavy wine, although it can fairly be said to be fleshy. It should be full, intense, deeply colored, and luxuriantly rich and involved. Actually, Chambertin is not the most extreme wine among the eight *grands crus* of Gevrey-Chambertin. Mazi-Chambertin is more forceful, almost brutish in its amplitude. Latricières-Chambertin is lighter, and consequently displays more apparent finesse. Ruchottes-Chambertin can be silkier.

So why is Chambertin accorded the rank of first among equals? The answer is similar to that offered in explaining the singularity of Volnay "Caillerets" or Meursault "Perrières," namely, that Chambertin consolidates more attributes than any other. It has almost as much sheer flavor as Mazi, but with the refinement of Ruchottes. It delivers this with as much finesse as Latricières. It is an amalgam and an amplification of all of the virtues of Gevrey-Chambertin. If it were human, we would call it "saintly."

This is Chambertin at its best. Regrettably, there isn't much of this sort of Chambertin around. The reasons include the usual roundup of suspects: excess yields; lesser clones; uninspired winemaking; and above all, the security of knowing that no matter what is offered, it will sell without question or cavil. Not to be ignored is that a goodly portion of the vineyard is planted to relatively young vines. The fact that few Chambertins offered today are worthy of either the name or the price is of no consequence whatever. In this, it resembles Montrachet, which also rarely rises to the promise of its name and or delivers on the potency of its site.

THE VINEYARD

Chambertin is 28.2918 ha/69.9 acres divided between two vineyards: Chambertin (12.9031 ha/31.9 acres) and Chambertin-

Clos de Bèze (15.3887 ha/38 acres). Wine made exclusively from Chambertin-Clos de Bèze can be sold either as Chambertin or Chambertin-Clos de Bèze. That from Chambertin can be sold only as Chambertin. Wine made from both vineyards can be sold only as Chambertin.

Chambertin

	Hectares	Acres	Cases*
M. Adrien Belland and Mme. Veuve Baron Antoine Vieillard	0.1015	0.3	47
Mme. Adrien Belland and Mme. Veuve Baron Antoine Vieillard	0.2028	0.5	94
Mme. Gilbert Bertin and Mme. Veuve Baron Antoine Vieillard	0.2028	0.5	94
Maison Albert Bichot	0.1727	0.4	80
Bouchard Père et Fils	0.1470	0.4	68
GFA Léon Camus Père et Fils	1.6938	4.2	783
GFA du Domaine des Chezeaux	0.1430	0.4	66
GFA Coribel	0.0986	0.2	46
Domaine Pierre Damoy	0.4759	1.2	220
M. Gaston Dupont	0.05037	0.1	25
M. et Mme. Robert Dupont	0.0538	0.1	25
SC des Grandes Appellations d'Origine	0.2016	0.5	93
M. et Mme. Ferdinand Launay	0.1586	0.4	73
SA Nouvelle Elvina et Leroy Vins et Alcools	0.1000	0.2	46
Domaine des Enfants de Marcilly	0.1486	0.4	69
SC Particulière Domaine Jacques Prieur	0.8397	2.1	388
SC du Domaine Henri Rebourseau	0.4612	1.1	213
M. Marie-François Remy and Mme. Veuve Marie Remy	0.3206	0.8	148
M. Marie-Philippe Remy	0.4003	1.0	185
Mme. Michel Rolland	0.8114	2.0	375
Domaine Armand Rousseau	0.2865	0.7	132
SC d'Exploitation du Domaine Armand Rousseau	0.0768	0.2	35
M. Charles Rousseau	1.5849	3.9	732
SCI du Clos du Thorey (Moillard)	0.0537	0.1	25
M. et Mme. Gabriel Tortochot	0.3983	1.0	184
M. François Trapet	0.2013	0.5	93

*Cases calculated on the *rendement de base* of 35 hl/ha plus 20 percent

	Hectares	Acres	Cases*
SC d'Exploitation du Domaine Louis Trapet	0.3715	0.9	172
M. Louis Trapet	1.6935	4.2	782
M. Louis Trapet and Mme. Jacques Rossignol	0.5720	1.4	264
M. Jean Trapet and M. Louis Trapet	0.5720	1.4	264
M. et Mme. Georges Vachet	0.2743	0.7	127

Clos de Bèze

	Hectares	Acres	Cases*
M. André Bart	0.4165	1.0	192
M. Michel Clair (et Copropriétaires)	0.9802	2.4	453
Consortium Viticole et Vinicole de Bourgogne	1.2942	3.2	598
Domaine Pierre Damoy	5.2764	13.0	2438
M. et Mme. Philippe Duroche	0.2530	0.6	117
M. Stephan Gelin	0.6025	1.5	278
M. et Mme. Robert Groffier	0.4066	1.0	188
SC d'Exploitation Drouhin-Laroze	1.3089	3.2	605
SCI Domaine Drouhin-Laroze	0.1582	0.4	73
M. Henri Marion	1.9225	4.8	888
M. Roger Peirazeau	0.1868	0.5	86
Mlle. Anne Pradal and Mme. Henri Pradal	0.1235	0.3	57
SC Particulière Domaine Jacques Prieur	0.1460	0.4	67
SC du Domaine Henri Rebourseau	0.3313	0.8	153
SC d'Exploitation du Domaine Armand Rousseau	0.7110	1.8	328
SCI du Clos du Thorey (Moillard)	0.2392	0.6	111
M. Jacques Vernet	0.4165	1.0	192
M. Marc Zibetti	0.2325	0.6	107
M. Jean-Marie Zibetti	0.2325	0.6	107

---

*Cases calculated on the *rendement de base* of 35 hl/ha plus 20 percent.

Mazi-
Chambertin

One of the fascinations of the Gevrey-Chambertin *grands crus* is how different they can be from each other. Mazi-Chambertin, for example, shares the same alignment on the slope as Chambertin-Clos de Bèze, which it adjoins. The wines surely are similar. Yet when one is faced with good examples of both wines from the same vintage and producer (such as those from Leroy or Domaine Armand Rousseau), there's no denying that they are not the same. Mazi-Chambertin seems more aggressive and intense, what the French call *sauvage* (wild). Indeed, there is a wild flavor to it in the same sense that vegetables plucked from the wild are more pungent, if less refined, than carefully nurtured varieties.

Perhaps because of this pungency, Mazi-Chambertin often can be a better bet than Chambertin itself. Partly this may be due to the vineyard boasting a large number of older vines compared to

Chambertin. It rarely, however, offers the same degree of finesse or refinement as Chambertin. For some reason, it seems to mature sooner as well, perhaps because its lacks the almost gyroscopic equilibrium present in the best Chambertins. Still, a Mazi-Chambertin needs ten years in a good vintage, so it hardly can be considered precocious.

One of the curiosities of Mazi-Chambertin was that it once was considered not only inferior to Chambertin and Chambertin-Clos de Bèze, but was divided into lower and upper portions. Yet nothing about the soil or the exposition or the slant of the slope is known—at least to me—that distinguishes one part from the other. Moreover, in 1860 when the Agriculture Committee of Beaune classified the vineyard, it branded a section of the lower part third class, with the upper part made a respectable second class. Today, both parts are *grand cru* and deservedly so, although the ownership records of the *cadastre* still divide the vineyard into *bas* (lower) and *haut* (upper).

THE VINEYARD

Mazi-Chambertin has 9.1034 ha/22.5 acres, divided into two *climats*: Les Mazis-Bas (4.5611 ha/11.27 acres) and Les Mazis-Hauts (4.5423 ha/11.22 acres).

Les Mazis-Bas

	Hectares	Acres	Cases*
Mme. Alice Bizot and Mme. Veuve Denis Bizot	0.1757	0.4	86
M. Félicien Caillet	0.0438	0.1	21
GFA Léon Camus Perè et Fils	0.3737	0.9	182
M. Stéphen Gelin	0.2673	0.7	130
M. Lucien Geoffroy	0.1727	0.4	84
M. et Mme. Michel Goudot	0.1202	0.3	59
M. Alain Langlais and Mme. Veuve Henri Langlais	0.1480	0.4	72
SCI Domaine Drouhin-Laroze	0.1240	0.3	61
M. et Mme. André Lucot	0.0506	0.1	25

*Cases calculated on the *rendement de base* of 37 hl/ha plus 20 percent

	Hectares	*Acres*	*Cases**
M. Bernard Maume and M. Jacques Maume	0.6727	1.7	328
M. Pierre Menneveau	0.0366	0.1	17
M. Émile Rebourseau and M. Jacques Rebourseau and coproprietors	0.9634	2.4	470
M. Charles Rousseau	0.5317	1.3	259
Mme. Veuve Ernest Tisserandot and M. Ernest Tisserandot	0.2074	0.5	101
M. Félix Tortochot	0.4183	1.0	204
M. et Mme. Georges Vachet	0.2520	0.6	123

Les Mazis-Hauts

	Hectares	*Acres*	*Cases**
M. Étienne Beaumont and Mme. Robert Girard	0.1943	0.5	95
Mme. Alice Bizot and Mme. Veuve Denis Bizot	0.2481	0.6	121
M. Eugène Chouiller and M. René Chouiller and Mme. Yvonne Chouiller	0.0205	0.1	10
Commune de Gevrey-Chambertin	0.0079	0.0	4
Consortium Viticole et Vinicole de Bourgogne	0.2044	3.0	588
M. Stéphen Gelin	0.1108	0.3	54
M. et Mme. Michel Goudot	0.3800	0.9	185
Hospices Civils de Beaune	1.5862	3.9	774
M. Roger Huguenot	0.0998	0.2	49
Mme. Veuve François Jacqueson and M. René Jacqueson	0.0945	0.2	46
M. et Mme. René Jacqueson	0.0685	0.2	33
M. Paul Jeanniard and Mme. Michel Papillaud	0.0387	0.1	19
M. Alain Langlais and Mme. Veuve Henri Langlais	0.3220	0.8	157
M. et Mme. André Lucot	0.3900	1.0	190
M. et Mme. Pierre Marchand	0.0395	0.1	19
M. René Masson	0.1065	0.3	52
M. Pierre Naigeon			

---

*Cases calculated on the *rendement de base* of 37 hl/ha plus 20 percent

	Hectares	Acres	Cases*
Mme. Veuve Pierre Naigeon	0.1406	0.3	69
M. Robert Newman (et Copropriétaires)	0.1890	0.5	92
Mme. Louis Noblet	0.0950	0.2	46
Mme. Louis Noblet	0.4352	1.1	212
M. et Mme. Henri Perrot-Minot	0.2086	0.5	102
M. et Mme. Jean Raphet	0.4476	1.1	218
M. Émile Rebourseau M. Jacques Rebourseau (et Copropriétaires)	0.5315	1.3	259
M. et Mme. Joseph Roty	0.1640	0.4	80
M. Charles Rousseau	0.5064	1.3	247
M. Aristide Sequin	0.0546	0.1	27
M. Stanislas Serafin	0.1255	0.3	61
Mlle. Suzanne Thomas	0.3818	0.9	186
Mme. Veuve Ernest Tisserandot M. Ernest Tisserandot	0.3132	0.8	153

---

*Cases calculated on the *rendement de base* of 37 hl/ha plus 20 percent

Latricières-Chambertin

Latricières-Chambertin brackets the southern end of Chambertin, just as Mazi-Chambertin is the northern bracket alongside Chambertin-Clos de Bèze. And just like its fellow bracket, Latricières shares seemingly the same slope, the same alignment, and apparently the same soil. Yet the wine bears surprisingly little resemblance to that of its famous neighbors. It always is lighter, more early-maturing, somehow lacking the stuffings of Chambertin, Clos de Bèze, or Mazi.

In a more logical Burgundian world (now there's an oxymoron), Clos de la Roche would switch places with Latricières-Chambertin. Somehow it seems more reasonable that a neighbor to Chambertin would be more like the sturdy, well-stuffed Clos de la Roche than the lacier, lighter-weight wine that is Latricières.

The temptation is always to compare Latricières with Chambertin, but a more enlightening comparison would be between Latricières and its adjacent vineyard, the *premier cru* Aux Combottes, which is the last vineyard stop in Gevrey-Chambertin before crossing the line into Morey-Saint-Denis. Both share a similar (relative) lightness. But here the breed of Latricières becomes evident. The difference is that Combottes, as the name suggests (*combe* is "a valley"), is situated in a hollow where cold air collects, making for a cooler microclimate. Latricières suffers no such problem, although a 1.1-acre slice of Aux Combottes was included in Latricières-Chambertin during the Appellation Contrôlée deliberations, which inclusion makes one suspect heavy-duty political lobbying at the time on the part of its owner, Domaine Léon Camus Père et Fils.

THE VINEYARD

Latricières-Chambertin 7.3544 ha/18.2 acres, divided into two *climats*: Latricières (17.1 acres) and a piece of Aux Combottes (1.1 acres)

Latricières

	Hectares	Acres	Cases*
GFA Léon Camus Père et Fils	0.0634	2.6	519
Consortium Viticole et Vinicole de Bourgogne	0.2067	3.0	589
M. Robert Newman (et Copropriétaires)	0.3830	0.9	187
SCI Domaine Drouhin-Laroze	0.6745	1.7	329
M. Ferdinand Launay	0.1677	0.4	82
M. Christopher Newman and M. Robert Newman and Mme. Robert Newman	0.1470	0.4	72
M. Marie-François Remy and Mme. Veuve Marie Remy (plot purchased in 1989 by Domaine Leroy)	0.5807	1.4	283
Mlle. Anne-Marie Remy (now Domaine Leroy)	0.1654	0.4	81
M. Michel Remy (now Domaine Leroy)	0.1539	0.4	75
M. Marie-Philippe Remy (now Domaine Leroy)	0.5715	1.4	279

*Cases calculated on the *rendement de base* of 37 hl/ha plus 20 percent

	Hectares	Acres	Cases*
M. Louis Trapet and Mme. Jacques Rossignol and M. Jean Trapet	0.0300	0.1	15
M. Louis Trapet and Mme. Jacques Rossignol	0.7340	1.8	358
M. Louis Trapet M. Jean Trapet	0.7340	1.8	358
Mme. Michel Vallée	0.2757	0.7	135
Aux Combottes			
GFA Léon Camus Père et Fils	0.4478	1.1	218

---

*Cases calculated on the *rendement de base* of 37 hl/ha plus 20 percent

Charmes-Chambertin and Mazoyères-Chambertin

T he reason that Charmes-Chambertin and Mazoyères-Chambertin are discussed jointly is simply that they are one and the same vineyard. On wine maps, they always are distinguished: Mazoyères is located below Latricières-Chambertin and abuts Morey-Saint-Denis; Charmes lies below Chambertin itself. But the law lets both be sold as Charmes-Chambertin.

One would think that the proximity of the actual Charmes vineyard to Chambertin would make it superior, but no one seems to think so. Part of the reason surely is the slope of the land. Right across the road that intersects Charmes from Chambertin, the vineyard drops sharply to a lower plane. In fact, there are several crevasses in it against the road, the vertical walls of which show clearly how different is the exposition of the two vineyards.

Technically, a grower with a holding only in Mazoyères can

choose that name, rather than the better-known Charmes. I only know of one producer to do so regularly, Domaine Camus. The owner listings to follow do, however, reveal which parcels are in Mazoyères and which are in Charmes.

The name "Charmes" was well-chosen. Of all the *grands crus*, Charmes is the easiest. It matures sooner than any of the others, is softer, and is the most apparently fruity. Rarely, if ever, would one describe a Charmes-Chambertin as austere, although there's no reason that winemaking couldn't push it in that direction. Frankly, it is the least distinctive of the *grands crus*, although still enjoyable all the same.

More than any other *grand cru*, Charmes-Chambertin is a specialty of *négociants*. It is the largest *grand cru* and *négociants* are thus able to obtain a supply. Several shippers' bottlings, notably those from Louis Jadot and Joseph Drouhin, are usually among the best.

THE VINEYARD

There are 30.8324 ha/76.2 acres divided between two *climats*: Aux Charmes (12.2456 ha/30.3 acres) and Mazoyères ou Charmes (18.5868 ha/ 45.9 acres).

Aux Charmes

	Hectares	Acres	Cases*
M. Bernard Bachelet	0.4338	1.1	212
SC Vignoble Bernard Bourée and M. Gaston Bourée	0.5923	1.5	289
GFA Léon Camus Père et Fils	0.0345	7.5	1481
M. Claude Dugat	0.3061	0.8	149
M. et Mme. Pierre Dugat	0.2388	0.6	117
SC d'Exploitation du Domaine Dujac	0.3094	0.8	151
M. Gaston Dupont	0.0615	0.2	30
M. et Mme. Philippe Duroche	0.3699	0.9	181
M. et Mme. Edmond Geantet	0.4500	1.1	220
GFA Huguenot Père et Fils	0.1143	0.3	56
M. Jean Mouchet and M. Dantes Adiba	0.3790	0.9	185
SC du Domaine Henri Rebourseau	0.7872	1.9	384

*Cases calculated on the *rendement de base* of 37 hl/ha plus 20 percent

	Hectares	Acres	Cases*
SC du Domaine Vitocole de la Guyonnière	0.0865	0.2	42
Mazoyères ou Charmes			
M. Pierre Amiot	0.1893	0.5	92
GFA Domaine Arlaud Père et Fils	0.1897	0.5	93
M. Étienne Beaumont and M. Marcel Beaumont	0.1616	0.4	79
Mme. Marcel Beaumont and Mme. Veuve Pierre Trivier	0.2731	0.7	133
M. et Mme. Robert Bolnot	0.1688	0.4	82
Mme. Veuve Gustave Bourgeot and M. Henri Bourgeot	0.4010	1.0	196
GFA Léon Camus Père et Fils	3.8731	9.6	1890
M. André Charlopin	0.1759	0.4	86
M. André Coquard	0.2111	0.5	103
M. Louis Coquard and M. Raymond Coquard	0.3230	0.8	158
SC d'Exploitation du Domaine Dujac	0.3865	1.0	189
M. et Mme. Bernard Dupont	0.3614	0.9	176
M. Jean-Baptiste Gibourg	0.1334	0.3	65
M. et Mme. Roger Humbert	0.1979	0.5	97
M. Michel Jouan	0.1986	0.5	97
M. Jean-Pierre Jouan	0.1302	0.3	64
Mlle. Paulette Lambert and Mme. Veuve Paul Defrance	0.6454	1.6	315
GFA Domaine Georges Lignier Père et fils	0.0852	0.2	42
M. et Mme. Bernard Magnien	0.2785	0.7	136
M. Félix Magnien	0.1992	0.5	97
M. et Mme. Claude Marchand	0.0466	0.1	23
Mme. Isabelle Marchand	0.0929	0.2	45
M. Bernard Maume	0.1256	0.3	61
M. Bernard Maume and M. Jacques Maume	0.0465	0.1	23
M. Armand Noirot	0.3093	0.8	151
Mme. Roger Peirazeau	0.2185	0.5	107
M. Roger Peirazeau	0.2313	0.6	113
M. et Mme. Henri Perrot-Minot	0.3498	3.3	659

*Cases calculated on the *rendement de base* of 37 hl/ha plus 20 percent

	Hectares	Acres	Cases*
Petits-Fils de Pierre Ponnelle	0.7350	1.8	359
M. Alfred Rang and Mme. Gaetan Mariotti	0.8603	2.1	420
M. Henri Richard	1.1105	2.7	542
M. et Mme. André Seguin	0.4517	1.1	220
M. Germain Tardy	0.0900	0.2	44
M. et Mme. Jean Taupenot	1.4407	3.6	703
M. Félix Tortochot	0.3495	0.9	171
M. et Mme. Gabriel Tortochot	0.2205	0.5	108
M. et Mme. Jacky Truchot	0.6544	1.6	319
M. et Mme. Gilbert Vadey	0.3960	1.0	193
M. Paul Valby	0.3561	0.9	174
SC du Domaine des Varoilles	0.6395	1.6	312
Mme. Veuve Baron Antoine Vieillard and M. Baron Jacques Vieillard	0.2029	0.5	99
Mme. Veuve Baron Antoine Vieillard and M. Baron Jean-Charles Vieillard	0.1014	0.3	49

---

*Cases calculated on the *rendement de base* of 37 hl/ha plus 20 percent

Griotte-Chambertin

Every Burgundy lover has his or her affections. Mine is Griotte-Chambertin. Though it's not as profound as either Chambertin or Mazi-Chambertin, or as elegant as Ruchottes-Chambertin, I nevertheless have an abiding affection for Griotte-Chambertin. Perhaps it's the name: *griotte* is a wild cherry, and damned if I don't find that exact scent in the wine. Maybe it's just the power of suggestion, but I don't think so.

The problem with Griotte-Chambertin is finding some. It is the smallest *grand cru*, producing not much more than fourteen hundred cases total. Actually, an average of the yield of this vineyard over the last fifteen years shows that Griotte-Chambertin issues fewer than eight hundred cases a year, well below what it legally could offer. This could explain the unusually high quality of the wine.

Griotte-Chambertin is voluptuously fruity when young, and

seems to mature relatively early. It is also somehow sleek and very fine. This conclusion, though, may be due to the wines with which I have the most familiarity: the Griotte-Chambertin of Joseph Drouhin and that from Domaine Ponsot. Both are superb. But both producers also specialize in creating intensely fruity, early-maturing wines. Nevertheless, I always look for more, so they must be doing something right.

THE VINEYARD

There are 2.6918 ha/6.65 acres in Griotte-Chambertin.

En Griotte

	Hectares	Acres	Cases*
GFA du Domaine des Chezeaux (Domaine Ponsot)	0.8856	2.2	432
Société Domaine Joseph Drouhin	0.5066	1.3	247
Mlle. Françoise Dugat and M. Maurice Dugat	0.1519	0.4	74
M. et Mme. Philippe Duroche	0.0192	0.05	9
M. et Mme. Jean-Claude Fourrier	0.2593	0.6	127
M. et Mme. Claude Marchand	0.1260	0.3	61
M. et Mme. Joseph Roty	0.0779	0.2	38
Mlle. Suzanne Thomas	0.6780	1.7	331

*Cases calculated on the *rendement de base* of 37 hl/ha plus 20 percent

Chapelle-Chambertin

T he curiouser and curiouser quality of the *grands crus* is fully in evidence with Chapelle-Chambertin. On the map, it looks like nothing so much as an extension or a subdivision of Griotte-Chambertin. In fact, they share an identical exposure. Yet side by side, the two wines are not at all identical. Chapelle-Chambertin is lighter and much less infused with that extraordinary wild-cherry scent found in Griotte-Chambertin.

The lightness may partially be due to the fact that Chapelle-Chambertin offers higher yields than occur in Griotte-Chambertin. Since 1971, the average yield in Chapelle-Chambertin has been around 36 hl/ha compared to Griotte-Chambertin's 25 hl/ha. This may be due to younger vines or more vigorous rootstocks or greedier growers. But it may also be due to Chapelle-Chambertin having slightly richer soil than is found in Griotte-Chambertin, or so the growers report. Whatever the source, Chapelle-Chambertin consistently is the lightest of the *grands crus*, although it does offer abundant bouquet and real finesse.

The vineyard takes its name from a chapel built on the site by the Abbey of Bèze in 1155, which was demolished during the Revolution of 1789. Also, Chapelle-Chambertin is divided into two *climats*: Chapelle and Les Gémeaux (twins). Les Gémeaux is an odd name, even by Burgundian standards. Marie-Hélène Landrieu-Lussigny, in her unique book on the origins of Burgundian vineyard place names *Les Lieux-Dits Dans Le Vignoble Bourguignon* (1983), reports that she has heard that the name somehow is in honor of Castor and Pollux, the mythological twin brothers. Alternatively, she says, it may have to do with mounds (of earth) that were hauled away two by two, which called to mind the mythological twins.

THE VINEYARD

Chapelle-Chambertin has 5.4853 ha/13.55 acres, divided into two *climats*: En la Chapelle (3.6924 ha/9.12 acres) and Les Gémeaux (1.7929 ha/4.43 acres).

En la Chapelle

	Hectares	Acres	Cases*
M. Jean-Marie Thomas Collignon	0.5127	1.3	250
Domaine Pierre Damoy	2.2182	5.5	1082
SCI Domaine Drouhin-Laroze Mme. Jacques Rossignol	0.5148	1.3	251
M. Jean Trapet and M. Louis Trapet	0.5562	1.4	271
M. Louis Trapet	0.4032	1.0	197

Les Gémeaux

	Hectares	Acres	Cases*
M. Robert Faye and Mme. Chatin Jacques	0.3625	0.9	177
M. Gaston Livera	0.3996	1.0	195
Mme. Frédéric Martin	0.0407	0.1	20
GFA du Domaine Ponsot	0.4673	1.2	228
M. Louis Trapet and Mme. Jacques Rossignol	0.1354	0.3	66
M. Roger Trinquier	0.3874	1.0	189

*Cases calculated on the *rendement de base* of 37 hl/ha plus 20 percent

Ruchottes-
Chambertin

T he location of this 8.2-acre vineyard helps explain its very particular character. It edges up farther on Montagne de la Combe-
Grise, against the slope of which nestle Latricierès-Chambertin,
Chambertin, Chambertin-Clos de Bèze, and Mazi-Chambertin. The
site of Ruchottes-Chambertin is atop Mazi-Chambertin. The topsoil
is sparse; the subsoil extremely pebbly.

The vineyard is divided into Ruchottes du Bas (lower) and
Ruchottes du Dessus (upper), separated by a track not much wider
than the tractors that traverse it. The upper portion is thought to
be better exposed and contains within it the Clos de Ruchottes-
Chambertin, which is a *monopole* of Domaine Armand Rousseau.
Inexplicably, this 2.5-acre (approximately) parcel was not listed in
the *cadastre* records, even though it was purchased by Domaine Rousseau from the *négociant* Thomas-Bassot in 1977.

Ruchottes-Chambertin is the most austere of the *grands crus*, its structure and character no doubt informed by the meager soil in which the vines are rooted. The yields also tend to be lower as a result. A good Ruchottes is a wine of minerally, as opposed to earthy, *goût de terroir*; slightly higher acidity than in the other *grands crus*; and a piercing flavor that is as much an expression of the soil as the grape. Its opposite would be the easygoing, grapey Charmes-Chambertin. The role of soil and exposure is best seen by comparing Ruchottes-Chambertin with its neighbor Mazi-Chambertin lower on the slope, with its richer, clayey soil and choicer exposure. Ruchottes-Chambertin is always leaner and less stuffed with fruit. The bottlings of Domaine Armand Rousseau tell this tale best, as Rousseau has prime plots in both vineyards and the vinification is identical.

THE VINEYARD

Ruchottes-Chambertin has 3.3037 ha/8.2 acres divided into two *climats*: Ruchottes du Bas (1.3114 ha/3.24 acres) and Ruchottes du Dessus (1.9923 ha/4.92 acres).

Ruchottes du Dessus

	Hectares	Acres	Cases*
M. Michel Bonnefond and Mlle. Odile Bonnefond	0.4271	1.1	208
M. et Mme. Jean-Claude Bourtourault	0.0976	0.2	48
M. et Mme. Henri Magnein	0.0811	0.2	40
M. Jean Rousseau	0.1300	0.3	63
M. François Trapet	0.2088	0.5	102

Ruchottes du Bas

M. et Mme. Hubert Grillot	0.0770	0.2	38
M. et Mme. Henri Magnien	0.0820	0.2	40
M. et Mme. Georges Mugneret	0.6397	1.6	312

---

*Cases calculated on the *rendement de base* of 37 hl/ha plus 20 percent

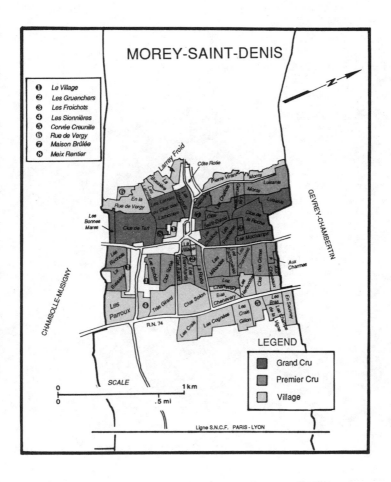

MOREY-SAINT-DENIS

Legend:
1. Le Village
2. Les Gruenchers
3. Les Froichots
4. Les Sionnières
5. Corvée Creunille
6. Rue de Vergy
7. Maison Brûlée
8. Meix Rentier

GEVREY-CHAMBERTIN

CHAMBOLLE-MUSIGNY

Larrey Froid

Côte Rotie

Pierre Virant

Monts

Luisante

Monts

Luisante

En la Rue de Vergy

Les Larrets ou Clos des Lambrays

La Riotte

La Bussière

Clos Saint-Denis

Clos de la Roche

Les Bonnes Mares

Clos de Tart

Les Verroilles

Les Mochamps

Les Ruchots

Les Sorbé

Clos Sorbé

Aux Charmes

Les Mazelières

Les Charrières

Aux Charmes

Les Chenevery

Clos Baulet

Les Parroux

Très Girard

Clos Solon

Bas Chenevery

Les Gaudichots

Les Bras de la Vigne

Les Cognées

Les Crais Gillon

En Seuvrey

R.N. 74

Les Crais

LEGEND

- Grand Cru
- Premier Cru
- Village

SCALE

0 ___ 1 km

0 ___ .5 mi

Ligne S.N.C.F. PARIS - LYON

Morey-Saint-Denis

We then made a survey of that delightful little commune of Morey St. Denis, the birthplace of many a beautiful wine, with the celebrated Clos de Tart, and Bonnes Mares in the vicinity. The district is all agog with fine vineyards.

—CHARLES WALTER BERRY, *In Search of Wine* (1935)

The old London wine merchant Charles Walter Berry got it right: Morey-Saint-Denis is indeed agog with fine vineyards. Its five *grands crus* (just barely, considering that one, Bonnes Mares, has only a 3.75-acre toehold in Morey-Saint-Denis) are just the beginning. More revealing is this: More than half of its total acreage is either *premier* or *grand cru*—57 percent, to be precise. That's more than in Vosne-Romanée.

The overall standard in Morey-Saint-Denis is rivaled only by Volnay. If you don't know anything about the producer or the vintage or even Burgundy itself, Morey-Saint-Denis is one of the safest blind bets you can place. It has an unusually high-minded cadre of growers. It's a stronghold of red Burgundy (and a very little white) as it should be made.

You would think that Morey-Saint-Denis would be a name as

familiar as Vosne-Romanée or Volnay, but apparently not. Partly this is due to its stepchild existence prior to domaine bottling. Before World War II, really before the 1960s, much of the wine of Morey-Saint-Denis was siphoned by *négociants* and sold either as Gevrey-Chambertin or Chambolle-Musigny, depending upon the style of the wine. Therein lies a hint as to the identity problem of this appellation: Its wines are not homogenous.

The usual descriptions have the northern end of Morey-Saint-Denis creating harder, more sinewy wines that are akin to Gevrey-Chambertin. The epitome of this is the *grand cru* Clos de la Roche, which bulges with muscular fruit and is counted among the longest-lived wines in Burgundy.

In fact, it's not so much the northern end that creates this style of wine. Rather, it's the upper slope throughout the length of the commune. Nearly all of the vineyards located between the 280-meter mark and 300 meters—which is high up on the slope—create rich, intense, sinewy wines: Clos de la Roche; Clos Saint-Denis; Clos des Lambrays; Clos de Tart; and Bonnes Mares. All of these are *grands crus*. The vineyards farther down the slope—lying between 260 meters and 275 meters—create softer wines, closer in style to those associated with Chambolle-Musigny. This narrow swath—just three football fields wide—encompasses all but three of the twenty *premiers crus* in Morey-Saint-Denis.

The *premiers crus* offer a suppleness and delicacy that make them some of the most elegant wines in Burgundy, rivaled only by neighboring Chambolle-Musigny and Volnay. The Côte de Nuits backbone shows itself in the age-worthiness of these wines. Although rarely "chewy" or weighty, they tend to be so well balanced and characterful that they age far longer than one might suspect. A good Morey-Saint-Denis *premier cru* from a good vintage is at its fullest expression only after ten years.

THE GRANDS CRUS

CLOS DE LA ROCHE—16.9027 ha/41.8 acres divided among eight *climats*: Les Genavrières (2.2 acres); Monts Luisants (9.2 acres); Clos de la Roche (11.3 acres); Les Mochamps (6.3 acres); Les Froichots (1.6 acres); Les Fremières (5.6 acres); Les Chabiots (5.3 acres); Les Chaffots (0.17 acre)

Clos de la Roche vies with Bonnes Mares as being one of the

longest-lived wines in Burgundy. A really good example will be very deep in color, almost black, with a dense, almost impenetrable quality when young. Only after several years in the bottle will it open up. Then it will require ten or more years to fully unfurl. The greatest examples can go thirty years or more, outdistancing all but the finest Chambertins. The quality can be stellar, yet Clos de la Roche remains relatively unheralded compared to other *grands crus*, notably those of Gevrey-Chambertin, most of which are lesser wines than a good Clos de la Roche.

Clos de la Roche

	Hectares	Acres	Cases*
SC d'Exploitation du Domaine Dujac	0.5903	1.5	273
GFA Domaine Georges Lignier Père et Fils	0.0601	0.2	28
GFA du Domaine Ponsot	1.8403	4.6	850
M. Gérard Raphet	0.3809	1.0	176
Mlle. Anne Remy	0.1430	0.4	66
M. Marie-François Remy			
Mme. Veuve Marie Remy	0.4990	1.2	231
M. et Mme. Michel Remy	0.1411	0.4	65
M. Marie-Philippe Remy	0.1774	0.4	82
M. Jean Rousseau	0.3845	1.0	178
M. et Mme. Jacky Truchot	0.3727	0.9	172

Les Mochamps

	Hectares	Acres	Cases*
M. Pierre Amiot	0.4286	1.1	198
GFA Domaine Arlaud Père et Fils	0.4390	1.1	203
M. Louis Coquard	0.4138	1.0	191
M. Raymond Coquard			
M. Georges Lignier	0.0055	0.01	3
GFA Domaine Georges Lignier Père et Fils	0.4492	1.1	208
M. Marie-François Remy			
Mme. Veuve Marie Remy	0.1660	0.4	77
M. Marie-Philippe Remy	0.2011	0.5	93
M. et Mme. Gilbert Vadey	0.4640	1.2	214

Les Froichots

	Hectares	Acres	Cases*
Mme. Paul Amiot			
Mme. Veuve Jean Bertrand	0.2206	0.5	102
Mme. Veuve Jean Bertrand	0.2207	0.6	102
Mme. Jeannine Bertrand			

*Cases calculated on the *rendement de base* of 35 hl/ha plus 20 percent

	Hectares	Acres	Cases*
M. Maurice Ducherpozat	0.0555	0.1	26
SC d'Exploitation du Domaine Dujac	0.1455	0.4	67

Les Fremières

M. Jean-Louis Amiot	0.1136	0.3	52
M. Philippe Batacchi	0.1999	0.5	92
M. Maurice Ducherpozat	0.1172	0.3	54
SC d'Exploitation du Domaine Dujac	0.1251	0.3	58
M. et Mme. Marcel Jeanniard	0.1808	0.5	84
GFA Domaine Georges Lignier Père et Fils	0.1863	0.5	86
M. et Mme. Bernard Magnien	0.0446	0.1	21
M. Alfred Rang	1.0997	2.7	508
M. Jean-Francois Rang			
M. et Mme. Jacky Truchot	0.0968	0.2	45
M. et Mme. Gilbert Vadey	0.1200	0.3	55

Les Chabiots

M. Pierre Amiot	0.2448	0.6	113
M. Robert Bordet	0.1663	0.4	77
Mme. Jean Chatelet	0.1689	0.4	78
M. Louis Coquard	0.4551	1.1	210
M. Raymond Coquard			
M. Raymond Coquard	0.2995	0.7	138
SC d'Exploitation du Domaine Dujac	0.4281	1.1	198
GFA Domaine Georges Lignier Père et Fils	0.2322	0.6	107
M. Claude Marchand	0.0675	0.2	31

Genavrières

GFA Domaine Georges Lignier Père et Fils	0.0435	0.1	23
SCI du Domaine des Monts Luisants	0.0354	0.1	19
M. et Mme. Roger Peirazeau	0.8028	2.0	371

Monts Luisants

M. et Mme. Pierre Albert	0.1626	0.4	75
M. Pierre Amiot	0.2518	0.6	116
SC d'Exploitation du Domaine Dujac	0.4703	1.2	217
M. Robert Gibourg	0.0656	0.2	30
M. Henri Jeanne	0.1738	0.4	80

---

*Cases calculated on the *rendement de base* of 35 hl/ha plus 20 percent

	Hectares	Acres	Cases*
M. Fernand Lecheneaut	0.0828	0.2	38
M. et Mme. Hubert Lignier	0.4821	1.2	223
M. Jacques Lignier	0.1370	0.3	63
M. et Mme. Maurice Lignier	0.1905	0.5	88
SCI du Domaine des Monts Luisants	0.0305	0.1	14
M. et Mme. Bernard Magnien	0.0050	0.01	2
M. et Mme. Michel Magnien	0.1493	0.4	69
GFA du Domaine Ponsot	0.9034	2.2	417
Mme. Jean Porcherot	0.1172	0.3	54
M. Marie-Philippe Remy	0.2865	0.7	132

CLOS SAINT-DENIS—6.6260 ha/16.37 acres divided among four *climats*: Clos Saint-Denis (5.3 acres); Calouère (3.2 acres); Les Chaffots (3.3 acres) and Maison Brûlée (4.5 acres)

The namesake vineyard of the town (it appended "Saint-Denis" to "Morey" in 1927) ironically is the least of the *grands crus*, which is only feinting with damn (good) praise. Clos Saint-Denis has the most finesse and delicacy of the *grands crus*, which says something about the values and tastes of the Moreyins circa 1927. It is too easy to dismiss Clos Saint-Denis as something lesser compared to, say, Clos de la Roche or Clos des Lambrays. But to do so is to miss an unusually refined wine. Good Clos Saint-Denis is a rare confluence of force and subtlety. It's not extravagantly perfumy like Romanée-Saint Vivant, or even richly fruity. But the more you savor a mature example, the more insinuating it becomes. It grows on you.

Clos Saint-Denis

	Hectares	Acres	Cases*
M. et Mme. Paul Amiot	0.1696	0.4	78
M. Pierre Amiot	0.1072	0.3	50
GFA Domaine Arlaud Père et Fils	0.1264	0.3	58
M. Philippe Charlopin	0.1696	0.4	78
GFA Domaine des Chezeaux	0.2693	0.7	124
M. Louis Coquard	0.1190	0.3	55
M. Raymond Coquard			
SC d'Exploitation du Domaine Dujac	0.2727	0.7	126
M. et Mme. Henri Jouan	0.1271	0.3	59
GFA Domaine Georges Lignier Père et Fils	0.1449	0.4	67

*Cases calculated on the *rendement de base* of 35 hl/ha plus 20 percent

	Hectares	Acres	Cases*
M. Antoine Magnien	0.2916	0.7	135
M. et Mme. Gilbert Vadey	0.3515	0.9	162

Calouère

SC d'Exploitation du Domaine Dujac	1.0062	2.5	465
M. et Mme. Stanislas Heresztyn	0.2323	0.6	107
M. et Mme. Gérard Peirazeau	0.0700	0.2	32

Maison Brûlée

Domaine Bertagna	0.5310	1.3	245
M. et Mme. Henri Jouan	0.2335	0.6	108
M. Georges Lignier	0.0738	0.2	34
GFA Domaine Georges Lignier Père et Fils	0.6405	1.6	296
M. et Mme. Roger Seguin	0.0493	0.1	23

CLOS DES LAMBRAYS—8.8394 ha/21.8 acres divided among three *climats*: Meix Rentier (2.8 acres); Clos des Lambrays or Les Larrets (14.1 acres), and Les Bouchots (4.9 acres)

Clos des Lambrays is the comeback story of Burgundy. Passed over for *grand cru* status in the 1930s (even though it was long recognized as a great vineyard), Clos des Lambrays never emerged as the contender it should have been. (The old label read "Grand Cru Classé," even though it technically wasn't.) Nearly all of the vineyard was owned by the Cosson family, which allowed the vineyard to decline over the decades and the wines to remain in barrel far longer than was advisable. It finally was purchased by the Saier brothers of Mercurey, along with a third investor (Roland de Chambure), in 1979 after the death of Madame Cosson, reportedly for 10 million French francs. What they found was a debilitated vineyard with seventy-five-year-old vines in weakened condition and a winery badly in need of complete overhaul. They replanted the vineyard as carefully as possible and rejuvenated the winemaking facilities. They also petitioned for an upgrade from *premier cru* to *grand cru*. This was granted in 1981, the first since the creation of Appellation Contrôlée in Burgundy. (It looks as if La Grande Rue in Vosne-Romanée will be the second; the application still is pending—but expected to be approved—at this writing.)

---

*Cases calculated on the *rendement de base* of 35 hl/ha plus 20 percent

In the past, the wine of Clos des Lambrays was dull and merely meaty. The new owners have struggled to return the wine to its proper regard. They have made recognition more difficult for themselves in creating an old-fashioned wine—in the best sense of that term. The problem is that such wine, which is tannic and closed when young, does not lend itself to the huzzahs of the barrel tasters who seek to divine the quality of a wine when it is just months old.

A good example can be found with the 1985 vintage, which can be said to be the first truly great Clos des Lambrays of the new regime. The early reports were lukewarm. It wasn't panned, but it failed to excite. Upon release, it was clearly dense, implacably tannic, and downright inscrutable. Yet five years later, a tasting of the '85 Clos des Lambrays allowed one to discover an extraordinary wine, suffused with an intense *goût de terroir* allied with massive yet graceful fruit. It was only just beginning to open up, and needs another decade. It was also seemingly as fresh as it was upon release. It will likely be one of the great sleepers of the 1985 vintage, the sort of Burgundy that everyone says he wants, with the concentration and longevity one finds in the best vintages of the 1950s.

Les Larrets or Clos des Lambrays

	Hectares	Acres	Cases*
Domaine des Lambrays	5.7187	14.1	2642

Meix Rentier

Domaine des Lambrays	0.9521	2.4	440
SC d'Exploitation Merme-Morizot	0.0430	0.1	20

Les Bouchots

Domaine des Lambrays	1.9910	4.9	920

CLOS DE TART—7.5328 ha/18.6 acres divided between two vineyards: Clos de Tart (17.9 acres) and a slice of Bonnes Mares (0.7 acre)

A *monopole* of the *négociant* Mommessin, Clos de Tart has had varying success over the years. At its best, it shares the richness and longevity of Clos de la Roche and Clos des Lambrays. But too often

---

*Cases calculated on the *rendement de base* of 35 hl/ha plus 20 percent

it has come off as coarse and a bit rustic, although the 1985 vintage certainly was all one could ask.

Clos de Tart has one of the most impressive pedigrees of any vineyard in Burgundy. The vineyard has not changed in size since 1250, when it was assembled by the Cistercian nuns of Notre Dame de Tart of Genlis, a small town between Dijon and Dole. They retained the vineyard until dispossessed of it by the Revolution of 1789. It was sold in one piece and, unusually, has remained a *monopole* ever since, right up to the Mommessin family purchase in 1932. It now is their *monopole*.

The seller was Mme. Guillemette Marey-Monge de Blic, who had purchased Clos de Tart from her sister, who had herself inherited it from their father. The Marey-Monge family is most famous for having owned since the Revolution a large portion of the *grand cru* Romanée Saint-Vivant in Vosne-Romanée, which was sold in 1989 to the Domaine de la Romanée-Conti for between $9 million and $10 million.

The Clos de Tart vineyard has been carefully replanted over the years, with half of it planted to vines averaging sixty years old. Oddly, the vines are planted horizontally along the slope, rather than the usual vertical or diagonal pattern.

Given such an extraordinary history, it is sad that the wine of Clos de Tart is so variable. It should be among the finest and most reliable *grands crus* of Burgundy and yet it cannot be considered so, although it always is a satisfying wine. In some vintages, it can be inspirational. Clos de Tart is always worth investigating, especially in the best vintages.

Clos de Tart

	Hectares	Acres	Cases*
Mommessin	7.2548	17.9	3352

BONNES MARES—The 3.74-acre portion of Bonnes Mares that sits on the Morey-Saint-Denis side is said to contain more limestone in the subsoil than is found in the rest of the vineyard. The wine from the Morey-Saint-Denis side is said to be harder and firmer even than the usual Bonnes Mares. Part of it (0.7 acre) is owned by

*Cases calculated on the *rendement de base* of 35 hl/ha plus 20 percent

Mommessin and is legally part of Clos de Tart, even though it does have the right to sell the wine as Bonnes Mares instead. It never has.

Bonnes Mares (Morey-Saint-Denis side)

	Hectares	Acres	Cases*
M. Bernard Clair (now Louis Jadot)	0.3363	0.8	155
M. Bernard Clair and Mme. Veuve Joseph Clair (now Louis Jadot)	1.1792	2.9	545
Mommessin	0.2780	0.7	128

THE PREMIERS CRUS

Clos Baulet—0.8703 ha/2.2 acres

M. et Mme. Jean-Marie Chassel	0.1235	0.3	65
M. Henri Cosson	0.3287	0.8	174
Mlle. Marthe Liebaut	0.2807	0.7	148
M. et Mme. Bernard Magnien	0.0780	0.2	41
M. Bernard Raphet	0.0594	0.2	31

Les Blanchards—1.9923 ha/4.9 acres

M. et Mme. Guy Coquard	0.2743	0.7	145
M. Henri Cosson	0.2758	0.7	146
M. et Mme. Marcel Jeanniard	0.4877	1.2	258
Mlle. Marthe Liebaut	0.0210	0.1	11
M. et Mme. Bernard Magnien	0.0239	0.1	13
M. et Mme. Michel Magnien	0.0475	0.1	25
M. Bernard Raphet	0.0342	0.1	18
M. Albert Seguin	0.0835	0.2	44
Mme. Veuve Elios Sorakatyj	0.1457	0.4	77
M. et Mme. Jacky Truchot	0.2926	0.7	154

La Bussière—2.5925 ha/6.4 acres

M. Jean-Marie Roumier	2.5425	6.3	1342

Les Chaffots—2.6186 ha/6.5 acres

GFA Domaine Georges Lignier Père et Fils	0.0728	0.2	38

---

*Cases calculated on the *rendement de base* of 35 hl/ha plus 20 percent for Bonnes Mares; 40 hl/ha plus 20 percent for the *premiers crus*

	Hectares	Acres	Cases*
M. et Mme. Bernard Magnien	0.0550	0.1	29
M. et Mme. Roger Seguin	0.0617	0.2	33
M. Pierre Amiot	0.0972	0.2	51
GFA Domaine Arlaud Père et Fils	0.0504	0.1	27
M. Jean Aucour	0.0358	0.1	19
M. Charles Beuchotte			
GFA Domaine des Chezeaux	0.1083	0.3	57
M. Louis Coquard	0.0492	0.1	26
M. Raymond Coquard			
SC d'Exploitation du Domaine Dujac	0.1950	0.5	103
M. et Mme. Marcel Jeanniard	0.1235	0.3	65
M. et Mme. Michel Jeanniard	0.1929	0.5	102
M. et Mme. Hubert Lignier	0.4507	1.1	238
GFA Domaine Georges Lignier Père et Fils	0.6692	1.7	353
M. Antoine Magnien	0.0264	0.1	14
M. et Mme. Bernard Magnien	0.1808	0.5	95
M. et Mme. Michel Magnien	0.5144	1.3	272
M. et Mme. Gérard Peirazeau	0.4135	1.0	218
Mme. Michel Rousseau	0.2366	0.6	125
Mme. Veuve Maurice Seguin	0.1535	0.4	81
M. et Mme. Roger Seguin	0.2887	0.7	152

Aux Charmes—1.1731 ha/2.9 acres

	Hectares	Acres	Cases*
M. Pierre Amiot	0.4672	1.2	247
M. et Mme. Maurice Lignier	0.2476	0.6	131
M. et Mme. Bernard Magnien	0.1410	0.4	74
M. et Mme. Robert Mazoyer	0.1500	0.4	79
M. Jean Raphet			
M. Louis Raphet	0.3342	0.8	176
M. et Mme. Germain Tardy	0.0913	0.2	48
Mme. Veuve Félix Tortochaut	0.1526	0.4	81
M. Gabriel Tortochaut	0.0734	0.2	39

Les Charrières—2.2676 ha/5.6 acres

	Hectares	Acres	Cases*
M. Philippe Batacchi	0.1292	0.3	68
Mme. Marius Ecard	0.2250	0.6	119
M. et Mme. Victor Gibourg	0.1084	0.3	57
M. Maurice Jeanniard			
M. Paul Jeanniard	0.2161	0.5	114
M. Jean-Pierre Jouan	0.0483	0.1	26
M. Fernand Lecheneaut	0.1420	0.4	75

*Cases calculated on the *rendement de base* of 40 hl/ha plus 20 percent

	Hectares	*Acres*	*Cases**
GFA Domaine Georges Lignier Père			
et Fils	0.3735	0.9	197
Mme. Jean Procherot	0.1699	0.4	90
M. et Mme. Roger Seguin	0.1095	0.3	58
M. et Mme. Maurice Sigaut	0.6154	1.5	325
M. et Mme. Germain Tardy	0.1303	0.3	69

Les Chéneverey—1.9009 ha/4.7 acres

M. Pierre Amiot	0.2784	0.7	147
M. et Mme. Edouard Bryczek	0.2254	0.6	119
M. et Mme. Wojcieck Bryczek	0.2460	0.6	130
M. et Mme. Michel Jeanniard	0.2870	0.7	152
Mlle. Odile Jeanniard			
M. Paul Jeanniard	0.0856	0.2	45
M. et Mme. Hubert Lignier	0.3570	0.9	188
M. et Mme. Maurice Lignier	0.4710	1.2	249
M. et Mme. Edmond Porcherot	0.2180	0.5	115
Mme. Jean Porcherot	0.2167	0.5	114

Aux Cheseaux—1.4947 ha/3.7 acres

M. Hervé Arlaud	0.7137	1.8	377
M. et Mme. Wojcieck Bryczek	0.0183	0.1	10
M. et Mme. André Coquard	0.0230	0.1	12
M. Armand Noirot	0.0538	0.1	28
M. Marie-François Remy			
Mme. Veuve Marie Remy	0.1363	0.3	72
M. et Mme. Germain Tardy	0.3061	0.8	162
M. et Mme. Jean Tardy	0.0505	0.1	27
M. et Mme. Jacky Truchot	0.0678	0.2	36
M. et Mme. Gilbert Vadey	0.1416	0.4	75

Côte Rôtie—1.2298 ha/3 acres

Les Faconnières—1.6651 ha/4.1 acres

M. et Mme. Jean-Marie Chassel	0.1725	0.4	91
M. et Mme. Roger Galla	0.2110	0.5	111
M. Jacques Lignier	0.3301	0.8	174
GFA Domaine Georges Lignier Père			
et Fils	0.1767	0.4	93
M. Antoine Magnien	0.2028	0.5	107
M. Jean-Paul Magnien			
M. Claude Marchand	0.0110	0.0	6

*Cases calculated on the *rendement de base* of 40 hl/ha plus 20 percent

	Hectares	Acres	Cases*
Mme. Jean Porcherot	0.3430	0.9	181
M. et Mme. Henri Schneider	0.1942	0.5	103

Les Genavrières—1.1910 ha/2.9 acres

	Hectares	Acres	Cases*
SCI du Domaine Des Monts Luisants	0.3296	0.8	174
M. Claude Marchand	0.0794	0.2	42
M. et Mme. Roger Peirazeau	0.6789	1.7	358

Les Gruenchers—0.5082 ha/1.25 acres

	Hectares	Acres	Cases*
M. et Mme. Jean-Marie Chassel	0.2517	0.6	133
GFA Domaine Georges Lignier Père et Fils	0.2565	0.6	135

Les Millandes—4.2123 ha/10.4 acres

	Hectares	Acres	Cases*
M. et Mme. Pierre Albert	0.0258	0.1	14
M. Jean-Louis Amiot	0.4228	1.0	223
Domaine Jean André	0.3397	0.8	179
M. Hervé Arlaud	0.0390	0.1	21
GFA Domaine Arlaud Père et Fils	0.3759	0.9	198
M. Jean Balland	0.0400	0.1	21
Mme. Georges Barbanchon			
M. Georges Barbanchon	0.1109	0.3	59
Mme. Veuve Roger Baron	0.1047	0.3	55
M. Philippe Batacchi	0.1210	0.3	64
M. Étienne Beaumont	0.1630	0.4	86
Mme. Jeannine Bertrand			
Mme. Veuve Jean Bertrand	0.1042	0.3	55
Mme. Paul Amiot			
Mme. Veuve Jean Bertrand	0.4578	1.1	242
M. et Mme. André Coquard	0.0384	0.1	20
SC d'Exploitation du Domaine Dujac			
Mme. Robert Girard	0.0758	0.2	40
GFA Domaine Georges Lignier Père et Fils	0.2150	0.5	114
M. et Mme. Bernard Magnien	0.1259	0.3	66
M. et Mme. Michel Magnien	0.2253	0.6	119
M. Claude Marchand	0.1160	0.3	61
M. Armand Noirot			
Mme. Veuve Clement Noirot	0.1276	0.3	67
Mme. Veuve Edmond Porcherot	0.1639	0.4	87
M. Jean Porcherot			

---

*Cases calculated on the *rendement de base* of 40 hl/ha plus 20 percent

	Hectares	Acres	Cases*
M. et Mme. Maurice Sigaut	0.3370	0.8	178
M. Paul Valby	0.2862	0.7	151

Monts Luisants—5.3889 ha/13.3 acres

Mme. Veuve Roger Berthier			
M. Roger Berthier	0.0525	0.1	28
Mme. Louis Charles	0.0582	0.1	31
Mme. et M. Michel Jeanniard	0.4756	1.2	251
M. Fernand Lecheneaut	0.0245	0.1	13
SCI du Domaine des Monts Luisants	1.9717	4.9	1041
M. et Mme. Bernard Magnien	0.0854	0.2	45
M. et Mme. Jean-Paul Magnien	0.1357	0.3	72
GFA du Domaine Ponsot	1.9616	4.9	1036
M. Jean-Marie Ponsot	0.0287	0.1	15
M. et Mme. Bernard Simon	0.5406	1.3	285
M. et Mme. Paul Tartarin	0.0198	0.1	10

Clos des Ormes—3.1522 ha/7.8 acres

Mme. Jean Chatelet	0.0830	0.2	44
M. et Mme. Justin Folletet	0.0483	0.1	26
M. et Mme. Roger Galla	0.1724	0.4	91
M. et Mme. André Gueneret	0.2477	0.6	131
M. et Mme. Marcel Jeanniard	0.3760	0.9	199
GFA Domaine Georges Lignier Père et Fils	1.5655	3.9	827
M. Paul Magnien	0.1569	0.4	83
M. Marie-François Remy			
Mme. Veuve Marie Remy	0.0460	0.1	24
M. Félix Tortochaut	0.0504	0.1	27
M. et Mme. Jacky Truchot	0.0864	0.2	46
M. Paul Valby	0.3196	0.8	169

La Riotte—2.4659 ha/6.1 acres

Mme. Veuve Jean Bertrand	0.0828	0.2	44
M. et Mme. Marcel Jeanniard	0.2260	0.6	119
M. Michel Jovan	0.1879	0.5	99
SCI Drouhin-Laroze	0.1496	0.4	79
M. et Mme. Henri Perrot Minot	0.5781	1.4	305
M. Armand Noirot	0.1175	0.3	62
Mme. Amiot Paul			
Commune de Morey-St.-Denis	0.3779	0.9	200

---

*Cases calculated on the *rendement de base* of 40 hl/ha plus 20 percent

	Hectares	Acres	Cases*
Mme. Jean Claude Taupenot	0.5684	1.4	300
M. Paul Valby	0.1777	0.4	94

Les Ruchots—2.5774 ha/6.4 acres

GFA Domaine Arlaud Père et Fils	0.5945	1.5	314
M. Georges Barbanchon	0.0770	0.2	41
Mme. Georges Barbanchon			
SC d'Exploitation du Domaine Dujac	0.2743	0.7	145
M. Michel Jouan	0.2234	0.6	118
M. et Mme. Bernard Magnien	0.2830	0.7	149
M. Paul Magnien	0.1084	0.3	57
M. Armand Noirot			
M. Armand Noirot	0.2977	0.7	157
Mme. Veuve Clement Noirot	0.2320	0.6	122
Mme. Veuve Kléber Olivier	0.1109	0.3	59
M. et Mme. Edmond Porcherot	0.2459	0.6	130
M. et Mme. Jacky Truchot	0.1303	0.3	69

Clos Sorbè—3.3263 ha/8.2 acres

Mme. Paul Amiot			
Mme. Veuve Jean Bertrand	0.1383	0.3	73
M. et Mme. Wojcieck Bryczek	0.0964	0.2	51
M. Henri Cosson	0.7704	1.9	407
SC d'Exploitation du Domaine Dujac	0.0793	0.2	42
M. et Mme. Henri Jouan	0.3159	0.8	167
Mme. Henri Legros	0.1694	0.4	89
GFA Domaine Bernard Serveau et Fils	0.0198	0.1	10
M. Germain Tardy			
M. Joseph Tardy	0.2992	0.7	158
M. et Mme. Jacky Truchot	1.1740	2.9	620
M. Paul Valby	0.1823	0.5	96

Les Sorbès—2.6758 ha/6.6 acres

M. Albert Jouan	0.1879	0.5	99
GFA Domaine Georges Lignier Père et Fils	0.2231	0.6	118
M. et Mme. Henri Mauffre	0.2090	0.5	111
GFA Domaine Bernard Serveau et Fils	1.6360	4.0	864

Le Village—0.9036 ha/2.2 acres

---

*Cases calculated on the *rendement de base* of 40 hl/ha plus 20 percent

PRODUCERS WORTH SEEKING OUT

DOMAINE PIERRE AMIOT—Fine Clos de la Roche in the grapey style, but nevertheless with good detail and longevity. Not in the same league, though, as those from Rousseau or Dujac. Also similarly grapey, but lighter, *premiers crus* from Charmes and Ruchottes.

DOMAINE DUJAC—Likely the most famous producer in Morey-Saint-Denis, owner Jacques Seysses is as atypical a Burgundian grower as can be imagined. He was born in Paris, educated in England and the United States, married to an American, a banker by training, and is heir to a fortune from his father's cookie company (Belin) which was sold to Nabisco. Despite, or perhaps because, of all this, Seysses was drawn to Burgundy. He methodically purchased portions of vineyards in Morey-Saint-Denis, Gevrey-Chambertin, and Vosne-Romanée in the late sixties and early seventies. He also went to the enology school in Beaune, earning a degree in enology. Seysses is the winemaker. His hands get dirty. He is a true Burgundian in everything but family tree. Hence the name: Domaine du Jac(ques).

Still, he had different ideas about what he wanted his wines to be: unfiltered, unfined, and unchaptalized if possible. In the late 1960s, these were radical ideas. Seysses persisted, winning not only a coterie of admirers among foreign buyers, but also among the younger generation of Burgundian winegrowers, sons who were poised to take over their father's estates. They admired Seysses for his ideals and intellectual rigor, and still do.

The Seysses wines, however, are not as unmanipulated as the ideology would lead one to expect. All of the Dujac wines, regardless of origin, share a dramatically silky texture. It is a winemaking style that, however admirable, leaves a surprisingly strong signature. In a blind tasting, you can spot the Dujac wine in a lineup of other wines from the same vineyard or appellation. They often are oaky and heavily vanilla-scented when young. On the other hand, they are lovely wines that, signature aside, do display their respective *terroirs*. You can do a great deal worse that to choose a Dujac wine. Apart from the signature, Dujac represents a shining standard.

The finest Dujac wine is the Clos de la Roche, perhaps because the sheer power of this vineyard overrides the Dujac style more than any other except the Bonnes Mares. The Bonnes Mares is almost as fine, although I usually give the Clos de la Roche the edge in most tastings. Not to be ignored is Dujac's sterling Clos Saint-Denis, which responds to the silken Dujac touch, displaying the intrinsic finesse of this vineyard. There's also a superb Echézeaux, as well as lovely, delicate, perfumey Morey-Saint-Denis *premier cru* and first-rate commune-level Morey-Saint-Denis.

Seysses also offers some white wine from Meursault, made from purchased juice. It is sold under the name of Druid. The wines are good, if a little oaky.

DOMAINE GEORGES LIGNIER—One of the major producers of Morey-Saint-Denis with holdings in Clos de la Roche, Clos Saint-Denis, and Bonnes Mares, as well as the *premier cru* Clos des Ormes. The Lignier style is intensely grapey, too much so for this taster. Nevertheless, the concentration is there, the standard notable, and the effort to create fine wine very much present. Unlike Dujac, where the *terroirs* still shine through, here the intense grapiness obscures the distinctions of *terroir*. In that sense, the wines lack "taste transparency."

DOMAINE PONSOT/DOMAINE DES CHEZEAUX—As mentioned in the section on Gevrey-Chambertin, this is one of the most problematic producers in Burgundy. Sometimes, such as 1985, the wines are delightful: bursting at the seams with pure, opulent fruit. Other times, such as 1982 or 1986, the wines are flimsy, oxidized, and frankly shabby. Of course, the prices are always high.

Ponsot emphasizes a lustrous, tender fruitiness. In the great years, there can be superb concentration. One will have to look hard to find a richer Clos de la Roche than Ponsot's 1985 Vieilles Vignes or the Clos Saint-Denis from '85. The style seems to show best when young, although the jury still is out on the opulent '85s. Generally, I approach Ponsot wines with caution, but I still look for them all the same.

Ponsot also produces a rare white Morey-Saint-Denis from vineyards in Monts Luisants. The wine is not 100 percent Chardonnay, but a blend of Chardonnay, Pinot Noir Blanc (the mutant white Pinot Noir clone first isolated by Henri Gouges in Nuits-Saint-Georges), and some Aligoté from eighty-year old vines. It is a wine of surprising character, with a fierce, stony *goût de terroir*.

DOMAINE GEORGES ROUMIER—Roumier's one Morey-Saint-Denis wine is a *monopole*, a 6.4-acre *premier cru* called Clos de la Bussière. It is among the most reliable wines from the commune, not a heavy-weight, but pure, refined, and detailed. It usually seems to be at its best after five or six years.

DOMAINE BERNARD SERVEAU—For me, this is the supreme pro-ducer in Morey-Saint-Denis and one of the finest in Burgundy. The father, Bernard, is in poor health, but his sons apparently have no quarrel with their father's standards or winemaking approach. Ser-veau wines have no signature. This can be disturbing when tasting from the barrel, because they display surprisingly little at that stage. There's no apparent oak; there's no flamboyant, grapey concentra-tion. The wines are Cistercian-austere. Those who don't live with Serveau wines could be forgiven for assuming that they don't age or develop. Nothing could be further from the truth. Only now, seven years after the vintage, are the 1982s beginning to show them-selves in full glory. The 1985s need at least ten years from the vintage. Even Serveau's Bourgogne Rouge '85 has yet to open up five years after the vintage.

Serveau's signature wine in Morey-Saint-Denis is a superb *pre-mier cru* Les Sorbès (which Serveau labels Les Sorbets), seemingly light but as focused as a laser beam. Serveau also issues stunning Chambolle-Musigny (q.v.) and a Nuits-Saint-Georges from the tiny Chaines Carteaux *premier cru*. Regrettably, there are only about twelve hundred cases total produced by this winery.

DOMAINE ARMAND ROUSSEAU—The Gevrey-Chambertin pro-ducer is the source of some of the most profound, long-lived Clos de la Roche available. Along with Rousseau's Gevrey-Chambertin "Clos Saint-Jacques," this is the Rousseau wine I seek out more than any other. In good vintages, it demands at least a decade of aging. Clos de la Roche bottlings from the 1950s are still thriving.

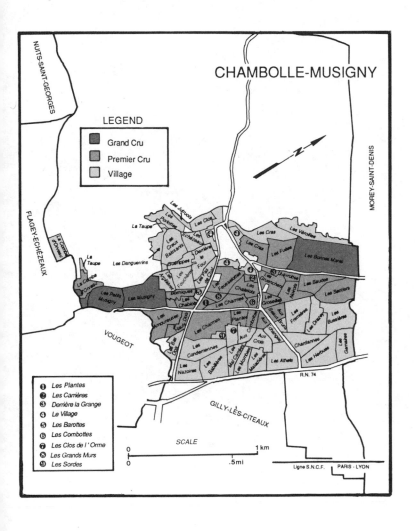

CHAMBOLLE-MUSIGNY

NUITS-SAINT-GEORGES

MOREY-SAINT-DENIS

FLAGEY-ECHÉZEAUX

LEGEND

Grand Cru
Premier Cru
Village

Les Jurools
Les
Porrottes
Les Clos
La Taupe
Les Creux
Les Baudaux
Echézeaux
Derrière
la
Four
La Taupe
Les Danguerrins
La Combe
L'Orveau
Les Petits
Musigny
Les Musigny
Les Argilliaces
Les Foucherts
Les Bornique
Les Chabiots
Les
Amoureuses
Haute Doix
Les Charmes
Les
Plantes
Les Combe
d'Orveau
La Taupe

Les Cras
Les Véroilles
Les Cras
Les Fuées
Les Bonnes Mares
Les Groseilles
Les Charmes
Les Baudes
Les Sentiers
Les Fremières
Les Cloizes
Les Bussières
Les Gruenchers
Aux Beaux Bruns
Chardannes
Les Herbues
Les Gamaires

VOUGEOT

Les Basse Doix
Les Condemennes
Les Nazoires
Les Babières
Mal Carrées
Les Hombres
Les Maladières
Les Athets
Aux Cras
Aux Echanges

R.N. 74

GILLY-LÈS-CITEAUX

1. Les Plantes
2. Les Carrières
3. Derrière la Grange
4. Le Village
5. Les Barottes
6. Les Combottes
7. Les Clos de l'Orme
8. Les Grands Murs
9. Les Sordes

SCALE

0   1 km
0   .5 mi

Ligne S.N.C.F.   PARIS - LYON

Chambolle-
Musigny

For once, the distinction of a Burgundy commune is reasonably easy to pinpoint: Chambolle-Musigny makes wines of grace. Their power derives not from mass but from a coordination of flavor with finesse: a kind of vinous jujitsu. Where Chambertin or Clos de la Roche can leave you in awe simply from their scale, only Bonnes-Mares achieves a similar presence in Chambolle-Musigny. Musigny, the most convincing wine of Burgundy, achieves its stature because of almost Gothic grace, rather than imposing weight.

There should always be some underlying strength, even in commune-level Chambolle-Musigny. It's too easy to confuse lightness with deftness. A good Chambolle-Musigny at whatever level should have backbone; one should be able to readily sense forceful flavor and see both structure and fruit.

Not least, there is—or should be—a distinctive *goût de terroir* to Chambolle-Musigny compared to other Côte de Nuits wines. This comes from an unusually abundant presence—for the Côte de Nuits—of limestone. Where Gevrey-Chambertin is earthy and Vosne-Romanée spicy, a good Chambolle-Musigny has an almost electric *goût de terroir*. This is the more apparent because of the taste transparency of the fruit of Chambolle-Musigny, again courtesy of the limestone-infused soil. Pinot Noirs grown on clayey soils have more weight and body than those grown on limestone soils.

A glance at the grower listings will reveal that the ownerships of the *premiers crus* are extraordinarily subdivided, even by Burgundian standards. As a result, one rarely sees many named-vineyard *premiers crus*. The notable exceptions to this are Les Amoureuses, the finest *premier cru* in the commune, and Les Charmes, the largest *premier cru*. Also, because of this extreme subdivision, Chambolle-Musigny is a commune where *négociants* thrive, performing like a type of winemaking bee, foraging for choice bits of nectar to be collected into a larger quantity back at the hive in Beaune or Nuits-Saint-George.

MUSIGNY

There are 10.7023 ha/26.44 acres divided among three *climats*: La Combe d'Orveau (1.5 acres); Les Petits Musigny (10.4 acres); and Les Musigny (14.6 acres).

The paeans to the qualities of Musigny have been sung over and over again. And why not? It is the ultimate wine of Chambolle-Musigny, and that means a supreme combination of flavor impact with finesse. The *grands crus* of Vosne-Romanée can be more dramatic, hinting even of addiction; Chambertin is undeniably richer. But Musigny has more finesse than all of them, more ethereal perfume of the purest sort, without the opiatic spice qualities of Romanée-Conti or La Tâche.

A tiny amount of white Musigny is produced, all from a three-quarter-acre plot planted to Chardonnay owned by Domaine Comte de Vogüé. The wine is exceptional to be sure, but not as exceptional a white wine as the red Musigny is a red wine. It is rich and forceful, although not as much as Corton-Charlemagne. But the *goût de terroir* is intense, and a note of almonds is found.

It is impossible to discuss Musigny without also discussing the

Domaine Comte de Vogüé. This producer dominates Musigny to a degree unmatched by any other producer in any other commune, even that of the Domaine de la Romanée-Conti in Vosne-Romanée. Although Musigny is not a *monopole* of de Vogüé, it very nearly is, as the estate owns 66.5 percent of it. For a vineyard of this size and acclaim, that is a remarkable dominance, especially considering that, unlike Romanée-Conti or La Tâche, Musigny has never has been under a single ownership.

For many Burgundy drinkers, the de Vogüé bottling *is* Musigny. Certainly, the wines of the 1950s and 1960s were unquestionably the standard against which all other versions were judged —and found wanting. No more. For a variety of reasons, most of them involving family difficulties, the Musigny of de Vogüé has declined. Considering the reputation of this property and the jewel of a vineyard that it possesses, that de Vogüé Musigny is no longer the reference standard is hard to accept. Yet a comparison tasting will show that it regularly is excelled by the Musignys of Leroy, Domaine Georges Roumier, and Louis Jadot, to name but three, with that of Joseph Drouhin very close behind these.

It's not that the de Vogüé Musigny is bad. Far from it. The 1985 vintage was its best vintage in years. Rather, it's uninspiring —for Musigny. It fails to deliver the exhilaration one has a right to expect from Musigny—and that once was obtained from the de Vogüé wine. Now, it lacks concentration and fullness of flavor. It tastes "safe." Musigny should be thrilling. Compare it to the other bottlings, and you will see for yourself. Some observers trace the decline to excessive yields; others look at the domaine's practice of filtering the wine. For this observer, it's all a sad mystery. Yet given the astonishing vineyard asset at its command, the Musigny of de Vogüé could return to form in a near-instant.

La Combe d'Orveau

	Hectares	Acres	Cases*
Domaine Jacques Prieur	0.6128	1.5	283

Les Petits Musigny

M. Georges de Vogüé	4.1935	10.4	1937

---

*Cases calculated on the *rendement de base* of 35 hl/ha plus 20 percent

	Hectares	Acres	Cases*
Les Musigny			
Consortium Viticole et Vinicole de Bourgogne	0.0338	0.1	16
M. Bernard Clair	0.0051	0.002	2
M. Jean Dufouleur	0.0980	0.2	45
Mme. Veuve Maurice Hudelot and Mme. Adrien Porteret	0.3093	0.8	143
M. Robert Jousset-Drouhin	0.6720	1.7	310
Nouvelle Elvina et Leroy Vins et Alcools	0.0800	0.2	37
M. Jacques Mugnier	1.1358	2.8	525
M. Pierre Ponnelle	0.2104	0.5	97
M. Christophe Roumier	0.0996	0.2	46
M. Roger Trinquier	0.1665	0.4	77
M. Georges de Vogüé	2.9273	7.2	1352

BONNES MARES

There are 15.0572 ha/37.2 acres divided between two communes: Chambolle-Musigny (13.5417 ha/33.46 acres) and Morey-Saint-Denis (1.5155 ha/3.74 acres).

In some ways, Bonnes Mares is not a Chambolle-Musigny. It really should be adjacent to Clos de la Roche, which, in turn, should be in Gevrey-Chambertin. All of which is to say that Bonnes Mares is a massive, chewy, tannic wine of formidable proportions and longevity. It, along with Clos de la Roche, would be the wine one would lay down on the birth of a child with every reason to expect something just coming into its prime—like the kid—upon turning twenty-one. Of course, the vintage and producer have to be right, but that's always a prerequisite.

A case could be made that Bonnes Mares is the most overlooked *grand cru* in Burgundy. Partly this is due to being overshadowed by Musigny, the only other *grand cru* in Chambolle-Musigny. Partly it is because it does not immediately offer the same degree of wafting perfuminess of cinnamon and stones provided by Musigny, or the silken refinement. All of that comes, in the particular fashion of

---

*Cases calculated on the *rendement de base* of 35 hl/ha plus 20 percent

Bonnes Mares, with time. A good Bonnes Mares is very nearly undrinkable until ten years have passed, at which point its substantial tannins will have diminished and the latent perfume emerges. At that point, or better yet, after another ten years, Bonnes Mares could well prove to be the most memorable red Burgundy you've had that year—or any other year. But who gets to drink ten- or twenty-year-old Bonnes Mares?

Happily, a number of producers in Bonnes Mares are creating just such a wine, notably Louis Jadot, Joseph Drouhin, Domaine Dujac, Domaine Robert Groffier, and Domaine Georges Roumier.

Bonnes Mares

	Hectares	Acres	Cases*
GFA du Domaine Arlaud Père et Fils	0.2081	0.5	96
Mme. André Bart	0.6690	1.7	309
GFA Bertheau et Fils	0.3444	0.9	159
Mlle. Josiane Charles	0.1113	0.3	51
M. Bernard Clair	0.1258	0.3	58
M. Christian Confuron	0.0636	0.2	29
M. Gabriel Delmas	0.0098	0.0	5
M. Bertrand de la Doucette and Mlle. Marie de la Doucette and Mme. Gérard de Vincens de Causans	0.5945	1.5	275
SCI Drouhin-Laroze	1.2933	3.2	598
SC d'Exploitation Drouhin-Laroze	0.4415	1.1	204
SC d'Exploitation du Domaine Dujac	0.4336	1.1	200
Mme. Veuve Louis Fournier and Mlle. Marguerite Fournier and M. Edouard Bart	0.3611	0.9	167
Mme. Paul Gauge	0.2159	0.5	100
M. et Mme. Robert Groffier	0.9748	2.4	450
Mme. Veuve Maurice Hudelot and Mme. Adrien Porteret	0.1656	0.4	77
Mme. Veuve Paul Hudelot	0.1229	0.3	57
Mme. Jean-Paul Husson	0.1738	0.4	80
M. Robert Jousset-Drouhin	0.2300	0.6	106
GFA Domaine Lignier Père et Fils	0.2860	0.7	132
M. Jacques Mugnier	0.3631	0.9	168

*Cases calculated on the *rendement de base* of 35 hl/ha plus 20 percent

	Hectares	Acres	Cases*
Mme. Veuve Pierre Naigeon and M. Pierre Naigeon	0.4983	1.2	230
M. Robert Newman and Mme. Robert Newman	0.3325	0.8	154
M. et Mme. Roger Peirazeau	0.4158	1.0	192
M. Pierre Ponnelle	0.0637	0.2	29
Petits-Fils de Pierre Ponnelle	0.6365	1.6	294
M. Jean Claude Roblot	0.0520	0.1	24
M. et Mme. Alain Roumier	0.4581	1.1	212
M. et Mme. Jacques Roumier	0.7390	1.8	341
M. Jean-Marie Roumier	0.1070	0.3	49
Mlle. Sylvie Roumier	0.3108	0.8	144
M. Henri Thomas	0.1465	0.4	68
M. Roger Trinquier	0.2716	0.7	125
Union Immobilière Commerciale Industrielle et Financière	0.2328	0.6	108
M. Georges de Vogüé	2.0745	5.1	958

THE PREMIERS CRUS

There are 60.7820 ha/150.2 acres in 24 vineyards.

	Hectares	Acres	Cases†
Les Amoureuses—5.4013 ha/3.3 acres			
GFA Bertheau et Fils	0.2676	0.7	159
M. Henri Felettig			
M. Bernard Grivelet	0.0645	0.2	38
M. et Mme. Robert Groffier	1.0723	2.6	637
Mme. Veuve Maurice Hudelot	0.1965	0.5	117
M. Robert Jousset-Drouhin	0.5288	1.3	314
M. Jacques Mugnier	0.5285	1.3	314
M. et Mme. Roger Peirazeau	0.2117	0.5	126
M. Roger Perrin	0.1243	0.3	74
Mme. Adrien Porteret			
M. Jean-Claude Roblot	0.1615	0.4	96
M. et Mme. Paul Roumier	0.3963	1.0	235
GFA du Domaine Bernard Serveau et Fils	0.3507	0.9	208

*Cases calculated on the *rendement de base* of 35 hl/ha plus 20 percent
†Cases calculated on the *rendement de base* of 45 hl/ha plus 20 pertcent

	Hectares	Acres	Cases*
Mme. Veuve Paul Tachot	0.4490	1.1	267
M. Georges de Vogüé	0.5607	1.4	333
M. et Mme. Edouard Zibetti	0.1158	0.3	69

Les Baudes—3.4161 ha/8.4 acres

M. et Mme. Jean Amiot	0.2746	0.7	163
SC du Domaine Jean-André	0.3164	0.8	188
Mme. Michel Barthod			
GFA Bertheau et Fils	0.3587	0.9	213
M. Guy Coquard	0.1520	0.4	90
M. et Mme. Pierre Courtmanche	0.0362	0.1	22
M. Georges Devogne	0.1328	0.3	79
SCI Drouhin-Laroze	0.1717	0.4	102
M. Jean Farcy	0.0504	0.1	30
M. Bernard Grivelet	0.3722	0.9	221
Grivelet Père et Fils	0.0688	0.2	41
Mme. Jean-Marie Gustin	0.1127	0.3	67
M. Robert Jousset-Drouhin	0.3375	0.8	200
M. et Mme. Hubert Lignier	0.1711	0.4	102
SCI du Domaine Veuve Paul Modot	0.2615	0.6	155
M. Marcel Noellat	0.1907	0.5	113
Bernard Roblot			
Paul Roblot	0.1342	0.3	80
SC du Domaine de la Tassée	0.2746	0.7	163

Aux Beaux Bruns—1.5386 ha/3.8 acres

Mme. Michel Barthod			
M. Edouard Mortet	0.4476	1.1	266
M. Marcel Noëllat	0.3380	0.8	201
M. Marcel Noëllat	0.3913	1.0	232
M. Michel Noëllat			
M. Jean-Marie Zibetti	0.3497	0.9	208

Les Borniques—1.4284 ha/3.5 acres

M. Pierre Arbinet	0.0538	0.1	32
M. Robert Jousset-Drouhin	0.2125	0.5	126
Mme. Rodolphe Graillot	0.1315	0.3	78
Mme. Veuve Maurice Hudelot	0.0625	0.2	37
Mme. Veuve Paul Hudelot	0.2310	0.6	137
M. Paul Hudelot			
Nouvelle Elvina et Leroy Vins et Alcools	0.0150	0.04	9

---

*Cases calculated on the *rendement de base* of 45 hl/ha plus 20 percent

	Hectares	Acres	Cases*
Mme. Adrien Porteret			
M. et Mme. Simon Regnier	0.1593	0.4	95
M. Bernard Roblot	0.4485	1.1	266
Mme. Veuve Paul Tachot	0.1143	0.3	68

Les Carrières—0.5256 ha/1.3 acres

M. et Mme. Bernard Amiot	0.0170	0.04	10
M. et Mme. Henri Felettig	0.4515	1.1	268

Les Chabiots—1.5031 ha/3.7 acres

GFA Bertheau et Fils	0.1525	0.4	91
Mme. Rodolphe Graillot	0.0740	0.2	44
Mme. Veuve Maurice Hudelot	0.0593	0.1	35
Mme. Adrien Porteret			
M. et Mme. Jean Prudhon	0.1362	0.3	81
M. Bernard Roblot	0.2703	0.7	161
GFA du Domaine Bernard Serveau et Fils	0.8108	2.0	482

Les Charmes—9.3193 ha/23 acres

M. Charles Allexant	0.0368	0.1	22
M. et Mme. Arsène Amiot	0.2665	0.7	158
M. et Mme. Bernard Amiot	0.3468	0.9	206
M. et Mme. Jean Amiot	0.2248	0.6	134
M. et Mme. Paul Amiot	0.2294	0.6	136
Mme. Michel Barthaud			
SC Bazin	0.6533	1.6	388
GFA Bertheau et Fils	0.6584	1.6	391
Mme. René Bourgeois			
M. et Mme. René Boursot	0.1095	0.3	65
Commune de Chambolle-Musigny	0.0026	0.006	2
Mlle. Josiane Charles	0.3398	0.8	202
GFA Domaine des Chezeaux	0.5833	1.4	346
M. Georges Clerget	0.2991	0.7	178
M. Michel Clerget	0.2990	0.7	178
M. et Mme. Michel Cluny	0.0825	0.2	49
M. Alain Collardot	0.1204	0.3	72
M. et Mme. Henri Felettig	0.1498	0.4	89
M. Georges Forey	0.2911	0.7	173
M. Bernard Grivelet	0.1100	0.3	65
Mme. Michel Guillaume	0.0758	0.2	45
M. Georges Hudelot	0.0896	0.2	53

*Cases calculated on the *rendement de base* of 45 hl/ha plus 20 percent

	Hectares	Acres	Cases*
M. Georges Hudelot	0.1192	0.3	71
M. et Mme. Joel Hudelot	0.4705	1.2	279
Mme. Veuve Joseph Hudelot	0.3386	0.8	201
M. Joseph Hudelot			
Mme. Veuve Maurice Hudelot	0.1880	0.5	112
Mme. Veuve Paul Hudelot	0.1565	0.4	93
M. et Mme. Michel Modot	0.0627	0.2	37
M. Marcel Noëllat	0.2520	0.6	150
Mme. Daniel Moine			
Mme. Henri Ouillon	0.0168	0.04	10
M. et Mme. Jean Prudhon	0.0286	0.1	17
M. et Mme. Bernard Ratheaux	0.0603	0.1	36
M. et Mme. Simon Regnier	0.0504	0.1	30
M. Bernard Roblot			
M. Paul Roblot	0.3105	0.8	184
M. Paul Roblot	0.3477	0.9	207
Mme. Jean Servelle			
M. et Mme. Jean Servelle	0.6790	1.7	403
M. Philippe Sigaut	0.1045	0.3	62
Mme. Veuve Paul Tachot	0.1725	0.4	102
M. Arthur Trapet			
Mme. Veuve Arthur Trapet	0.0684	0.2	41
M. Edouard Zibetti	0.7487	1.9	445

Les Châtelots—2.9639 ha/7.3 acres

	Hectares	Acres	Cases*
M. et Mme. Bernard Amiot	0.0459	0.1	27
M. et Mme. Bernard Amiot	0.0643	0.2	38
M. Gaston Barthod-Michel	0.0274	0.1	16
Mlle. Ghislaine Barthod-Michel	0.0159	0.04	9
Mme. Michel Barthod			
Mme. Veuve Ernest Boursot	0.0590	0.1	35
M. et Mme. Jean Boursot	0.0368	0.1	22
M. et Mme. René Boursot	0.0580	0.1	34
Mme. Veuve Brunet	0.1573	0.4	93
Mlle. Anne Confuron			
Mme. Veuve Jean Confuron	0.2345	0.6	139
Mlle. Sophie Confuron			
Mlle. Beatrice Coquard			
M. Guy Coquard	0.0704	0.2	42
Mlle. Thérèse Felettig	0.0513	0.1	30
M. et Mme. Henri Girard	0.0315	0.1	19
Mme. Rodolphe Graillot	0.0925	0.2	55
M. Bernard Grivelet	0.2991	0.7	178

*Cases calculated on the *rendement de base* of 45 hl/ha plus 20 percent

	Hectares	Acres	Cases*
M. Guy Hudelot	0.0755	0.2	45
Mme. Veuve Maurice Hudelot	0.0494	0.1	29
Mme. Veuve Paul Hudelot	0.0791	0.2	47
M. Paul Hudelot			
M. et Mme. Bernard Huelin	0.0357	0.1	21
SCI du Domaine Veuve Paul Modot	0.5377	1.3	319
M. Marcel Noëllat	0.0493	0.1	29
M. Marcel Noëllat	0.0425	0.1	25
Mme. Michel Noëllat			
Mme. Adrien Porteret			
M. et Mme. Bernard Ratheaux	0.0899	0.2	53
M. Henri Ratheaux	0.0391	0.1	23
M. et Mme. Simon Regnier	0.1117	0.3	66
M. et Mme. Louis Renard	0.1350	0.3	80
M. Hervé Sigaut	0.1555	0.4	92
M. et Mme. Maurice Sigaut	0.0578	0.1	34
M. Philippe Sigaut	0.0793	0.2	47
M. et Mme. Edouard Zibetti	0.0675	0.2	40

La Combe d'Orveau—2.3828 ha/5.9 acres

	Hectares	Acres	Cases*
Mme. Veuve Pierre Bordeaux Montrieux	0.2718	0.7	161
Consortium Viticole et Vinicole de Bourgogne (Faiveley)	0.2127	0.5	126
M. Alain Fauchier Delavigne			
M. Hervé Fauchier Delavigne	0.5437	1.3	323
M. Hervé Fauchier Delavigne			
M. Alain Fauchier Delavigne			
Mme. Henri Perrot Minot	0.4736	1.2	281
Domaine Jacques Prieur	0.2008	0.5	119
Mlle. Laure Rasse	0.0330	0.1	20
Mme. Jean Taupenot	0.4547	1.1	270

Les Combottes—1.5533/3.8 acres divided into two *climats*: Les Combottes (1.8 acres) and Aux Combottes (2 acres)

Aux Combottes

	Hectares	Acres	Cases*
M. et Mme. Bernard Amiot	0.0285	0.1	17
M. Pierre Bertrand	0.2875	0.7	171
M. et Mme. René Boursot	0.0369	0.1	22
M. Jacques Mugnier	0.0061	0.015	4
M. et Mme. Michel Noëllat	0.0922	0.2	55
M. et Mme. Simon Regnier	0.0497	0.1	30

---

*Cases calculated on the *rendement de base* of 45 hl/ha plus 20 percent

	Hectares	Acres	Cases*
M. et Mme. Guy Robin	0.1290	0.3	77
M. et Mme. Edouard Zibetti	0.1248	0.3	74

Les Combottes

	Hectares	Acres	Cases*
M. et Mme. Michel Modot	0.0150	0.04	9
SCI du Domaine Veuve Paul Modot	0.1668	0.4	99
Commune de Chambolle-Musigny	0.0065	0.0	4
M. Bernard Roumier	0.2747	0.7	163
M. et Mme. Edouard Zibetti	0.0588	0.1	35
M. Marc Zibetti	0.1340	0.3	80

Les Cras—3.4462 ha/8.5 acres

	Hectares	Acres	Cases*
Mme. Bernard Denizot	0.0836	0.2	50
Mme. Rodolphe Graillot	0.0985	0.2	59
M. et Mme. Joel Hudelot	0.3675	0.9	218
Mme. Gaston Barthod-Michel			
Mlle. Madeleine Noëllat			
M. Marcel Noëllat	0.4146	1.0	246
M. Marcel Noëllat	0.3673	0.9	218
Mme. Michel Noëllat			
Mme. Michel Noëllat			
M. et Mme. Noël Piquand	0.3416	0.8	203
M. Bernard Roumier	1.6013	4.0	951

Derrière la Grange—0.4700 ha/1.2 acres

	Hectares	Acres	Cases*
M. Marie Remy			
Mme. Marie Remy	0.4700	1.2	279

Aux Echanges—0.9260 ha/2.3 acres

	Hectares	Acres	Cases*
Société Consortium d'Études Commerciales et Industrielles	0.9260	2.3	550

Les Feusselottes—4.3958 ha/10.9 acres divided between two *climats*: Les Feusselottes (9 acres) and Les Grands Murs (1.9 acres)

Les Feusselottes

	Hectares	Acres	Cases*
Mme. René Bourgeois			
M. Christian Confuron	0.6344	1.6	377
M. Jean Farcy	0.0670	0.2	40
M. Bernard Grivelet	0.9457	2.3	562
M. Joseph Hudelot			

---

*Cases calculated on the *rendement de base* of 45 hl/ha plus 20 percent

	Hectares	Acres	Cases*
Mme. Veuve Joseph Hudelot	0.0366	0.1	22
GFA Glantenay Midan	0.0877	0.2	52
SCI du Domaine Veuve Paul Modot	0.3207	0.8	190
Mme. Daniel Moine	0.2970	0.7	176
M. Daniel Moine			
M. et Mme. Noël Piquand	0.4980	1.2	296
M. Jean Prudhon			
M. Paul Roblot	0.1695	0.4	101
Mlle. Sylvie Roblot	0.1372	0.3	81
M. Jacques Simeon	0.0574	0.1	34
M. Henri Stévignon	0.2463	0.6	146

Les Grands Murs

	Hectares	Acres	Cases*
Mme. Veuve Brunet	0.1235	0.3	73
M. Christian Confuron	0.2245	0.6	133
M. Rodolphe Graillot	0.1680	0.4	100
M. Joseph Hudelot			
Mme. Veuve Joseph Hudelot	0.2523	0.6	150

Les Fuées—4.3841 ha/10.8 acres

	Hectares	Acres	Cases*
M. et Mme. Jean Amiot	0.0690	0.2	41
Mme. Noël Boude	0.1000	0.2	59
Consortium Viticole et Vinicole de			
Bourgogne (Faiveley)	0.1897	0.5	113
M. et Mme. Jean Boursot	0.3045	0.8	181
M. et Mme. Remy Poinet Boursot	0.0570	0.1	34
M. et Mme. René Boursot	0.1669	0.4	99
M. Guy Coquard	0.1013	0.3	60
M. Georges de Vogüé	0.1461	0.4	87
M. et Mme. Henri Girard	0.1483	0.4	88
M. Joseph Hudelot			
Mme. Veuve Joseph Hudelot	0.0700	0.2	42
M. et Mme. Michel Modot	0.1588	0.4	94
M. Jacques Mugnier	0.7109	1.8	422
M. et Mme. Michel Noëllat	0.2413	0.6	143
M. et Mme. Louis Renard	0.0453	0.1	27
M. Bernard Roblot			
M. Bernard Roblot			
Mme. Bernard Roblot	0.1488	0.4	88
M. Jean-Claude Roblot	0.2822	0.7	168
M. Paul Roblot	0.0630	0.2	37
Mlle. Sylvie Roblot	0.4120	1.0	245

---

*Cases calculated on the *rendement de base* of 45 hl/ha plus 20 percent

	Hectares	Acres	Cases*
M. et Mme. Alain Roumier	0.1607	0.4	95
M. Jean-Marie Roumier	0.0680	0.2	40
M. et Mme. Paul Roumier	0.0120	0.03	7
Mme. Jean Servelle			
M. Hervé Sigaut	0.1678	0.4	100
M. Laurent Sigaut	0.1044	0.3	62
M. Philippe Sigaut	0.0650	0.2	39
Mlle. Denise Tachot	0.1508	0.4	90
Mme. Veuve Paul Tachot	0.0750	0.2	45
Mme. Veuve Paul Tachot	0.0455	0.1	27

Les Groseilles—1.3386 ha/3.3 acres

	Hectares	Acres	Cases*
M. et Mme. Jean Amiot	0.1434	0.4	85
GFA Bertheau et Fils	0.1503	0.4	89
M. Jean-Pierre Brunet	0.1153	0.3	68
Mme. Veuve Maurice Hudelot	0.3248	0.8	193
SCI du Domaine Veuve Paul Modot	0.2432	0.6	144
Mme. Daniel Moine			
M. Vittorio Moretti	0.0970	0.2	58
Mme. Henri Royer			
Mme. Veuve Philippe Sigaut	0.1632	0.4	97
M. Philippe Sigaut	0.1002	0.2	60

Les Gruenchers—2.8236 ha/7 acres

	Hectares	Acres	Cases*
M. et Mme. Bernard Amiot	0.0411	0.1	24
M. et Mme. Jean Amiot	0.0689	0.2	41
M. et Mme. Pierre Bertheau	0.0718	0.2	43
Mme. René Bourgeois			
M. Henri Charles	0.1520	0.4	90
SC d'Exploitation du Domaine Dujac	0.3259	0.8	194
M. Jean-Claude Fourrier	0.2906	0.7	173
Mme. Veuve Maurice Hudelot	0.0305	0.1	18
M. Pierre Julien	0.1597	0.4	95
Mme. Daniel Moine			
M. Vittorio Moretti	0.0635	0.2	38
M. Jean-Claude Roblot	0.6421	0.6	381
M. Paul Roblot	0.3622	0.9	215
Mme. Henri Royer			
M. et Mme. Jean Servelle	0.0247	0.1	15
M. et Mme. Maurice Sibaut	0.2099	0.5	125
M. Philippe Sigaut	0.2120	0.5	126
M. et Mme. Edouard Zibetti	0.1696	0.4	101

*Cases calculated on the *rendement de base* of 45 hl/ha plus 20 percent

	Hectares	*Acres*	*Cases**
Les Hauts Doix—1.7375 ha/4.3 acres			
M. Bernard Grivelet	0.0620	0.2	37
M. et Mme. Robert Groffier	1.0003	2.5	594
M. Robert Jousset-Drouhin	0.0695	0.2	41
M. et Mme. Roger Peirazeau	0.6057	1.5	360
Les Lavrottes—0.9195 ha/2.3 acres			
M. Christian Confuron	0.3204	0.8	190
SCI Drouhin-Laroze	0.0700	0.2	42
M. Pierre Julien	0.1498	0.4	89
M. et Mme. Michel Modot	0.3793	0.9	225
Les Noirots—2.8479 ha/ 7 acres			
M. et Mme. Jean Amiot	0.0915	0.2	54
GFA Bertheau et Fils	0.3197	0.8	190
Mme. Veuve Brunet	0.1012	0.3	60
M. et Mme. Michel Cluny	0.3990	1.0	237
M. Georges Delaye	0.1293	0.3	77
M. Bernard Grivelet	0.3834	0.9	228
M. Robert Jousset-Drouhin	0.0625	0.2	37
Mme. Henri Legros	0.2830	0.7	168
M. Marcel Noëllat	0.1073	0.3	64
M. et Mme. Michel Nöellat	0.1310	0.3	78
Mme. Michel Noëllat			
M. et Mme. Simon Regnier	0.1049	0.3	62
M. Bernard Roblot	0.2972	0.7	177
M. Bernard Roblot			
M. Jean-Claude Roblot	0.2173	0.5	129
M. Paul Roblot	0.2141	0.5	127
Les Plantes—1.7795 ha/4.4 acres			
M. et Mme. Arsène Amiot	0.2465	0.6	146
Domaines Bertagna	0.2320	0.6	138
Mlle. Catherine Bilik			
M. Joseph Bilik	0.0256	0.1	15
M. Jean-Pierre Brunet	0.0522	0.1	31
M. Jean Farcy	0.1620	0.4	96
M. Jean Fournier	0.0993	0.2	59
M. Émile Gibourg	0.0352	0.1	21
Mme. Rodolphe Graillot	0.0930	0.2	55
M. Robert Jousset-Drouhin	0.4026	1.0	239

*Cases calculated on the *rendement de base* of 45 hl/ha plus 20 percent

	Hectares	Acres	Cases*
M. Jacques Mugnier	0.4742	1.2	282
Mme. Henri Ouillon	0.2113	0.5	126
M. et Mme. Bernard Ratheaux	0.0085	0.0	5
M. et Mme. Paul Roumier	0.1830	0.5	109
M. et Mme. Jean Servelle	0.3405	0.8	202

Les Sentiers—4.8945 ha/12.1 acres

GFA du Domaine Arlaud Père et Fils	0.2300	0.6	137
Mme. Michel Barthod			
GFA du Domaine Bernard Serveau			
et Fils	0.4464	1.1	265
M. Nojcieck Bryczek	0.0465	0.1	28
M. André Coquard	0.0687	0.2	41
Mme. Justin Folletet	0.0694	0.2	41
M. René Gibourg	0.1492	0.4	89
M. et Mme. Victor Gibourg	0.1683	0.4	100
M. et Mme. Robert Groffier	1.0733	2.7	638
Mlle. Marthe Liebaut	0.0714	0.2	42
M. Antoine Magnien	0.1266	0.3	75
M. et Mme. Michel Magnien	0.1486	0.4	88
M. Jean-Paul Magnien			
Mme. Isabelle Marchand	0.1240	0.3	74
M. Marcel Noëllat	0.0700	0.2	42
Mme. Jean Porcherot	0.0299	0.1	18
M. Henri Schneider	0.2843	0.7	169
M. Jean Seguin	0.1780	0.4	106
M. et Mme. Maurice Sigaut	0.6235	1.5	370
M. Philippe Sigaut	0.0522	0.1	31
SC du Domaine de la Tassée	0.2745	0.7	163
M. et Mme. Jacky Truchot	0.6597	1.6	392

PRODUCERS WORTH SEEKING OUT (AND SOME NOT)

DOMAINE GEORGES CLERGET/DOMAINE MICHEL CLERGET—
One of the less-heralded (although by no means unknown) producers
of Chambolle-Musigny, Clerget creates some of the most luscious
red Burgundies available, invariably deeply colored and remarkably
concentrated. Although based in Vougeot, Clerget is notable for his
Chambolle-Musigny. There's a first-rate commune-level Chambolle-

---

*Cases calculated on the *rendement de base* of 45 hl/ha plus 20 percent

Musigny (except, curiously, in 1985, of all vintages), but the real specialty is a stunning, huge-scale *premier cru* Les Charmes. There're no winemaking tricks here. Rather, Clerget keeps the yields low, ferments the wines with only one quarter of the stems, and uses 50 percent new oak barrels. There's nothing in such a description that gives any clue to just how rich and full the Clerget wines are, save one: the low yields. Clerget's vineyards rarely exceed 30 hl/ha. In addition to the Chambolle-Musigny bottlings, Clerget also issues a profound Echézeaux from a rented plot with very old vines and the commune-level Vosne-Romanée "Les Violettes." This is a producer that excels in lesser vintages such as 1984 and 1986, which says something right there.

JOSEPH DROUHIN—The soft, supple Drouhin style shines in its wonderful bottling of Musigny. This is one of the most luscious of today's great Musignys, different in style from those of Leroy or Jadot or Roumier, but of a similar standard. It's worth seeking out.

DOMAINE DUJAC—Delectable Bonnes Mares offered in the silky, subtle, delicate Dujac style. But the Bonnes Mares muscularity and power still is unmistakable. Along with Clos de la Roche, this is Dujac's best wine.

DOMAINE ROBERT GROFFIER—The source of some very good, although slightly uneven from vintage to vintage, Chambolle-Musigny. Groffier offers a truly fine Les Amoureuses, as well as the *premier cru* Les Sentiers. The style here is for soft, delicate wines of good concentration and a touch of vanillin from 100 percent new oak barrels. The Bonnes Mares is, along with Les Amoureuses, the signature wine: intense, strong, yet still in the delicate Groffier style. This is a very good producer whose wines should be investigated.

LOUIS JADOT—The source of some of the greatest Bonnes Mares available today: exceptionally intense, concentrated, and made to age for decades.

Jadot purchased the former Clair-Daü estate in 1985, which

included 4.7 acres of Bonnes Mares planted to old vines. In this was the entire Morey-Saint-Denis portion (3.74 acres) of Bonnes Mares, which is famously hard, long-lived wine even by Bonnes Mares standards, with the balance in Chambolle-Musigny. Prior to that purchase, Jadot did not own any Bonnes Mares, although it did sell wines purchased from others. But with the Clair-Daü property, coupled with their own fastidious winemaking, Jadot has vaulted to the top rank among Bonnes Mares producers. Right behind it is a very fine, but not quite as inspirational, Musigny. And right behind that is a superb Les Amoureuses.

LABOURÉ-ROI—The Nuits-Saint-Georges *négociant* has increasingly specialized in seeking out small lots of Chambolle-Musigny in recent years, with the result that the shipper has become one of the most reliable sources of good commune-level Chambolle-Musigny that sell for quite reasonable prices. Also, it has recently become the distribution agent of Domaine Modot (q.v.), which is the source of yet more good Chambolle-Musigny.

LEROY—The source of some of the greatest Musigny made. Regrettably, there is isn't much of it. The newly formed Domaine Leroy made just one barrel (twenty-five cases) in the 1988 vintage. The Musignys offered by Leroy *négociant* (presumably from Leroy's tiny Musigny holding, augmented by the purchase of wine) are magnificent: The 1985 Leroy Musigny was one of the greatest wines made in that vintage. The 1969 still lingers in the mind—and it's not ready yet. Reference-standard.

DOMAINE GEORGES LIGNIER—A source for superb, intense Bonnes Mares that is packed with bright, fresh fruit in Lignier's grapey style. Still, the quality is powerfully present. Also, a pretty, easy-going commune-level Chambolle-Musigny of consistently good quality.

DOMAINE MICHEL MODOT—I came across the wines of this producer at a tasting offered by the *négociant* Labouré-Roi, which has taken on the unusual role (for a shipper) of representing some twenty domaine wines throughout Burgundy. Labouré-Roi bottles the wines under the domaine label, yet buys them outright from the domaines, leaving the domaines all the glory but none of the risk. In Chambolle-Musigny, Labouré-Roi discovered Domaine Modot, which, as the grower listings reveal, owns some choice parcels in Les Lavrottes, Les Fuées, Les Charmes, Les Combottes, Les Groseilles, Les Châtelots, and Les Feusselottes. I really don't know what all gets done with all of these wines. So far, all I've tasted was an extraordinary Chambolle-Musigny 1986 that was perhaps the finest commune-level Chambolle that I can recall. Surely it couldn't have been composed only of commune-level vines. Equally exciting was a stunning Bourgogne Rouge 1986 that turned out to be from Fixin. This is a producer to watch.

DOMAINE JACQUES PRIEUR—Based in Meursault, this domaine has long held a choice piece of Musigny: all 1.5 acres of the climat La Combe d'Orveau, a triangular plot that is almost directly in line with the château in Clos de Vougeot. So far, the wine is pleasant, but hardly exceptional. I keep waiting for this estate to wake up. New partners may prove just the jostle it needs. Certainly, the raw materials in the form of Musigny and other great vineyards (such as Montrachet) are present.

DOMAINE GEORGES ROUMIER—At this point, one could easily submit that this domaine is one of the dozen strongest estates in Burgundy today. It just doesn't seem to miss, as is evidenced by superb 1982s and 1986s, light vintages where even some of the most renowned properties stubbed a toe. Roumier, instead, issued some of its prettiest wines from those vintages, especially in '86. The winemaking currently is in the hands of young Christophe Roumier, which means that we can expect this property to continue at this standard for years to come.

Sorting through the offerings is a delight. At the top is a mind-boggling Bonnes Mares, one of the reference standards for the *grand cru*. Equally eye-opening (and jaw-dropping) is Roumier's Musigny, which is also reference-standard—if you can find any. Rarer yet is the Les Amoureuses, in which Roumier offers one of the two best bottlings I know (the other is Serveau's). And so it goes. The commune-level Chambolle-Musigny is often better than some other producers' *premiers crus*. The winemaking style emphasizes bright, deep, concentrated fruit without a hint of grapiness or a note of excessive oak. The *terroirs* always shine through.

DOMAINE BERNARD SERVEAU—The Morey-Saint-Denis producer actually has his two best wines from Chambolle-Musigny: a lovely, ethereal Les Chabiots, in which Serveau is the largest owner, and a magnificent Les Amoureuses as tightly sprung as a sports car, with all the latent power. Along with the Amoureuses of Roumier, it is the best version of this acclaimed *premier cru* that I know.

DOMAINE COMTE GEORGES DE VOGÜÉ—The Musigny difficulties of this domaine have already been discussed. The de Vogüé holdings extend to large parcels in Bonnes Mares and Les Amoureuses. In the past, which is to say 1969 and earlier, these, along with the Musigny, were extraordinary. Today, they are merely good. The la Doucettes of Loire wine fame (and now Chablis in the form of the recent purchase of the shipper Albert Pic/A. Regnard) are related to the de Vogüé family and, as shown in the listings, own a piece of Bonnes Mares. Burgundian scuttlebut has it that the resolution to the de Vogüé malaise will come in the form of Patrick de la Doucette, who heads the family wine operations in the Loire and Chablis. We shall see.

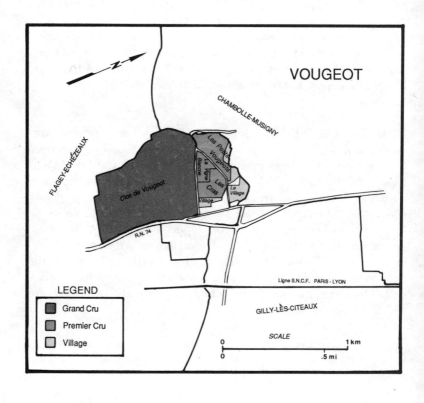

VOUGEOT

CHAMBOLLE-MUSIGNY

FLAGEY-ECHÉZEAUX

Les Petits Vougeots
La Vigne Blanche
Clos de Vougeot
Les Cras
Le Village
Village

R.N. 74

Ligne S.N.C.F.   PARIS - LYON

GILLY-LÈS-CITEAUX

LEGEND

Grand Cru
Premier Cru
Village

SCALE

0 _____ 1 km
0 _____ .5 mi

Vougeot

Stopped at Nuits for intelligence concerning the vineyards of this country, so famous in France, and indeed in all of Europe; and examine the Clos de Vougeot, of 100 journaux, walled in, and belonging to a convent of Bernardine monks. When are we to find these fellows choosing badly? The spots they appropriate show what a righteous attention they give to things of the spirit.

—ARTHUR YOUNG, *Travels in France* (1792)

No commune in Burgundy is more completely dominated by one *grand cru* vineyard than Vougeot. Very likely, the average Burgundy drinker draws no distinction between the wine of Clos de Vougeot and the commune of Vougeot, which name is derived from a nearby stream called the Vouge. After all, the 125 acres of Clos de Vougeot account for 75 percent of the total vineyard area of Vougeot. The rest is a matter of twenty-nine acres of *premier cru* vineyards and just twelve acres of commune-level wine entitled to be called Vougeot. There is a town, but it counts only 197 Vougeotins.

Why is the Clos de Vougeot so famous? History accounts for much of it; current wine quality far less so. The history is impressive. A creation of the Cistercian order of monks, the present 125 acres has not changed since at least 1336. It would seem to be the most

Burgundian of vineyards. Yet in one important feature, it is not: Clos de Vougeot was created on a model that wine drinkers today would describe as Bordeauxlike rather than Burgundian. It is a vineyard that achieved its acclaim by careful blending rather than from a finely wrought distinction of *terroir*. In the same way that Château Lafite-Rothschild is a wine assembled from a wide swath of vineyard of varying qualities, with each vat carefully analyzed and then blended (or eliminated) to make up the namesake wine, so, too, was Clos de Vougeot an assembled creation. Where the greatness of Romanée-Conti or Musigny lay in their profound site specificity, that of Clos de Vougeot was in its Cistercian caretakers' magnificently skilled blending ability.

The acclaim for Clos de Vougeot persisted after the vineyard was confiscated in May 1790, by a then-obscure second lieutenant named Napoleon Bonaparte. It was sold in one piece to one Jean Focard, who subsequently proved to be a deadbeat, being unable to come up with the whopping purchase price of 1,140,600 livres, which was twenty-two times the annual revenue of the property. (I am indebted to Jean-François Bazin's superb book *Le Clos de Vougeot* for these details.) After being sold again for the same price to two Parisian bankers, Louis and Pierre-Antoine Ravel, the dazzling *solitaire* of Clos de Vougeot looked to be on the verge of a breakup, as a third share was sold to a fellow banker. But in 1818 it returned to a single ownership, ostensibly that of Victor Ouvrard. He promptly gave it to his nineteen-year-old cousin Julien-Jules Ouvrard. This was because Julien-Jules's father, Gabriel-Julien Ouvrard, actually put up the money. His vast wealth was achieved from having supplied Napoleon's armies with war matériel.

Clos de Vougeot continued in its Bordelais fashion, thanks to its being under a single ownership. Ouvrard proved himself a serious steward, so much so that he became mayor of Vougeot and manager of the Romanée-Conti vineyard. The wines of that property actually were made in Ouvrard's cellars at Clos de Vougeot.

When he died in 1861 at the age of sixty-two, the vineyard passed to his sister's four children, who put it up for sale in pieces. Oddly, it was purchased (by Baron Thénard) only to be sold back again to descendants of the Ouvrard family. There, it remained under one cohesive ownership until 1889. By then phylloxera was taking its toll on the vineyard. Because of that, it fetched only 600,000 francs when purchased by fifteen Burgundian *négociants* who were motivated, in part, by a fear that the famous property would fall into British or German hands.

This was the beginning of the end for Clos de Vougeot. Incredibly, Clos de Vougeot had remained intact for at least seven hundred years under effectively just three owners: the Cistercian order from its inception in the 1100s to the confiscation in 1790; the Ravels from 1791 to 1818, and the Ouvrard family from 1818 to 1889.

Today, Clos de Vougeot is as much a myth as a wine, much as Château Lafite would be if it had eighty-plus owners all entitled to employ the fabled name. Keep in mind that where many other vineyards in the Côte d'Or are more fractionalized than Clos de Vougeot, none is as large. It's one thing for Pommard "Les Charmots" to have fifty-one owners in 14.5 acres. It's quite another to have it sprawled across 125 acres. (The same problem is present in Echézeaux.) When carefully assembled into a larger whole, lesser plots could play an auxillary role in the final blend, perhaps adding a bit of necessary acidity (from less perfectly ripened grapes) or some additional body from richer but less fine wine. But on their own, such wines are less than what one expects from a *grand cru*. Yet tradition accords these wines the rank of *grand cru*, ignoring the circumstances by which they achieved their original elevation.

Conventional wisdom has it that Clos de Vougeot is qualitatively divided into thirds. The top third of the slope is said to offer the finest wines, the middle less good, and the lowest portion the least. One thing is certain: The vineyards at the base suffer grievously from poor drainage. Clos de Vougeot is the only *grand cru* in the Côte d'Or that abuts the main road, N74, at the base of the slope.

Do we know for a fact that this ancient assertion about the divisions of the slope is accurate? We do not. Likely, it is true. Today, it is all but impossible to confirm, as the variables of winemaking technique from owner to owner and the extreme parceling of the vineyard will trip up even the most dedicated investigator. We do know that the monks—who reportedly made three *cuvées* of varying quality—did differentiate the 125 acres into fifteen *climats* with names such as Devant-la-Maison, Musigny-Melot, de la Combotte, and so forth. Whether these were merely administrative designations or reflected viticultural qualities is unclear. Probably, it was a bit of both.

What of Clos de Vougeot today? For the Burgundy buyer, it is a minefield. No other vineyard, certainly no other *grand cru*, is more likely to disappoint than Clos de Vougeot. One of the reasons for this is the dirty little secret of Burgundy: Too often a vineyard holding is too small to vinify separately, at least not without special pains. So the grower adds the grapes to a vat with grapes from other sites. The wine is made, and the legally allowed amount of Clos de Vougeot from whatever the size of the holding is siphoned off and sold—either domaine-bottled or to a *négociant*—as Clos de Vougeot. This practice occurs throughout the Côte d'Or, but one is led to believe that it is more prevalent in Clos de Vougeot due to the fame of the vineyard and the outsized number of owners.

Even at its best, Clos de Vougeot tends not to be a wine of marked character compared to, say, La Tâche or Clos de la Roche or Musigny. A really good Clos de Vougeot is richly perfumed, but in a less insinuating fashion than Musigny, although it shares with Musigny the distinction of an unusually long, lingering aftertaste. It should have stuffings, although never on the scale of Bonnes Mares or Richebourg. Instead, it should be a complete wine, in the sense of amalgamating the pronounced qualities of the best red Burgundies without any one feature standing out. It is no coincidence that Clos de Vougeot shares an ancient acclaim with other vineyards offering this same seamless consolidation of attributes: Chambertin, Volnay "Caillerets," Meursault "Perrières," and Montrachet, among others.

A tiny quantity of white wine is produced in the commune of Vougeot, none of it in the Clos de Vougeot itself. At one time, though, Clos de Vougeot was generously interplanted with Chardonnay and, probably, Pinot Gris. James Busby, in his *Journal of a Tour Through Some of the Vineyards of France and Spain* (1833), offers a detailed description of the winemaking at Clos de Vougeot, then under the Ouvrard stewardship. "They are getting rid of the white grapes in the Clos Vougeot, for the vines not only produce less, but the price of white wine never rises so high as that of the red wines. It is no uncommon thing for a hogshead of the latter to bring 1250 to 1500 francs, but the white wine never rises above 600 francs the hogshead."

Today, there exists a *premier cru* vineyard just outside the walls of Clos de Vougeot at the top of the slope called "Le Clos Blanc" or "La Vigne Blanche." It is this vineyard that creates what little white wine is produced. It is not a white Clos de Vougeot, but an entirely separate vineyard. The wine is interesting, but more as an oddity than as a compelling white Burgundy. It is a *monopole* of the Dijon shipper L'Héritier-Guyot.

THE VINEYARDS

There are 67.0867 ha/165.8 acres, of which 11.9 acres are commune-level; 28.9 acres are *premier cru*; and 125 acres are *grand cru* (Clos de Vougeot).

PREMIERS CRUS

Les Cras—2.9865 ha/7.4 acres
Le Clos Blanc or La Vigne Blanche—3.0495 ha/7.6 acres
Les Petits Vougeots—5.6432 ha/13.9 acres divided into two *climats*: Les Petits Vougeots (8.6 acres) and Clos de la Perrière (5.3 acres; a *monopole* of Domaine Bertagna)

GRAND CRU

CLOS DE VOUGEOT—50.5910 ha/125 acres

	Hectares	Acres	Cases*
Mme. Monique André and Mme. Marie-Christine Sesia	1.9720	4.9	912
M. Robert Arnoux	0.4280	1.0	198
Société Aujoux et Cie SA	0.2009	0.5	93
Mme. Michèle Beaufort-Noblet	0.1712	0.4	79
SC des Grands Appellations d'Origines (Domaine Bertagna)	0.3100	0.8	143
SA Maison Albert Bichot (4 parcels) (Domaine du Clos Frantin)	0.6302	1.6	291

*Cases calculated on the *rendement de base* of 35 hl/ha plus 20 percent

	Hectares	*Acres*	*Cases**
GFA François Capitain et Fils	0.1712	0.4	79
M. Denis Cheron (Domaine Misset) (2 parcels)	2.0626	5.1	953
Mme. Jean-Antide Charvet	0.3118	0.8	144
M. Daniel Chopin	0.3485	0.9	161
M. Bernard Clerc (2 parcels)	0.4047	1.0	187
M. Félix Clerget	0.3424	0.8	158
M. Guy Cocquard	0.2149	0.5	99
GAEC Coquard-Loison-Fleurot	0.2140	0.5	99
M. Christian Confuron	0.3424	0.8	158
M. Joseph Confuron	0.2539	0.6	117
Mme. Jean-Jacques Confuron (2 parcels)	0.5152	1.3	238
Consortium Vinicole et Viticole de Bourgogne (Joseph Faiveley) (2 parcels)	0.8280	2.0	383
Mme. Chantal Desmazieres (Ropiteau-Mignon)	0.2208	0.5	102
GFA de Coteaux Dorés (M. Gérard Loichet)	0.8353	2.1	386
Domaine Joseph Drouhin	0.2920	0.7	135
Mme. Monique Drouhin-Pradal	0.6210	1.5	287
SCE des Domaines Drouhin-Laroze	1.2544	3.1	580
M. Jean Dufouleur	0.2085	0.5	96
GAEC du Domaine René Engel	1.3696	3.4	633
M. Thierry Faiveley	0.4589	1.1	212
GAEC Gerbet Filles	0.3133	0.8	145
Enfants de M. Louis Gouroux and Mme. Yvonne Gouroux	0.6820	1.7	315
SC Jean Grivot	1.8675	4.6	863
Mme. Colette Gros and Mme. Marie-Louise Gros	1.5570	3.8	719
M. François Gros	0.9320	2.3	431
M. Michel Gros	0.2085	0.5	96
M. Alfred Haegelen-Jayer	0.3516	0.9	162
M. Henri Haegelen and M. Émile Haegelen	0.4030	1.0	186
L'Héritier-Guyot	1.0520	2.6	486
M. Noël Hudelot-Mongeard	0.4280	1.1	198
M. Alain Hudelot-Noëllat (3 parcels)	1.0480	2.6	484

*Cases calculated on the *rendement de base* of 35 hl/ha plus 20 percent

	Hectares	*Acres*	*Cases**
Domaine Louis Jadot (see also Pierre Mérat/Champy)	0.3212	0.8	148
SCI Domaine Jaffelin	0.6214	1.5	287
Mme. Jacqueline Labet and Mme. Nicole Dechelette (5 parcels) (Domaine du Château de la Tour)	5.4804	13.5	2532
M. François Lamarche and Mlle. Geneviève Lamarche	1.3589	3.4	628
Maison Legay-Lagoute	0.1880	0.5	87
Leroy (see also SC Charles Noëllat)	0.2083	0.5	96
Mme. Chantal Lescure	0.3129	0.8	146
M. René Leymarie	0.5260	1.3	243
Mme. Xavier Liger-Belair et Ses Enfants	0.7260	1.8	335
Mme. Comtesse Michel de Loisy	0.6470	1.6	299
M. Pierre-Yves Masson	0.4256	1.1	197
M. Jean Méo (Domaine Méo-Camuzet)	3.0343	7.5	1402
Colonel Pierre Mérat (Champy Père) (now Louis Jadot)	2.2566	5.6	1042
SCI Mongeard-Mugneret et Fils	0.2849	0.7	132
Mme. Jacqueline Porteret	0.1422	0.35	66
Dr. Georges Mugneret	0.3424	0.8	158
SC Charles Noëllat (now Domaine Leroy) (2 parcels)	1.6900	4.2	781
M. Jean Nourissat	0.1587	0.4	73
SA Pierre Ponnelle	0.3428	0.8	158
SCI Domaine Jacques Prieur	1.2500	3.1	577
M. Bernard Raphet	0.2387	0.6	110
M. Jean Raphet (2 parcels)	0.9442	2.3	436
Domaine Henri Rebourseau (2 parcels)	2.2100	5.5	1021
Mme. de Roubaix	0.4251	1.0	196
M. Bruno Roumier	0.5331	1.3	246
Mme. Sylvie Roumier	0.3211	0.8	148
SCI du Clos de Thorey (2 parcels) (Moillard)	0.6000	1.5	277
GFA Domaine Tortochot	0.2033	0.5	94
M. Robert Tourlière	0.6420	1.6	296
Mme. Marie-Annick Tremblay	0.2140	0.5	99
Mme. Odette Vadey-Rameau	0.4975	1.2	230
M. André Wilhelm-Lecrivain	0.3424	0.8	158

*Cases calculated on the *rendement de base* of 35 hl/ha plus 20 percent

PRODUCERS WORTH SEEKING OUT (AND SOME NOT)

DOMAINE DU CHÂTEAU DE LA TOUR—The largest single owner in Clos de Vougeot with 13.5 acres (nearly all in the midslope), it also is the only producer that is actually able to vinify the wine within the walls of the clos itself, courtesy of owning the namesake Château de la Tour. This mock fortress was built in 1890, and is the only other structure in the Clos de Vougeot besides the ancient Cistercian château that houses the old presses and now is headquarters for the Chevalier de Tastevin organization, which proselytizes Burgundy wines throughout the world through various chapters.

Originally owned by Jean Morin, the property succeeded to his two daughters in 1975, Jacqueline Labet and Nicole Dechelette. All of the wine is sold under one label. At one time, this property issued some of the best Clos de Vougeot, but the quality had been declining for years. Since 1987, the wines have been produced under the guidance of consulting enologist Guy Accad, who advocates fifteen- to twenty-five-day cold maceration of unfermented juice with the skins prior to fermentation. At Château de la Tour, they have modified this to a seven- to ten-day cold maceration. A tasting of the 1987, '88, and '89 vintages left me cold. The wines are dark, as are all Accad-influenced bottlings, but lacked detail or flavor definition. So far, Château de la Tour has not yet hit its stride on the comeback trail.

DOMAINE MICHEL CLERGET/DOMAINE GEORGES CLERGET— This fine producer offers one of the only *premier cru* Vougeots that I know, a Vougeot "Les Petits Vougeots." The wine lacks the depth of a Clos de Vougeot, perhaps due to young vines (planted in the mid-seventies), but still has distinction. It's worth keeping in mind that Les Petits Vougeots abuts Chambolle-Musigny "Les Amoureuses," yet there is surprisingly little similarity between the two wines that I can find except for a general perfuminess.

DOMAINE JACKY CONFURON-COTETIDOT—This Vosne-Romanée producer owns a 0.6-acre plot of Clos de Vougeot at the base of the slope. The vines, however, are fifty years old. Guy Accad also consults to this producer, and all of Confuron's wines are resultingly dark and strongly influenced by cold maceration. Nevertheless, Confuron's 1988 Clos de Vougeot is the most interesting, even exciting, wine I have tasted under the Accad regime, offering surprising depth, a bittersweet-chocolate scent, and superb perfume.

JOSEPH DROUHIN—The *négociant* owns two parcels in Clos de Vougeot, one in the midslope (1.5 acres) and another at the base (0.7 acre). Both contain young vines, much of the two plots replanted in the early eighties. This is one of the more reliable sources of good Clos de Vougeot, although rarely does the Drouhin rendition reach the inspirational stage.

DOMAINE DROUHIN-LAROZE—Not related to the wine-shipping firm Joseph Drouhin, this domaine owns a choice 3.1-acre plot at the top of the slope. Regrettably, I have tasted only a few Drouhin-Laroze wines, but the Clos de Vougeot bottling stood out as exceptional.

DOMAINE RENÉ ENGEL—One of the stellar producers of Clos de Vougeot; everything lines up here. The 3.4-acre plot is one of the best situated, right near the top of the slope. Moreover, the vines are venerable, having been planted in 1922. Best of all, the wine-making has been rejuvenated in recent years by Philippe Engel. His grandfather, René, was a university professor in Dijon and a beloved figure in Burgundian life. He died in 1986 at the age of ninety-two, having outlived his son Pierre, who died in 1981.

Based in Vosne-Romanée, this domaine has gone from strength to strength in recent years. Invariably, the Clos de Vougeot bottling has emerged as one of the stars among the impressive lineup of offerings. Here, the wine is of compelling concentration, but without flamboyant stylistic flourishes or obvious manipulation. This is Clos de Vougeot as it should be.

JOSEPH FAIVELEY—This *négociant* owns 3.2 acres of Clos de Vougeot in three parcels, two of which are located near the base, the third and smallest in the high midslope. The tough, rather dried-out Faiveley style is present in the Clos de Vougeot bottling as well. The fruit quality is present, but the delivery falls short for this palate.

DOMAINE JEAN GRIVOT—Another Vosne-Romanée domaine newly under the guidance of Guy Accad since the 1987 vintage. Grivot owns a 4.6-acre plot at the base of the slope. The Clos de Vougeot bottling was unidentifiable, by me, as anything resembling a *grand cru*. Here, the Accad method shows its heaviest, most suffocating hand. It is interesting to compare the Grivot Clos de Vougeot with that of Jacky Confuron-Cotetidot, especially since their respective plots are within 150 feet of each other. Yet the wines are dramatically different. Old vines may make the difference, although even the youngest vines in Grivot's plot now are twenty years old, with many twice that age.

DOMAINE GROS FRÈRE ET SOEUR—Massive wine from a 3.8-acre plot at the very top of the Clos de Vougeot. In fact, it is adjacent to Musigny. The winemaking style of this interesting domaine seeks almost extreme extraction. Frankly, I can't quite make up my mind about this producer's wines.

DOMAINE JEAN GROS—The Gros family has claims staked out in the best parts of Clos de Vougeot. Three different domaines, all vinified separately, exist: Gros Frère et Soeur, François Gros, and Jean Gros. It's a classic Burgundian inheritance situation.

Domaine Jean Gros now is in the hands of Jean's widow and their son, Michel, who made a superb Clos de Vougeot from 0.5-acre plot in the high midslope. The vines, however, were pulled up in 1986 and the vineyard replanted. Thus, we shall not see any more Clos de Vougeot from this estate for some years. However, should you come across one of the rare older bottlings, it's worth pursuing.

LOUIS JADOT—This *négociant* has, in recent years, created some of the best Clos de Vougeot available, even though the 0.8-acre parcel is at the base of the slope. Very likely it is augmented by wines purchased from other owners. But Jadot promises to become a leading supplier of top-echelon Clos de Vougeot, thanks to the purchase of the ancient *négociant* Champy Père et Cie and its vineyard holdings in November 1989. Champy was the oldest *négociant* firm in Burgundy, dating to 1720. The name likely will now cease to exist. Champy owned 5.6 acres of Clos de Vougeot in one parcel, running vertically from the base to the midslope.

DOMAINE CHANTAL LESCURE—Owner since 1976 of a beautifully sited 0.8-acre plot on the upper midslope. The winemaking has sometimes proved a bit oaky, but the 1988 and '89 Clos de Vougeot tasted from the barrel showed no evidence of this. The style is rich, intense, and supple. Excellent, first-rank Clos de Vougeot. The wines of this domaine are tended and distributed by the *négociant* Labouré-Roi.

LEROY—The newly created Domaine Leroy is the creator of superb Clos de Vougeot. The *négociant* Leroy has long been a source of reference-standard Clos de Vougeot, purchased from others. Until the purchase of the former Domaine Charles Noëllat, Leroy owned only a 0.5-acre parcel at the base of the slope. The vines in this plot were pulled up in late 1986. But in 1988, Leroy acquired Domaine Noëllat and with it 4.2 acres of Clos de Vougeot in two parcels, the larger of them at the base and midslope, the smaller at the topmost point of the slope. The vines are all at least thirty-five years old, with many older than that. The 1988 and '89 vintages were outstanding when tasted from the barrel.

DOMAINE MÉO-CAMUZET—One of the major owners of Clos de Vougeot, with 8.3 acres superbly sited on the upper slope adjacent to the château. For years, the vineyard was sharecropped with the now-retired Henri Jayer of Vosne-Romanée. Now, he consults to the newly revived domaine. The wines are a bit uneven, with the '86s depressingly light. Still, the 1985s were superlative, and one has every reason to expect ever-superior Clos de Vougeot to emerge from this estate.

DOMAINE MONGEARD-MUGNERET—Excellent, concentrated Clos de Vougeot in Mongeard-Mugneret's characteristic style, which is slightly rustic and a bit oaky. Nevertheless, this is top-rank Clos de Vougeot. The grapes come from two parcels on the upper slope, one of them owned by Domaine Mongeard-Mugneret. The other is a parcel owned by Enfants de M. Louis and Mme. Yvonne Gouroux, which is sharecropped by Mongeard-Mugneret.

DOMAINE GEORGES MUGNERET—The late Dr. Mugneret created stunning Clos de Vougeot from a 0.8-acre plot high up on the slope near the château. The vines now are thirty-six years old. This is reference-standard Clos de Vougeot, with the sort of detail and finesse too rarely found.

DOMAINE JACQUES PRIEUR—Owner of a 3.1-acre plot near the base of the slope. The vines are relatively young, with the oldest about twenty years old. Good Clos de Vougeot, but nothing stirring.

DOMAINE HENRI REBOURSEAU—One of the major owners in Clos de Vougeot, with 11.1 acres in the exact center of the clos. The wines are highly regarded. Regrettably, I have not tasted any.

DOMAINE DANIEL RION—Superb Clos de Vougeot from this rising domaine now under the direction of son Patrice Rion. The grapes come from a sharecropping arrangement with M. Denis Cheron (Domaine Misset) from the lower part of the midslope. If nothing else, this rendition proves that grapes from the lower end can create outstanding Clos de Vougeot in capable hands and from sufficiently mature vines (planted in 1956).

DOMAINE GEORGES ROUMIER—One of the outstanding producers of Clos de Vougeot, with 0.8 acre in two parcels, one running vertically from the base to the midslope; the other is situated on the upper slope in the center of the clos. This is reference-standard Clos de Vougeot. The Clos de Vougeot bottling also is sold under the name Hervé Roumier, but is made at Domaine Georges Roumier.

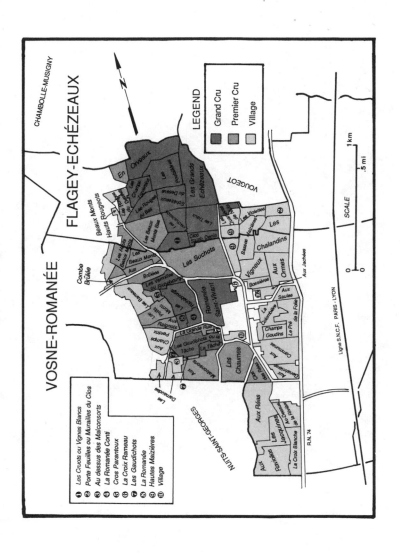

VOSNE-ROMANÉE

FLAGEY-ECHÉZEAUX

CHAMBOLLE-MUSIGNY

LEGEND

Grand Cru
Premier Cru
Village

En Orveaux
Les Poulaillères
Les Grands Echézeaux
Les Cruots
Echézeaux du Dessus
Les Rouges du Bas
Les Loächausses
Clos Saint-Denis
Beaux Monts Bas
Hauts Rougeois
Les Suchots
Beaux Monts Hauts
Les Hauts Beaux Monts
Aux Brûlées
Les Petits Monts
Les Verroilles ou Richebourg
La Grande Rue
Romanée Saint-Vivant
Les Reignots
Aux Raignots
Aux Malconsorts
Les Gaudichots ou la Tâche
La Tâche
Les Chaumes
Les Damaudes
Cros Parantoux
Combe Brûlée

Les Violettes
Les Basses Maizières
Les Chalandins
Vigneux
Aux Ormes
Aux Jachées
Boissières
Aux Saules
La Colombière
Champs Goudins
Le Pré de la Folle
Aux Communes
Aux Genaivrières
Aux Réas
Aux Ravlottes
Les Jacquines
Au Dessus de la Rivière
La Croix Blanche

VOUGEOT

NUITS-SAINT-GEORGES

R.N. 74

Ligne S.N.C.F. PARIS - LYON

SCALE

0   .5 mi
0   1 km

① Les Cruots ou Vignes Blancs
② Porte Feuilles ou Murailles du Clos
③ Au dessus des Malconsorts
④ La Romanée Conti
⑤ Cros Parantoux
⑥ La Croix Rameau
⑦ Les Gaudichots
⑧ La Romanée
⑨ Hautes Maizières
⑩ Village

Vosne-Romanée

No comment on Vosne-Romanée is more famous than that of the eighteenth century abbot and historian Courtépée. (His coauthor, a lawyer named Beguillet, somehow has long since been forgotten.) It's an airy, aristocratic observation. Too bad it's not true.

To be fair, in the context of most of the wines of Courtépée's day, the vulgarity of which could bring a horse back from a faint, it probably was an accurate commentary. Even poor Vosne wines have a refinement. But today, refinement has blossomed in the most unlikely places. Vosne-Romanée is no longer an isolated oasis of refinement. Now, there are too many common wines in Vosne. The fame is resounding, the prices correspondingly high, and the Vosniers, *à la* Liberace, coast all the way to the bank.

Commune-level Vosne-Romanée is the riskiest bet of any *village* wine in Burgundy. The name conjures up a vision of the spicy fragrance found in the *grands crus*. Too rarely is even a whiff of this found in the commune-level wines. That it could be achieved is proved by the occasional bottling of real quality. Of course, it won't have the stuffings or the breed of the *premiers* or *grands crus*, but the family resemblance is unmistakable.

Viticulturally, Vosne-Romanée embraces two communes: Vosne-Romanée proper and Flagey-Echézeaux, which lies sandwiched between Vosne-Romanée and Vougeot. All of the wines of Flagey-Echézeaux are entitled to be sold as Vosne-Romanée.

THE VINEYARDS

There are 98.5678 ha/243.6 acres of commune-level Vosne-Romanée. Of this, 210.2 acres are located in Vosne-Romanée and 33.4 acres in Flagey-Echézeaux.

The best producers of commune-level Vosne-Romanée are (not surprisingly) those who issue the best *premiers* and *grands crus*. Look for producers such as Domaine Jean Gros, Domaine Gros Frère et Soeur, Leroy, Domaine Georges Mugneret, Domaine René Engel, and Domaine Jean Grivot. (See the listings under The Premiers Crus.)

THE PREMIERS CRUS

It is at the *premier cru* level that the undeniable distinction of Vosne-Romanée makes itself known. Truly, there are no common Vosne-Romanée *premiers crus*. It is an exclusive club: just fifteen vineyards. Inevitably, some are better than others, but nearly all of them are worthy of investigation.

A good Vosne *premier cru* should project the velvety texture for which Vosne is famed, along with a pronounced earthy/spicy *goût de terroir*. The wine should not be at all grapey, but rather, should smack of a more resonant flavor allied with noticeable richness. It should be memorable.

LA GRANDE RUE—Pride of place belongs to this odd little vineyard. The oddness is not the wine, which is fine (although not great) but the fact that it is a *premier cru* rather than a *grand cru*. Wine lovers, poring over their maps, can surely be forgiven for wondering how a 3.5-acre slice of vineyard wedged between Romanée-Conti and La Tâche could possibly have escaped being *grand cru*.

A *monopole* of Domaine Lamarche, which acquired it in 1933, La Grande Rue was classed *premier cru* in 1936 because the owner, Henri Lamarche, refused to apply for *grand cru* status. His heirs say that he didn't want to shoulder the expense involved in applying for *grand cru* status, what with the cost of supplying the documentary evidence required for such consideration. After all, it was the Depression, and the prices fetched everywhere in Burgundy were derisory. Although this reluctance was understandable, even more likely was an unwillingness to pay the increased taxes that inevitably would follow from being classified *grand cru*. It is a supreme example of short-sightedness.

During the recalibration of the Burgundy vineyard performed by INAO in the early 1980s, the current owner of La Grande Rue, Henri's son, François, applied for an upgrade in 1984. With that, INAO initiated soil analyses of the vineyard (to compare it with neighboring *grands crus*), wine tastings, consultations with neighboring growers, and, above all, a general feeling out of the acceptability of such a move in the Burgundian community. Precedent for such an upgrade from *premier cru* to *grand cru* had been established with the elevation of Clos des Lambrays in Morey-Saint-Denis in 1981. It was the first such change since the original designations in the 1930s.

As of this writing, La Grande Rue has yet to be canonized *grand cru*. Such a ruling can, however, be made retroactive and apply to a vintage prior to the date of the formal declaration. Many observers expect the 1988 vintage, for example, to be allowed to be labeled *grand cru* should the ascension come to pass.

The wine itself, from the few bottles I've tasted, appears to be exceptionally refined, but nowhere in the same league as its neighbors. Nevertheless, it provides superb finesse, although one could wish for more stuffings. The winemaking is reported to be variable according to tasters who have had the opportunity to taste multiple vintages of La Grande Rue.

AUX MALCONSORTS—One of the three *premiers crus* adjoining Nuits-Saint-Georges (the others are Les Chaumes and Clos des Réas), it shares with them a characteristic meatiness and concentration. Regrettably, the major owner in Aux Malconsorts is the *négociant* Moillard, which issues a pasteurized, deeply colored, weighty but one-dimensional wine.

CLOS DES RÉAS—A monopole of Domaine Jean Gros, this exceptional vineyard should not be confused with the much larger, commune-level Aux Réas which is contiguous. As with Malconsorts, you find a knife-and-fork richness allied with the stirring *goût de terroir* that sets apart the best Vosne-Romanées from all other red Burgundies.

AUX BRÛLÉES AND CROS PARANTOUX—One of the grouping of *premiers crus* perched high on the slope. The others are the four *climats* of Les Beaux Monts. Aux Brûlées and Cros Parantoux have single-handedly been made famous by the remarkable winemaking of the now-retired Henri Jayer. In his hands, both vineyards displayed a profound earthiness that few other Vosne-Romanées could equal.

LES BEAUX MONTS—Actually composed of four *climats* sharing a common name, this vineyard issues lighter wines of unusually pronounced stoniness. Here, the higher elevation and stonier soils create intensely perfumed wine unlike the richer, meatier wines found near Nuits-Saint Georges, with less weight but undeniable flavor impact.

LES PETITS MONTS—Like the similarly named Beaux Monts, this fine vineyard is fascinating, if only because it is so different from the *grand cru* Richebourg, which it adjoins. But Petits Monts is at a higher elevation, with less rich soil. The resulting wine is strikingly earthy/spicy, but without the foundation-shaking weight of Richebourg. Beautifully fragrant wine, though.

LES SUCHOTS—The largest of the *premiers crus* and the least satisfying. This vineyard, too, is sandwiched between *grands crus*: Romanée-Saint-Vivant and Richebourg to the south and Echézeaux to the north. Yet no one would suggest that Les Suchots is of *grand cru* stature. The wine typically is light in weight and with little punch.

LES BEAUX MONTS—11.3871 ha/28.1 acres divided into four *climats*: Les Beaux Monts (5.8 acres); Les Hauts Beaux Monts (5 acres); Les Beaux Monts Bas (13.4 acres); and Les Beaux Monts Hauts (3.9 acres)

Les Hauts Beaux Monts

	Hectares	Acres	Cases*
M. et Mme. Maurice Chevallier	0.3277	0.8	173
Mme. Veuve Fernand Girardin and M. Gérard Girardin	0.3141	0.8	166
M. et Mme. Jean Grivot	0.1207	0.3	64
Mme. Pierre Lamadon	0.0270	0.1	14
M. et Mme. Jean-François Raillard	0.0450	0.1	24
M. et Mme. Daniel Rion	0.9678	2.4	511
Mme. Denis Tremblay	0.1493	0.4	79

Les Beaux Monts

	Hectares	Acres	Cases*
SCI Noëllat (now Domaine Leroy)	2.3550	5.8	1243

Aux Brûlées—4.5329 ha/11.2 acres divided into two *climats*: Aux Brûlées (9.3 acres) and La Combe Brûlée (1.9 acres)

Aux Brûlées

	Hectares	Acres	Cases*
GFA Les Arbaupins	0.6301	1.6	333
GFA Domaine Camuzet	0.7002	1.7	370
M. Serge Confuron	0.1173	0.3	62
M. René Engel	1.0513	2.6	555
M. et Mme. Jean Grivot	0.1435	0.4	76
M. Pierre Guyon	0.1521	0.4	80
Mme. Pierre Lamadon	0.1157	0.3	61
M. Gérard Mugneret			
Mme. Jacqueline Mugneret			
M. René Mugneret	0.0947	0.2	50
M. René Mugneret	0.1750	0.4	92
SCI Noëllat (now Domaine Leroy)	0.2713	0.7	143
M. Henri Noirot	0.0310	0.1	16
M. Serge Sirugue	0.0360	0.1	19

*Cases calculated on the *rendement de base* of 40 hl/ha plus 20 percent

	Hectares	Acres	Cases*
La Combe Brûlée			
M. et Mme. Jules Brosson	0.5482	1.4	289
M. et Mme. Michel Chevallier	0.3323	0.8	175
M. et Mme. Michel Chevigny	0.0524	0.1	28
M. René Engel	0.1671	0.4	88
GFA Domaine Gerbet	0.0184	0.1	10
M. et Mme. Bernard Thomas	0.0345	0.1	18
Les Chaumes—6.4555 ha/16 acres			
M. Robert Arnoux	0.7362	1.8	389
Mme. Albert Bedhet	0.1349	0.3	71
Maison Albert Bichot	0.1240	0.3	65
GFA du Domaine Camuzet	1.5498	3.8	818
M. Joseph Cathiard			
SCI Château de Vosne-Romanée	0.1175	0.3	62
M. Joseph Confuron	0.1664	0.4	88
M. Jean Grivot	0.1527	0.4	81
M. François Lamarche			
Mme. François Lamarche	0.4207	1.0	222
M. Henri Lamarche	0.1397	0.4	74
M. Pierre Magnien	0.1475	0.4	78
M. Jean Méo	0.4571	1.1	241
M. Marcel Mitre	0.0361	0.1	19
M. Robert Noblet	0.2423	0.6	128
M. Georges Noëllat	0.2378	0.6	126
M. Michel Noëllat	0.1296	0.3	68
Mme. Hervé Pacareau			
M. Daniel Rion	0.4106	1.0	217
M. Marcel Rion	0.4562	1.1	241
M. Georges Thomas	0.3644	0.9	192
M. François Tisserandot	0.0354	0.1	19
Mme. André Tupinier	0.3720	0.9	196
Mme. André Wilhelm	0.3943	1.0	208
Clos des Réas—2.1245 ha/5.2 acres			
GFA Jean Gros	2.1166	5.2	1118
La Croix Rameau—0.5987 ha/1.4 acres			
Mme. Veuve Denis Bizot	0.2020	0.5	107
M. et Mme. Jacques Cacheux	0.1560	0.4	82
Mme. Jacques Coudray			

---

*Cases calculated on the *rendement de base* of 40 hl/ha plus 20 percent

	Hectares	Acres	Cases*
M. Henri Lamarche and Mme. Hervé Pacareau	0.1483	0.4	78
Mme. Hervé Pacareau	0.0622	0.2	33

Cros Parantoux—1.0127 ha/2.5 acres

GFA Domaine Camuzet	0.2950	0.7	156
M. Henri Jayer	0.7177	1.8	379

Les Gaudichots—1.0283 ha/2.5 acres

M. Jean Forey	0.0953	0.2	50
M. Pierre Hudelot	0.2009	0.5	106
M. François Lamarche and M. Henri Lamarche	0.2318	0.6	122
SC Domaine de la Romanée-Conti	0.0829	0.2	44
Mme. Veuve André Thomas and Mme. Odile Thomas	0.1957	0.5	103
SCI du Clos de Thorey (Moillard)	0.2365	0.6	125

La Grande Rue—1.4207 ha/3.5 acres

M. François Lamarche and M. Henri Lamarche	1.4207	3.5	750

Aux Malconsorts—5.8583 ha/14.5 acres

Maison Albert Bichot	1.7766	4.4	938
M. André Cathiard	0.7435	1.8	393
M. Alain Hudelot	0.1370	0.3	72
M. Henri Lamarche and Mme. Hervé Pacareau	0.4999	1.2	264
SCI du Clos de Thorey (Moillard)	2.7013	6.7	1426

En Orveaux—1.7855 ha/4.4 acres

Les Petits Monts—3.6681 ha/9.1 acres

Mme. Marie Boquillon-Liger-Belair	0.0973	0.2	51
M. Gabriel Bonot	0.1189	0.3	63
M. Michel Chevigny	0.0533	0.1	28
SCI Domaine Clair-Daü-Bartet	0.0780	0.2	41
GFA Domaine Gerbetsi	0.2844	0.7	150

---

*Cases calculated on the *rendement de base* of 40 hl/ha plus 20 percent

	Hectares	Acres	Cases*
Mme. Veuve Fernand Girardin and M. Guy Girardin	0.1849	0.5	98
Mme. Veuve Fernand Girardin and M. Gérard Girardin	0.1849	0.5	98
Mme. Alain Hudelot	0.2154	0.5	114
M. Lucien Jayer	0.0658	0.2	35
Mme. Pierre Lamadon	0.1297	0.3	68
M. Paul Magnien	0.1150	0.3	61
M. René Magnien and Mme. Veuve René Magnien	0.1764	0.4	93
M. Marcel Mitre	0.0932	0.2	49
M. André Noblet	0.1718	0.4	91
M. Georges Noëllat	0.2138	0.5	113
M. Pierre Pasquier	0.1627	0.4	86
Mme. Eugène Picard and Mme. Veuve Eugène Picard	0.1698	0.4	90
SC Domaine de la Romanée-Conti	0.4050	1.0	214
Safer	0.3021	0.8	160
M. Serge Sirugue	0.3438	0.9	182
M. Roland Vigot	0.1799	0.4	95

Aux Raignots—1.6180 ha/4 acres

	Hectares	Acres	Cases*
M. Robert Arnoux	0.2202	0.5	116
M. Alfred Cathiard	0.2438	0.6	129
Mme. Jacqueline Jayer	0.0746	0.2	39
M. Louis Michaudet	0.0435	0.1	23
M. Marcel Mitre	0.0943	0.2	50
Mme. Eugène Pernin and M. André Pernin	0.0508	0.1	27
M. Jean Picard	0.0446	0.1	24
SC Domaine de la Romanée-Conti	0.0360	0.1	19
M. Serge Sirugue	0.0345	0.1	18
SCI Domaine de Vosne-Romanée	0.6959	1.7	367

Les Rouges du Dessus—2.6195 ha/6.5 acres

Les Suchots—13.0760 ha/32.3 acres

	Hectares	Acres	Cases*
M. Robert Arnoux	0.4290	1.1	227

---

*Cases calculated on the *rendement de base* of 40 hl/ha plus 20 percent

	Hectares	Acres	Cases*
M. Lucien Audidier and GFA Maitrot Audidier	0.2443	0.6	129
M. Jean Claude Blée and Mme. Veuve Louis Blée	0.2159	0.5	114
Mme. Veuve Louis Blée and	0.2159	0.5	114
Mme. Alain Boigey	0.6832	1.7	361
M. Alain Bourcier and SC Domaine André Bourcier	0.2244	0.6	118
M. Gabriel Boyeaux			
M. Jules Brosson	0.2159	0.5	114
M. Jacques Cacheux	0.4266	1.1	225
Mme. René Cacheux	0.9531	2.4	503
M. André Cathiard	0.1630	0.4	86
M. Roger Chevallier and M. Yves Chevallier	0.3224	0.8	170
M. Jacky Confuron	0.3409	0.8	180
M. Joseph Confuron	1.3432	3.3	709
M. Joseph Confuron and M. Serge Confuron	0.2568	0.6	136
Mme. Veuve Henri Gouroux and Mme. René Moissenet	0.5018	1.2	265
Mme. Alain Hudelot	0.4535	1.1	239
Mme. Pierre Lamadon	0.2192	0.5	116
M. Henri Lamarche and Mme. René Pacareau	0.3652	0.9	193
GFA Domaine Chantal Lescure	0.4252	1.1	225
M. Marc Manière	0.8216	2.0	434
Mme. Jacqueline Mugneret and M. René Mugneret	0.1861	0.5	98
M. René Mugneret and M. Gérard Mugneret	0.1861	0.5	98
Mme. Lucette Noëllat	0.5728	1.4	302
M. Michel Noëllat	0.7994	2.0	422
M. Georges Poinsot	0.4253	1.1	225

---

*Cases calculated on the *rendement de base* of 40 hl/ha plus 20 percent

	Hectares	Acres	Cases*
M. Michel Roblin	0.8504	2.1	449
SC Domaine de la Romanée-Conti	1.0190	2.5	538
Mme. Veuve André Thomas and Mme. Odile Thomas	0.2158	0.5	114

PRODUCERS WORTH SEEKING OUT (AND SOME NOT)

ALBERT BICHOT/DOMAINE DU CLOS FRANTIN—One of the largest *négociants*, Bichot offers some of its choicest wines under the Clos du Frantin label: Clos de Vougeot; Echézeaux; Grands Echézeaux; and Vosne-Romanée "Les Malconsorts," along with a commune-level Gevrey-Chambertin and Nuits-Saint-Georges. The wines are variable in quality, usually hard, tannic, and sometimes tasting a bit "cooked," like so many of Bichot's regular offerings. In a good vintage such as 1985 or '88, they are worth investigating. Rarely, if ever, are they top rank.

DOMAINE MICHEL CLERGET—The Chambolle-Musigny producer is the source of some of the most intense, concentrated, sublime Echézeaux from very old vines.

DOMAINE JACKY CONFURON-COTETIDOT—The controversial Vosne-Romanée producer has been discussed elsewhere (See Cold Maceration). The wines are produced under the guidance of consulting enologist Guy Accad: Vosne-Romanée; Vosne "Suchots"; Clos de Vougeot; Nuits-Saint-Georges Premier Cru (partly from Aux Murgers); commune-level Nuits-Saint-Georges and Chambolle-Musigny; and a Bourgogne *rouge* from vines just outside of Vosne-Romanée.

The Accad influence is all over these wines: They are dark and opulently fruity but deprived of detail or *terroir*. They have appeal, but only to the extent that they are pleasant drinking for those unconcerned with the distinctions of site.

---

*Cases calculated on the *rendement de base* of 40 hl/ha plus 20 percent

JOSEPH DROUHIN—Excellent Grands Echézeaux from a 1.25-acre plot; good Echézeaux from a one-acre plot; and reliable commune-level Vosne. Among the *négociants*, all of whom have a difficult time obtaining a supply of grapes or wines from Vosne-Romanée, Drouhin is among the most reliable.

DOMAINE DUJAC—The Morey-Saint-Denis producer issues top-rank Echézeaux from a 1.6-acre parcel. The Dujac style lends itself superbly to the light elegance of Echézeaux.

DOMAINE RENÉ ENGEL—Philippe Engel has improved the wines from this Vosne-Romanée-based estate after taking over the domaine upon the untimely death of his father in 1981. The current style emphasizes freshness and bright, clean fruit, but not at the expense of overwhelming or obscuring the *terroir*. The commune-level Vosne-Romanée is always a good buy and one of the best renditions of this beleaguered category. The Echézeaux is lovely, but inevitably is dwarfed by the concentration and intensity of the Grands Echézeaux. The Vosne-Romanée "Les Brûlées" comes from young vines, and consequently lacks the stuffings this vineyard can offer. Still, it's appealing drinking.

DOMAINE JEAN GRIVOT—This estate came under the guidance of consulting enologist Guy Accad, starting with the 1987 vintage. Amazingly, Grivot subjected all of his vineyards to Accad's extended cold-maceration technique. One cannot doubt Grivot's conviction as to its merit. Barrel samples of the 1987s, '88s, and '89s of Grivot's Vosne-Romanée "Les Beaumonts," Echézeaux, Clos de Vougeot, and Richebourg left me profoundly depressed. The *terroirs* were nowhere to be found, not even in the Richebourg. All of the wines certainly were dark to the point of opaque and seemed enormously fruity. But the fruit was mute. Maybe time in the bottle will amplify the voice of the land that I couldn't discern.

DOMAINE JEAN GROS—One of the top domaines of Vosne-Romanée. Keeping the wines of the Gros family straight can be a challenge. The original estate was Domaine Louis Gros. He had four children: Jean, François, Gustave, and Colette. When he died, the property was divided among his widow, Marie-Louise Gros, and their children. Three domaines emerged: Gros Frerè et Soeur; François Gros; and Jean Gros.

Domaine Jean Gros is owned by the widow of the late Jean Gros. Their son Michel is the winemaker. The signature wine of this estate is the *premier cru* Clos des Réas, which is a *monopole*. It is classic Vosne, with all the spice and violets one seeks but too rarely finds. Far finer, of course, is the Richebourg, which is massively concentrated, tannic, and reference-standard. This is one of the great estates of Vosne-Romanée, producing concentrated, finely detailed wines. These are wines against which others are judged.

DOMAINE GROS FRÈRE ET SOEUR—Domaine Gros Frère et Soeur is the domaine created by Colette (*soeur*) and the late Gustave (*frère*). The wine is made by Colette's nephew, Bernard, who is the son of her brother, the late Jean Gros. Bernard's brother, Michel, makes the wine for Domaine Jean Gros.

The style of winemaking here is different from that of Domaine Jean Gros: more exuberantly fruity, softer and accessible sooner. The concentration is undeniable, but sometimes the sheer fruitiness of the wines can be fatiguing. The intensity of the extraordinary *cassis* taste can make you wonder.

DOMAINE FRANÇOIS GROS—I am unfamiliar with the wines of this domaine, the third division of the former Louis Gros estate. The wines are made by Anne Gros, who is the young cousin of Michel and Bernard.

DOMAINE HENRI JAYER—The legendary Burgundy winemaker of the 1980s Henri Jayer retired from active, full-time winemaking with the 1988 vintage, after a lifetime (born 1922) of meticulous vine-tending and winemaking. Jayer's wines captured the attention of Burgundy connoisseurs for the intensity and purity of the fruit, the unusually deep color, and the profundity of the wines over time.

One of Jayer's innovative techniques was the cold maceration of unfermented grape juice with the skins (and no stems) for four to six days before starting the fermentation. The fermentation then is allowed to begin, but Jayer prolongs it as long as possible. The newly made wine thus spends about three weeks on the skins, in addition to the weeklong prefermentation cold maceration.

Less frequently noted is that Jayer's vines are pruned severely for reduced yields, well below the ostensible maximum yields set by the regulations. Cold maceration surely gave the wines unusually deep color. Jayer says that it also adds more fragrance and richness to the wines. But the undeniable character comes from the grapes. Jayer is, above all, a vineyardist.

He has tended two sets of vines: his own holdings and some of those of what is now called Domaine Méo-Camuzet. Jayer's holdings are small, less than six acres. Most of what was issued under the Henri Jayer label came from the holdings of the Camuzet family, whose vineyards Jayer tended *en métayage* since 1944. He took care of the vines and made the wine, getting half of the production for his services. Until 1983, they sold their portion to *négociants*. With his contract with the Méo family ending in the mid-'80s, Jayer decided it was time to retire. His nephew, Emmanuel Rouget, who has worked with Jayer since 1982, will work Jayer's vines in Echézeaux and Cros Parantoux under a similar sharecropping arrangement. Wines already have appeared under his own label, starting with the 1985 vintage. Henri Jayer now consults under contract to Domaine Méo-Camuzet through 1992, as well as to his nephew and others.

DOMAINE JACQUELINE JAYER—The wines of Jacqueline Jayer are made at Domaine Jean Grivot, as Jean Grivot is her brother-in-law. The wines include a commune-level Vosne-Romanée, Vosne-Romanée "Les Rouges," Nuits-Saint-Georges "Les Lavières," and an Echézeaux. Presumably, they will be made in the same Guy Accad–influenced fashion as Grivot's own wines.

DOMAINE ROBERT JAYER-GILLES—Yet another Jayer, although how Robert Jayer is related to the others I do not know (I think that Henri and Jacqueline are his cousins). One thing is certain: He makes lovely wines, although not much of them. The Jayer-Gilles specialty is Hautes Côtes de Nuits and Hautes Côtes de Beaune, both of which are superb if overly oaky. He often uses uses 100 percent new oak for his red wines (there is a white Hautes Côtes de Beaune made from Pinot Blanc, as well) and the lighter weight of the Hautes Côtes wines do not seem to support the vanilla oakiness as well as could be hoped. But the quality and purity of the fruit is superb. The same applies to his Côte de Nuits-Villages.

The standout wine though, is the Echézeaux. Here, the oak presents no problem: The concentration and definition are outstanding. This is reference-standard Echézeaux.

DOMAINE HENRI LAMARCHE—One of the major landholders in Vosne-Romanée. Lamarche owns plots in Suchots, Malconsorts, Echézeaux, Grands Echézeaux, and the *monopole* of La Grande Rue, as well as a plot in Clos de Vougeot. The wines are variable. This is a producer worth investigating in the strongest and best vintages, but worth watching all the same.

LOUIS LATOUR—Latour's presence in Vosne-Romanée is found in their Romanée Saint-Vivant "Les Quatre Journaux." A *journal* is an ancient measurement of area, usually related to a day's work by a man. Many parts of France employed the term *journal*, but the area differed, depending upon the type of work being done. In Burgundy, where vine-tending is time-consuming, a *journal* was 0.8 acre. This really was about a week's work. Burgundy's term for a day's work was the *ouvrée*, one tenth of an acre. Eight *ouvrées* made a *journal*. (In Lorraine, a *journal* was one half acre; in the Landes district near Bordeaux it was one acre for poor land, but a little less for good land.)

Les Quatre Journaux should, literally, be about 3.4 acres. The Latour holding actually is 1.9 acres. Presumably, it came from a larger plot of that name that has since been subdivided. The name is more charming than the wine, which is inexcusably light and lacking in flavor definition, even in vintages as ripe as 1985.

DOMAINE LEROY—The *négociant* Leroy purchased the former Domaine Charles Noëllat in July 1988 for a reported $11.2 million for about thirty-five acres of vines, the 1987 crop, the substantial inventory of older bottlings, the winery, and houses of the estate. Now Domaine Leroy, it rightfully should be called Domaine Lalou, because it is the creation and life's ambition of majority owner Lalou Bize-Leroy (born 1932).

I happened to be with Lalou the day she took possession of the property, tramping the vineyards to examine the often-ancient vines and witnessing her unconcealed dismay at the shabbiness of the winery facilities. By her side was André Porcheret, the former wine-maker of the Hospices de Beaune whom Lalou lured away by offering him a reasonable recompense compared to the pittance of a salary paid by the Hospices. (They were outraged at Lalou's audacity, demanding him back. Porcheret refused to return, even after they offered him a matching salary to that of Domaine Leroy.)

I did not visit the property again until late 1989. The winery was virtually unrecognizable from the tatty shambles I first saw. Only the walls remained. Everything else was removed. In an amazingly short time, in fact just days before the 1989 harvest was about to begin (and it was early that year), Lalou Bize-Leroy and André Porcheret had the winery of their dreams. It is a jewel, an amalgam of tradition and high-tech.

The grapes arrive in small plastic baskets designed to prevent the crushing of the grapes, and are transferred directly to a mesh conveyor belt that shakes the clusters gently to rid the grapes of any excess moisture clinging to them. The clusters then pass through three powerful blowers, the first two with cool air, the final one with warm air. The clusters then gently fall into small stainless-steel bins like those of a hod carrier. These are carried off by forklift to a crusher to gently rupture the skins and are then carried off to large, upright, open-topped oak casks for the fermentation and maceration. The grapes are tipped into the cask.

The perimeter of the fermentation room is lined with these upright oak casks. Above them, mounted on the ceiling, is a steel rail. This rail carries an overhead hydraulic plunger that can descend to within a few inches of the base of the cask. It replicates the traditional punching-down action that growers once had to do by hand (and still do), using long-handled poles with a flat plate at the end.

Interestingly, the oak casks are temperature-controlled by a flexible plastic *drapeur* (radiator) through which cold or hot water runs as needed. The temperature of each cask is monitored by computer and controlled to within one degree of the desired temperature. This particular *drapeur* is essential to the system because, being flexible, it can be carried down by the hydraulic plunger without harm. The fermentation and maceration typically extend for about three weeks, whereupon the must is pressed and the wines transferred to 100 percent new oak barrels.

When I tasted the wines from these new barrels, I was surprised that none of them, including the first-ever 1988 vintage, which was just about ready for bottling, tasted the least bit oaky. I asked Porcheret how he managed to avoid this common pitfall in using new oak barrels, and he explained that he cleaned each barrel with salt, and multiple rinsings of water, before using it.

Since the original Noëllat purchase in 1988, Leroy also purchased Domaine Remy in Gevrey-Chambertin with 8.5 acres, thereby adding to an already formidable collection of vineyards in Chambertin, Latricières-Chambertin, and Clos de la Roche. Yet another purchase snared one acre in Puligny-Montrachet "Les Folatières" and a parcel of Corton "Renardes." The total now is about sixty-two acres, including the vineyards previously owned by the *négociant* business of Leroy. "Domaine Lalou" is now one of the most important estates in Burgundy.

And how are the wines? Based upon tastings only from the barrel—keeping in mind that Leroy's record for cellaring and bottling is beyond reproach—they are stunning. No doubt the prices will be, too. Nevertheless, the Richebourg and Romanée Saint-Vivant of Domaine Leroy will likely equal or exceed the magnificent standard already set by the Domaine de la Romanée-Conti. However, side-by-side tastings are not yet possible, so this is speculation at present. (Such comparisons, which are inevitable, will probably exacerbate the friction already caused by Lalou Bize's decision not to fold these two holdings into the DRC portfolio and, instead, issue competing wines.)

The style of all of the wines is characteristically Leroy: massive concentration allied to almost digital definition of the individual *terroirs*. The red wines are structured for long aging, a Leroy signature. The white wines are rich, opulent, and, like the Leroy whites, somehow old-fashioned.

DOMAINE MÉO-CAMUZET—This is a label that did not exist until the 1983 vintage. It is a choice example of how new Burgundy estates emerge seemingly from nowhere. The Camuzet and Méo families have long owned prime parcels in Clos de Vougeot, Richebourg, and Corton, and multiple *premiers crus* in Vosne-Romanée and Nuits-Saint-Georges. The two families are related. Étienne Camuzet (who died in 1946) was the great-uncle of Jean Méo.

The Camuzet vines were tended by Henri Jayer, who also made the wine under a sharecropping arrangement. When Mme. Camuzet, who was childless, died in 1959, she left the vineyards to her cousin Jean Méo. A graduate of the prestigious École Polytechnique, which has long been the feeder university for high-level French bureaucrats, Méo, now sixty-three, had a distinguished career under President Charles de Gaulle, which included a stint as the head of the state-owned ELF petroleum company. Later, he became the head of an advertising agency and a deputy to the European Parliament in the early 1980s.

A domaine of some twenty-five acres, Méo-Camuzet blazed onto the Burgundian scene with unusual brightness, courtesy of the prominent vineyard holdings. The association with Henri Jayer (who tended only the former Camuzet vines, not those of Méo) certainly added luster to the brand-new estate. Management of the estate is newly in the hands of Jean Méo's son, Jean-Nicolas. Henri Jayer was retained as a consultant through 1992.

The wines of this promising property, Jayer's involvement notwithstanding, have been disappointingly uneven. The '83s suffered from the taste of rot and hail (as did so many other producers' wines); the '84s were diluted beyond redemption; but the '85s were stunning and made one hunger for future Méo-Camuzet bottlings. Regrettably, the '86s did not show well at all, having failed to overcome the dilution problem of that wet, but redeemable, harvest. The '87s and '88s are reported to be promising, so I await with anticipation. Given the superb vineyards and the consulting presence of Henri Jayer, this could prove to be one of the star estates of the 1990s. We shall see.

MOILLARD/CLOS DE THOREY/DOMAINE THOMAS-MOILLARD—

Moillard wines seem to attract those who want their Burgundies to resemble Cabernets: inky-dark, powerfully fruity, and fairly tannic. Distinctions of *terroir* take a backseat, if they are admitted at all. Moillard delivers these goods, pasteurizing them along the way just to make sure that nothing gets lost. Nothing does—except *terroir*.

Domaine Thomas-Moillard is the new name used for some of Moillard's estate-bottlings, notably the Vosne-Romanée "Les Malconsorts." "Clos de Thorey" was previously used, and is still found on the label as well.

DOMAINE GEORGES MUGNERET/MUGNERET-GIBOURG—One of the great Burgundy producers. The wines of the late Dr. Georges Mugneret also are sold under the Mugneret-Gibourg name. This particular Mugneret (there are at least half a dozen in Vosne-Romanée) issues some of the most beautifully detailed Echézeaux available. Also, top-rank commune-level Vosne-Romanée, as well as great Clos de Vougeot; Ruchottes-Chambertin, Chambolle-Musigny "Les Feusselottes," and Nuits-Saint-Georges "Les Chaignots." The style is pure, accurate, and high-impact, without a great show of weight.

DOMAINE MONGEARD-MUGNERET—This estate has a great many fans and with good reason. I can't say that I am one of them, although I can easily see the attraction. On the plus side, Mongeard-Mugneret not only owns parcels in Richebourg, Echézeaux, Grands Echézeaux, Clos de Vougeot, and Vosne-Romanée "Les Suchots," among others, but clearly provides the goods. The wines usually have excellent concentration and depth. However, they too often appear overly rustic and too oaky for this palate. They are good wines, but I think that they could be better yet—more refined, less oaky, and with even greater definition. Still, they are far better than many others and worth searching out.

DOMAINE PERNIN-ROSSIN—I have not tasted Pernin-Rossin's wines in recent years. It should be noted that this domaine now retains Guy Accad as a consultant for its winemaking.

DOMAINE DANIEL-RION—The Nuits-Saint-Georges producer issues two superb bottlings of Vosne *premiers crus*: Les [Hauts] Beaux Monts and Les Chaumes, as well as an excellent commune-level Vosne-Romanée. The bright fruitiness of the Rion style serves these wines well, as the earthy qualities are heightened without being blurred.

DOMAINE ROBERT SIRUGUE—A small domaine with a piece of Grands Echézeaux and Vosne "Petits Monts" that creates lovely wines. The only drawback is that they can be a little oaky. That aside, this is a top-rank producer.

DOMAINE DE LA ROMANÉE-CONTI—For many Burgundy drinkers, this is *the* domaine. And who could blame anybody for thinking so? After all, DRC (which abbreviation seems to be exclusively an American fashion) owns all of Romanée-Conti; all of La Tâche; half of Romanée Saint-Vivant; one third of Richebourg; one third of Grands Echézeaux; 1.05 acres of Echézeaux; and 1.7 acres of Le Montrachet. All of these are estate-bottled.

What is less well known is what *else* the Domaine de la Romanée-Conti owns: a half-acre of Bâtard-Montrachet; 3.8 acres of *premier cru* Vosne-Romanée (2.7 acres of Suchots and one acre of Les Petits Monts, among others); and 8.27 acres of commune-level Vosne-Romanée. These wines or grapes are sold in bulk to *négociants*.

Indisputably, it is an extraordinary estate, with equally extraordinary resources. It is owned by two families: de Villaine and Leroy. Aubert de Villaine, fifty, and Lalou Bize-Leroy, fifty-eight, are the co-directors of the property, both representing their respective family interests. The origins of the Domaine de la Romanée-Conti began in 1867, when the namesake Romanée-Conti vineyard was sold to a *négociant* in Santenay named J. M. Duvaut-Blochet, who already had amassed significant vineyard holdings. Over the years, Duvaut-Blochet assembled what we now know as the Domaine de la Romanée-Conti. And his family owned it all.

In 1942, Aubert de Villaine's father (a descendant of the Duvaut-Blochets) sold half of the Domaine de la Romanée-Conti to his longtime friend Henri Leroy, a *négociant* in Auxey-Duresses who had made his fortune selling bulk wine and brandy from the Cognac region to Asbach, the big German brandy producer. Henri Leroy (who died at eighty-five in 1979) had two daughters, each of whom owns one quarter of the Domaine de la Romanée-Conti: Lalou Bize-Leroy and her sister, Pauline, who lives in Switzerland. The de Villaine shares are more fragmented: ten in all.

The Domaine de la Romanée-Conti can point to two achievements. It has, more often than not, lived up to the obligation of its vineyards. Other producers own extraordinary vineyards and yet fail to issue equally extraordinary wines. Although there have been lapses, the Domaine de la Romanée-Conti feels its charge keenly and has been faithful to it.

Its other achievement is commercial. The Domaine de la Romanée-Conti has convinced buyers that it alone is somehow exempt from the notorious variability of Burgundy. The Domaine de la Romanée-Conti has come to be considered a guarantee of great Burgundy, regardless of vintage. It is the only true brand name in Burgundy. This was achieved as a result of a sincere and often expensive effort in the vineyard and winery. It also came from a savvy recognition of the necessity for publicity, which has now become as much a burden as a benefit for the two co-directors.

The domaine goes to great lengths to point out to visitors and, especially, journalists, its expensive risk-taking in harvesting grapes later than just about any other grower. You will see photographs of grapes being harvested in the snow. Its yields are significantly, even dramatically, lower than those of many other estates. Over and over, the degree of painstaking, almost monkish care that the domaine bestows upon its wines has been drummed into buyers' minds through a ceaseless flow of articles in magazines and newspapers. And it is all true. Aubert de Villaine and Lalou Bize-Leroy are committed with full heart to what they themselves recognize is a moral, rather than a mercantile, duty—a guardianship rather than an ownership. In a cynical age, such an assertion may be difficult to swallow, but nothing that I have seen or heard leads me to any other conclusion.

That said, it must also be pointed out that the Domaine de la Romanée-Conti is not exempt from Burgundian realities. Its track record is not that much better than that of a dozen other top domaines in Burgundy. All of their sincere care and all of your money do not add up to infallibility.

Where do the lapses occur? Until the 1985 vintage, all of the wines were bottled directly from the barrel. The owners submitted time and again that this was best for the wine. To the extent that limited handling is always to be preferred for Pinot Noir, this was undoubtedly true. But it also spawned a surprising degree of bottle variation. And some of those bottles were nowhere near as good as others. Variation from barrel to barrel happens in every estate and, spoilage notwithstanding, is inexplicable. The problem is that buyers have come to believe that the Domaine de la Romanée-Conti label is a warranty against just such variability. Finally, with the 1985 vintage and afterward, the practice was altered. Now, six barrels are blended together and then bottled. Perhaps a certain greatness from a certain barrel has been lost, but the buyer finally has achieved at least one measure of security that was previously lacking.

Another lapse has been a reluctance upon the part of the Domaine de la Romanée-Conti to remove certain vintages from the market. This is a sensitive area. Keep in mind the kind of money involved. The domaine produces, on average, about ninety-thousand bottles of wine annually. For the sake of perspective, if you figure an average selling price of fifty dollars a bottle (which probably is on the low side), that would mean foregoing all or part of at least $4.5 million. Of course, even if a vintage wasn't issued, it would not require a total loss. The wine simply would be sold to *négociants*—at a far lower return, to be sure.

Clearly, to remove even some wine from even a single vintage would be a staggering financial blow. Nevertheless, it has been done before. In the 1950 and '51 vintages, only La Tâche was released; In the 1960 vintage, only La Tâche and Romanée-Conti were sold; In the 1963 and '65 vintages, no Echézeaux was released; In the 1968 vintage no red wines were sold at all, only Le Montrachet.

The stakes were lower back then. Now, if not prohibitive, they are at least pause-giving. Some might say that not since 1968 has Burgundy experienced a vintage poor enough to warrant withholding a wine from the market. Yet most recently the '83s were badly marked by hail. The 1974 vintage was miserable, as was 1975. Then there were 1977, '81, and '84. The Domaine de la Romanée-Conti released all of its wines in all of these vintages, to mixed receptions.

The issue is not whether the Domaine de la Romanée-Conti can create better wines than other producers in an off-vintage. They can and they do. Nor is it an issue of failing to recognize that every vintage has its particular character. No one has a right to expect a 1979, which was a light but fine vintage, to offer the concentration of its predecessor, the opulent 1978 vintage. Both were good years, in their fashion. But when that fashion incorporates a strong taste of hail, such as in 1983, is it enough to say that this, after all, was the taste of the vintage, and let it go at that? Given the premium exacted by the Domaine de la Romanée-Conti—and the perception of assured quality that makes such a premium possible—the notion that certain wines or vintages do not merit being sold under the DRC label is worth considering. Nor is it without precedent elsewhere, at similar financial burden. Château d'Yquem produces sixty-thousand bottles of its famous wine at a price comparable to the wines of the Domaine de la Romanée-Conti. Yet no Yquem was issued in 1964, '72, and '74. In 1965, only 50 percent of its production was released; in 1968, only 10 percent; in 1973, only 12 percent; in 1978 only 15 percent; and in the fairly good vintage of 1982, the figure was still just 33 percent.

Such reservations about DRC are worth airing. But with that comes the obligation to acknowledge, indeed to celebrate, the exceptional achievement of many DRC vintages. Are the wines of the Domaine de la Romanée-Conti worth the price? The answer has to be yes. In fact, in the very best vintages, they can be said to be cheap relative to the rarity of the production and the breathtaking sensory experience they provide. You will have to search long and hard to find a more memorable wine-drinking moment than any of the 1985s, with the possible exception of the Echézeaux, which was merely outstanding. The 1988s engrave themselves on the mind with comparable incision. Partly it is due to the grandeur of the vineyards. After all, nobody really *makes* La Tâche, Richebourg, Romanée Saint-Vivant, Grands Echézeaux, or Le Montrachet. They are veins of flavor in the earth. But they can be refined. This the Domaine de la Romanée-Conti strains to do—and frequently achieves.

The most consistent wine surely is La Tâche, followed by Richebourg, Romanée-Conti, and Grands Echézeaux. In fact, Grands Echézeaux probably is the bargain wine of DRC, as it sells for only one third more than the Echézeaux, yet is easily two or three times the wine in terms of concentration and complexity. The Montrachet is reference-standard, the one by which others are judged (and almost always found wanting).

Much is made of the manner in which the Domaine de la Romanée-Conti sells its wines. Knowing that everyone wants Romanée-Conti, it uses it as a locomotive to sell the other wines. The formula is simple: A merchant can get one bottle of Romanée-Conti for every fifteen bottles of other wines of the same vintage. Alternatively, a twelve-bottle case is offered at a fixed price. The formula here changes occasionally. For the 1987 vintage, it was: one bottle of Romanée-Conti; three bottles of La Tâche; three bottles of Romanée Saint-Vivant; three bottles of Echézeaux; one bottle of Richebourg; and one bottle of Grands Echézeaux. The Montrachet is far rarer: One bottle is available for every fifty bottles purchased from the same vintage, but only if the total order exceeds fifty cases of assorted wines from the same vintage.

No Burgundy producer is more involved in futures offerings than the Domaine de la Romanée-Conti. Partly this is due to the fame and prestige of the producer. Burgundy lovers want to get in on the deal as soon as possible. Merchants, as always, are happy to allow their customers to assume the risk and financial burden. But the Domaine de la Romanée-Conti is also a player. It demands of the merchants that they pay for the wines in full *before* their arrival. Because of this, merchants are more inclined than ever to offer the wines on futures.

Should you buy DRC futures? Probably not, unless you want multiple cases. Like all Burgundy futures, they are only reservations, rather than any sort of price break. And the quantities involved are such that DRC wines always resurface on the market. Take, for example, the 1985 vintage, which was, until the '88s, the highest-priced DRC wines ever. In the fall of 1987, Marin Wine Cellar in San Rafael, California, which specializes in the rarest wines (selling them at good prices, too), offered futures on the 1985 DRCs as follows: La Tâche $150; Richebourg $150; Grands Echézeaux $125; Romanée Saint-Vivant $146; Echézeaux $90.

By the summer of 1988, Marin's catalog offered the 1985s as follows: Richebourg $225; Grands Echézeaux $140; Echézeaux $79. La Tâche and even Romanée-Conti were available on a "Please Inquire" basis.

In August 1989, Premier Cru wine merchant in Oakland, California, offered '85 La Tâche and Richebourg for $229 a bottle. The Burgundy Wine Company in New York had '85 Romanée Saint-Vivant for $168.75 and La Tâche at $222.50 in July '89.

Clearly, the price increases were not that significant, especially given the already high cost of the wines. And this was for a stupendous vintage that more than lived up to its promise. Certainly, futures buyers made out well with '85s. But not by that much. And less-publicized vintages don't necessarily see price spurts over the years. Unlike Bordeaux wines, Burgundies come in high but rarely rise much in price later on, including the wines of the Domaine de la Romanée-Conti. For example, you can find many 1982 DRC wines selling today for not much more, if any more, than what they commanded upon release. And 1982 was a good vintage for DRC.

But after you get past all the wheeling and dealing; when you have read all of the reports and tasting notes; when you finally get down to actually drinking a bottle of one of the wines of the Domaine de la Romanée-Conti, there is one inescapable conclusion: They are magnificent.

DOMAINE DE LA SCI DU CHÂTEAU DE VOSNE-ROMANÉE— This is the proper name of the estate of the Liger-Belair family, which owns the *grand cru monopole* Romanée, as well as 1.7 acres of of Aux Raignots, the largest holding in that *premier cru* vineyard. The wines are hard, tannic, and long-lived, with real quality, although not of notable finesse or polish. The cellaring, bottling, and distribution are performed by the *négociant* Bouchard Père et Fils.

Romanée-Conti

It took me twenty years to see why Romanée-Conti is the greatest vineyard.

—LALOU BIZE-LEROY,
Co-owner of the Domaine de la Romanée-Conti

I was surprised when Lalou Bize-Leroy confided the remarkable admission quoted above. It was said to me during a conversation on my first visit to the Domaine de la Romanée-Conti ten years ago. I had asked Mme. Bize if she would be willing to walk through the vineyards with me. (I long ago discovered that you can extract more insightful observations about wine from winegrowers while walking through their vineyard than you can across a tableful of wine bottles or playing peek-a-boo among the barrels.) She consented with pleasure.

We strode about the vineyards, climbing higher up the slope along the narrow track that runs between Romanée-Conti and La Grande Rue. It takes you, with a bit of huffing, to the summit. There you can look down on the *grands crus* of Vosne-Romanée, as well as a commanding sweep of the neighboring communes and the vast, flat plain in front of the slope. It is one of the choicest viewpoints in the Côte d'Or. (The other is in Volnay.)

From this spot, it takes little imagination to see Burgundy as it was centuries ago. Here are the most individual vineyards in the world, their boundaries calibrated with pinpoint accuracy to a single vine. Yet one is unable to distinguish one plot from another. The vineyard distinctions are only revealed through wine, in the same way that a drab rock turns dazzling when exposed to ultraviolet light.

We stood gazing at the vineyards, speaking little, if at all. I asked Mme. Bize (who insisted that I, like everyone else, call her Lalou) to point out La Tâche to me. After sighting it, I said, "I'm sure that it's just a matter of inexperience, but I always seem to prefer La Tâche to Romanée-Conti." To my surprise, Lalou replied, "That's how I used to feel. It took me twenty years to see why Romanée-Conti is the greatest vineyard. Before that, my heart belonged to La Tâche."

Romanée-Conti has achieved its renown not because it is dramatically superior to La Tâche or Richebourg, but because it is a "perfect sphere" of a wine. A perfect sphere can be subjected to any pressure without it breaking because the pressure is equal on all sides at all times. Romanée-Conti is the perfect Vosne-Romanée. It consolidates all of the distinctions of Vosne-Romanée, which then are amplified, without distortion. It is never as massive as Richebourg. Nor is it as intense and *sauvage* as La Tâche. Is it "better" than those two giants? Not really. But its completeness, coupled with its extraordinary refinement, makes it unique. The telling point is that, despite its unending complexity, one is never fatigued by it.

What does Romanée-Conti taste like? Above all, it is spicy. The forcefulness of this is so strong that it can almost seem unnatural. It has what all the great Burgundies offer: a sense of the grape as vehicle. The famed earthiness of Vosne-Romanée is captured more completely, with greater nuance, in Romanée-Conti than in any other wine. It is ethereal, yet capable of aging far longer than its "weight" would lead one to expect.

Is it worth the price? Whenever Romanée-Conti is discussed, someone feels compelled to decry the price, righteously declaring it "obscene" that a wine sells for five hundred dollars a bottle or more upon release. Oddly, some of these same debunkers are equally vehement in their defense of the free market. The price of Romanée-

Conti is a function of its fame and its minute supply. Keep in mind the number of people in the world who have an income of, say, $1 million a year or more, which income works out to eighty-three thousand dollars a month—before taxes, admittedly. Still, according to *The Wall Street Journal*, in 1987 the Internal Revenue Service had 35,875 Americans reporting adjusted gross incomes of $1 million or more. What's six thousand bucks for a case of Romanée-Conti? Their problem is not affording it, but finding it. Happily, only a fraction of the world's rich have a passion for wine. Imagine what the price would be if it were otherwise.

Romanée-Conti—1.8050 ha/4.46 acres

	Hectares	Acres	Cases*
SC Domaine de la Romanée-Conti	1.8050	4.46	667

---

*Cases calculated on the *rendement de base* of 35 hl/ha

La Tâche

For reasons that cannot be explained, wine lovers feel compelled to declare their undying admiration and devotion to a particular wine. "If I had to drink but one wine, it would be such and such," the statement goes. Like certain animals, they seem to think that they should mate for life.

This said, I must confess that I, too, feel a mating call—for La Tâche. It is the most gratifying of all Burgundies, the one I want to spend my life with. Its siren call is its astounding *goût de terroir*: intense, wild, and magnificently earthy. La Tâche is also, in recent years, the most reliable wine in Burgundy. A *monopole* of the Domaine de la Romanée-Conti, it manages to be DRC's most consistent wine. In almost any vintage you care to name, La Tâche almost invariably turns in the strongest performance, relative to the vintage. For example, where the 1980 Romanée-Conti was a bit watery, the

1980 La Tâche was provokingly intense, with its characteristic *goût de terroir* shining through a remarkable (for the vintage) concentration of fruit. Not even the DRC Richebourg rivaled it in concentration that year, although in other vintages Richebourg can proffer a greater "fatness." As a student in one of my wine-tasting classes once put it, "We're not talking about wine here, we're talking about personalities."

Just why La Tâche should be so consistent is one of those Burgundian mysteries that not even the owners of the Domaine de la Romanée-Conti can explain, try as they might. All the usual answers are present: old vines; very low yields; late harvesting; punctilious winemaking. Yet somehow La Tâche turns in a superior performance across the vintages than the others. Unsatisfying as it may be to those with insistently rational minds, one answer presents itself: The site is powerfully strong.

The limits of this strength were found to stretch beyond the boundaries of the original vineyard of La Tâche ("the task"). Prior to 1932, La Tâche was smaller even than Romanée-Conti, comprising just 3.5 acres. But a court in Dijon ruled, upon application by the owners of the Domaine de la Romanée-Conti, that an additional 11.43 acres from the neighboring vineyard of Les Gaudichots could legally be called La Tâche. The Domaine de la Romanée-Conti was able to demonstrate that what was sold as La Tâche in preceeding years was, in fact, also from Les Gaudichots and indistinguishable from the original 3.5-acre namesake vineyard.

Les Gaudichots still exists, although just barely. It is fragmented into three tiny pieces, scattered around the edges of La Tâche. One piece is at the topmost tip of La Tâche; another is sandwiched between Aux Malconsorts and the midsection of La Tâche; and a third actually pokes into La Grande Rue at the bottom of the slope. Part of it (.0526 ha/.13 acre) is classed as commune-level. Another part (1.0283 ha/2.5 acres) is classed as *premier cru*. In fact, the Domaine de la Romanée-Conti still owns two tenths of an acre of *premier cru* Les Gaudichots.

La Tâche—6.0620 ha/14.98 acres divided into two *climats*: La Tâche (1.4345 ha/3.5 acres) and Les Gaudichots ou La Tâche (4.6275 ha/11.43 acres)

La Tâche

	Hectares	Acres	Cases*
SC Domaine de la Romanée-Conti	1.4345	3.5	530

Les Gaudichots ou La Tâche

SC Domaine de la Romanée-Conti	4.6275	11.4	1710

---

*Cases calculated on the *rendement de base* of 35 hl/ha

Richebourg

R ichebourg is the most succulent wine in Burgundy, perhaps the world. It is aptly named: No red Burgundy is richer or more abundantly endowed than Richebourg. In one sense, Richebourg is truly a modern wine, in that it displays the power and amplitude so prized by wine lovers today. If the Burgundian slate were wiped clean and a new hierarchy established, it's a fair guess that Richebourg, rather than Romanée-Conti, would be anointed the greatest of all red Burgundies. Where once a coarse, rustic world prized refinement and finesse, a more refined but sensorily oversaturated modern world craves stronger, more vibrant flavors.

The greatness of Richebourg is that it supplies an imposing amount of supremely complicated flavors—the signature spiciness; violets; chocolate—with a resonance unrivaled in any other red Burgundy. Moreover, this is delivered with great finesse allied with the most satiny texture of any of the *grands crus* of Burgundy. At its best, Richebourg is incomparable.

Like La Tâche, the vineyard of Richebourg was expanded in the Appellation Contrôlée deliberations of the 1930s. When granted *grand cru* status in September 1936, the vineyard was officially expanded from its original 12.5 acres to its present 19.85 acres because of the inclusion of the Les Verroilles vineyard, which lies higher up on the slope between the *premiers crus* Aux Brûlées and Cros Parantoux.

Richebourg—8.0345 ha/19.85 acres divided into two *climats*: Les Richebourgs (5.0518 ha/12.5 acres) and Les Verroilles ou Richebourgs (2.9827 ha/7.4 acres)

Les Richebourgs

	Hectares	Acres	Cases*
GFA Domaine Camuzet	0.0462	0.1	17
Mme. Alain Hudelot	0.2817	0.7	104
SCI Noëllat (now Domaine Leroy)	0.7765	1.9	287
SC Domaine de la Romanée-Conti	2.5704	6.4	950
Safer	0.6313	1.6	234

(Two owners with holdings in Les Richebourgs are not listed above: M. Marie Bocquillon-Liger-Belair and coproprietors; and M. and Mme. Jean Vienot. Between them they own 0.7457 ha/1.8 acres unaccounted for in this listing.)

Les Verroilles ou Richebourgs

	Hectares	Acres	Cases*
Maison Albert Bichot	0.0733	0.2	27
GFA Domaine Camuzet	0.3061	0.8	113
M. François Gros	0.4384	1.1	162
GFA Jean Gros	0.3775	0.9	139
Mme. Veuve Louis Gros and Mme. Colette Gros	0.4719	1.2	174
M. Gustave Gros and Mme. Veuve Louis Gros	0.3785	0.9	140
SC Domaine de la Romanée-Conti	0.9370	2.3	346

---

*Cases calculated on the *rendement de base* of 35 hl/ha

Romanée
Saint-Vivant

Romanée Saint-Vivant is the unsung *grand cru* of Vosne-Romanée, if a vineyard as famous as this could ever be said to lack celebration. Nevertheless, when the rhapsodies are recited, Romanée Saint-Vivant is usually an afterthought. The reason, one suspects, is its lack of obvious weight and stuffings. Compared to La Tâche or Richebourg, the wine of Romanée Saint-Vivant is lighter and less dramatically powerful. But its virtue rests in an extraordinary scent, exceeded in this quality only by Romanée-Conti itself.

Another feature of Romanée Saint-Vivant is that it is more early-maturing than any of the other *grands crus* except Echézeaux. Perhaps this is a function of its lacy, delicate texture. Also, it seems to degenerate more readily when poorly shipped or when cellared in a too-warm environment. *Fragile* is the term that often comes to mind with Romanée Saint-Vivant. But at its best, it is sensational:

powerfully perfumed with the intoxicating spiciness of Vosne-Romanée, and equally generous with that same quality in the aftertaste.

For centuries, the dominant owner of Romanée Saint-Vivant was the Marey family, which purchased the entire vineyard in 1790. Over the centuries, various parcels were sold, although the descendants, the Neyrand family, still owned half of Romanée Saint-Vivant until 1988, when the entire 13.1-acre holding was sold to the Domaine de la Romanée-Conti for a reported $9 million to $10 million, or $700,000 to $800,000 an acre. The Domaine de la Romanée-Conti had long tended the parcel and produced the wine, selling it under the DRC label with the additional citation "Marey-Monge." The long-term contract had given the Domaine de la Romanée-Conti the option to purchase the property should it become available. Reportedly, it was sold because of the prohibitive death taxes imposed by the French government, which call for a cash payment of 40 percent of the value of the estate within one year of the death of the owner.

The other great transfer in Romanée Saint-Vivant came with the purchase of the former Domaine Charles Noëllat by the *négociant* Leroy in 1988 (the owners of which, the Leroy family, also are co-owners of the Domaine de la Romanée-Conti). The newly formed Domaine Leroy is now the second-largest owner in Romanée Saint-Vivant with 3.7 acres.

Romanée Saint-Vivant—9.4374 ha/23.32 acres

	Hectares	Acres	Cases*
GFA Domaine de Corton-Grancey (Louis Latour)	0.7630	1.9	282
Mme. Veuve André Galtie and Mme. Julien Perrin	0.6779	1.7	250
Mme. Alain Hudelot	0.4777	1.2	177
SCI Noëllat (now Domaine Leroy)	1.4913	3.7	551
M. Henri Poinsot	0.7417	1.8	274
CFA Domaine de la Romanée Saint-Vivant (now Domaine de la Romanée-Conti)	5.2858	13.1	1954

---

*Cases calculated on the *rendement de base* of 35 hl/ha

Romanée

R omanée, or La Romanée as it is often called, is the smallest
appellation contrôlée in France. (Château Grillet in the Rhône sometimes is mistakenly cited as being the smallest, but it is 6.2 acres
compared to Romanée's 2.1 acres.)

The history of the vineyard is a capsule example of Burgundy
itself. It is a *monopole* of the Liger-Belair family, which owns the
Château de Vosne-Romanée. The current owner is the eighty-five-
year-old abbot, M. Juste Liger-Belair. His family once was one of
the great landowners of the Côte de Nuits, owning portions of what
are now La Tâche and La Grande Rue.

According to M. Liger-Belair, Romanée-Conti and Romanée
were one vineyard, divided into eight small pieces. This story is
disputed by the owners of the Domaine de la Romanée-Conti. These
eight pieces, he says, were put up for sale in 1763. Jean-François de

Bourbon, the prince de Conti, purchased the largest of the eight pieces, all called Romanée. That parcel was a 4.5-acre plot. He changed its name to Romanée-Conti. A member of the Liger-Belair family, a general under Napoleon Bonaparte, already owned one of the remaining seven parcels, and over the years acquired the balance, consolidating them into the 2.1-acre plot known today as Romanée, which is located directly above Romanée-Conti.

For their part, the owners of the Domaine de la Romanée-Conti point to records indicating the plot of Romanée-Conti itself only acquired its Romanée name in 1651. And that the current Romanée used to be identified as being *au dessus de la Romanée*[-Conti], or "above the vineyard called Romanée." This would indicate that it was never part of what is now Romanée-Conti, or considered so.

Whatever the truth, Romanée inevitably is compared to Romanée-Conti. The wines certainly are similar, but Romanée-Conti always emerges as more fragrant and perfumed, while Romanée is harder and less forthcoming, at least in its youth. How much of this is winemaking as opposed to *terroir* cannot be easily, if at all, ascertained. Regardless, Romanée is one of the greatest red Burgundies and always worthy of investigation—if only it could be found.

Romanée is cellared, bottled, and distributed (if that is the word, given the infinitesimal quantity) by the *négociant* Bouchard Père et Fils under the Château de Vosne-Romanée label. It assumed this role with the 1976 vintage. Previously, the *négociant* Albert Bichot performed that function for years.

Romanée—0.8452 ha/2.1 acres

	Hectares	Acres	Cases*
SCI Château de Vosne-Romanée	0.8452	2.1	312

---

*Cases calculated on the *rendement de base* of 35 hl/ha

Grands Echézeaux

W hoever named Grands Echézeaux clearly recognized the dramatic difference in quality between the sprawling 93-acre Echézeaux and the compact, 22.6-acre site of Grands Echézeaux. Apart from a similarity in names, they have little in common. Grands Echézeaux is an authentic *grand cru*. In fact, it is one of the most reliable, rewarding *grands crus* in Burgundy.

Grands Echézeaux is a remarkably concentrated wine. It is reminiscent of a delightful hard candy of intense and multiple flavors. Just when you think you have reached the soft center, you discover a kernel of even more concentrated flavor awaiting within. In this sense, Grands Echézeaux has much more in common with Richebourg, Romanée, and La Tâche than it does with Echézeaux. If it has a lack, it is that Grands Echézeaux cannot be said to offer the ethereal, spicy scents so prominent in Romanée Saint-Vivant or Romanée-Conti.

Another point of interest is Grands Echézeaux's distinctiveness from Clos de Vougeot, with which it is contiguous. Very few bottlings of Clos de Vougeot can equal the concentration and intensity of a good Grands Echézeaux. Yet few Grands Echézeaux are as perfumed as a good Clos de Vougeot. The *terroir* clearly is different.

There are twenty-two owners of Grands Echézeaux, a number of them issuing superb wines. The reference-standard surely is the Domaine de la Romanée-Conti, which now owns the largest plot, of 7.7 acres. In 1988, they sold one acre of their original 8.7-acre holding in Grands Echézeaux to Assurances du Crédit Mutuel-Vie, an insurance company in Strasbourg. Other top-drawer bottlings are found from domaines René Engel; Mongeard-Mugneret; and Robert Sirugue. Joseph Drouhin owns a 1.25-acre parcel, from which they make superb wine.

GRANDS ECHÉZEAUX—9.1445 ha/22.6 acres

Echézeaux

Echézeaux is in the commune of Flagey-Echézeaux, all of the wines of which are sold as Vosne-Romanée. Only the *grands crus*, Echézeaux and Grands-Echézeaux, preserve the name. These two vineyards account for 45 percent of the vines in this otherwise anonymous village. The Flageotins are not complaining.

Echézeaux is the least satisfying of the *grands crus* of Vosne-Romanée, displaying fewer of the familial characteristics of Vosne-Romanée than any other. Echézeaux is eleven *climats* cobbled together. But as with Clos de Vougeot, all are entitled to the *grand cru* designation and only occasionally does anything of *grand cru* caliber emerge from this vineyard. The problem is scale. Echézeaux is too big to offer the consistency of greatness required of a *grand cru*, with ninety-three acres and eighty-four owners. It is the second-largest *grand cru* sold under only one name (unlike Corton) after Clos de Vougeot (125 acres).

On the other hand, when Echézeaux is good, it is very, very good. One need only taste the Echézeaux bottlings from domaines Henri Jayer; Dujac; Michel Clerget; René Engel; Georges Mugneret; Mongeard-Mugneret; or the Domaine de la Romanée-Conti to see what this vineyard can offer. At its best, Echézeaux can be a richly fruity wine of considerable earthiness with a good, solid middle taste. Rarely is it massive (although the Echézeaux bottlings of Michel Clerget and Henri Jayer can be so described), but it can—and should—have guts. Too often, though, many bottlings of Echézeaux are excessively light and thin, almost ghostly in their flavor definition and weight.

The Echézeaux of the Domaine de la Romanée-Conti is always the most expensive, but unlike their renditions of Richebourg, Romanée Saint-Vivant, or Grands-Echézeaux—all of which compete against other bottlings—the DRC version is not supreme. It is merely excellent. The youth of the vines may play a role here.

In fact, the Domaine de la Romanée-Conti now owns only 1.05 acres of Echézeaux, even though it continues to produce the same quantity of Echézeaux as before. In 1988, DRC sold a 4.24 ha/10.5-acre parcel of its Echézeaux holding to the Strasbourg insurance company Crédit Mutuel-Vie, as well as one acre in Grands-Echézeaux. The price was undisclosed. The vineyard was sold in order to purchase the Marey-Monge parcel of Romanée Saint-Vivant. The Domaine de la Romanée-Conti continues to tend their former Echézeaux vines on behalf of the new owner, as well as make and sell the wine under the DRC label.

ECHÉZEAUX—37.6922 ha/93.1 acres in 11 *climats*: Les Treux (12.2 acres); Clos Saint-Denis (4.2 acres); Les Cruots ou Vignes Blanches (7.8 acres); Les Loachausses (7.7 acres); Echézeaux du Dessus (8.8 acres); Les Rouges du Bas (9.7 acres); Les Beaux Monts Bas (0.35 acre); Les Champs Traversins (7.1 acres); Les Pouaillères (13 acres); En Orveaux (19.8 acres); and Les Quartiers de Nuits (2.4 acres).

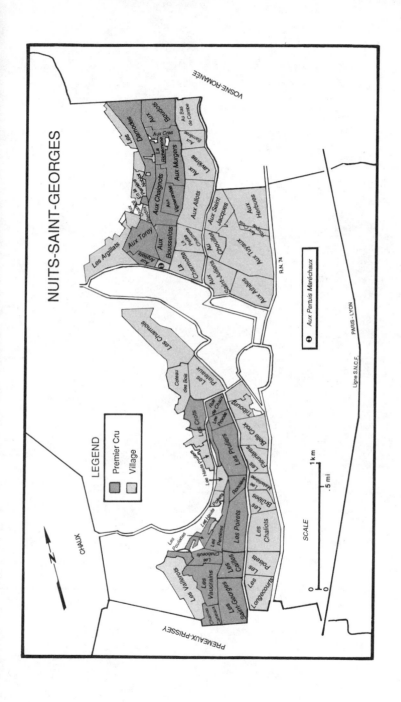

NUITS-SAINT-GEORGES

LEGEND

Premier Cru

Village

SCALE

0 .5 mi

0 1 km

CHAUX

VOSNE-ROMANÉE

PREMEAUX-PRISSEY

① Aux Pertuis Maréchaux

R.N. 74

Ligne S.N.C.F.

PARIS - LYON

Les Damodes
Aux Boudots
Aux Cras
Au Bas de Combe
Aux Murgers
Aux Vignerondes
Aux Bas
La Richemone
Aux Chaignots
En la Perrière Noblot
Les Crots
Aux Thorey
Aux Bousselots
Aux Damodes
Aux Argillas
Les Argillats
La Roncière
Aux Lavières
Aux Allots
Aux Saint Jacques
Aux Herbues
Aux Chamonotte
La Chaboeufs
Au Chouillot
Rue de Chaux
Aux Crots
Saint-Julien
Aux Thorey
Aux Athies
Aux Tuyaux
Les Chamois
Coteau des Bois
Les Plateaux
Rue de Chaux
La Poule
Tibourg
Les Croix
Belle Croix
Les Fleurières
Les Damodes
Les Hauts Pruliers
Les Pruliers
Les Roncières
Les Brûlées
Les Makereaux
Les Chaillots
Les Poirets
Les Poisets
Les Longecourts
Les Chaines Carteaux
Les Vallerots
Les Vaucrains
Saint-Georges
Les Cailles
Les Perrières
Les Poulettes
Les Chaboeufs
Les Crots

Nuits-Saint-Georges

No *appellation* is more of a challenge for the Burgundy amateur than Nuits-Saint-Georges. It has more *premiers crus*—thirty-eight—than any other. Yet it has no *grands crus*. Moreover, the elongated length of Nuits-Saint-Georges is divided into two distinct zones: the *zone Vosnoise* north of the town of Nuits-Saint-Georges; the *zone de Saint-Georges* south of the town. Some observers distinguish yet a third zone, that of the commune of Prémeaux-Prissey, which comprises the southern end of the *appellation*, the wines of which are entitled to be sold as Nuits-Saint-Georges.

Because of these complications, Nuits-Saint-Georges is a challenge. The wines, though, can be stimulating. Good ones are difficult to find, as Nuits, unlike Volnay or Morey-Saint-Denis, cannot be said to be a stronghold of high-minded growers. Happily, several are outstanding, and they should be pursued.

A good Nuits-Saint-Georges, even a commune-level bottling, should be a rugged wine when young: tannic, robust, richly concentrated, and unbending. Not for Nuits is the suppleness of Morey-Saint-Denis or the opulence of neighboring Vosne-Romanée. They are wines of structure and scale, built for aging and rewarding those who wait with an earthiness different from any other. A mature Nuits, especially from a good *premier cru*, can be a revelation. More than one taster has cried, upon sampling a mature Nuits-Saint-Georges, "This is what I always imagined Burgundy to be like!"

The problem is that in past times Nuits-Saint-Georges, like Pommard and Beaune, became emblematic of a particular kind of Burgundy—never mind whether it came from Nuits or even was composed exclusively of Pinot Noir. It is best not to dwell on how much wine from the Rhône—Syrah and Grenache—was passed off as Nuits-Saint-Georges.

Because of the size of the district, and because the town is second only to Beaune in population, Nuits-Saint-Georges is a stronghold of *négociants*. Some of them took advantage of this, issuing top-drawer Nuits. Others took a different sort of advantage, displaying the address of the firm prominently on the label of an otherwise ordinary red wine to mislead a gullible, non-French-speaking public into thinking that the wine came from the famous Nuits-Saint-Georges. Such practices are largely behind us now. Still, there's a surprising amount of insipid wine issued under the rubric of Nuits-Saint-Georges. And not all of it, by any means, comes from just the *négociants*. Life is easy when you can sell your wine under a name that is very nearly synonymous with red Burgundy.

THE PREMIERS CRUS

Zone Vosnoise (the northern end)

LES DAMODES—One of two *premiers crus* contiguous with Vosne-Romanée. (The other is Aux Boudots.) Les Damodes has the highest elevation of any of the *premiers crus*, sited between 280 meters and 340 meters (840 feet and 1,020 feet). The soil is a brown calcareous type with fine gravel mixed into it, especially toward the southern end of it, where the soil is the most gravely and least deep. As a result of both the soil and the elevation, the wines of Les Damodes are lighter and finer than some others, with a whiff of violets reminiscent of neighboring Vosne-Romanée.

AUX BOUDOTS—Located below Les Damodes, the elevation is lower on the slope and the soil deeper and richer, with more pebbles and less gravel. As a result, Aux Boudots offers richer, fuller, fatter wine, similar in body to Vosne-Romanée. It is an exact continuation (geographically speaking) of Vosne-Romanée "Aux Malconsorts," with which it shares common characteristics.

LA RICHEMONE—A small vineyard (4.8 acres) of exceptional quality. The soil of Richemone is similar to that of Les Damodes, but with more flat rocks and some sand, as well as a lower elevation. The vineyard is only 400 feet wide and lies between the 270-meter mark and 280 meters (810 feet and 840 feet). The wines are relatively light, but with a powerful, earthy pungency.

AUX MURGERS—On the same alignment as Aux Boudots; the soil is the same. But the wine is different, somehow less under the sphere of influence of Vosne-Romanée and more classically Nuits-Saint-Georges: hard, almost severe, with the stony, earthy/animal scents characteristic of Nuits-Saint-Georges *premiers crus*.

AUX CHAIGNOTS—The name comes from a local patois for iron-rich minerals, at least according to one source. Despite that, the soil actually is the usual brown calcareous sort, with quite a bit of clay. The resulting wine, no doubt thanks to the clay, is firm and solid, with a good deal of substance and longevity. It is considered the biggest wine in the *zone Vosnoise*: fat, rich, long-lived, and even a bit coarse.

AUX TOREY AND AUX BOUSSELOTS—These two *premiers crus* share similar qualities, with differences traceable to elevation. Aux Torey is the higher of the two, with a steeper slope and more gravelly soil. It lies between the 255-meter mark and 280 meters (765 feet and 840 feet) with a 10 percent to 15 percent slope. In comparison,

Aux Bousselots has only a 2 percent to 5 percent slope, and is found between 250 meters and 260 meters (750 feet and 780 feet). The wines can display the concentrated, jammy scent found in the more robust *premiers crus*. Aux Torey, not surprisingly, is a little lighter than Bousselots, courtesy of its elevation.

Zone de Saint-Georges (central)

RUE DE CHAUX—A small vineyard of just 5.25 acres. A strongly calcareous soil seems to result in relatively light wines with some earthiness.

LES PRULIERS—One of the great *premiers crus*: strongly mineral, with overtones of chocolate and leather. Pruliers is classic Nuits-Saint-Georges, long-lived and intense. The soil has some sand and siliceous earth; The southern end has finer gravel than the northern.

LES POIRETS—Very gravelly soil with the usual brown calcareous underlay. The *climat* Clos des Porret is a *monopole* of Domaine Henri Gouges.

LES PERRIÈRES, LES HAUTS POIRETS, AND LES POULETTES —All three *premiers crus* occupy high elevations: Les Perrières at 250 meters to 265 meters; Les Hauts Poirets at 250 meters to 300 meters; and Les Poulettes at 265 meters to 300 meters. The soil in all three is very pebbly and stony. The wines are lighter, with higher acidity and, in good vintages, great finesse.

LES CAILLES—One of the choicest vineyards in Nuits, creating rich, intense, beautifully structured wines. The soil is described as *très caillouteux*—very stony—by the local growers' association.

LES SAINT-GEORGES—This would be the *grand cru* of Nuits-Saint-Georges. As in so many other signature vineyards elsewhere in the Côte d'Or, the greatness of Les Saint-Georges is its completeness:

It is rich, intense, concentrated, and profound, while offering the greatest degree of finesse. It also is among the longest-lived Nuits wines. The dominant owner is Domaine Henri Gouges, which owns 44 percent of the vineyard.

LES VAUCRAINS—Along with Les Cailles, this is a runner-up to Les Saint-Georges as the best vineyard in Nuits. One of the richest, most intense aromatic wines, perhaps with more concentration than any other. Vaucrains creates some of the most consistently fine Nuits. What it lacks is the degree of finesse of either Les Cailles or Les Saint-Georges, but not by much.

CHAINES CARTEAUX—One of the many small (6.25 acres) *premiers crus* of Nuits-Saint-Georges. The high elevation of 260 meters to 300 meters (780 feet to 900 feet) helps result in light wines. The slope is one of the steepest in Nuits, from 18 percent to 20 percent. The wines can display an intensely stony *goût de terroir*.

PRÉMEAUX-PRISSEY

AUX PERDRIX AND AUX CORVÉES—Stony and gravelly soils. The wines are both characteristically Prémeauxlike: hard, even tough, with firm, unyielding fruit that takes years to open up. The wines of both vineyards can be very fine.

LES ARGILLIÈRES—For this taster, Les Argillières is the finest vineyard in Prémeaux and coequal with Les Cailles and Vaucrains. The key to Les Argillières is an extraordinarily intense minerally *goût de terroir*. The wine is firm, as all Prémeaux vineyards seem to be, but the finesse is unusual. This is one of the finest Nuits *premiers crus*.

CLOS DE LA MARÉCHALE—A *monopole* of Joseph Faiveley, which does not own the vineyard but leases it under a long-term contract. The Faiveley style is for hard, long-lived wines, and this Prémeaux vineyard responds to that like a well-trained horse under a properly placed spur. The wine is concentrated, meaty, and tannic. It is not a wine of finesse, but of great "chewiness." It is good, but not great.

Aux Argillas—1.8869 ha/4.7 acres

	Hectares	Acres	Cases*
M. et Mme. Marcel Chauvenet	0.1400	0.4	74
M. et Mme. Maurice Chevillon	0.3592	0.9	190

Aux Boudots—6.3018 ha/15.6 acres

GFA du Domaine Camuzet	1.0441	2.6	551
M. et Mme. René Cavin	0.0466	0.1	25
M. Maurice Chevallier	0.2493	0.6	132
M. Michel Chevallier	0.2492	0.6	132
Hospices de Nuits-Saint-Georges	0.2052	0.5	108
M. et Mme. Jean Grivot	0.8496	2.1	449
M. et Mme. Henri Lamy	0.0642	0.1	34
Mme. Marc Manière	0.2330	0.6	123
M. Vincent Mongeard	0.1283	0.3	68
SC Mongeard-Mugneret et Fils	0.2572	0.6	136
M. Georges Noëllat	0.3320	0.8	175
Mme. Lucette Noëllat	0.4607	1.1	243
SCI Noëllat (now Domaine Leroy)	1.4903	3.7	787
Mme. Jacques Saconnet	0.3330	0.8	176
Mme. Georges Teyssie	0.0868	0.2	46

Aux Bousselots—4.2433 ha/10.5 acres

M. et Mme. Jean Chauvenet	0.5483	1.4	290
M. Georges Chevillon	0.4038	1.0	213
M. et Mme. Maurice Chevillon	0.5245	1.3	277
M. Michel Chevillon	0.1278	0.3	67
M. et Mme. Michel Gavignet	0.4398	1.1	232
SCI Gille	0.2154	0.5	114
M. Gérard Julien	0.7035	1.7	371
M. Henri Legros	0.1927	0.5	102
M. Marcel Legros	0.1190	0.3	63
M. Gilles Remoriquet	0.1434	0.4	76
M. Maurice Ruinet	0.3492	0.9	184
M. Jean Trapet	0.3428	0.9	181
Société Exploitation Vignobles la Roncière	0.2832	0.7	150

Les Cailles—3.8063 ha/9.4 acres

---

*Cases calculated on the *rendement de base* of 40 hl/ha plus 20 percent

	Hectares	Acres	Cases*
M. Jean Boillot	1.0675	2.6	564
M. Jean-Pierre Dubrule	0.3393	0.8	179
Mme. Jean-Pierre Dubrule	0.5355	1.3	283
M. Marcel Gesseaume	0.2458	0.6	130
SCI Gille Am	0.4239	1.1	224
SCI du Domaine Les Cailles Misserey	1.1943	3.0	631

Les Chaboeufs—2.8090 ha/6.9 acres

M. Jean Confuron	0.4794	1.1	253
M. Marcel Gavignet	0.4991	1.2	264
M. Michel Gavignet	0.9899	2.5	523
SC du Domaine de la Poulette	0.6090	1.5	322
M. André Vauthier	0.1185	0.3	63
M. Gabriel Vauthier	0.1131	0.3	60

Aux Chaignots—5.8585 ha/14.5 acres

M. Gabriel Boyeaux	0.1590	0.4	84
M. et Mme. Maurice Chevillon	1.5280	3.8	807
M. Daniel Chopin	0.3977	1.0	210
M. et Mme. Daniel Chopin	0.1840	0.5	97
Consortium Viticole et Vinicole Bourgogne (Faiveley)	0.7261	1.8	383
M. Marius Ecart	0.3795	0.9	200
M. et Mme. Marcel Gavignet	0.2019	0.5	107
SC du Domaine Henri Gouges	0.4718	1.2	249
M. Georges Mugneret	1.2700	3.1	671
M. Marcel Rion	0.3720	0.9	196
M. Louis Tissot	0.1435	0.4	76

Chaines Carteaux—2.5323 ha/6.3 acres

M. André Dupasquier	0.3919	1.0	207
M. et Mme. Roger Dupasquier	0.1427	0.4	75
Mme. Arnaud Gilles	0.1330	0.3	70
M. Marcel Gouges	0.0612	0.2	32
M. Michel Gouges	0.0612	0.2	32

Aux Champs Perdix—0.7357 ha/1.8 acres

M. Georges Chevillon	0.0957	0.2	51
M. et Mme. Maurice Chevillon	0.1170	0.3	62
M. Marius Ecard	0.2767	0.7	146
Mme. Veuve Marius Ecart	0.2460	0.6	130

---

*Cases calculated on the *rendement de base* of 40 hl/ha plus 20 percent

	Hectares	Acres	Cases*
GFA Jean Gros	0.7134	1.7	377
M. Fioravente Dal Molin	0.0652	0.2	34
M. Alain Pelletier	0.0947	0.2	50
M. Louis Tissot	0.2393	0.6	126

Aux Cras—2.9993 ha/7.4 acres

Mme. Marcel Bouquin	0.1124	0.3	59
M. Gilbert Girardin	0.1123	0.3	59
M. et Mme. Pierre Lamadon	0.4297	1.1	227
Mme. Pierre Lamadon	0.3962	1.0	209
M. et Mme. Henri Lamy	0.2656	0.7	140
M. Patrick Lamy	0.1460	0.4	77
M. Patrick Lamy	0.0180	0.04	10
M. Jean Mugneret	0.2705	0.7	143
Mme. Veuve Marcel Mugneret	0.4350	1.1	230
M. Marcel Mugneret	0.1736	0.4	92
M. Georges Noëllat	0.8040	2.0	425

Les Crot—4.0233 ha/9.9 acres divided into two *climats*: Les Crot (2.9 acres) and Château Gris (7.1 acres)

M. et Mme. Bernard Aimé	0.1945	0.5	103
M. Benigne Bichot	0.3940	1.0	208
Société Château Gris	2.7693	6.8	1462
M. Georges Chevillon	0.2445	0.6	129
M. Marcel Gouges	1.1072	2.7	585
Mme. Jacqueline Jouan	0.5035	1.2	266
M. Henri de Mayol de Luppe	0.0835	0.2	44
M. Adrien Pouilly	0.0390	0.1	21
M. Daniel Rion	0.4192	1.0	221

Les Damodes—8.5456 ha/21.1 acres

M. et Mme. Marcel Béthanie	0.3183	0.8	168
M. Benigne Bichot	0.7426	1.8	392
M. Jean-Claude Boisset	0.9143	2.3	483
M. Gabriel Bonnet	0.0930	0.2	49
M. et Mme. Pierre Boudier	0.1866	0.5	99
M. et Mme. René Cavin	0.3686	0.9	195
M. et Mme. Marcel Chantin	0.7287	1.8	385
M. et Mme. Marcel Chantin	0.0540	0.1	29
M. Maurice Chevallier	0.2875	0.7	152
M. Michel Chevallier	0.2682	0.7	142
M. Maurice Chevillon	0.0450	0.1	24
M. André Chopin	0.1246	0.3	66

*Cases calculated on the *rendement de base* of 40 hl/ha plus 20 percent

	Hectares	Acres	Cases*
M. et Mme. Yves Chopin	0.1824	0.5	96
M. Roger Gaheri	0.1666	0.4	88
M. et Mme. René Gandrey	0.2540	0.6	134
M. François Gouges	0.0179	0.04	9
M. Alfred Haegelen	0.2284	0.6	121
M. Robert Jayer	0.1121	0.3	59
M. Alexis Lagnier	0.0508	0.1	27
M. et Mme. Pierre Lamy	0.2198	0.5	116
M. Fernand Lescheneaut	0.4089	1.0	216
GFA Domaine Chantal Lescure	0.5394	1.3	284
M. et Mme. Armand Machard de Gramont	0.3448	0.9	182
Mme. Armand Machard de Gramont	0.2217	0.6	117
M. René Magnien	0.1600	0.4	84
Mme. Marc Manière	0.7309	1.8	386
Mme. Alain Michelot	0.0443	0.1	23
M. Louis Moreau	0.3164	0.8	167
M. et Mme. Marcel Mutin	0.1423	0.4	75
Mme. Josette Normand	0.1076	0.3	57
M. Arthur Poillot	0.0159	0.04	8
M. et Mme. Jean-Pierre Poulet	0.1300	0.3	69
M. Henri Remoriquet	0.1818	0.5	96
Mme. Jacques Saconney	0.1643	0.4	87
M. Jean Trapet	0.0890	0.2	47
M. Michel Trapet	0.2553	0.6	135

Les Hauts Pruliers—0.2060 ha/0.5 acre

Mme. Veuve Maxime Machard de Gramont	0.0465	0.1	25
M. Georges Pillot	0.1007	0.25	53

Aux Murgers—4.8911 ha/12.1 acres

GFA Les Arbaupins	0.1138	0.3	60
GFA du Domaine Camuzet	0.7497	1.9	396
M. Marie-Joseph Catniard	0.4566	1.1	241
M. et Mme. Marcel Chauvenet	0.4067	1.0	215
M. et Mme. André Chopin	0.2144	0.5	113
Hospices de Nuits-Saint-Georges	0.1703	0.4	90
Mme. Alain Hudelot	0.6765	1.7	357
Société Louis Robin	0.9975	2.5	527
M. René Magnien	0.1505	0.4	79
M. Marc Misserey	0.2360	0.6	125

*Cases calculated on the *rendement de base* of 40 hl/ha plus 20 percent

	Hectares	Acres	Cases*
SCI du Domaine Misset	0.1970	0.5	104
M. Marcel Rion	0.1815	0.5	96
Mme. Denis Tremblay	0.1708	0.4	90

Les Perrières—3.3488 ha/8.3 acres

M. Robert Chevillon	0.4426	1.1	234
Mme. Jean Forey	0.4213	1.0	222
SC du Domaine Henri Gouges	0.3983	1.0	210
M. Georges Jeanniard	0.2200	0.5	116
M. Paul Jouan	0.9315	2.3	492
M. Timothy Marshall	0.2455	0.6	130
Société Exploitation de Vignobles la Roncières	0.4493	1.1	237

En La Perrière Noblot—0.2987 ha/0.74 acre

M. et Mme. Jean Pierre Bony	0.1460	0.4	77
M. Marius Ecart	0.4585	1.1	242
Mme. Veuve Marius Ecart	0.0695	0.2	37
M. et Mme. Machard de Gramont	0.2779	0.7	147
Mme. Armand Machard de Gramont	0.2436	0.6	129
GFA Jean Gros	0.1739	0.4	92
M. et Mme. Gilles Remoriquet	0.0637	0.2	34

Les Poirets—7.1501 ha/17.7 acres divided into two *climats*: Porrets Saint-Georges (8.8 acres) and Clos des Porrets Saint-Georges (8.9 acres)

M. Régis Dubois	0.4628	1.1	244
M. Robert Dubois	0.1132	0.3	60
Hospices de Nuits-Saint-Georges	0.1896	0.5	100
Mme. Jean Ledy	0.5494	1.4	290
SCI du Clos du Thorey (Moillard)	0.5360	1.3	283
Consortium Viticole et Vinicole de Bourgogne (Faiveley)	1.6996	4.2	897

Clos des Porrets

SC du Domaine Henri Gouges	3.5993	8.9	1900

Les Poulettes—2.1350 ha/5.3 acres

M. et Mme. Aimé Bernard	0.0600	0.2	32
M. et Mme. Jean Chevaunet	0.1728	0.4	91
SCI du Domaine Guy Dufouleur	0.3415	0.8	180
M. et Mme. Christian Gavignet	0.1080	0.3	57
Mme. Armand Machard de Gramont	0.0610	0.2	32

*Cases calculated on the *rendement de base* of 40 hl/ha plus 20 percent

	Hectares	*Acres*	*Cases**
M. Fioravente Dal Molin	0.2657	0.7	140
M. Daniel Pillot	0.0862	0.2	46
SC du Domaine de la Poulette	0.9396	2.3	496
Société Vinicole Commercial de France	0.1099	0.3	58

Les Pruliers—7.6849 ha/19 acres divided into two *climats*: Les Pruliers (17.6 acres) and Les Procès (3.3 acres)

Les Pruliers

M. Louis Boillot	0.2666	0.7	141
M. Pierre Boillot	0.2666	0.7	141
M. et Mme. Maurice Chevillon	0.2742	0.6	145
M. Robert Chevillon	0.4277	1.1	226
M. Auguste Chicotot	0.0960	0.2	51
M. Marcel Gesseaume	0.5517	1.4	291
SC du Domaine Henri Gouges	1.3085	3.2	691
Mme. Aristide Grivot	0.7600	1.9	401
M. et Mme. Jean Guy	0.5226	1.3	276
M. Pierre Masson	1.5682	3.9	828
M. Jean-Marie Zibetti	1.0652	2.6	562

Les Procès

M. et Mme. Robert Arnoux	0.6205	1.5	328
M. Jean Dufour	0.1613	0.4	85
M. Gaston Garrigues	0.7293	1.8	385
SC du Domaine Henri Gouges	0.5676	1.4	300
Mme. Veuve Maurice Grandne	0.0200	0.1	11
M. Michel Guy	0.0428	0.1	23
Mlle. Georgette Jeanniard	0.1630	0.4	86
M. Timothy Marshall	0.1828	0.5	97
M. Pierre Masson	0.2783	0.7	147
M. René Tardy	0.3920	1.0	207
M. et Mme. Maurice Vigot	0.1428	0.4	75

La Richemone—1.9691 ha/4.9 acres

M. et Mme. Jean Chauvenet	0.0638	0.2	34
M. Pascal Mairet	0.4497	1.1	237
Mlle. Marie Michelot	0.5565	1.4	294
M. Jean Mugneret	0.1707	0.4	90
M. Jean Thomas	0.8244	2.0	435
Mme. Veuve Jean Thomas	0.1038	0.3	55
M. Pierre Thomas	0.0676	0.2	36

*Cases calculated on the *rendement de base* of 40 hl/ha plus 20 percent

	Hectares	Acres	Cases*
Roncière—2.1895 ha/5.4 acres			
Mme. Henri Caillot	1.0087	2.5	533
M. Maurice Chevillon	0.0815	0.2	43
Mme. Veuve René Julien	0.3108	0.8	164
Mme. René Julien	0.1920	0.5	101
M. et Mme. Robert Lavocat	0.0920	0.2	49
Société d'Exploitation de Vignobles le Roncière	0.5045	1.3	266
Rue de Chaux—2.1271 ha/5.3 acres			
Mme. Gilbert Besancenot	0.2801	0.7	148
Mme. Guy Chevrot	0.1220	0.3	64
M. Alexis Chicotot	0.2880	0.7	152
M. Auguste Chicotot	0.2882	0.7	152
Mme. Veuve Albert Goze	0.2321	0.6	123
Hospices de Nuits-Saint-Georges	0.2935	0.7	155
M. et Mme. Henri Remoriquet	0.3958	1.0	209
Société d'Exploitation de Vignobles la Roncière	0.2264	0.7	120
Les Saint-Georges—7.5212 ha/18.6 acres			
Consortium Viticole et Vinicole Bourgogne (Faiveley)	0.2314	0.6	122
GFA Audidier Maitrot	0.6313	1.6	333
M. Jean-Pierre Delahoutre	0.1597	0.4	84
Mme. Jean-Pierre Dubrule	0.1926	0.5	102
Mme. Michael Frisby	0.4525	1.1	239
SC du Domaine Henri Gouges	3.3644	8.3	1776
Hospices de Nuits-Saint-Georges	0.9516	2.4	502
Mme. Jean-Claude Laporte	0.1926	0.5	102
M. et Mme. Gilles Remoriquet	0.1814	0.5	96
M. Marc Zibetti	0.5393	1.3	285
Aux Torey—4.9962 ha/12.3 acres			
Mme. Marcel Chantin	0.0175	0.04	9
M. et Mme. Marcel Chauvenet	0.1147	0.3	61
Mme. Veuve Maurice Grandne	0.3460	0.9	183
M. Michel Guy	0.0532	0.1	28
M. et Mme. Louis Legros	0.6387	1.6	337
M. Michel Legros	0.0852	0.2	45
M. Pierre Masson	0.5667	1.4	299
SCI du Clos de Thorey (Moillard)	3.4384	8.5	1815

*Cases calculated on the *rendement de base* of 40 hl/ha plus 20 percent

	Hectares	Acres	Cases*
Les Vallerots—0.8679 ha/2.1 acres			
M. et Mme. Jean-Pierre Bony	0.0500	0.1	26
M. Bertrand Machard de Gramont	0.4500	1.1	238
M. et Mme. Xavier Machard de			
Gramont	0.3977	1.0	210
SC du Domaine de la Poulette	0.3333	0.8	176
M. André Vauthier	0.2343	0.6	124
Les Vaucrains—6.2099 ha/15.3 acres			
M. Christian Confuron	0.2565	0.6	135
Mlle. Odile Darthenay	0.5160	1.3	272
M. Jérome Deharveng	0.5172	1.3	273
M. André Dupasquier	0.1765	0.4	93
M. Michel Dupasquier	0.0990	0.2	52
M. et Mme. Roger Dupasquier	0.1508	0.4	80
SC du Domaine Henri Gouges	0.9890	2.4	522
GFA Audidier Maitrot	0.2105	0.5	111
Mme. Garnier des Garets d'Ars Marcel	0.5160	1.3	272
M. Alain Michelot	0.6800	1.7	359
SC du Domaine de la Poulette	1.1104	2.7	586
Aux Vignerondes—3.8455 ha/9.5 acres			
GFA les Arbaupins	0.1571	0.4	83
Consortium Viticole et Vinicole			
Bourgogne (Faiveley)	0.4623	1.1	244
Hospice Nuits-Saint-Georges	0.9942	2.5	525
M. Georges Missey	0.3577	0.9	189
Mlle. Marie-Christine Mugneret	0.2605	0.6	138
SCI Noëllat (now Domaine Leroy)	0.3780	0.9	200
M. Daniel Rion	0.4624	1.1	244

PRÉMEAUX-PRISSEY

Les Argillières—4.4417 ha/11 acres divided into two *climats*: Les Argillières (0.5 acre) and Clos des Argillières (10.4 acres)
Clos Arlot—5.4460 ha/13.5 acres
Aux Corvées—7.5429 ha/18.6 acres divided into three *climats*: Clos des Corvées (12.7 acres); Clos des Corvées Pagets (3.7 acres) and Clos Saint-Marc (2.3 acres)
Les Didiers—2.4520 ha/6.1 acres

---

*Cases calculated on the *rendement de base* of 40 hl/ha plus 20 percent

Les Forêts or Clos des Forêts Saint-Georges—7.1117 ha/17.6 acres

Les Grandes Vignes or Clos des Grandes Vignes—2.2126 ha/5.5 acres

Clos de la Maréchale—9.5500 ha/23.6 acres

Aux Perdrix—3.4973 ha/8.6 acres

PRODUCERS WORTH SEEKING OUT (AND SOME NOT)

BOUCHARD PÈRE ET FILS—The *négociant* owns the 2.3-acre *monopole* Clos Saint-Marc, a *climat* of Aux Corvées. This is one of Bouchard's better bottlings, with good structure and better than usual concentration for this producer.

DOMAINE ROBERT CHEVILLON—Simply put, this is the supreme domaine in Nuits-Saint-Georges. That title used to go to Domaine Henri Gouges (which still has the best vineyard holdings), but that once-fabled estate has long since been shouldered aside by the stellar winemaking of Robert Chevillon. This is Nuits-Saint-Georges as it should be but so rarely is: concentrated, tannic, almost painfully intense, yet with no apparent winemaking signature. Chevillon's Les Argillières, Les Vaucrains, and Les Cailles are among the great red Burgundies of our time. The Les Saint-Georges is a masterpiece and shows just what this vineyard can achieve. Robert's brother Maurice issues wines under his own label, but I have not tasted any. The reports, however, are that they are very good, although the winemaking is performed separately from that of his brother.

DOMAINE GEORGES CHICOTOT—One of the early disciples of enologist Guy Accad. I have not tasted the wines, but it should be noted that Chicotot owns parcels of Pruliers, Les Saint-Georges, and Les Vaucrains. If nothing else, the Accad approach of prolonged cold maceration is enjoying the benefit of some of the best vineyards in Burgundy.

JOSEPH FAIVELEY—This Nuits-based *négociant* has a strong following. I cannot count myself among them, although I would like to. This is a serious *négociant* striving for the highest quality. Yet the winemaking is old-fashioned in the less attractive sense of the term. Faiveley's signature wine is the *monopole* Clos de la Maréchale.

DOMAINE HENRI GOUGES—It's time to take the gloves off: The wines of Domaine Henri Gouges are second-rate and have been for years. No domaine in Burgundy has coasted longer on a once-lustrous reputation than this one. At one time—i.e., in the 1960s and earlier—Gouges was the standard-bearer for Nuits-Saint-Georges. The late Henri Gouges amassed a stunning collection of vineyards: the lion's share of Les Saint-Georges, all of the Clos des Porrets; 3.2 acres of Les Pruliers; 2.4 acres in Les Vaucrains; and smaller parcels in several other *premiers crus*. It is an extraordinary estate. Yet the wines are lackluster.

The reasons for this are not entirely clear. Certainly, the relatively brief fermentation period of roughly ten days is one reason. Perhaps the removal of all the stems might be another. A third may well be their practice of fermenting the grapes virtually uncrushed in closed concrete vats, in effect a variation on the carbonic maceration employed in the Beaujolais region. To be fair, the wines do display their *terroirs*. But they are so thin that in some vintages, such as 1982, they border on the anorexic. If you want to see just what a faint echo the Gouges wines have become, simply taste a wine from Leroy, Robert Chevillon, Alain Michelot, or Daniel Rion alongside. It is a depressing, even frustrating experience, as the Gouges name was once synonymous with outstanding quality. No more.

HOSPICES DE NUITS—This is the Nuits-Saint-Georges counterpart to the Hospices de Beaune. The wines are exclusively *premiers crus* from Nuits-Saint-Georges. The Hospices owns about twenty acres. Unlike the Hospices de Beaune auction, which occurs on the third Sunday in November after the harvest, the timing of the auction of the Hospices de Nuits is more rational: usually on the Sunday before Palm Sunday, which puts it in late March or early April. By then the wines have finished their malolactic fermentations and are able to be reasonably assessed. The quality appears to be consistently good, but as always, too much depends upon who buys the wine and how it is cellared. Prices tend to be a more reasonable than those of the Hospices de Beaune.

DOMAINE ROBERT JAYER-GILLES—This small producer offers just one Nuits wine, a superb Les Damodes. Regrettably, he only owns one quarter-acre, enough for about fifty cases, with a good portion of that going to the three-star Paris restaurant Taillevent. At least it's going to a good home.

LABOURÉ-ROI—This Nuits-based *négociant* has successfully specialized in locating small batches of various Nuits *premiers crus*, many of them of superior quality. The prices are usually more reasonable than others for the quality level, as well. Worth watching.

LEROY—The *négociant* Leroy is one of the great Nuits-Saint-Georges specialists. The muscular Leroy style is ideal for the intrinsically muscular Nuits character. With the purchase of Domaine Charles Noëllat, the newly created Domaine Leroy now owns vines in Aux Boudots and Aux Vignerondes. The price for the Leroy Nuits wines is high even by Leroy standards, but the quality is unmatched.

DOMAINE MACHARD DE GRAMONT—The owner of some excellent vineyards, this estate's wines seem excessively variable. Too often they seem a little "slippery," perhaps from excessive chaptalization? Still, they are worth investigating in the best years, as occasionally there have been some fine bottlings.

DOMAINE MÉO-CAMUZET—Two Nuits bottlings from this potentially good estate: Aux Murgers and Les Boudots. If, under Henri Jayer's consulting tutelage, they can issue a Nuits "Aux Murgers" of the caliber of that produced by Henri Jayer, then the wine will be nothing short of sensational. So far, the results are mixed, but there's reason for hope.

DOMAINE ALAIN MICHELOT—One of the best estates in Nuits-Saint-Georges. Michelot's wine almost always displays concentration and depth. If there's a drawback, it's that the wines can be a little oaky. But the quality is exemplary.

DOMAINE GEORGES MUGNERET—The only Nuits from this Vosne-Romanée estate is a superb Les Chaignots. The style, as always, emphasizes powerful impact without massive weight. This wine delivers.

DOMAINE DANIEL RION—This estate is one of the best examples of a younger generation assuming command from the older, and in the process catapulting the wines into a different orbit of quality. It doesn't always work that way, but here it did. Patrice Rion, in his early thirties, took over from his father, Daniel, in the 1979 vintage. The wines have improved noticeably every year.

Rion strives for a sharp burst of well-defined and very fresh-tasting fruit. The wines almost invariably offer superb concentration and lovely flavor definition. The Clos des Argillières is a masterpiece. Close on its heels are Les Hauts Pruliers, Vignerondes, and Grandes Vignes. This is a top-ranked producer. Also superb Chambolle-Musigny "Beaux Bruns" and good Clos de Vougeot, as well as ex-cellent Vosne *premiers crus*.

DOMAINE BERNARD SERVEAU—The Chambolle-Musigny producer owns a parcel in Chaines Carteaux. (It's not listed in the grower listings for reasons that escape me.) The Serveau style strives for delicacy. Chaines Carteaux rewards this, being an intrinsically delicate Nuits wine because of its elevation. The wine is extremely peppery.

CÔTE DE
BEAUNE

Côte de Beaune- Villages and Côte de Beaune

CÔTE DE BEAUNE-VILLAGES

With these two *appellations*, one really has stepped down the rabbit hole of Burgundy's Alice-in-Wonderland wine regulations. The first thing to remember is that, despite the close similarity of names, Côte de Beaune and Côte de Beaune-Villages are not the same.

Côte de Beaune-Villages is a catchall designation for any red wine that is grown within the *appellation* boundaries of any *appellation* in the Côte de Beaune *except* Beaune, Aloxe-Corton, Pommard, and Volnay. If the wine comes only from one *appellation*, it may substitute its name in conjunction with the term "Côte de Beaune," e.g. Monthelie–Côte de Beaune. If wine from two or more *appellations* is blended together, the wine can then only be called Côte de Beaune-Villages.

Clearly, this is a trading device for the wine shippers. It allows them to combine batches of red wines from widely varying locations and of widely varying qualities. Usually, Côte de Beaune-Villages wines are light, ready for drinking upon release, and, if you land on a good one, can be a good buy. (Do not conclude from this that Côte de Nuits-Villages is the same for the northern part of the Côte d'Or. It is much more restrictive and nowhere near as all-encompassing. See Côte de Nuits-Villages.)

CÔTE DE BEAUNE

Côte de Beaune is a goofy designation that applies only to the wines of Beaune and to four vineyards high on the Montagne de Beaune that are not entitled to the Beaune *appellation* designation. They are Dessus des Marconnets, La Grande Châtelaine, Les Mondes Rondes, and Pierres Blanches.

Why the *appellation* Côte de Beaune exists is one of those quirks of Burgundian logic, if that's the word. The gist is that prior to the creation of Appellation Contrôlée in the late 1930s, many blended wines were sold under the name Côte de Beaune. The shippers of Beaune decided that the Beaune name was too precious to be lavished on others. They insisted that consumers would automatically assume that such a wine must come from Beaune itself. (The fact that they themselves benefitted from this purported confusion before Appellation Contrôlée somehow was ignored.) Therefore, only wine from the commune of Beaune, plus the additional four vineyards, should be entitled to use the precious "Côte de Beaune" designation. Everyone else had to use the name "Côte de Beaune-Villages."

Today, one sees very little wine labeled "Côte de Beaune." The most prominent exception to this is La Grande Châtelaine, owned by Domaine Chantal Lescure and distributed by the *négociant* Labouré-Roi. Both red and white La Grande Chatelaine are made. The wines are light but flavorful. They also are bargains, selling for about fifteen dollars a bottle.

Ladoix-Serrigny

The Ladoisiens, as they call themselves, must surely feel themselves forever bridesmaids and never brides. A few of their vineyards are allowed to be called Aloxe-Corton, and so they take that name. A more privileged few are counted among the *grands crus* of Corton, and that's that. Most of the rest of the wine of Ladoix-Serrigny winds up being sold as Côte de Beaune-Villages, even though it often is better than what usually is sold under that name. Ladoix-Serrigny stands for nothing.

This is a pity, if only because the wines of Ladoix, red and white, are rewarding, if not necessarily exciting. They tend to be sturdy, mouth-filling wines, often with refreshing acidity. They age well, although with little transformation. They do have the redeeming virtue of value: They are relatively inexpensive.

The commune comprises three villages: Ladoix, which straddles

N74, the main road to Beaune; Buisson, which is the northernmost outpost of the Côte de Beaune and lies—what there is of the village—amid the vineyards; and Serrigny, which lies about one mile away from Ladoix across N74 on the flat plain.

Like everything else on or near the hill of Corton, Ladoix-Serrigny has its own complicated geology. But rarely do the exposures bring the subsoils to life via Pinot Noir and Chardonnay. Those that do are brought into the Corton or Aloxe-Corton fold.

THE PREMIERS CRUS

Bois Roussot—1.7845 ha/4.4 acres
Le Clou d'Orge—1.5840 ha/3.9 acres
La Corvée—7.1404 ha/17.6 acres
Les Joyeuses—0.7599 ha/1.9 acres
La Micaude—1.6382 ha/4 acres
Mourottes—1.4736 ha/3.6 acres divided into two *climats*: Basses Mourottes (2.3 acres) and Hautes Mourottes (1.3 acres). This is only part of each *climat*; the balance in both is Corton and Corton-Charlemagne.

PRODUCERS WORTH SEEKING OUT

I rarely see Ladoix-Serrigny in the States. Because of that, I always seek it out on restaurant lists in Burgundy and Paris. It's always a good buy.

CAPITAIN-GAGNEROT/DOMAINE FRANÇOIS CAPITAIN—First-rate red Ladoix from a 3.4-acre holding in the *premier cru* La Micaude. Also, a white Les Gréchons of good report (haven't had it) from a vineyard high up on the slope.

CHÂTEAU CORTON ANDRÉ/PIERRE ANDRÉ—This producer—owned by the *négociant* La Reine Pédauque—issues a very reliable commune-level red Ladoix called Clos des Chagnots, which is a *monopole*. Its ownership listings frequently are under Société d'Élévage et de Diffusion des Grands Vins.

CHEVALLIER PÈRE ET FILS—I've seen this producer's Ladoix wines, red and white, more than any other. Always good quality, they are sturdy wines, well made and properly priced. The white is less good than the red, but still worth drinking.

NAMES THAT COME RECOMMENDED (BUT NOT YET TRIED)

Domaine André Nudant and Gaston and Pierre Ravaut.

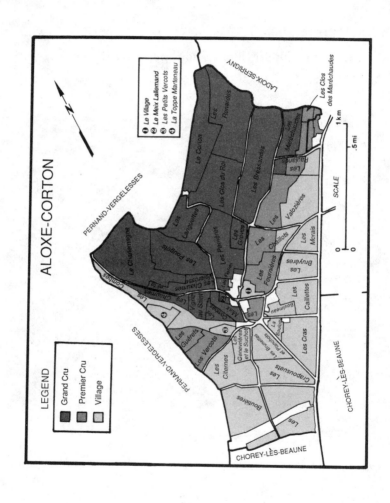

ALOXE-CORTON

LEGEND
- Grand Cru
- Premier Cru
- Village

PERNAND-VERGELESSES

PERNAND-VERGELESSES

LADOIX-SERRIGNY

CHOREY-LÈS-BEAUNE

CHOREY-LÈS-BEAUNE

SCALE
0 — .5mi
0 — 1 km

① Le Village
② Le Meix Lallemand
③ Les Petits Vercots
④ La Toppe Marteneau

Le Corton
Les Renardes
Les Pougets
Le Charlemagne
Les Languettes
Les Combes
Les Chaumes et la Voierosse
Les Paulands
Les Maréchaudes
Les Clos des Maréchaudes
Les Clos du Roi
Les Bressandes
Les Grèves
Les Perrières
Les Valozières
Les Chaillots
Les Moraix
Les Fournières
Les Bruyères
Les Guérets
Les Vercots
Les Citernes
Les Boutières
Les Grands Lolières
Les Genevrières et le Suchot
Les Boulmeau
Les Caillettes
Les Crapousuets
Les Cras
La Boulotte et Vignotte
Les Petites Lolières
La Vigne au Saint
Aux Meix
Boulmeau

Corton

One of the disappointments of Burgundy is that, so often, the
greatest vineyards don't look the part. You visit Romanée-Conti for
the first time, a-tingle with anticipation, only to discover a patch of
vineyard no different from any other on the slope. The same is true
for Montrachet and Chambertin. But it's not true for Corton. It
looks like a *grand cru*, a majestic uplift.

The fact that the hill of Corton stands freely from the slope
means that it alone has exposures found almost nowhere else in the
Côte d'Or. Some of its vineyards actually face west, although not
the best ones. But that does tell us how aloof the hill is from the
general run of the slope.

If the signature of a great wine is that the drinker senses strongly
that it couldn't come from just anywhere, then Corton is indisputably
grand cru. It is like no other red Burgundy: severe, intense, long-

lived. Neither as opulent as La Tâche nor as massive as Chambertin, a great Corton is a clarification of the possibilities of Pinot Noir. As with other great Burgundies, you can say of it that nowhere else is there such an articulation. The shadings of flavor and character are evident as you taste first a Renardes, then Clos du Roi right next to it, and finally Bressandes, which lies below them both, parallel to their combined lengths. There's no mistaking the distinctions. They all share the same southeast exposure.

When you steer along the curve of the hill, toward Perrières and Pougets, you discover a different wine: lighter, less resonantly rich, a tenor of a Pinot Noir rather than a baritone. The exposure has changed—it's more southerly—but so too has the soil. Now, it's more chalk and marl, where before it was clay and iron. But the wine is still uniquely expressive. Finally, you swing around the curve and leave red wine behind altogether. What once was Corton suddenly is Corton-Charlemagne. The chalky white soil is the tip-off.

Corton has been heralded for centuries. When Cyrus Redding reported on it in 1833, it then was 46 hectares (114 acres), producing the equivalent of just 10 or 15 hectoliters per hectare. It was a complicated vineyard then, with numerous climats and considerable interplanting of Aligoté and Pinot Gris (called Pinot Beurot) with Pinot Noir. The wine was always sold simply as Corton.

In addition to being majestic, the hill of Corton also is a monument—to the complications of Appellation Contrôlée regulations. To anatomize Corton today is to participate in an angel-sexing exercise. All of the legal punctilio involving Corton reflects the Appellation Contrôllée catechism of "*loyal, locale et constant.*" What was traditional, individual to the area, and long-term in Corton was a lot of wine from a big hill being blended together and sold under a simple catchall name. And it still is.

With the exception of Clos de Vougeot, no other *grand cru* in the Côte d'Or has available to it so many opportunities for blending within its *appellation.* Although Clos de Vougeot is cited (accurately) as the largest single vineyard in the Côte d'Or, in practical reality it's really Corton. The difference is that we still have in use all of the individual vineyard names in Corton. Any or all of the twenty-eight vineyards authorized to grow *grand cru* red Corton can be blended and sold as "Corton." In comparison, with Clos de Vougeot we have long since forgotten the fifteen *climat* names that once subdivided it.

Corton is the most convenient *grand cru* in Burgundy. It suits the purposes of wine shippers for whom blending vineyards to create one single, easily remembered wine is their stock-in-trade. Almost nowhere else in Burgundy (except the *premiers crus* of Chablis) can so many named vineyards be so freely combined and yet sold as being from one vineyard, let alone a *grand cru*.

The growers benefit equally. A glance at the ownership listings reveals the usual pattern of fragmented holdings, with the usual lucky handful of owners clutching to scraps of more than one vineyard. They too can and do combine their wines under the proud banner of Corton. It's a testament to the stubborn devotion of the Burgundian winegrower to his land that so many single-vineyard Cortons are issued.

THE VINEYARD

The Corton *appellation* is exclusively *grand cru*. A number of vineyards that are, in fact, devoted exclusively to white wine (Corton-Charlemagne) are also listed under the Corton *appellation*. Depending upon what's planted, they can swing either way. This reflects the pre-Appellation Contrôlée interplanting of red and white grapes on the hill of Corton.

The name of any of the twenty-eight vineyards entitled to be sold as "Corton" can also be added to the label, provided that the wine in the bottle comes exclusively from the vineyard named and no other, e.g., Corton "Bressandes." It also can just be called "Corton." Wine made from two or more vineyards can only be labeled "Corton" or "Le Corton."

The Corton *appellation* crosses three commune boundaries: Pernand-Vergelesses, Aloxe-Corton, and Ladoix-Serrigny.

En Charlemagne—17.2589 ha/42.6 acres

(See Corton-Charlemagne)

In Aloxe-Corton

	Hectares	Acres	Cases*
Les Bressandes—17.4181 ha/43 acres			
M. Patrick Belgrand	0.2190	0.5	101
M. Hubert Bouzereau	0.1430	0.4	66

*Cases calculated on the *rendement de base* of 35 hl/ha plus 20 percent

	Hectares	Acres	Cases*
M. Philippe Bouzereau	0.1482	0.4	68
Domaine les Bressandes	0.9925	2.5	459
GFA du Domaine Chandon de Briailles	1.8945	4.7	875
M. et Mme. Jean Cornu	0.5688	1.4	263
M. Jacques Deligny	0.2566	0.6	119
M. et Mme. Charles de Mérode	0.3775	0.9	174
M. Florent de Mérode	0.8169	2.0	377
M. Pierre Dubreuil and Mme. Maurice Maratray	0.7125	1.8	329
M. Bernard Dubreuil and M. Pierre Dubreuil	0.7703	1.9	356
Domaine Viticole de la Guyonnière	0.4319	1.1	200
Hospices Civils de Beaune	1.9236	4.8	889
M. André Hypolyte and Mme. Veuve André Hypolyte	0.2062	0.5	95
M. Michel Jaboulet-Vercherre	0.4845	1.2	224
Maison Louis Latour and GFA du Domaine de Corton-Grancey	0.7875	2.0	364
M. Jean-Louis Latour and M. Louis Latour and Maison Louis Latour	0.3855	1.0	178
Maison Louis Latour	1.6393	4.1	757
GFA du Domaine de Meix (Domaine Senard)	0.6273	1.6	290
M. et Mme. André Nudant	0.6058	1.5	280
Mlle. France Poisot	0.4352	1.1	201
Mlle. Anne Pradal and Mme. Henri Pradal	0.2525	0.6	117
M. et Mme. Louis Prin	0.4239	1.1	196
M. et Mme. Pierre Ravaut	0.4263	1.1	197
M. et Mme. Léon Sordoillet	0.1134	0.3	52
SC du Domaine Hippolyte Thévenot	0.4275	1.1	198
GFA Tollot-Beaut et Fils	0.9121	2.3	421

Le Charlemagne—16.9472 ha/41.9 acres

Les Chaumes et la Voierosse—6.6478 ha/16.4 acres divided into two *climats*: Les Chaumes et la Voierosse (9.6 acres) and Les Chaumes (6.8 acres)

---

*Cases calculated on the *rendement de base* of 35 hl/ha plus 20 percent

	Hectares	*Acres*	*Cases**
Les Chaumes et la Voierosse			
GFA du Domaine Chandon de Briailles	0.1168	0.3	54
GFA de Corton Louis Chapuis et Fils	0.6125	1.5	283
Hospices Civils de Beaune	1.1362	2.8	525
SC du Domaine Louis Jadot	0.1867	0.5	86
Mlle. Thérèse Jadot and SC du Domaine Louis Jadot	0.2463	0.6	114
M. Jacques Latour and Mme. Michel Rolland	0.0120	0.03	6
M. et Mme. Léon Sordoillet	0.6259	1.6	289
GFA du Domaine Robert Rapet	0.3882	1.0	179
M. Roland Rapet	0.0845	0.2	39
M. Vincent Rapet	0.1250	0.3	58
SC du Domaine Hippolyte Thévenot (Antonin Guyon)	0.2432	0.6	112
Les Chaumes			
M. Robert Barberet	0.2630	0.7	122
GFA du Domaine Belgrand-Latour	0.7293	1.8	337
M. Jacques Latour and Mme. Michel Rolland	0.5132	1.3	237
M. et Mme. René Quenot	0.3075	0.8	142
Les Combes—1.6917 ha/4.2 acres			
Domaine de la Juvinière (Pierre André/ Reine Pédauque)	0.5667	1.4	337
SC du Domaine Latour	0.5224	1.3	310
GFA Maigne-Ocquidant	0.2887	0.7	171
GFA Tollot-Beaut et Fils	0.3139	0.8	186
Le Corton—11.6727 ha/28.8 acres			
Maison Bouchard Père et Fils	6.8448	16.9	3162
M. et Mme. Jean Boudier	0.0614	0.2	28
Mme. Henri Chabot	0.2239	0.6	103
M. Félix Clerget	0.1993	0.5	92
M. Marcel Doudet	0.4611	1.1	213
Maison Louis Latour	0.5700	1.4	263

*Cases calculated on the *rendement de base* of 35 hl/ha plus 20 percent

	Hectares	Acres	Cases*
M. et Mme. Pierre Maldant	0.3278	0.8	151
M. Paul Moreau	0.0868	0.2	40
M. Maurice Poisot	0.5700	1.4	263
SC du Domaine Hippolyte Thévenot (Antonin Guyon)	0.2910	0.7	134
M. et Mme. Yvés Thomas	0.2321	0.6	107
GFA Tollot-Beaut et Fils	0.2412	0.6	111
M. Claude Viellard	0.4291	1.1	198
Consortium Vinicole et Viticole (Joseph Faiveley)	0.3275	0.8	151
M. et Mme. Michel Voarick	0.3408	0.8	157

Les Fiètres—1.1053 ha/2.7 acres

	Hectares	Acres	Cases*
Hospices Civils de Beaune	0.4015	1.0	185
GFA Émile Voarick	0.6969	1.7	322

Les Grèves—2.3169 ha/5.7 acres

	Hectares	Acres	Cases*
M. et Mme. Adrien Belland	0.5500	1.4	254
Hospices Civils de Beaune	0.1200	0.3	55
Maison Louis Latour	0.9180	2.3	424
M. Jean-Louis Latour and M. Louis Latour and Mme. Veuve Louis Latour	0.2922	0.7	135
Mlle. Geneviève Poisot	0.4367	1.0	202

Les Languettes—7.2375 ha/17.9 acres

	Hectares	Acres	Cases*
Maison Albert Bichot	1.2004	3.0	634
Mme. Gérard Blanc	0.1850	0.5	98
GFA de Corton Louis Chapuis et Fils	0.8526	2.1	450
Domaine Joseph Drouhin	0.3364	0.9	178
Mme. Gabriel Logier d'Ardhuy	0.5092	1.3	269
M. Jacques Latour and Mme. Michel Rolland	1.9580	4.8	1034
Mme. Gérard Mestre	0.1850	0.5	98
M. et Mme. Louis Petitjean	1.1723	2.9	619
GFA du Domaine Lequin-Roussot	0.3700	0.9	195
M. et Mme. Michel Voarick	0.4664	1.2	246

---

*Cases calculated on the *rendement de base* of 35 hl/ha plus 20 percent, except for Les Languettes at 40 hl/ha plus 20 percent

	Hectares	*Acres*	*Cases**
Les Maréchaudes—4.4597 ha/11 acres			

Clos des Maréchaudes

SCA du Domaine Saier	0.6835	1.7	316

Les Maréchaudes

Mlle. Isabelle Doudet and M. Marcel Doudet	0.1927	0.5	89
M. et Mme. Marcel Goyet	0.0012	0.0	1
Mlle. Marie Maldant	0.2310	0.6	107
M. et Mme. Michel Mallard	0.0924	0.2	43
M. Maurice Maratray	0.1675	0.4	77
M. Florent de Mérode	0.5656	1.4	261
M. et Mme. Gaston Ravaut	0.0717	0.2	33

Clos des Meix—2.7143 ha/6.7 acres divided into two *climats*: Le Meix Lallemand (1.4 acres) and Les Meix (5.3 acres)

GFA du Domaine des Meix (Domaine Senard)	2.0323	5.0	939
M. Daniel Senard	0.0835	0.2	39

Les Paulands—1.0513 ha/2.6 acres

M. Louis Denis and Mme. Veuve Louis Denis	0.2170	0.5	100
GFA du Domaine de Meix (Domaine Senard)	0.8343	2.1	385

Les Perrières—9.8771 ha/24.4 acres divided into two *climats*: Les Perrières (23.6 acres) and Le Village (0.8 acre)

Les Perrières

M. et Mme. Adrien Belland	0.6858	1.7	317
Mme. Pierre Belgrand and Mme. Veuve Louis Latour	0.8540	2.1	395
Mme. Veuve Pierre Château and Mme. Pierre Heron	1.0684	2.6	494
GFA de Corton Louis Chapuis et Fils	0.5442	1.3	251

---

*Cases calculated on the *rendement de base* of 35 hl/ha plus 20 percent

	Hectares	Acres	Cases*
Mme. Henri Georget	0.1428	0.4	66
GFA du Domaine de Corton-Grancey	1.7241	4.3	797
M. Henri Latour	0.3512	0.9	162
M. Jacques Latour and Mme. Michel Rolland	0.1414	0.4	65
M. Louis Latour and M. Jean-Louis Latour	0.0113	0.02	5
Maison Louis Latour	0.6387	1.6	295
Mme. Gérard Mestre	0.2910	0.7	134
M. et Mme. Jean Meuneveaux	0.2654	0.7	123
M. Joseph Mugnier	0.6031	1.5	279
M. Paul Poisot	1.2525	3.1	579
M. et Mme. René Quenot	0.2486	0.6	115
Mme. Roland Rapet and M. Roland Rapet	0.1580	0.4	73
M. et Mme. Léon Sordoillet	0.5321	1.3	246

Le Village

Société d'Élevage et de Diffusion des Grands Vins (Pierre André/Reine Pédauque)	0.3710	0.9	171

Les Pougets—9.8240 ha/24.3 acres

Mlle. Thérèse Jadot and SC du Domaine Louis Jadot	2.5699	6.4	1187
SC du Domaine Louis Jadot	0.2623	0.7	121
GFA du Domaine Belgrand-Latour	0.7482	1.9	346
M. Jacques Latour and Mme. Michel Rolland	0.9340	2.3	432
Maison Louis Latour	1.2397	3.1	573
GFA du Domaine Marchal-Latour	1.3391	3.3	619
M. Joseph Marchal	0.0088	0.0	4
M. André Prudhon	0.1653	0.4	76
M. Roland Rapet	0.4565	1.1	211
M. et Mme. Léon Sordoillet	0.3635	0.9	168
M. Pierre Taste	1.4598	3.6	674

Les Renardes—14.3539 ha/35.5 acres

---

*Cases calculated on the *rendement de base* of 35 hl/ha plus 20 percent

	Hectares	Acres	Cases*
Hospices Civils de Beaune	1.5135	3.7	699
M. Félix Clerget	0.0480	0.1	22
M. Jean-Pierre Colin	0.4278	1.1	198
Mme. Patrick Delattre	0.3912	1.0	181
M. Florent de Mérode	0.5081	1.3	235
Société d'Élevage et de Diffusion des Grands Vins (Pierre André/Reine Pédauque)	0.4405	1.1	204
GFA du Domaine François Capitain et Fils	0.3288	0.8	152
Mme. Veuve Alexandre Gaunoux and M. Alexandre Gaunoux	1.3027	3.2	602
M. et Mme. François Gay	0.2139	0.5	99
M. et Mme. Michel Gay	0.2139	0.5	99
M. Pierre Gille	0.1625	0.4	75
Mme. Georges Gouvernet	0.3913	1.0	181
M. André Gros	0.4138	1.0	191
Maison Louis Latour	0.3184	0.8	147
M. Roger Liger	0.1700	0.4	79
M. Hubert Maldant	0.3322	0.8	153
M. Paul Moreau	1.0068	2.5	465
M. et Mme. Louis Petitjean	0.4145	1.0	191
M. Pierre Petitjean	0.5014	1.2	232
M. Jean Pierre	1.4492	3.6	670
M. et Mme. Louis Prin	0.0682	0.2	32
Mme. Jean-Claude Sauvageot	0.4278	1.1	198
SC du Domaine Hippolyte Thévenot (Antonin Guyon)	0.2170	0.5	100
M. Paul Viellard	0.8469	2.1	391
Consortium Vinicole et Viticole (Joseph Faiveley)	0.2095	0.5	97

Le Clos du Roi—10.7270 ha/26.5 acres

	Hectares	Acres	Cases*
Mme. Pierre André	0.4176	1.0	193
Mme. Patrick Boura	0.2837	0.7	131
GFA du Domaine Chandon de Briailles	0.4465	1.1	206
SCI du Clos de Thorey	0.4176	1.0	193
M. Bernard Collenet	0.2837	0.7	131
M. Florent de Mérode	0.5721	1.4	264
M. et Mme. Bernard Dubreuil	0.2680	0.7	124

---

*Cases calculated on the *rendement de base* of 35 hl/ha plus 20 percent

	Hectares	Acres	Cases*
Mme. Veuve Michel Frisby and M. Michel Frisby and Mme. Veuve Léon Bruck	2.8314	7.0	1308
Hospices Civils de Beaune	0.8397	2.1	388
GFA du Domaine Marchal-Latour	0.3700	0.9	171
Mme. Maurice Maratray and M. Bernard et M. Pierre Dubreuil	0.7099	1.8	328
GFA du Domaine de Meix (Domaine Senard)	0.5385	1.3	249
M. et Mme. Louis Petitjean	0.5006	1.2	231
Les Petits-Fils de Pierre Ponnelle	0.4970	1.2	230
M. Daniel Senard	0.1038	0.3	48
SC des Domaines Thénard	0.9085	2.2	420
SC du Domaine Hippolyte Thévenot	0.5478	1.4	253
M. Claude Vieillard	0.3897	1.0	180

La Vigne au Saint—2.4622 ha/6.1 acres

	Hectares	Acres	Cases*
M. et Mme. Adrien Belland	0.4660	1.2	215
GFA du Domaine de Corton-Grancey SC du Domaine Latour	0.4839	1.2	224
Maison Louis Latour	1.4923	3.7	227

In Ladoix-Serrigny

Les Carriéres—0.5053 ha/1.2 acres

	Hectares	Acres	Cases*
M. et Mme. Georges Chevalier	0.2628	0.7	121
M. et Mme. Maxime Jacob	0.1275	0.3	59

Les Grandes Loliéres—3.0440 ha/7.5 acres

	Hectares	Acres	Cases*
GFA Domaine François Capitain et Fils	0.7112	1.8	329
M. et Mme. Georges Chevalier	0.2533	0.6	117
M. et Mme. Marcel Goyet	1.2295	3.0	568
M. Alain Maillard	0.1890	0.5	87
Mlle. Marie Maldant	0.2693	0.7	124
M. et Mme. Patrick Mallard	0.2585	0.6	119
M. et Mme. Paul Mancins	0.0426	0.1	20
M. et Mme. Maurice Maratray	0.9060	2.2	419

Basses Mourottes—0.9481 ha/2.3 acres

	Hectares	Acres	Cases*
Mme. Patrick Boura	0.0267	0.07	12

*Cases calculated on the *rendement de base* of 35 hl/ha plus 20 percent

	Hectares	Acres	Cases*
GFA Domaine François Capitain et Fils	0.2063	0.5	95
Mme. Georges Gouvernet	0.0169	0.04	8
M. Raymond Jacob and M. Robert Jacob	0.1943	0.5	90
M. Maxime Jacob and M. Robert Jacob	0.2592	0.6	120
M. Maxime Jacob and M. Raymond Jacob	0.2446	0.6	113

Hautes Mourottes—1.9292 ha/4.8 acres

Mlle. Marie Bachelet	0.1400	0.3	65
Mlle. Michelle Bachelet	0.1400	0.3	65
M. et Mme. Raymond Bachelet	0.0700	0.2	32
GFA Domaine François Capitain et Fils	0.0850	0.2	39
Mlle. Georges Gouvernet	0.1927	0.5	89
M. Maxime Jacob and M. Raymond Jacob	0.1770	0.4	82
M. Maxime Jacob and M. Robert Jacob	0.1675	0.4	77
M. et Mme. Pierre Ravaut	0.3425	0.8	158
Mme. Charles Viénot	0.1888	0.5	87

Les Moutottes—0.8459 ha/2.1 acres

GFA Domaine François Capitain et Fils	0.8460	2.1	391

Le Rognet et Corton—11.5948 ha/28.6 acres

M. Jean Allexant and M. Charles Allexant	0.3347	0.8	155
GFA du Domaine Camuzet	0.4520	1.1	209
M. et Mme. Claude Chevalier	0.2178	0.5	101
M. et Mme. Georges Chevalier	0.5107	1.3	236
M. François Collenet	0.7297	1.8	337
Consortium Viticole et Vinicole de Bourgogne (Joseph Faiveley)	2.9037	7.2	1342
M. Charles Deligny and M. Jacques Deligny	0.3230	0.8	149
Mme. Veuve Henri Dufouleur and M. Henri Dufouleur	0.1771	0.4	82
SCI de Domaines Dupray	0.6467	1.6	299
M. André Gros	0.2454	0.6	113

---

*Cases calculated on the *rendement de base* of 35 hl/ha plus 20 percent

	Hectares	Acres	Cases*
M. Michel Lucotte	0.3606	0.9	166
M. et Mme. Marcel Lucotte	0.4074	1.0	188
M. Pierre Masson	0.2827	0.7	131
M. et Mme. André Pathiaux	0.2803	0.7	129
Safer de Bourgogne	2.2900	5.7	1058
Mme. André Vercherre	0.3206	0.8	148
M. Claude Vieillard et Copropriétaires	0.6990	1.7	323
M. Claude Vieillard	0.0592	0.1	27

La Toppe au Vert—0.1080 ha/0.3 acre

	Hectares	Acres	Cases*
GFA Domaine François Capitain et Fils	0.1080	0.3	50

Les Vergennes—3.4517 ha/8.5 acres

	Hectares	Acres	Cases*
M. et Mme. Maurice Cachat	1.4250	3.5	658
M. Pierre Masson	2.0255	5.0	936

LES POUGETS—Because of the limestone and chalk soil, this vineyard creates strong yet lighter-weight Corton compared to Bressandes, Clos du Roi, or Renardes. Nevertheless, it is the essence of "breed." All of the distinction of Corton is present here. It can be austere and hard at first, later maturing into a wine of great finesse with a spicy scent and a metallic aftertaste.

LA VIGNE AU SAINT—As with Pougets, the soil is chalkier and the resulting wine lighter. Vigne au Saint is almost, but not quite, a *monopole* of Louis Latour. The other owner is Domaine Adrien Belland.

LE CORTON—It is difficult to know when one is drinking an actual Le Corton, for nomenclatural reasons explained previously. Nevertheless, the vineyard of Le Corton, located as it is at the crest of the hill, creates a distinct wine: hard, lean, with a relatively thin "middle taste" and an intense, aggressive *goût de terroir* in both the scent and the aftertaste. It lacks the roundness of Clos du Roi and Renardes below it. This is due to the high limestone content of the soil. It is

---

*Cases calculated on the *rendement de base* of 35 hl/ha plus 20 percent

interesting to note that in the 1860 vineyard classification of the Agricultural Committee of Beaune, Le Corton was ranked "third class," which was damning indeed. I think that they were a bit severe. Part of Le Corton is planted to Chardonnay and is sold as Corton-Charlemagne.

LE CLOS DU ROI—Along with Les Bressandes, this is the richest, fullest, most corpulent of the Cortons. It is Corton at full throttle. It also is one of the most reliable of Cortons, as it is difficult not to create something really fine from this choice vineyard. The soil is a mix of clay and iron with some limestone.

LES BRESSANDES—It's always a tie between Bressandes and Clos du Roi for the honor of richest, most concentrated Corton. Bressandes seems a bit firmer and tougher than Clos du Roi, perhaps because of some limestone (part of it was formerly a quarry). But that's just a supposition. It usually is the most expressive, long-lived Corton, and rarely does one come across a bottling that isn't at least satisfying. At best, though, it is the supreme Corton.

LES RENARDES—One supposes that foxes were once seen in this vineyard, given the name. Or maybe it's just the "gamy" taste that everyone—present company included—always seems to find in Renardes. Contiguous to both Clos du Roi and Bressandes, there is no question that Renardes is distinct from either of them. Certainly, it is in the plump, concentrated category of Cortons; it shares similar soil and exposure to its neighbors. But it somehow lacks the authority of Bressandes and the soft gentility of Clos du Roi. It is *sauvage* (wild).

PRODUCERS WORTH SEEKING OUT (AND SOME NOT)

DOMAINE ADRIEN BELLAND—The source of some good, but not great, Corton "Grèves." The Belland style leans toward a supple, almost slippery style emphasizing bright, fresh fruit. It can sometimes lack detail as a result. Belland is the minority owner of La Vigne au Saint, but I've never tasted Belland's version.

DOMAINE BONNEAU DU MARTRAY—Great as its Corton-Charlemagne is, the Bonneau du Martray red Corton is a fine but not great wine. The problem may be a matter of clonal selection. Its Corton vineyard was one of the first to be replanted using what's called *sélection clonale*, a few strains of Pinot Noir isolated for attributes of deep color, disease-resistance, and good yield. The wine is good, but a bit grapey. Maybe with older vines it will acquire greater nuance.

BOUCHARD PÈRE ET FILS—Good Corton of some austerity but no great depth. A major owner in the Le Corton vineyard.

DOMAINE CHANDON DE BRIAILLES—This domaine can be a frustration, if only because it issues some of the purest, most delicately drawn bottlings of Corton "Bressandes" and "Maréchaudes" (from the upper portion near Bressandes). The problem is that sometimes the wines go "off," for reasons unknown. It may be a matter of microbial spoilage or bad bottling or just poor shipping. But at their best, they are elegant Bressandes. Not the biggest, but with great finesse and detail.

DOMAINE CHEVALIER—This producer is best known for excellent Ladoix-Serrigny, a rarely seen labeling. Nevertheless, Chevalier makes fine straightforward Corton "Rognet."

JOSEPH FAIVELEY—This *négociant* is one of two privileged producers of a brand-name red Corton. (Latour's Château Corton-Grancey is the other.) In 1930, a court in Dijon granted the Faiveley family the right to call its 7.2-acre parcel of Rognet et Corton under the brand name of Clos des Cortons Faiveley. The date here is important: It was before the installment of Appellation Contrôlée in Corton in 1937. Since Faiveley had already been granted a legal right to use the name, the precedent stood. Rognet et Corton, by the way, does not refer to a kidney. Rather, according to Faiveley, it is a corruption of *rogne es Corton*, meaning "a vineyard taken from the main part of Corton to provide a daughter with a dowry," which event occurred after the Revolution.

Clos des Cortons Faiveley is a rich, beefy wine of considerable tannins and a certain coarseness. Nevertheless, it is one of the better Cortons available, although not of the same class as a great Bressandes or Clos du Roi. The Faiveley holdings are listed by the corporate name: Consortium Viticole et Vinicole de Bourgogne.

ANTONIN GUYON—Based in Savigny-lès-Beaune, in the late 1960s this *négociant* acquired Domaine Hippolyte Thévenot. It issues wine under a variety of names, although I've never seen the Cortons sold under anything other than Domaine Antonin Guyon. The wines are intense, a bit oaky, but structured to last. There's good concentration. Worth watching.

HOSPICES DE BEAUNE—Two *cuvées* of red Corton are offered:

Cuvée Charlotte Dumay—Les Renardes (2 ha/5 acres); Les Bressandes (1 ha/2.5 acres); and Le Clos du Roi (0.5 ha/1.2 acres)

Cuvée Docteur Peste—Les Bressandes (1 ha/2.5 acres); Les Chaumes et la Voierosses (1 ha/2.5 acres); Le Clos du Roi (0.5 ha/1.2 acres); Les Fiètres (0.4 ha/1 acre); Les Grèves (0.1 ha/0.2 acre)

One *cuvée* of white Corton (which is technically not a *grand cru*) is offered:

Cuvée Paul Chanson—Les Vergennes (0.32 ha/0.8 acre)

LOUIS JADOT—The source of superb Pougets. Jadot is the reference standard for this vineyard. Also stunning Bressandes, long-lived, fleshy, and detailed.

LOUIS LATOUR—As with Corton-Charlemagne, Louis Latour is more closely assocated with red Corton than any other producer. The firm also is the largest landholder of the *grand cru*, with some forty-two acres of Corton. Most, although not all, of the wine is bottled under the brand name of Château Corton-Grancey, which is a blend of multiple vineyards. Recently, there is a new label called

Corton Domaine Latour, which is a different blend, I'm told. It sells for less money too. Latour also issues a single vineyard bottling in its Clos de la Vigne au Saint, which it owns almost outright.

Opinions about the Latour Cortons (and other reds) are divided. For some, Château Corton-Grancey is the ideal red Corton. Others are disturbed by the Latour practice of flash-pasteurizing their wines to prevent spoilage. The present Louis Latour (the sixth of that name, with a seventh being groomed to take over) defends the practice, declaring it to be less disruptive to wine than many forms of filtration. Others are less convinced.

One thing is certain: The Latour style for red wines veers toward the light side, courtesy of a relatively brief (seven- to ten-day) fermentation and maceration period. As for Château Corton-Grancey, it is a good, but by no means great, red Corton. It is a sturdy, undoubtedly long-lived wine, but of no great breed or flavor definition. It often seems "blurry." The Clos de la Vigne au Saint is a much more interesting wine, albeit unnecessarily light, even for its chalky-soil vineyard location. Still, it does retain some defined character, which seems lacking in Château Corton-Grancey.

DOMAINE LEROY—The newly created Domaine Leroy in Vosne-Romanée has added to a piece of Corton "Renardes" from which winemaker André Porcheret has created a superb, wonderfully intense wine in the 1989 vintage. A producer to watch. The *négociant* firm of Leroy, of which Domaine Leroy is a part, did not own any vineyards in Corton until this new purchase. But various older bottlings of various single-vineyard Cortons have usually proved to be exceptional.

DOMAINE MÉO-CAMUZET—This Vosne-Romanée domaine is in a period of transition. For years, much of its vineyard holdings were in metayage with Henri Jayer. Recently, the contracts have expired, with all of the grapes reverting to Méo-Camuzet. They make superb Corton from 1.1 acres in Le Rognet et Corton. It is worthwhile comparing the elegant yet rich Méo-Camuzet wine with that from Clos des Corton Faiveley.

DOMAINE PRINCE FLORENT DE MÉRODE/CHÂTEAU DE SERRIGNY—Mixed reviews for this important estate based in Ladoix-Serrigny. I have had some good bottles over the years, but the wines are exceedingly variable—sometimes overchaptalized, sometimes thin. I would seek them out only in the best vintages. This is too bad, because de Mérode could be in the top rank, given the old vines (thirty to forty years old) and the vineyards owned.

DOMAINE DANIEL SENARD—Daniel (father) and Philippe (son) Senard offer wine under several labels. There's the mainstay label of Domaine Daniel Senard. Philippe Senard has his own label. There's also the *monopole* on Corton "Clos des Meix," bottled under the Domaine des Meix label. And there's a *négociant* business under the name of Paul Bocion. This is a problematic property. For years, the Senards have issued traditional, finely detailed wines from Poulands, Bressandes, and Clos du Roi.

Beginning with the 1988 vintage, Philippe Senard (who is in charge of the winemaking) has thrown in his lot with the enologist Guy Accad. As a result, who knows what will happen with these wines?

A tasting of Senard's 1988s in November '89, showed them to have the uniformly deep color characteristic of Accad-influenced Burgundies, as well as that curious slippery texture. Still, the substantial tannins, typical of '88s, were present, and most important, vineyard distinctions were to be found. That said, when Philippe Senard brought out a bottle of his '86 to compare with the "new, improved" '88 of the same vineyard, the jig was up: The traditionally made '86 displayed much more precise detail than the richer, deeper-hued '88. And it wasn't a matter of the benefit of two years' more age. Senard also bottles a Corton-Charlemagne *rouge* from a one-acre plot of fifteen-year-old vines. I didn't know such a thing was authorized. (Maybe it isn't.) It was just what you'd expect: light, a bit thin with a chalky *goût de terroir*.

DOMAINE TOLLOT-BEAUT—When they're "on," no producer makes greater Cortons than Tollot-Beaut. Some of my fondest wine memories revolve around the Tollot-Beaut Cortons: a profound Bressandes, like a bass blast from a pipe organ and a beautiful, precisely defined Le Corton. The oaky Tollot-Beaut style seems supportable in Corton. Regrettably, the wines can be variable. Light vintages such as 1982 and 1986 are nothing to sing about.

Corton-
Charlemagne

Ripeness is all.

—WILLIAM SHAKESPEARE, *King Lear*

Corton-Charlemagne is the most dramatic Chardonnay in the world. It is not just a matter of fruit, with which Corton-Charlemagne is famously endowed, courtesy of an almost enchanted exposure on the hill of Corton. It's also a matter of a *goût de terroir* so pronounced that only *grand cru* Chablis, Chevalier-Montrachet, and Le Montrachet can rival or exceed it. The combination makes for high drama in the glass. To be fair, Corton-Charlemagne does have one deficiency: Compared to Le Montrachet, Meursault "Perrières," and Chevalier-Montrachet, it can be said to lack finesse.

Corton-Charlemagne is a wine of texture. It should give the sensation of heaviness without actually being heavy. Each mouthful is its own universe of flavor, never capable of being fully explored. There should be abundant, almost aggressive mineraliness. Although Chardonnay has proved the ideal vehicle, one is not drinking Chardonnay with Corton-Charlemagne: One is drinking *terroir*.

The uniqueness is due to an unrivaled pairing of soil and exposure. The hill of Corton is almost a free market of exposures, with options ranging from nearly due north to due east, almost 280 degrees around. And around that configuration is embedded an array of soils ranging from almost pure chalk to iron-rich red clay. The white wines do best where the soil is chalky and the exposure south and southwesterly. Technically, the soil is blue or white marl, which is a kind of chalky clay that adds richness to white wines. That is Corton-Charlemagne. (There are a few minor exceptions on the east side of the hill in Ladoix-Serrigny with chalky soils.)

The astonishment of Corton-Charlemagne is that it came to Chardonnay—and thus to grace—so late. The vineyard itself, as the name suggests, is centuries old. Whether Charlemagne himself, in 775, did donate his domaine in Aloxe-Corton to the abbey of Saint-Androche in Saulieu can never be proved. The church records were destroyed by fire in 1360. Nevertheless, it was at least possible and maybe even likely.

According to Claude Chapuis in his book *Corton*, the original donation in the vineyard now called Le Charlemagne was 36 or 40 *ouvrées* (3.7 acres or 4.2 acres). By the time this plot was sold *bien national* during the Revolution of 1789, the abbey's Charlemagne. plot had almost doubled to 70 *ouvrées* or 7.4 acres. Today, all of Corton-Charlemagne is effectively 85 acres.

That should be history enough for any vineyard. But the real history of this extraordinary vineyard only began when Corton-Charlemagne allied itself to Chardonnay. You would think that had happened almost from the start. Instead, it is traced only to the late 1800s when the great-grandfather of the current Louis Latour replanted part of his holdings in Corton-Charlemagne to Chardonnay.

This was revolutionary. Prior to this break with tradition, the wine of Corton-Charlemagne came from three grapes: Aligoté, Pinot Blanc, or Pinot Gris (called Pinot Beurot). Doubtless these were the most magnificent examples imaginable. The Senard family still makes some Pinot Gris for private consumption, and it is stunning—and the vines aren't even in the Corton-Charlemagne appellation. It was only in 1948 that Aligoté was finally forbidden.

This recent conversion to Chardonnay helps explain why Corton-Charlemagne is not counted among the greatest white Burgundies by eighteenth- and nineteenth-century writers. Rather, it was various Meursaults and, above all, Montrachets, that garnered the huzzahs.

Today, no one disputes the supremacy of Corton-Charlemagne. The only thing left to be lamented is that, too often, the wine is not drunk sufficiently mature. A good Corton-Charlemagne needs eight to ten years of age for its full majesty to be revealed. The problem is, it's so luscious at so young an age, who can be blamed for drinking it so soon? Nevertheless, patience is advised. Also sympathetic food. Because of its richness, you don't want to trundle out a mature— or even an immature—Corton-Charlemagne with any old piece of fish or chicken. Complementary richness is called for: salmon with Béarnaise or Hollandaise sauce; a cream soup; and above all others, lobster. The delicate richness of lobster seems to find its fated partner in Corton-Charlemagne.

THE VINEYARD

Corton-Charlemagne is exclusively *grand cru*. The appellation crosses three communes: Pernand-Vergelesses, Aloxe-Corton, and Ladoix-Serrigny. It is almost a contiguous sweep of vineyard along the south and southwesterly face of the hill of Corton, except for isolated, minor outposts of plots on the east face in Ladoix-Serrigny.

The complication of Corton-Charlemagne—really, the whole hill of Corton and its wines—is that a number of vineyards known for and planted to Pinot Noir, such as Les Pougets, Les Renardes, Le Corton, Le Rognet et Corton, are also authorized to grow Chardonnay and are entitled to call the wine "Corton-Charlemagne." This is because these and other vineyards traditionally grew white wine, which was called Corton-Charlemagne prior to Appellation Contrôlée.

Also, there exists—as a technicality—a white wine appellation simply called "Charlemagne." It has fallen entirely out of use, but it still exists on the Appellation Contrôlée books. The following vineyards are entitled to use the name: En Charlemagne, Le Charlemagne, Les Pougets, Les Languettes, and Le Corton.

There is such a thing as a white Corton. It is not a *grand cru*. Nor is it another name for Corton-Charlemagne. The name (and a very little wine) exists because of the presence of white wine grapes in what are now the *grand cru* vineyards of Corton. The vineyards entitled to create Corton-Charlemagne cannot create white Corton, nor vice-versa.

The Hospices de Beaune offers a white Corton: Cuvée Paul

Chanson, who in 1974 gave a 0.32 ha/0.8-acre piece of Corton "Les Vergennes" to the Hospices. It is 100 percent Chardonnay. Another notable white Corton comes from Domaine Chandon de Briailles, which has part of its plot in Les Bressandes planted half to Chardonnay and half to Pinot Blanc.

The vineyards entitled to create Corton-Charlemagne are as follows (for other ownership listings see "Corton"):

In Pernand-Vergelesses

En Charlemagne—17.2589 ha/42.6 acres

	Hectares	Acres	Cases*
Mme. Jean-Paul le Bault de la Morinière and M. Jean-Charles le Bault de la Morinière	4.5229	11.2	2388
Mme. Georges Belin	0.4360	1.1	230
M. Serge Blosse and Mme. Serge Blosse	0.4029	1.0	213
M. Lucien Chabot	0.1674	0.4	88
Mme. Marius Delarche and M. Marius Delarche	0.9831	2.4	519
M. Louis Denis Mme. Veuve Louis Denis	0.0192	0.5	10
M. Louis Denis M. Raoul Denis Mme. Raoul Denis	0.0436 0.2243	0.1 0.6	23 118
M. et Mme. Roland Denis	0.1108	0.3	59
Mme. Bernard Dubreuil and M. Bernard Dubreuil	0.0605	0.1	32
M. Pierre Dubreuil and M. Bernard Dubreuil and Mme. Maurice Maratray	1.0345	2.6	546
M. Eugène Gauffroy	0.5062	1.3	267
M. et Mme. Jean Gauffroy	0.4877	1.2	258
M. Félix Gauthey	0.2790	0.7	147
M. et Mme. Henri Glantenet	0.1250	0.3	66
Mlle. Lucienne Glantenet	0.1266	0.3	67

---

*Cases calculated on the *rendement de base* of 40 hl/ha plus 20 percent

	Hectares	*Acres*	*Cases**
M. et Mme. Antonio Gordo	0.2727	0.7	144
Mme. Veuve Bruno Hartwagner	0.2373	0.6	125
Mme. Veuve Bruno Hartwagner and M. Bruno Hartwagner	0.3200	0.8	169
Mme. Marcel Klein	0.1190	0.3	63
M. Henri Marey	0.1170	0.3	62
M. et Mme. Pierre Marey	0.4325	1.1	228
Mme. Veuve Mijo Muskovac and M. Mijo Muskovac	0.3425	0.8	181
M. et Mme. André Nudant	0.1505	0.4	79
GFA du Domaine Pauelo	0.6000	1.5	317
M. et Mme. Regis Pavelot	0.1232	0.3	65
Commune de Pernard-Vergelesses	0.4652	1.1	246
M. Bernard Pialat and M. Raymond Pialat	0.0935	0.2	49
M. Roland Rapet	0.7244	1.8	382
M. Vincent Rapet	0.1007	0.2	53
GFA du Domaine Robert	1.3653	3.4	721
Mme. Jean Roumier	0.2040	0.5	108
M. et Mme. André Thiely	0.4996	1.2	264
Mme. Veuve Fernand Vannet and M. Fernand Vannet	0.0880	0.2	46

In Aloxe-Corton

Le Charlemagne—16.9472 ha/41.9 acres

M. Jean-Charles le Bault de la Morinière and Mme. Jean-Paul le Bault de la Morinière (Domaine Bonneau du Martray)	6.5713	16.2	3470
M. Jean-Charles le Bault de la Morinière and Mme. Jean-Paul le Bault de la Morinière (Domaine Bonneau du Martray)	0.0618	0.2	33
Hospices Civils de Beaune	0.4793	1.2	253
GFA du Domaine François Capitain et Fils	0.1200	0.3	63
M. Émile Cauvard	0.0934	0.2	49

*Cases calculated on the *rendement de base* of 40 hl/ha plus 20 percent

	Hectares	Acres	Cases*
Mme. Henri Chabot	0.2210	0.6	117
GFA de Corton Louis Chapuis et Fils	0.3036	0.8	160
Mme. Pierre Château	2.1759	5.4	1149
M. et Mme. Jean-Claude Fontaine	0.5721	1.4	302
M. Roger Gagnerot	0.1466	0.4	77
GFA du Domaine Belgrand-Latour	0.9031	2.2	477
M. Jacques Latour	0.5190	1.3	274
Maison Louis Latour	1.1900	2.9	628
GFA du Domaine Marchal-Latour	0.7874	2.0	416
Mme. René Laurent	0.2294	0.6	121
M. et Mme. Claude Lessaque	0.1672	0.4	88
M. Paul Louis and Mme. André Guenard and M. Marcel Louis	0.2179	0.5	115
Mme. Veuve Hubert Maldant and M. Hubert Maldant	0.1940	0.5	102
Mlle. Berthe Morey	0.0573	0.1	30
GFA du Domaine Pavelot	0.1453	0.7	77
M. Maxime Perronnet	0.1057	0.3	56
Mlle. Yvonne Perronnet	0.1091	0.3	58
Mme. Veuve Jules Podechard and Mme. Michel Lucotte	0.1057	0.3	56
GFA du Domaine Jean Prudhon	0.3361	0.8	177
GFA du Domaine Robert Rapet	0.1668	0.4	88
Mme. Michel Rolland			
Mme. Simone Serre	0.1254	0.3	66
Mme. Simone Serre	0.1233	0.3	65
M. et Mme. Leon Sordoillet	0.4558	1.1	241
Mme. Veuve Eugène Terrand and M. Eugène Terrand	0.0598	0.2	32
SC du Domaine Hippolyte Thévenot	0.2635	0.7	139

LES POUGETS—9.8240 ha/24.3 acres

LES LANGUETTES—7.2375 ha/17.9 acres

LE CORTON—11.6727 ha/28.8 acres

---

*Cases calculated on the *rendement de base* of 40 hl/ha plus 20 percent

LES RENARDES—2.8892 ha/7.1 acres (this is only one quarter of the Renardes vineyard)

In Ladoix-Serrigny

(See "Corton" for holdings entitled to the Corton-Charlemagne *appellation*.)

BASSES MOUROTTES—0.9481 ha/2.3 acres

HAUTES MOUROTTES—1.9292 ha/4.8 acres

LE ROGNET ET CORTON—3.1766 ha/7.8 acres (this is one third of the Rognet et Corton vineyard)

PRODUCERS WORTH SEEKING OUT

DOMAINE BONNEAU DU MARTRAY—Without question, one of the leading estates in Corton-Charlemagne. The owner, Comte Jean le Bault de la Morinière, submits that this large parcel of Corton-Charlemagne includes the original plot owned by Charlemagne. Given the choice location, smack in the heart of the En Charlemagne and Le Charlemagne vineyards, it seems entirely possible. In any judging of Corton-Charlemagne, the wine of Bonneau du Martray is destined to emerge in the top rank. It has the succulence, the texture and the profound richness that one has a right to expect. It also ages magnificently. It is one of the consistently great Corton-Charlemagnes.

BOUCHARD PÈRE ET FILS—A major owner of Corton-Charlemagne with some eight acres, Bouchard Père makes a good but not great wine. Too often it lacks depth and breed. Because of the inherent generosity of Corton-Charlemagne, it can taste pretty good on its own, but when put into play against the same vintage from Bonneau du Martray or Tollot-Beaut or Coche-Dury, you can see how far short it falls.

DOMAINE JEAN-FRANÇOIS COCHE-DURY—In 1986, the Meursault producer purchased 0.3350 ha/0.8 acre of Corton-Charlemagne. From this minuscule plot, Coche-Dury makes one of the most profound examples of *appellation*. Typical of the austere Coche-Dury style, it is evident that the wine will require years of age for it to evolve. But the concentration and, above all, the definition of flavors, is already evident. The price, alas, is bizarre, courtesy of Coche-Dury's reputation in the States and—let's be honest—the outsized profit-taking of his importers.

JOSEPH DROUHIN—The Beaune *négociant* owns little Corton-Charlemagne vineyard—0.8 acre, according to Claude Chapuis's book *Corton*—but the firm does buy from others. Corton-Charlemagne is one of Drouhin's most successful white wines. The soft, full Drouhin style lends itself admirably to Corton-Charlemagne. For a surprising exercise, you might try comparing a bottle of Drouhin's white Beaune "Clos des Mouches" against a Drouhin Corton-Charlemagne of the same vintage. They are not equal, but there is a curious familial resemblance.

JOSEPH FAIVELEY—The Nuits-Saint-Georges *négociant* offers a stunning Corton-Charlemagne: rich, opulent, and full-bodied. Regrettably, there isn't much of it. Faiveley owns about 1.5 acres. To the best of my knowledge, the wine comes exclusively from this holding.

HOSPICES DE BEAUNE—The Hospices de Beaune has one *cuvée* from Corton-Charlemagne. It invariably is the most expensive wine at the auction. The 1.2-acre plot (according to the *cadastre* records) is in the En Charlemagne vineyard. The wine is usually excellent.

Cuvée Francois de Salins—0.4793 ha/1.2 acres

LOUIS JADOT—One of the great Corton-Charlemagne producers, the Jadot style is evident in its Corton-Charlemagne as well: austere, tightly closed-in youth and demanding long bottle-aging. Jadot's

Corton-Charlemagne is not as opulent as that from Bonneau du Martray or Tollot-Beaut. Nevertheless, it still retains the characteristic creamy texture and, above all, the detail and *goût de terroir*. Jadot owns slightly less than 3.5 acres in Corton-Charlemagne.

LOUIS LATOUR—The patriarchal name of Corton-Charlemagne, as well as one of the largest property owners with a whopping twenty-five acres. Not surprisingly, the Latour Corton-Charlemagne is the best-known bottling in the world. It is most drinkers' introduction to the vineyard, and sometimes the only version they know. They could do worse. They also could do better. The Latour style in all of its wines, red and white, veers toward lightness. This is not to say that the wines necessarily lack character or definition, but rather, amplitude. One wishes for more. There is a sense of dilution. This also applies to Latour's Corton-Charlemagne. It is always at least a rewarding wine, but when you taste a Latour Corton-Charlemagne next to one of the exemplar bottlings, it is like going from monaural to stereo. This is too bad, as no producer has a greater opportunity—or the historical right—to be considered the supreme source for Corton-Charlemagne.

DOMAINE GEORGES ROUMIER—This Chambolle-Musigny domaine owns a tiny (half-acre) slice on the westerly face of En Charlemagne in Pernand-Vergelesses. As young Christophe Roumier ruefully admits, the exposure will never allow him to create a truly opulent Corton-Charlemagne. That said, Roumier still does an outstanding job, creating a full-bodied wine of breed. But not much of it, of course.

DOMAINE TOLLOT-BEAUT—Far better known for its superb red Cortons, this producer makes, for me, one of the most memorable of all Corton-Charlemagnes: unusually luscious, profound wine with all of the greenish-gold color and unending stony aftertaste that one could wish. One also could wish for more. Tollot-Beaut owns just 0.6 acre.

Aloxe-Corton

Burgundy buyers are forever complaining about the lack of availability of good-value red Burgundies. Granted, "good value" is a relative term, but within the context of the Côte d'Or, some of the best red wines for the money are commune-level and, especially, *premier cru* Aloxe-Corton.

Inevitably, they are overshadowed—literally and figuratively —by Corton. Wines labeled Aloxe-Corton (locally pronounced *Ahh-losse*) come from the lower flanks of the hill or from the flat plains surrounding it. The wines are almost exclusively red, with a minute amount of white Aloxe-Corton.

Why are they such good deals? Simply because although they don't have the breed of Corton, they do have the stuffings. A well-made Aloxe-Corton from a good vintage is a mouthful, reminiscent of a cross between Nuits-Saint-Georges and Beaune. And like Corton, they require at least five years, sometimes ten, to fully reveal their attributes.

This is not lost on *négociants*, who find Aloxe-Corton choice pickings. As for choosing a producer, a good rule of thumb is—not surprisingly—anyone who makes a good Corton is likely to make an equally good Aloxe-Corton.

There are relatively few *premiers crus*. The importance of exposure is absolute: All the *premiers crus* adjoin the *grands crus*. They literally cannot make the grade. They simply are too low on the hill to achieve greatness. But they do offer more finesse and flavor distinction than the commune-level Aloxe-Corton, although not as much as Corton itself. The Aloxois point to Les Fournières, Les Paulands, Les Maréchaudes, Les Valozièrès, and Les Petites Lolières.

THE PREMIERS CRUS

The twelve *premiers crus* of Aloxe-Corton cross the commune boundary into neighboring Ladoix-Serrigny, where five of them are located. These five vineyards invariably are labeled "Aloxe-Corton." The acreages shown below represent only the *premier cru* portions of the vineyards, several of which also have *grand cru* portions. The *grand cru* sections are found in "Corton."

In Aloxe-Corton

Les Chaillots—4.6312 ha/11.4 acres
Les Fournières—5.5697 ha/13.8 acres
Les Guérets—2.5590 ha/6.3 acres
Les Meix or Clos du Chapitre—1.9042 ha/4.7 acres
Les Paulands—1.5997 ha/4 acres
Les Valozières—6.5899 ha/16.3 acres
Les Vercots—4.1903 ha/10.3 acres

In Ladoix-Serrigny

La Coutière—2.5154 ha/6.2 acres
Les Maréchaudes or Clos des Maréchaudes—3.7118 ha/9.2 acres
Les Moutottes—0.9425 ha/2.3 acres

Les Petites Lolières—1.6425 ha/4.1 acres
La Toppe au Vert—1.7299 ha/4.3 acres

PRODUCERS WORTH SEEKING OUT

Consult the listings under Corton and Corton-Charlemagne. Many reputable *négociants* offer good Aloxe-Corton. Louis Latour in particular specializes in it. I have always enjoyed the commune-level Aloxe-Corton from Tollot-Beaut, which has added to it some *premier cru* wine. A well-reputed domaine (whose wines I have not tasted) is Domaine Michel Mallard, a major owner in several *premiers crus*.

Pernand-Vergelesses

P ernand-Vergelesses is reminiscent of one those villages that scratch out an existence on the side of a volcano. The life of the townspeople is forever fixed on that one compelling fact. You always come back to the fact that it is attached to the hill of Corton. Never mind that some of its best vineyards lie completely free of the Corton hill (which was, in fact, of volcanic origin). Never mind that the Pernandais appended the name of Vergelesses, rather than say, Pernand-Charlemagne. After all, Pernand's greatest vineyard is En Charlemagne, which creates the great Corton-Charlemagne.

To judge from the number of visitors, one gets the impression that relatively few tourists make it up to the town, which lies wedged, like a boulder stuck in a narrow crevasse, in the valley formed between the Corton hill and the escarpment of the Côte d'Or itself. Many of its vineyards are located behind the town, farther up on the slopes. Exposure is everything in Pernand-Vergelesses. This explains why its five *premiers crus* all are located away from Corton, on the slope that segues into Savigny-lès-Beaune.

What is a little odd about Pernand-Vergelesses is how much more red wine it produces than white: almost five bottles of red for every one of white. And of the white it produces, a significant percentage is reported to be Aligoté. The soil explains why: Much of it is iron-infused clay, which lends itself more to Pinot Noir than Chardonnay. Where the soil is chalky, Chardonnay or Aligoté is planted.

The red wine of Pernand-Vergelesses is for the cognoscenti. If you want to convert someone to Burgundy, you haul out a Volnay or a Vosne-Romanée or a Chambolle-Musigny. They are joy in the glass and irresistible. Pernand-Vergelesses, on the other hand, is unbending, like an old Maine farmer. It takes years for the wine to unveil itself, and even then, you will discover not something entrancing, but characterful and still a bit austere. But after enough Volnays and Vosnes, you find it a delight. At best, red Pernand-Vergelesses is a mingling of earth and soft berries. But you have to nurture it first in a cool cellar for at least five years, preferably more in rich vintages.

The white Pernand-Vergelesses is similarly earthy, but without the finesse that the best reds can deliver. It too ages well, and like white Savigny-lès-Beaune, it can surprise you with its almost fierce *goût de terroir*. Along with Ladoix-Serrigny, I always look for both red and white Pernand-Vergelesses on restaurant wine lists. The price invariably is attractive.

THE PREMIERS CRUS

Technically, Pernand-Vergelesses has one *grand cru* vineyard, the 42.6 acre En Charlemagne vineyard, which lies entirely within the Pernand-Vergelesses commune. All of its wine is entitled to be called Corton-Charlemagne if Chardonnay; Corton if Pinot Noir.

En Caradeux—14.3804 ha/35.5 acres
Creux de la Net—3.4429 ha/8.5 acres
Les Fichots—11.2252 ha/27.7 acres

Île des Vergelesses or Île des Hautes Vergelesses—9.4065 ha/23.2 acres
Les Basses Vergelesses or Vergelesses—18.0559 ha/44.6 acres

PRODUCERS WORTH SEEKING OUT

DOMAINE CHANDON DE BRIALLES—One of the leading producers of red Île des Vergelesses, Chandon de Briailles creates a wine of considerable subtlety and finesse. As always, the wines of this producer are variable, but in the best vintages this is a Pernand-Vergelesses to look for.

CHANSON—The light touch found in all of this shipper's wines seems to work well in Pernand-Vergelesses. They issue an excellent red Vergelesses.

DOMAINE DEBREUIL-FONTAINE—One of the leading producers in Pernand-Vergelesses, excelling in both red and white. Pierre Debreuil's commune-level Clos Berthet *monopole* is excellent red Pernand, best drunk in the short term. Also very good red Île de Vergelesses *premier cru*.

DOMAINE JACQUES GERMAIN—François Germain makes some of the best white Pernand-Vergelesses, although not much of it.

HOSPICES DE BEAUNE—One *cuvée* of red Pernand-Vergelesses is offered:

Cuvée Rameau-Lamarosse—Les Basses Vergelesses (0.6 ha/1.5 acres)

DOMAINE LALEURE-PIOT—Very good commune-level white Pernand-Vergelesses; the red Les Vergelesses from a five-acre parcel is exceptionally good, perfumy wine.

LOUIS JADOT—Lovely white Pernand, structured for long life in Jadot's characteristic austere style. Red Pernand "Clos de la Croix de Pierre" is a superb, 3.7-acre *monopole* in the *premier cru* vineyard, En Caradeux.

LOUIS LATOUR—Anything on or near the hill of Corton finds its way into the Latour lineup. Nicely crafted red Île de Vergelesses, albeit in the light Latour style.

DOMAINE RAPET PÈRE ET FILS—One of the top estates, offering exceptionally good red Les Vergelesses and Île de Vergelesses. It's interesting to compare the two, if only to discover the greater depth and character of Île de Vergelesses over Vergelesses, perhaps because of old vines in their Île de Vergelesses plot. The wines are famously long-lived.

DOMAINE MAURICE ROLLIN ET FILS—Intense, concentrated red, especially from Île des Vergelesses. Also, very good, graceful commune-level white.

DOMAINE ANDRÉ THIELY—Powerful, perfumy white Pernand not often seen in the States.

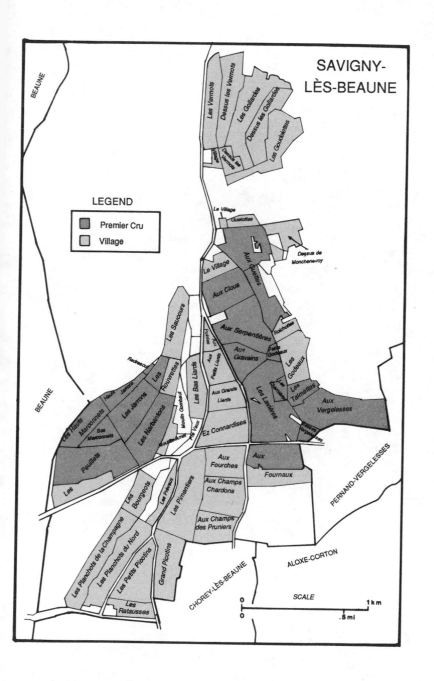

Savigny-lès-Beaune

*Art is the understanding of beauty through the senses, through
all the senses, and in order to understand the dream of a Vinci,
or the inner life of a Bach, one must, I repeat, be capable of
adoring the scented and fugitive soul of a passionate wine.*

—MARCEL ROUFF, *La Vie et la Passion de Dodin-Bouffant*
(1924)

"The scented and fugitive soul of a passionate wine." In this one
evocative phrase, the Swiss writer Marcel Rouff captured the particular appeal of Savigny-lès-Beaune. I'm sure that it wasn't Savigny
he had in mind. Clearly, any fine wine will do. But there is something
about Savigny that lends itself especially well: It *does* seem to have
a scented and yet fugitive soul. Both the red and the very little
amount of white offer a passion of sorts in the form of a surprisingly
pungent *goût de terroir*. It is surprising because Savigny-lès-Beaune
abuts Beaune, which does not have much *goût de terroir* in its wines.

Still, Savigny is inextricably tied to Beaune. Not only does
Beaune shoulder its way into the village name, it even accounts for
the unusual addition of an *accent grave* in "lès". Serena Sutcliffe in
her richly detailed *Pocket Guide to the Wines of Burgundy* tells us that
it is there because the "lès" derives from the Latin *latus*, "at the side"
(of Beaune).

Savigny-lès-Beaune is a complicated commune. It offers multiple subsoils and a baffling variety of exposures ranging from prime southeast to north and northeast. And to confound wine-writing pundits, some of the northeast exposures—which, in theory, should be doom—produce some of Savigny's best wines, such as Serpentières and Lavières.

The source of Savigny's complication is a valley, through which runs the stream called the Rhoin. On the side next to Beaune, on the slope called Mont Battois, you have one sort of Savigny. Across the valley, next to Pernand-Vergelesses, is a strikingly different version. The village of Savigny sits at the "headwaters" between the côtes, like a referee separating two glaring fighters.

Not surprisingly, the Beaune-slope vineyards—Marconnets, Jarrons, Narbantons—create Beaunelike wines: knife-and-fork wines. They are the richest, most concentrated Savignys. In a lush vintage, they can trick you into thinking that you're drinking something other than Savigny, maybe commune-level Vosne-Romanée or a good Pommard. They distinguish themselves from Beaune by an earthy *goût de terroir*.

Across the valley, the Pernand-side vineyards—Serpentières, Lavières, Vergelesses—deliver a different Savigny: lighter but with an eye-opening pungency. Here, the *goût de terroir* is different, with a deeply etched stoniness aided by a strawberry-scented fruitiness. The wines are delicate yet sturdy. Which is better? Those who prize meatiness in their Pinot Noirs will opt for a Savigny "Marconnets" or "Narbantons." Those who savor pronounced *goût de terroir* delivered in a light yet strong manner—one thinks of raw silk—will seek Serpentières or Lavières.

One point about red Savigny-lès-Beaune is worth noting: its ability to age. Although both côtes in Savigny are rewarding when young, the best wines are structured to age for at least ten years, gaining in complexity and, especially, bouquet, along the way. The lightness of the Pernand-side Savignys can be deceptive.

White Savigny-lès-Beaune is another matter. Little is produced. Savigny-lès-Beaune cranks out substantial quantities of red. It is third after Beaune and Pommard in Côte de Beaune red wine production. White wine accounts for just half of one percent of Savigny's total wine production. Moreover, not all of it is Chardonnay. An unknown quantity of Pinot Blanc makes up some of Savigny's white wine production. The Pinot Blanc is interesting, but coarse. The

Chardonnay of is something else again: It can be eye-opening, filled with a fierce *goût de terroir* that calls to mind *premier cru* Chablis.

THE PREMIERS CRUS

The Beaune Side

LES MARCONNETS—Potentially the richest, most concentrated of the Savigny *premiers crus*. It is interesting to compare a Beaune "Marconnets" with a Savigny-lès-Beaune "Marconnets." The fleshy, rounded similarities are present in both, but in Savigny the wine seems earthier. The soil is more calcareous on the Savigny side, and the exposure almost due east rather than southeasterly in Beaune "Marconnets." A good Marconnets needs at least five years of age, preferably more, to show its breed. The top of Marconnets got scalped by the A6 freeway, which is too bad. On the other hand, the original routing had it running through Le Montrachet.

LES JARRONS—Another of the dense, packed Savignys requiring extended aging. The soil here is a mix of sand and clay, different from the more limestone-infused subsoil of Marconnets. Les Jarrons is composed of two *climats*: Hauts Jarrons at the top and, farther down the flank of the Mont Battois, what used to be called "La Dominode des Jarrons" and now is simply "Les Jarrons." Many producers still label their wine Dominode (Vineyard of the Lord). The two *climats* are both *premier cru*. But in 1860 Haut Jarrons was considered lesser to Dominode. The reason likely is soil: Les Jarrons or Dominode has a clayey/sandy soil, no doubt washed down from the top of Mont Battois over the millennia. Haut Jarrons, closer to the crest of the chalky Mont Battois, has some of this chalk mixed into its subsoil, along with gravel.

LES NARBANTONS—At the base of the flank of Mont Battois is Les Narbantons. As you might expect, here the soil is an accumulation of millennia of runoff. Les Narbantons has an intermixed subsoil of clay, silt (from the river Rhoin) and sand. It too offers full, rounded wine, although a bit lighter than Jarrons or Marconnets.

LES PEUILLETS—Below Marconnets and adjacent to Les Narbantons, Les Peuillets seems to be a combination of the two. It boasts the dark color characteristic of Marconnets, but is softer and rounder, resembling Narbantons in that respect. As with the others, it too is a wine that calls for extended aging for its pungency to emerge.

The Pernand-Vergelesses Side

AUX SERPENTIÈRES—The source of this amusing name appears to be in dispute. Some say it is because snakes are found in the vineyard. Yet Anthony Hanson in *Burgundy* reports, "The name of Aux Serpentières is thought to have come not from finding serpents in this particular vineyard, but from the snakings of the boundaries between the many holdings." I like the idea of snakes myself.

Serpentières has the most passionate, scented, and fugitive soul of any of the *premiers crus*. Nothing about the color or weight of most Serpentières wines would lead one to expect the whacking great force of its flavor. After being lulled by its medium scarlet hue and light texture, you discover a hard kernel of fruit that clamps onto your palate and won't let go. (There's that snake.) It has the most finesse of the *premiers crus*, as well as a strident *goût de terroir*, what the Savigniens call the "fire" in their wines. The exposure is due south and the soil gravelly.

AUX CLOUS—Adjacent to Serpentières, it is less often seen, but very fine. It has less finesse than Serpentières, most likely due to its having more clay in the soil. The color is often deeper (clay, again) and the wine is firm. It can be one of the most concentrated of the Pernand-side Savignys and worth seeking out.

LES LAVIÈRES—In the same way that Eskimos distinguish various types of snow, the Burgundians are connoisseurs of rocks. They've got names for all sorts of sizes, shapes, and types of rocks that they have laboriously hauled out of their vineyards. Les Lavières is named after one of these species of rocks, a flat, broad piece of stone called a *lave*. The larger sizes became tombstones; the smaller ones were used as roofing tiles. (The largest roof still using *laves* in France is the forbidding fourteenth-century fortress Château de Rully in the Côte Chalonnaise, which was reroofed not long ago.) Anyway, Les Lavières had plenty of these rocks. It is one of the most appealing Savignys, delicate, strawberry-scented, and more early-maturing than some others.

AUX GUETTES—The source of some of the sternest, firmest Savigny seems to be Aux Guettes. The soil changes a bit in Guettes, although whether that contributes to its concentrated firmness I wouldn't venture to say. Whatever the source, Aux Guettes appears to produce long-lived, rewarding Savigny. The name is thought to derive from its elevated position on the slope, a lookout post (*guet*).

AUX VERGELESSES—The soil here is different yet again, with substantial quantities of brown oolitic limestone and clay. Like its Pernand counterpart of the same name, the Savigny version has a firmness allied with great finesse and noticeable *goût de terroir*. I never have tried both a Savigny "Vergelesses" and a Pernand "Vergelesses" side by side, but I wouldn't expect many differences, if any. Generally, you can expect Vergelesses to be perfumy, but not weighty.

LES CHARNIÈRES—2.0720 ha/5.1 acres

AUX CLOUS—9.9240 ha/24.5 acres

AUX FOURNAUX—7.8998 ha/19.5 acres divided into two *climats*: Aux Fournaux (15.9 acres) and Champ Chevrey (3.6 acres)

AUX GRAVAINS—6.1490 ha/15.2 acres

AUX GUETTES—14.0832 ha/34.8 acres

LES JARRONS—13.7948 ha/34.1 acres divided into three *climats*: Les Jarrons or La Dominode (19.5 acres); Les Jarrons (3.6 acres); and Hauts Jarrons (11 acres)

LES LAVIÈRES—17.6634 ha/43.6 acres

LES MARCONNETS—8.3319 ha/20.6 acres divided into two *climats*: Bas Marconnets (7.4 acres) and Hauts Marconnets (13.2 acres)

LES NARBANTONS—9.4865 ha/23.4 acres

PETITS GODEAUX—0.7115 ha/1.8 acres

LES PEUILLETS—16.1685 ha/40 acres

REDRESCUT OR REDRESCUL—0.5995 ha/1.5 acres

LES ROUVRETTES—2.8317 ha/7 acres

AUX SERPENTIÈRES—12.3371 ha/30.5 acres

LES TALMETTES—3.0964 ha/7.6 acres

AUX VERGELESSES OR LES VERGELESSES—18.8705 ha/46.6 acres divided into three *climats*: Aux Vergelesses (38 acres); Vergelesses-Batailliere (4.5 acres); and Basses Vergelesses (4.1 acres)

PRODUCERS WORTH SEEKING OUT

DOMAINE SIMON BIZE—Very fine Vergelesses, Marconnets, and Guettes are produced by one of the rising young winemakers, Patrick Bize.

DOMAINE CHANDON DE BRIAILLES—More famous for its Corton, this domaine actually is based in Savigny-lès-Beaune and produces a lovely, compelling Lavières from a 6.4-acre holding. Good commune-level Savigny as well. Classic, delicate winemaking.

DOMAINE BRUNO CLAIR—When the old Clair-Daü domaine in Marsannay was sold to Maison Louis Jadot in 1985, the son, Bruno Clair, started his own estate, which includes a 4.1-acre parcel in Jarrons–La Dominode from the Clair-Daü property. Beautiful, graceful winemaking is found here, with the characteristic Jarrons fleshiness.

DOMAINE MAURICE ÉCARD—Savigny-lès-Beaune boasts several great names offering reference-standard examples. Maurice Écard is one of them. An easy-going, unpretentious sort, the Écard style is signature-free. You don't find anything except the distinction of the *terroir*. The style is delicate but potent. Superb Serpentières from a five-acre plot; Narbantons from a 4.4-acre holding; Les Clous; and Peuillets. Écard also produces a very fine white Savigny made entirely from Pinot Blanc. Écard is the first to point out that it cannot rival Chardonnay as a grape. Still, if you see it, taste it. Domaine Louis Écard-Guyot is another label.

DOMAINE PIERRE GUILLEMOT—Another of the great Savigny names. Guillemot offers lovely Serpentières and Jarrons, as well as the best white Savigny-lès-Beaune that I have tasted—from Pinot Blanc no less. Domaine Anne-Marie Guillemot is another label. The wines are the same.

HOSPICES DE BEAUNE—Three *cuvées* from Savigny-lès-Beaune are offered:

Cuvée Forneret—Les Vergelesses (1 ha/2.5 acres) and Aux Gravains (0.66 ha/1.6 acres)

Cuvée Fouquerand—Basses Vergelesses (1 ha/2.5 acres); Les Talmettes (0.66 ha/1.6 acres); Aux Gravains (0.33 ha/0.8 acre); and Aux Serpentières (0.14 ha/0.3 acre)

Cuvée Arthur Girard—Les Peuillets (1 ha/2.5 acres) and Les Marconnets (0.8 ha/2 acres)

LEROY—This *négociant* somehow manages to offer unusually rich, fruity Savigny-lès-Beaunes unlike any others. One wonders where Madame Bize-Leroy locates them. A Savigny "Marconnets" 1985 still reverberates in the taste memory: powerful, chocolaty, impossibly rich for Savigny, yet still graceful. Other offerings, notably Serpentières, are similarly endowed, vintage and vineyard permitting.

LOUIS JADOT—The source for superb white Savigny-lès Beaune of great breed.

DOMAINE JEAN-MARC PAVELOT—Yet another resonant name in Savigny. Rich, intense wines from slightly less than one acre in Narbantons; a muscular Les Guettes from a 3.5-acre holding; and a classically rich Jarrons–La Dominode.

DOMAINE TOLLOT-BEAUT—Based in Chorey-lès-Beaune, this highly regarded producer also issues a pretty Les Lavières, from forty-five-year-old vines. Tollot-Beaut has the 3.6-acre *monopole* Champ Chevrey (Aux Fournaux) which, regrettably, is not sent to the States. If there's a drawback, it's that the wines don't support the oaky Tollot-Beaut style, which is a pity because the underlying fruit and *terroir* are very pure.

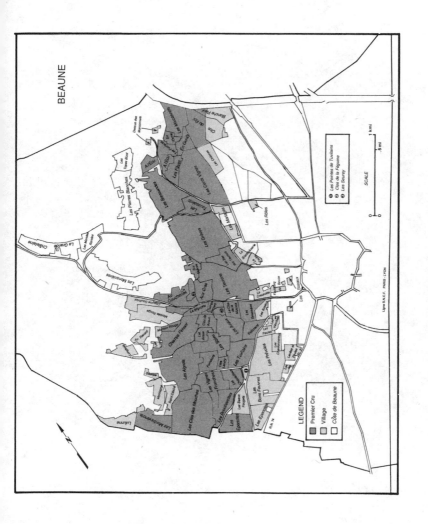

BEAUNE

LEGEND

■ Premier Cru
□ Village
□ Côte de Beaune

① Les Pointes de Tvelians
② Côte de la Féguine
③ Les Sceurey

SCALE

Ligne S.N.C.F. PARIS - LYON

Beaune

An apocryphal story used to circulate in the London wine trade of the country wine merchant who, instructing his staff in the mysteries of Burgundy, would tell them "There are two sorts: Beaune, and the rest. We sell Beaune."

—GERALD ASHER, *On Wine* (1986)

Beaune, like Pommard, used to be a convenient deception. For centuries, it has been the center from which wine shippers ruled viticultural Burgundy almost as preemptorily as the Burgundian dukes previously ruled political Burgundy. The shippers reported not to the land, but to the market. Since they owned most of the best vineyards in Beaune, it was in their best interests to ally the name Beaune with wine quality. After all, what kind of shipper would locate himself in a town with third-rate wine?

Beaune offered other conveniences. Shippers could expand their cellars into the medieval burrowings that honeycomb subterranean Beaune. Another is that it lies at the foot of a slope with an unusually broad swath of uniformly good vineyards. Only six communes in the Côte d'Or have more vineyard land—commune-level, *premier cru* and *grand cru* combined—than Beaune has in *premiers crus* alone.

The Beaunois cup runneth over in another way: The once-formidable moat around the town was filled by springs emerging from the base of the slope.

So, as with Pommard, Nuits-Saint-Georges, and Chambertin, wines of a certain style were baptized "Beaune," never mind where they came from or even whether they were composed exclusively of Pinot Noir. That these fraudulent but satisfying creations were a hit is not surprising. After all, they were created in a very pleasant image: the true wine of Beaune.

What Beaune stood for then is what Beaune still is about: a plump, succulent, fruity wine. The difference now is the delivery of these attributes. Authentic Beaune has far greater delicacy and refinement than the worked-on, amplified Beaunes of more deceitful times.

Beaune at its best is more an expression of the grape than of *terroir*. It is often observed that the wines have a sameness about them. Yet in the same way that Chinese characters change meaning based on subtle tonalities in pronunciation, the distinctions of the Beaune vineyards become evident upon close attention.

Still, the presence of distinctive *terroirs* is not insistent. Geologically, the slope has relatively few variations compared to the geological jumble of other communes. Climatically, its broad southeastern face affords many vineyards a common exposure. Differences do emerge, sometimes forcefully. But usually they are discreet. There is a common *terroir* to Beaune wines, in the broadest sense of that notion. It translates itself to a rich, grapey quality. But rarely do the individual vineyards offer a pronounced *goût de terroir*.

THE VINEYARDS

Beaune has 449.7877 ha/1,111 acres of vineyard of which 795 acres are *premier cru*. There are thirty-nine *premiers crus*, and no *grands crus*.

The vineyards of Beaune can be roughly classified into two groups: those south of the route de Bouze, a road that runs straight up the slope from the southern end of the town through a narrow valley, and those north of this valley. The southern vineyards toward Pommard generally yield more delicate wines, although by no means always thin or light. The vineyards toward Aloxe-Corton and Savigny-lès-Beaune tend to be more dense and concentrated.

THE PREMIERS CRUS

Les Aigrots—18.6365 ha/46 acres

	Hectares	*Acres*	*Cases***
Commune de Beaune	0.0955	0.2	50
M. Roger Billard	0.7430	1.8	392
Maison Bouchard Père et Fils	8.0460	19.9	4248
M. Edmond Bourrud and M. Jean-Baptiste Bourrud	0.3680	0.9	194
M. Victor Briotet	0.1840	0.5	97
Caves du Couvent des Cordeliers	0.2263	0.6	119
M. Fèlix Clerget and M. Pierre Masson	2.2804	5.6	1204
M. Hughes Devevey and M. Jean-Marie Devevey and M. Philippe Laroche	1.0010	2.5	529
M. Bernard Dury	0.2697	0.7	142
M. Marie Durand de Gevigney	0.4484	1.1	237
Hospices Civils de Beaune	0.4270	1.1	225
M. Christian Janet	0.6622	1.6	350
M. Paul Passerotte	0.5300	1.3	280
M. Robert Passerotte	0.6648	1.6	351
M. Roger Rossignol	0.6514	1.6	344
GFA Domaine Voiret	0.3976	1.0	210

Les Avaux—15.6251 ha/38.6 acres in three *climats*: Les Avaux (29.5 acres); Clos des Avaux (4.6 acres); and Champs Pimont-Clos des Avaux (4.5 acres)

Maison Bouchard Père et Fils	2.9581	7.3	1562
M. Jean-Clovis Colin	0.4496	1.1	237
Comptoir Vinicole d'Achat	0.2839	0.7	150
Designation Absente	1.4804	3.7	782
M. Jacques Floquet	0.4473	1.1	236
M. Jean-Pierre Floquet	0.0480	0.1	25
M. Jean-Pierre Floquet and M. Pierre Floquet	0.4072	1.0	215
Mme. Émile Fontaine	0.1866	0.5	99
M. Daniel Germain	0.1996	0.5	105
Hospices Civils de Beaune	3.2470	8.0	1714
SCI Domaine Jaffelin	0.3136	0.8	166
M. Alain Jobard	0.6401	1.6	338
M. Raymond Lamalle	0.2416	0.6	128

---

*Cases calculated on the *rendement de base* of 40 hl/ha plus 20 percent

	Hectares	Acres	Cases*
M. Gilbert Lecuelle	0.2416	0.6	128
M. Pierre Mérat	1.4258	3.5	753
M. Edmond Mocquin	0.2573	0.6	136
M. Jean Sauvageot	0.0970	0.2	51
GFA Domaine Voiret	0.4671	1.2	247

Le Bas des Teurons—6.3167 ha/15.6 acres

	Hectares	Acres	Cases*
GFA Arnoux	0.4815	1.2	254
M. Jacques Bergeret	0.8087	2.0	427
M. Bernard Besancenot	0.4490	1.1	237
Maison Bouchard Père et Fils	1.4968	3.7	790
M. Philippe Bouzereau	0.0523	0.1	28
SCI du Clos de Thorey	0.6675	1.6	352
Mme. Simone Duchet	0.1322	0.3	70
M. Jacques Floquet	0.0901	0.2	48
M. Pierre Floquet	0.3076	0.8	162
GAEC Martin Maurice et Fils	0.2398	0.6	127
Hospices Civils de Beaune	0.4798	1.2	253
M. Michel Lafarge	0.1470	0.4	78
M. Pierre Masson	0.0114	0.03	6
M. Edmond Mocquin	0.1724	0.4	91
GFA du Domaine Bernard d'Orgeval	0.4934	1.2	261
M. Henri Pradal	0.3784	0.9	200
GFA Domaine Voiret	0.2631	0.7	139

Belissand—4.8843 ha/12.1 acres

	Hectares	Acres	Cases*
Maison Bouchard Père et Fils	1.5818	3.9	835
M. Bertrand Darviot	0.3291	0.8	174
M. Didier Darviot	0.4485	1.1	237
M. Alexandre Devaux	0.2828	0.7	149
GFA Domaine Bernard d'Orgeval	1.5712	3.9	830
M. Raymond Durieux	0.4670	1.2	247
M. Pascal Faivre	0.2190	0.5	116

Les Boucherottes—8.5428 ha/21.1 acres

	Hectares	Acres	Cases*
Maison Bouchard Père et Fils	0.2695	0.7	142
M. Jean-Baptiste Dechaume	0.3615	0.9	191
M. Maurice Dechaume	0.3646	0.9	193
GFA Domaine Delagrange SC	0.3680	0.9	194
Domaine Joseph Drouhin	0.0041	0.01	2
M. Alexandre Gaunoux	0.1363	0.3	72
M. François Gaunoux	0.0510	0.1	27

---

*Cases calculated on the *rendement de base* of 40 hl/ha plus 20 percent

	Hectares	Acres	Cases*
SCI Domaine Paul Germain	0.9553	2.4	504
Hospices Civils de Beaune	0.6924	1.7	366
Mme. Jeanne Jadot	1.3197	3.3	697
M. Louis Jadot	1.1898	2.9	628
M. Jean-Baptiste Joliot	0.2770	0.7	146
M. Roland Joliot	0.2138	0.5	113
M. Louis Latour	0.1232	0.3	65
Maison Louis Latour	1.0587	2.6	559
M. Bernard Lochardet	0.3570	0.9	188
SC du Domaine Parent	0.3008	0.8	163
GFA Domaine Pothier-Rieusset	0.4624	1.1	244

Les Bressandes—16.9705 ha/41.9 acres

	Hectares	Acres	Cases*
M. Charles Allexant	0.7924	2.0	418
M. Jacques Bergeret	0.5240	1.3	277
Maison Bouchard Père et Fils	0.1785	0.4	94
GFA Bressandes Fondations SC	1.2440	3.1	657
Maison Chanson Père et Fils	1.3369	3.3	706
M. Georges Constant	0.0674	0.2	36
M. Guy Constant	0.0790	0.2	42
Comptoir Vinicole d'Achat	0.1557	0.4	82
M. Julien Doussot	0.7755	1.9	409
M. Paul Dubois	0.7703	1.9	407
Mme. Simone Duchet	0.8986	2.2	474
M. Yves Ferrand and M. Louis Deveney	0.3980	1.0	210
Mme. Émile Fontaine	0.3448	0.9	182
Hospices Civils de Beaune	3.5060	3.7	795
Domaine Louis Jadot	0.9432	2.3	498
SA Jobe	0.6225	1.5	329
Lycée Agricole et Viticole	0.3727	0.9	197
M. Francois Marion	0.2120	0.5	112
M. Albert Morot	1.2715	3.1	671
M. Robert Passerotte	0.2170	0.5	115
Remoissenet Père et Fils	0.1157	0.3	61
M. Benjamin Thoenig	0.3745	0.9	198
M. Jean-Claude Thoenig	0.1158	0.3	61
M. Michel Jaboulet-Vercherre	0.5297	1.3	280

Les Cents Vignes—23.5004 ha/58.1 acres

	Hectares	Acres	Cases*
GFA Arnoux	0.4952	1.2	261
Commune de Beaune	0.6298	1.6	333

*Cases calculated on the *rendement de base* of 40 hl/ha plus 20 percent

	Hectares	Acres	Cases*
GFA Domaine Besancenot-Mathouillet	3.2613	8.1	1722
M. Pierre Bize	0.1197	0.3	63
M. Jean Boillot	0.4790	1.2	253
M. Joseph Bouchard	0.2702	0.7	143
Maison Bouchard Père et Fils	2.2089	5.5	1166
Mme. Émile Cauvard	0.5251	1.3	277
Maison Chanson Père et Fils	0.6477	1.6	342
M. Louis Coron	0.4067	1.0	214
Comptoir Vinicole d'Achat	0.9103	2.2	481
M. Julien Doussot	0.2420	0.6	128
M. Paul Dubois	0.2175	0.5	115
Mme. Simone Duchet	0.4739	1.2	250
M. André Gagey and M. Jacques Saconney	0.0054	1.0	219
M. Daniel Germain	0.3935	1.0	208
SCI Domaine Paul Germain	0.5768	1.4	305
Hospices Civils de Beaune	2.9170	7.2	1540
M. Frederic Mazilly	0.1892	0.5	100
M. René Monnier	0.8550	2.1	451
M. Hubert Monnot	1.8405	2.1	444
M. Albert Morot	1.2708	3.2	675
M. Marcel Pape and M. Gérard Descotes	0.3026	0.7	160
M. Charles Podechard and M. Marcel Ducret	0.1853	0.5	98
M. Hubert Prieur	1.2510	3.1	661
GFA Domaine Robert Rapet	0.2215	0.5	117
M. Bernard Sessiaume and M. Henri Sessiaume	1.1605	2.9	615
M. Jean-Louis Tourlière	0.0063	0.6	119
M. Pierre Verne	0.0067	0.6	130

Champs Pimont—16.3601 ha/40.4 acres in two *climats*: Champs Pimont (40.1 acres) and Champs Pimont-Les Longes (0.3 acre)

Champs Pimont-Les Longes

M. André Royer	0.1095	0.3	58

Champs Pimont

M. Pierre Balizet	0.5014	1.2	265

---

*Cases calculated on the *rendement de base* of 40 hl/ha plus 20 percent

	Hectares	Acres	Cases*
Commune de Beaune	0.3603	0.9	190
Maison Bouchard Père et Fils	0.7225	1.8	381
Maison Chanson Père et Fils	3.0810	7.6	1627
M. Louis Coron	0.8750	2.2	462
M. Jacques Floquet	1.3125	3.2	693
M. Jacques Floquet	0.9858	2.4	521
M. Pierre Floquet	0.8422	2.1	445
Mme. Émile Fontaine	0.4800	1.2	253
M. Marie-Joseph Durand de Gevigney	0.1900	0.5	100
Mme. Marie Durand de Gevigney	1.7055	4.2	901
Hospices Civils de Beaune	1.4526	3.6	767
Domaine des Enfants de Marcilly	0.2948	0.7	156
M. François Pascaut	4.9818	12.3	2630

Les Chouacheux—5.0379 ha/12.4 acres

	Hectares	Acres	Cases*
GFA Domaine Cretal Bouchez	0.4977	1.2	263
M. André Gagey and M. Jacques Saconney	0.6685	1.7	353
Domaine Louis Jadot	0.3743	0.9	198
GFA Domaine Chantal Lescure	1.5130	3.7	799
M. Michel Rebourgeon	0.2565	0.6	135
M. Alain Repolt	0.0746	0.2	39
M. Jean-Claude Sabre	0.2539	0.6	134
M. Edward Sturmer	0.9929	2.5	524
GFA du Domaine Voiret	0.4065	0.1	25

Aux Coucherias—9.5623 ha/23.6 acres in two *climats*: Aux Coucherias (19 acres) and Aux Coucherias-Clos de la Féguine (4.6 acres). Maison Louis Jadot distinguishes a five-acre subplot it owns under the name of "Clos de Couchereaux."

	Hectares	Acres	Cases*
M. Jean-Baptiste Allexant	0.6363	1.6	336
M. André Bardon	0.1960	0.5	101
M. Bernard Caillet	0.5470	1.4	289
Domaine Louis Jadot	2.0351	5.0	1075
M. Pierre Labet	0.4258	1.1	225
M. André Laubron	0.2686	0.7	142
Domaine des Enfants de Marcilly	0.7100	1.8	375
M. Julien Montchovet	0.9385	2.3	496
Domaine Jacques Prieur	1.7457	4.3	922
M. Hector Ronsin	0.1878	0.5	99
M. Daniel Senard	0.2895	0.7	153

---

*Cases calculated on the *rendement de base* of 40 hl/ha plus 20 percent

	Hectares	Acres	Cases*
Aux Cras—4.9961 ha/12.3 acres			
M. Charles Collin	0.3248	0.8	171
M. Jacques Floquet	0.4267	1.1	225
M. Pierre Floquet	0.3869	1.0	204
SCI Domaine Paul Germain	1.2908	3.2	682
Maison Louis Latour	0.5403	1.3	285
M. Marcel Naudin and M. Paul Naudin	0.0503	0.1	27
M. François Pascaut	1.5173	3.7	801
GFA du Domaine Voiret	0.3249	0.8	172

À l'Écu—5.0173 ha/12.4 acres in two *climats*: À l'Écu (6.5 acres) and Clos de l'Écu (5.9 acres)

	Hectares	Acres	Cases*
M. Jacques Bergeret	0.1930	0.5	102
Maison Bouchard Père et Fils	0.5357	1.3	283
Maison Chanson Père et Fils	1.1199	2.8	591
Maison Louis Latour	0.6214	1.5	328
M. Michel Jaboulet-Vercherre	2.3703	5.9	1252

Les Epenotes—7.9612 ha/19.7 acres in two *climats*: Les Epenotes (19 acres) and Les Beaux Fougets-Epenotes (0.7 acre)

	Hectares	Acres	Cases*
M. Phillippe Ballot	0.4251	1.1	224
M. Gabriel Billard	0.1960	0.5	101
M. Georges Billard	0.1724	0.4	91
M. Jean Boillot	0.6372	1.6	336
M. Pierre Boillot	0.2406	0.6	127
M. André Buisson	0.1605	0.4	85
M. François Charles	0.6155	1.5	325
M. Bernard Eloy	0.2705	0.7	143
M. Marie-Joseph Durand de Gevigney	1.2173	3.0	643
M. André Loubet and M. Jean Dewailly	0.4469	1.1	236
M. Pierre Millot	0.2013	0.5	106
M. André Mussy and M. Michel Meuzard	0.9576	2.4	506
SC Domaine Parent	1.7488	4.3	923
M. Georges Parigot and M. Jean Demougeot	0.1623	0.4	86
M. Henri Pradal	0.9121	2.3	482

---

*Cases calculated on the *rendement de base* of 40 hl/ha plus 20 percent

	Hectares	Acres	Cases*
Les Fèves—4.4165 ha/10.9 acres			
Maison Chanson Père et Fils	3.7905	9.4	2001
Comptoir Vinicole d'Achat	0.6137	1.5	324
En Genêt—4.3489 ha/10.7 acres			
M. Michel Arnoux	0.8737	2.2	461
Maison Bouchard Père et Fils	1.2649	3.1	668
M. André Gaffie	0.2608	0.6	138
M. Jean-Marc Genot	0.2246	0.6	119
Hospices Civils de Beaune	0.4222	1.0	223
Remoissenet Père et Fils	1.2835	3.2	678
Les Grèves—31.3330 ha/77.4 acres			
Commune d'Allerey (Bureau d'Aide Sociale)	0.5831	1.4	308
GFA Domaine Besancenot-Mathouillet	0.4378	1.1	231
Maison Bouchard Père et Fils	5.7308	14.2	3026
M. François Carimentran	0.2313	0.6	122
SCI du Clos de Thorey (Moillard)	1.5301	3.8	808
M. Félix Clerget	0.1833	0.5	97
Maison Chanson Père et Fils	0.7770	1.9	410
M. Louis Coron	0.1796	0.4	95
Comptoir Vinicole d'Achat	2.2015	5.4	1162
M. Yves Darviot	0.6793	1.7	359
M. Desmazières	0.7374	1.8	389
Mme. Simone Duchet	0.0003	0.7	158
M. Jacques Floquet	0.7569	1.9	400
M. Pierre Floquet	0.0011	1.9	407
M. Charles Genot	1.0382	2.6	548
GFA Domaine Goud de Beaupuis	1.2735	3.1	672
M. André Guillemard	0.2418	0.6	128
Hospices Civils de Beaune	2.4162	6.0	1276
M. Michel Lafarge	0.3750	0.9	198
Maison Louis Latour	0.1815	0.4	96
M. Alain Maillard	0.3622	0.9	191
M. Philippe Petitjean de Marcilly	0.7917	2.0	418
M. Marie-Fernand Masson	0.7143	1.8	377
M. Pierre Masson	0.4249	1.0	224
M. Evelyne Moine and Mme. Henri Moine and M. Jean-Pierre Moine	1.3057	3.2	689

---

*Cases calculated on the *rendement de base* of 40 hl/ha plus 20 percent

	Hectares	Acres	Cases*
Albert Morot	0.1253	0.3	66
M. Régis Parigot	0.4357	1.1	230
M. François Pascaut	1.1668	2.9	616
Les Petits-Fils de Pierre Ponnelle	0.3275	0.8	173
M. Marc Rageneau and Mme. Véronique Barrois	1.3793	3.4	728
Remoissenet Père et Fils	0.5809	1.4	307
GFA Tollot Beaut et Fils	0.5942	1.5	314
M. Robert Tourlière	0.7793	1.9	411
M. Jean-Baptiste Virely	0.5367	1.3	283
GFA Domain Voiret	0.4455	1.1	235

Clos Landry or Clos Saint-Landry—1.9769 ha/4.9 acres

Maison Bouchard Père et Fils	1.9384	4.8	1023

Les Marconnets—9.3911 ha/23.2 acres

M. Joseph Bouchard	1.5220	3.8	804
Maison Bouchard Père et Fils	2.3227	5.7	1226
M. Maurice Boudras	0.3167	0.8	167
GFA Domaine Bernard d'Orgeval	0.6842	1.7	361
Maison Chanson Père et Fils	3.7788	6.9	1467
M. Albert Morot	0.6700	1.7	354
M. Benjamin Thoenig	1.47	0.3	55

La Mignotte—2.4058 ha/5.9 acres

Hospices Civils de Beaune	2.0770	6.8	1463
M. Abel Malgat	0.3090	0.8	163

Montée Rouge—3.7569 ha/9.3 acres

M. François Carimentran	0.2315	0.6	122
M. Henri Chambrette	0.3483	0.9	184
M. Roger Dessertau	0.1787	0.4	94
M. Henri Fumey	0.2086	0.5	110
Hospices Civils de Beaune	1.6470	4.1	870
M. Marcel Louis and M. Paul Louis and M. André Guenard	2.3505	5.8	1241
M. Gabriel Tainturier	0.1214	0.3	64

Les Montrevenots—8.4240 ha/20.8 acres

---

*Cases calculated on the *rendement de base* of 40 hl/ha plus 20 percent

	Hectares	Acres	Cases*
Mme. Monique Belorgey and M. Jean Charlut	0.2274	0.6	120
GFA Pommard Belorgey	0.5535	1.4	292
M. Jacques Bergeret and M. Jacques Marie-Joseph Bergeret	0.2731	0.7	144
M. Henri Chauvenet and M. Jacques Chauvenet	0.1420	0.4	75
M. Armand Dancer	0.1543	0.4	81
M. Bernard Dubreuil	0.3156	0.8	167
Hospices Civils de Beaune	2.1107	5.2	1114
M. Louis Jovard	0.4135	1.0	218
M. Dominique Lahaye	0.0856	0.2	45
M. Bernard Lochardet	0.1611	0.4	85
Mme. Denise Loget	0.6512	1.6	344
M. André Loubet and M. Jean Dewailly	0.3589	0.9	189
M. Christian Menaut	0.2057	0.5	109
M. François Michelot	0.1418	0.4	75
M. Jean Monnier			
Mme. Yvette Monnier	0.5340	1.3	282
Mme. Émile Mouillot	0.1452	0.4	77
M. André Mussy and M. Serge Mussy	0.2780	0.7	147
M. André Mussy and M. Michel Meuzard	0.2510	0.6	133
M. Serge Mussy	0.8977	2.2	474
SC Domaine Parent	0.2565	0.6	135
M. Michel Parigot and M. Paul Moingeon and M. Jean Benoit	0.0856	0.2	45
Safer	0.3873	1.0	204

Le Clos des Mouches—25.1847 ha/62.2 acres in two *climats*: Le Clos des Mouches (62.1 acres) and Boucherottes-Clos des Mouches (0.1 acre)

M. Michel Arcelain	0.1988	0.5	105
Commune de Beaune	0.3313	0.8	175
GFA Domaine Gonnet Billard	0.1247	0.3	66
Maison Chanson Père et Fils	3.2729	8.1	1728
M. Louis Coron	0.1440	0.4	76
M. Henri Darviot	0.4760	1.2	251

*Cases calculated on the *rendement de base* of 40 hl/ha plus 20 percent

	Hectares	Acres	Cases*
Domaine Joseph Drouhin	1.5158	3.7	800
Maison Joseph Drouhin	0.2240	0.6	118
M. Robert Jousset-Drouhin	0.9216	2.3	487
M. Robert Jousset-Drouhin and Domaine Joseph Drouhin	10.2477	25.3	5411
GFA Domaine Edmond	0.7263	1.8	383
M. Jean Garaudet and M. Marc Garaudet	0.1503	0.4	79
M. François Gaunoux	0.6680	1.7	353
M. Daniel Gerbeaut	0.1552	0.4	82
M. Henri Girardin	0.3518	0.9	186
GFA Jules Guillemard	0.4726	1.2	250
Hospices Civils de Beaune	0.2905	0.7	153
M. Louis Jadot	0.0120	0.03	6
M. Denis Marion	0.5320	1.3	281
M. Jacques Marion	0.2330	0.6	123
M. Maurice Marion	0.3850	1.0	203
M. Pierre Mérat	0.2775	0.7	147
M. François Pascaut	2.2047	5.4	1164
Mme. Eugène Rossignol	0.2753	0.7	145

Le Clos de la Mousse—3.3650 ha/8.3 acres

Maison Bouchard Père et Fils	3.3626	8.3	1775

En l'Orme—2.0220 ha/5 acres

Commune d'Allerey (Bureau d'Aide Sociale)	2.0002	5.0	1067

Les Perrières—3.2001 ha/7.9 acres

M. André Bouzereau	0.2242	0.6	118
M. Jean-Pierre Floquet	0.6370	1.6	336
M. François Gay	0.2568	0.6	136
Hospices Civils de Beaune	0.7735	1.9	408
M. Louis Latour	0.7036	1.7	372

Pertuisots—5.2732 ha/13 acres

Commune d'Allerey, Bureau d'Aide Sociale	0.4037	1.0	213
M. Fernand Baudrand	0.4485	1.1	237

---

*Cases calculated on the *rendement de base* of 40 hl/ha plus 20 percent

	Hectares	Acres	Cases*
Commune de Beaune, Bureau d'Aide Sociale	0.7366	1.8	389
Maison Bouchard Père et Fils	0.4532	1.1	239
M. Pierre Bouzereau	0.7370	1.8	389
M. François Carimentran	0.2160	0.5	114
Mme. Simone Duchet	0.2325	0.6	123
M. Pierre Masson	0.5167	1.3	273
GFA Domaine Voiret	1.2305	3.0	650

Les Reversées—4.7814 ha/11.8 acres

	Hectares	Acres	Cases*
Linda et Sandrine Berti	0.2242	0.6	118
M. Aimé Bollotte	0.0428	0.1	23
M. Christian Bouley	0.5823	1.4	307
M. Fernand Carre	0.3430	0.8	181
M. Henri Faivre	0.2694	0.7	142
M. Marcel Gagnerot	0.2670	0.7	141
M. Marc Garot and M. René Stehly	0.2672	0.7	141
SCI Domaine Jaffelin	0.2448	0.6	129
M. Bernard Jeannet	0.3333	0.8	176
M. Edmond Joly and M. André Bouillet	0.2670	0.7	141
M. Christian Rossignol	0.3198	0.8	169
M. Jean-Claude Thoenig	0.8395	2.1	443

Clos du Roi—8.7687 ha/21.7 acres in two *climats*: Clos du Roi (20.8 acres) and Blanche Fleur-Clos du Roi (0.9 acre)

	Hectares	Acres	Cases*
M. Jacques Bergeret	0.9600	2.4	507
GFA Domaine Besancenot-Mathouillet	0.3286	0.8	174
M. Jean Boillot	0.6985	1.7	369
M. André Boisseaux and M. Jacques Boisseaux and M. Pierre Boisseaux	0.2583	0.6	136
M. Joseph Bouchard	0.4081	1.0	215
Maison Bouchard Père et Fils	0.8294	2.0	438
Maison Chanson Père et Fils	2.6993	6.7	1425
SA Aujoux et Cie	0.0666	0.2	35
M. Louis Coron	0.0554	0.1	29
M. Jérome Doudet and M. Marcel Doudet	0.0631	0.2	33
Maison Louis Latour	0.4205	1.0	222

---

*Cases calculated on the *rendement de base* of 40 hl/ha plus 20 percent

	Hectares	Acres	Cases*
Les Petits-Fils Pierre de Ponnelle	0.0165	0.04	9
M. Chantal Prieur and M. Claude Uny	0.3955	1.0	209
GFA Tollot-Beaut et Fils	0.9182	2.3	485

Blanche Fleur-Clos du Roi

Maison Chanson Père et Fils	0.3558	0.9	188

Les Seurey—1.2325 ha/3 acres

Maison Bouchard Père et Fils	0.3990	1.0	211
Hospices Civils de Beaune	0.8333	2.1	440

Les Sizies—8.5522 ha/21.2 acres

M. André Bardon	0.6730	1.7	355
Maison Bouchard Père et Fils	3.1396	7.8	1658
M. Roger Bouchotte	0.5305	1.3	280
M. Jean-Pierre Colin	0.6462	1.6	341
M. Henri Faivre	0.2008	0.5	106
M. Jean-Pierre Floquet	0.5673	1.4	300
M. Jean-Pierre Floquet and M. Pierre Floquet	1.0520	3.7	793
Hospices Civils de Beaune	0.3203	0.8	169
M. Alain Jobard	0.0848	0.2	45
M. Raymond Lamalle	0.1367	0.3	72
M. Michel Prunier	0.2296	0.6	121
M. Paul Rousseau	0.4705	1.2	248
M. Jean Sauvageot	0.5430	1.3	287

Sur les Grèves—3.6217 ha/8.9 acres in two *climats*: Sur les Grèves (7.1 acres) and Sur les Grèves-Clos Sainte-Anne (1.8 acres)

Maison Bouchard Père et Fils	1.1605	2.9	613
M. Jean Bouley	0.7260	1.8	383
Domaine Joseph Drouhin	0.7595	1.9	401
M. Pierre Floquet	0.0692	0.2	37
SCI Domaine Paul Germain	0.1255	0.3	66
M. Edmond de Marcilly	0.6373	1.6	336

Les Teurons—21.0404 ha/52 acres

M. André Barolet	0.3468	0.9	183
Maison Bouchard Père et Fils	2.5597	6.3	1352

*Cases calculated on the *rendement de base* of 40 hl/ha plus 20 percent

	Hectares	*Acres*	*Cases**
M. Philippe Bouzereau	0.3991	1.0	211
M. François Carimentran	0.5410	1.3	286
Mme. Émile Cauvard	0.5274	1.3	278
Maison Chanson Père et Fils	3.8015	9.4	2007
Comptoir Vinicole d'Achat	0.5397	1.3	285
M. Robert Ferrain	0.4361	1.1	230
SCI Domaine Paul Germain	2.0305	5.0	1072
Hospices Civils de Beaune	2.0074	5.0	1060
Domaine Louis Jadot	0.5012	1.2	265
Mme. Martine Jadot and Mme. Thérèse Jadot	0.5013	1.2	265
M. Robert Marot	1.6908	4.2	893
M. Albert Morot	0.9888	2.4	522
M. Michel Pernot and M. Paul Pernot	0.2165	0.5	114
M. François Rossignol and M. Régis Rossignol	0.6160	1.5	325
M. François Rossignol and M. Michel Rossignol	0.6160	1.5	325
M. François Rossignol and M. Yves Rossignol	0.6160	1.5	325
M. Jacques Rossignol	1.1735	2.9	620

Les Toussaints—6.4179 ha/15.9 acres

GFA Domaine Besancenot-Mathouillet	0.5810	1.4	307
Maison Bouchard Père et Fils	0.6015	1.5	318
Comptoir Vinicole d'Achat	1.4385	3.6	760
M. Michel Gay	0.2092	0.5	110
M. Daniel Germain	0.5276	1.3	279
M. René Monnier and M. Hubert Monnot	0.8035	2.0	424
M. Albert Morot	0.7714	1.9	407
M. Henri Puthod	0.2183	0.5	115
Remoissenet Père et Fils	0.3768	0.9	199
M. Robert Tourlière	0.8901	2.2	470

Les Tuvilains—8.9352 ha/22.1 acres

Commune de Beaune, Bureau d'Aide Sociale	0.9561	2.4	505

---

*Cases calculated on the *rendement de base* of 40 hl/ha plus 20 percent

	Hectares	Acres	Cases*
Maison Bouchard Père et Fils	4.0360	10.0	2131
M. Denis Clement	0.3093	0.8	163
Comptoir Vinicole d'Achat	0.7200	1.8	380
M. Henri Faivre	0.2520	0.6	133
M. Jean-Pierre Floquet	0.4055	1.0	214
M. Edmond Mocquin	0.3088	0.8	163
M. Jacques Rossignol	0.2644	0.7	140
M. Robert Tourlière	0.5552	1.4	293
GFA Domaine Voiret	1.0762	2.7	568

Les Vignes Franches—9.7674 ha/24.1 acres in two *climats*: Vignes Franches (21 acres) and Clos des Ursules (3.1 acres)

	Hectares	Acres	Cases*
M. Michel Bouzereau and M. Leon Ozga	0.4945	1.2	261
Maison Chanson Père et Fils	0.0950	0.2	50
M. Bernard Eloy	0.3023	0.7	160
SCI Domaine Paul Germain	0.9595	2.4	507
GFA Domaine Goud de Beaupuis	1.6075	4.0	849
Hospices Civils de Beaune	0.2112	0.5	112
M. Georges Jacquet	0.5703	1.4	301
Domaine Louis Jadot	2.7468	6.8	1450
Maison Louis Latour	1.5747	3.9	831
M. Frédéric Mazilly	0.2893	0.7	153
M. Henri Rebourgeon	0.6125	1.5	323

VINEYARDS WORTH SEEKING OUT

All *premiers crus* are not created equal in Beaune. The stars are: Clos du Roi, Cents Vignes, Bressandes, Grèves, Marconnets, Les Fèves, Teurons, Avaux, Vignes Franches, and Clos des Mouches. Several producers offer prominently named subplots in these vineyards such as Jadot's Clos des Ursules (Vignes Franches); Bouchard Père's Vigne de l'Enfant Jésus (Grèves); Louis Jadot's Clos des Chouchereaux (Aux Coucherias); and Jaboulet-Vercherre's Clos de l'Écu (À l'Écu). One sometimes finds wines labeled "Beaune Premier Cru." If the price is right, these can be outstanding wines for the money.

---

*Cases calculated on the *rendement de base* of 40 hl/ha plus 20 percent

LES CHOUACHEUX—This vineyard has long fascinated me because it consistently produces a lighter, more early-maturing wine than its neighbor right above it, Vignes Franches, which is a richer, beefier wine. To look at the usual vineyard map tells us little, save that it is lower on the slope than some of the choicer *premiers crus*. A geological map, however, gives us some hints. Where the upper part of Vignes Franches has a subsoil of what's called brown oolitic limestone, this is absent in Chouacheux, which is more pebbly, which likely makes for a lighter-weight wine.

But it was when I walked through the Beaune vineyards with Pierre-Henry Gagey of Maison Louis Jadot that another important difference was revealed. Jadot produces a superb Vignes Franches from a subplot called Clos des Ursules. And it also owns slightly less than one acre of Chouacheux. Pierre-Henry confirmed my impression that Chouacheux always is lighter and more early-maturing than Vignes Franches. When pressed for a reason, he pointed to Chouacheux as we stood in Vignes Franches. "You see how the slope gently dips there?" he instructed. "I think that air drainage is a factor. The cool air slides right through Vignes Franches and then collects in that dip where Chouacheux is located. I'll bet you that it has a cooler microclimate." And I'll bet you that he's right.

LE CLOS DES MOUCHES—Contrary to the usual explanation, Clos des Mouches does not mean the enclosed vineyard of the flies, but rather, of the wasps (*guêpes*). Some say it's bees, which in fact adorn Maison Drouhin's charming Clos des Mouches label. The locals must be tough customers, brushing off wasps like flies. (There is also a Clos de la Mousse, but that's altogether different.)

Clos des Mouches is one of the most famous Beaune *premiers crus* and one of the most satisfying. Maison Drouhin dominates in vineyard holdings (twenty-nine acres; almost half the vineyard) and in carrying the fame of the vineyard farthest. Happily, the Drouhin version is outstanding. Clos des Mouches is quintessential Beaune: fleshy, warm, grapey, and round. If a wine could be cuddly, it would be Clos des Mouches. It's usually at its best between five and ten years of age.

LES VIGNES FRANCHES—One of the most rewarding of the *premiers crus*. *Chewy* is a word that keeps cropping up in my notes.

Although Vignes Franches adjoins Clos des Mouches, the wines share only certain characteristics: Both are fleshy and deeply colored. But Vignes Franches seems richer and fuller, better-defined. It has more backbone. It is one of the top five *premiers crus* of Beaune.

CLOS DU ROI—I've often suspected that one could do worse than to choose Burgundies based only on certain vineyard names, no matter what the commune. One name would be Clos du Roi or another regal or ducal variation thereof. Along with Marconnets, the Clos du Roi vineyard creates some of the most intense, almost stern wine of Beaune. At its best, Clos du Roi is the most concentrated, voluptuous wine of Beaune. One possible reason for only the upper half of Clos du Roi being classified *premier cru* is geological: the line seems to adhere almost exactly to a shift in subsoils, the *premier cru* section having oolitic brown limestone that is absent farther down the slope.

LES CENTS VIGNES—Although adjacent to Clos du Roi, Les Cents Vignes, or the Hundred Vines, usually emerges as a slightly more delicate wine, plump to be sure, but not quite as densely packed a wine. Still, it shares the richness and intensity common to the best of the *premiers crus* north of route de Bouze.

LES BRESSANDES—Another of the meaty, concentrated wines of the northern part of Beaune.

LES GRÈVES—A notable exception to the idea that the vineyards north of the route de Bouze are all heavyweights. The gravelly soil of Les Grèves leads to a lighter-textured wine than is found from its neighbors. Its distinction is a remarkable delicacy allied with powerful flavor impact. Grèves offers what Bressandes and Clos du Roi too often lack: finesse.

LES TEURONS—This vineyard often is spelled "Theurons." A difficult one to get a handle on. I've found Teurons to be a lean, firm wine that doesn't have quite the breed or depth of neighboring Grèves. But I wouldn't care to swear to that.

LES AVAUX—South of the route de Bouze, the few times I've had a Beaune "Avaux," I've found a lovely perfuminess coupled with forthright fruitiness. *Pretty* is the term that shows up in my notes.

PRODUCERS WORTH SEEKING OUT (AND SOME NOT)

DOMAINE BESANCENOT-MATHOUILLET—A tongue-twister of a name, but wines worth wrapping your palate around. Amazingly concentrated, intense wines that are almost—but not quite—ponderously so. Outstanding Cent-Vignes (the largest owner), Grèves, and Clos du Roi.

BOUCHARD PÈRE ET FILS—In a *négociant*-dominated commune, Bouchard Père is king of the hill. The wines are issued with the Domaines du Château de Beaune label. The most famous is their Vigne de l'Enfant Jésus bottling from the Grèves vineyard, which can be a lush, velvety wine in good years. They also have the *monopole* on the 4.9-acre Clos Saint-Landry, from which comes a rare white Beaune of good quality. Also there's the *monopole* of the 8.3-acre Clos de la Mousse. The *négociant* also issues both a red and a white blend of *premiers crus* under the brand name Beaune du Château. Bouchard is a continuing frustration: so many vines, so little ambition. No *négociant* owns more *premier* and *grand cru* vineyards than Bouchard Père, yet what emerges is mediocre.

CHANSON PÈRE ET FILS—Another *négociant* with substantial vineyard holdings in Beaune: 8.1 acres in Clos des Mouches; the 9.3-acre *climat* Clos des Marconnets; the 9.4-acre Clos des Fèves; 9.4 acres of Teurons. These and other wines are sold under the Domaine Chanson label. They are the best wines of Chanson, a *négociant* whose other wines are lackluster: slight, blurred, and boring. And even these domaine bottlings could be better, with more stuffings and flavor impact.

JOSEPH DROUHIN—One of the ranking *négociants*, Drouhin's signature wine surely is Clos des Mouches. The question is really whether the rare white Clos des Mouches is even better than the red. Few white Beaunes are issued, with Drouhin's Clos des Mouches *blanc* being by far the best known. It has some of the voluptuousness of no less a wine than Corton-Charlemagne, although not its profound *goût de terroir*. Still, the resemblance is there. The Drouhin style for red wines, no matter what the vineyard, is for early-maturing, deeply colored wines that pop with fresh, bursting fruit. Some in the trade call them restaurant wines, as they are so immediately accessible. For that style, no one does it better than Drouhin.

DOMAINE JACQUES GERMAIN—If you had to choose just one source for Beaune, you could do worse than this estate, impeccably run by François Germain. Stunning Teurons, Vignes Franches, and Cent Vignes, as well as a stylish, straightforward commune-level Beaune. Germain's signature-free style presents some of the clearest vineyard differences, as well as displaying the delicacy that Beaune can deliver.

HOSPICES DE BEAUNE—The Hospices de Beaune, an ancient charitable institution providing medical and nursing-home care, is the spoiled child of doting Burgundian parents. Its wines sell for ever-higher prices at an auction on the third Sunday in November without regard for quality. Supporters indulgently suggest that it is, after all, a charity auction. Anyone who believes that is still in short pants. The Hospices has effectively sold itself to the world as the source of uniquely fine red and white Burgundies. It does own choice vineyards. And it has issued some very fine wines over the years. The irony is that no label is less reliable that that of the Hospices.

The reason for this is twofold. First, the wines made by the Hospices are auctioned in November and must be carted off by the successful bidders no later than the following March. That means that virtually all of the critical cellaring techniques are performed by others, who may or may not be any good at it. All of these wines are stored in new oak barrels. Too often, Hospices wines are excessvely marked by oakiness, as the *négociant* who purchases the wines at auction is not likely to transfer the wine to a different barrel, understandably figuring that a new oak barrel is superior to anything else, never mind the structure or depth of the wine that's in it. In short, a Hospices wine is often no better than the *négociant*—it's never a domaine—who cellars and bottles it.

A second reason, often overlooked, is the pressure on the Hospices to complete the fermentations—primary and malolactic—as soon as possible, so as to have presentable wines by the third week of November, when bidders get a chance to taste the wines from the barrel. Although the public stance is that the Hospices does whatever the wines need, the private reports are that the Hospices winemakers are acutely aware of the time pressure and make vinification decisions accordingly.

At this writing, the gap between quality and price is greater than ever. The quality of Hospices wines rose dramatically after the arrival in 1977 of André Porcheret, who left ten years later to make the wines for the newly created Domaine Leroy. Since his departure, the wines have slumped again. Yet the prices fetched by the 1989 vintage were the highest ever. The wines, especially the reds, should have been spectacularly good. Instead, they were painfully light and thin. The whites were better, but of no extraordinary standard.

Who was buying these wines? Not the best *négociants*, not at those prices—and that quality. There are exceptions, of course. Maison Joseph Drouhin always buys the first lot of Cuvée Maurice Drouhin, the vineyards for which were donated by the current owner's late uncle. It is expected of him. But most of the purchases were on behalf of Japanese clients and various Swiss, German, Belgian, and British restaurateurs. They wanted to touch the fashionable hem.

The serious *négociants* know better. What would you do if you saw lackluster red Pernand-Vergelesses being sold for the same (barrel) price as Chambertin? You'd sit on your not-so-charitable hands. (Both barrels went to private buyers.) How about a Corton-Charlemagne of good but not great quality that sold for the equivalent of $167 a bottle? No *négociant* in his right mind spends that kind of money for a barrel of Corton-Charlemagne—maybe one fifth that price. Yet a private British buyer bought all five barrels, dropping $250,000 in the process.

What does this mean for the serious Burgundy lover? Namely that not only is there nothing magical about the quality of the Hospices wines, but that the premium you are being asked to pay is akin to buying a five-dollar chip in Las Vegas for ten dollars—and then betting at the same odds as everybody else. You have to be very charitable, both in palate as well as pocketbook. The nine Beaune wines of the Hospices are as follows:

Cuvée Nicolas Rolin—Les Cents Vignes (1.5 ha/3.7 acres); Les Grèves (0.8 ha/2 acres); and En Genêt (0.4 ha/1 acre)

Cuvée Guigone de Salins—Les Bressandes (1 ha/2.5 acres); Les Seurey (0.8 ha/2 acres); Champs Pimont (0.6 ha/1.5 acres)

Clos des Avaux—2 ha/4.9 acres

Cuvée Brunet—Les Teurons (0.88 ha/2.2 acres); Les Bressandes (0.66 ha/1.6 acres); La Mignotte (0.5 ha/1.2 acres); Les Cents Vignes (0.33 ha/0.8 acre)

Cuvée Maurice Drouhin—Les Avaux (0.8 ha/2 acres); Les Boucherottes (0.4 ha/1 acre); Champs Pimont (0.6 ha/1.5 acres); Les Grèves (0.4 ha/1 acre)

Cuvée Hugues et Louis Bétault—Les Grèves (0.88 ha/2.2 acres); La Mignotte (0.5 ha/1.2 acres); Les Aigrots (0.4 ha/1 acre); Les Sizies (0.33 ha/0.8 acre); Les Vignes Franches (0.2 ha/0.5 acre)

Cuvée Rousseau-Deslandes—Les Cent Vignes (1 ha/2.5 acres); Les Montrevenots (0.66 ha/1.6 acres); La Mignotte (0.4 ha/1 acre); Les Avaux (0.33 ha/0.8 acre)

Cuvée Dames Hospitalières—Les Bressandes (1 ha/2.5 acres); La Mignotte (0.66 ha/1.6 acres); Les Teurons (0.5 ha/1.2 acres); Les Grèves (0.33 ha/0.8 acre)

Cuvée Cyrot Chaudron—1 hectare of unspecified Beaune vineyard donated in 1979. There is also a Cuvée Cyrot-Chaudron for Pommard, also unspecified.

LOUIS JADOT—Close on François Germain's heels as the supreme source of Beaune wines, the signature Jadot wine surely is its Clos des

Ursules bottling from Vignes Franches. The Jadot style has evolved in recent years. In the 1970s, the red wines tended toward a certain dryness, the wines never quite blossoming the way one hoped for. Maybe it was too much tannin or too high a fermentation temperature. Whatever the cause, the difficulty has since been finessed. Today, the Jadot reds retain a superb austerity, but are informed with greater suppleness and tender fruit. Lovely Boucherottes and Teurons; good Chouacheux. They make a Beaune *premier cru* under the brand name Beaune Tradition. Also a wine labeled "Clos des Couchereaux" a five-acre subplot in Aux Coucherias.

DOMAINE MICHEL LAFARGE—The Volnay producer issues a superb Beaune "Grèves" that displays the lacy delicacy of the Grèves vineyard.

LEROY—This *négociant* also has a strong showing in Beaune, producing voluptuous, reference-standard examples of many different vineyards over the years. Like all Leroy wines, they are vinified for long life, which the quality rewards. I know of no other *négociant* offering as many different vineyards of Beaune at such a high standard of quality. It is the more impressive considering that Leroy does not own any vineyards in Beaune.

DOMAINE CHANTAL LESCURE—The largest holder in Chouacheux, this domaine is improving yearly. The Chouacheux is a soft, pretty wine that matures early but with satisfying achievement of flavor. Also, it's a good buy.

DOMAINE MUSSY—The Pommard producer retains his touch in Beaune, with top-rank Epenottes, as well as rarely seen Montrevenots. The same vineyards also are issued by André Mussy's nephew and heir, Bernard Fèvre of Saint-Romain.

DOMAINE JACQUES PRIEUR—The Meursault-based domaine has the *monopole* on the 4.6-acre Clos de la Féguine *climat* of Aux Cras. Good wine but not top rank.

DOMAINE TOLLOT-BEAUT—This is the estate that calls to mind the phrase "When they're good, they are very, very good. . . ." For an admirably long time, Tollot-Beaut represented some of the best in Burgundy. The winemaking is old-fashioned, striving for depth and intensity and vineyard definition. True, it has an identifiable style: It's a bit "jammy," almost glossy. There's a lot of oak. But the purity is there as well. However, in recent vintages, notably 1982 and 1986, it is hard to believe that such slight, poorly fashioned wines could have emerged from Tollot-Beaut. The '85s, happily, were extraordinary. Still, this is a producer that cannot (and should not) be ignored. Look for profound Grèves and extraordinary Clos du Roi.

Chorey-
lès-
Beaune

O n the flatlands opposite the hill of Corton are the vineyards of Chorey-lès-Beaune, which create pleasant, Beaunelike wines of no great depth or staying power. Still, they are superior to basic Bourgogne *rouge*. At one time, Chorey-lès-Beaune was cited as bargain red Burgundy. It once was. It no longer is, at least by the time it gets to the States and is marked up two or three times.

For example, the excellent Chorey-lès-Beaune 1985 of Domaine Jacques Germain cost twenty-four dollars retail in the States. Good as it is, that's a lot of money for what is, after all, still only a good basic Pinot Noir of no great breed. You can buy a red Chassagne-Montrachet Premier Cru for the same money. Most of the forty-five thousand cases of red wine produced from its 415.5 acres of vines—all of them commune-level—are sold as Côte de Beaune-Villages.

Chorey-lès-Beaune also is noted for a different reason: It is home to several top-ranked producers, all of whom own vineyards in the commune and issue pleasing wines. Two stand out: Domaine Tollot-Beaut and Domaine Jacques Germain, which is housed in the Château de Chorey.

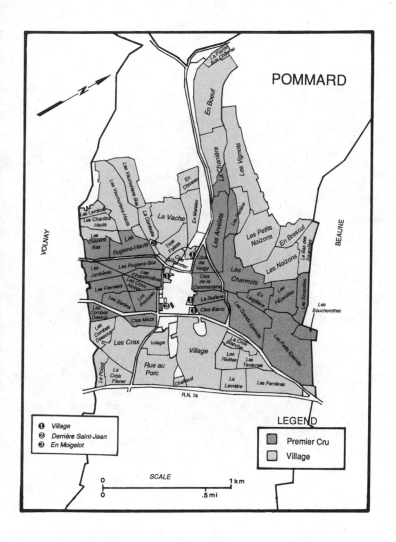

POMMARD

VOLNAY

BEAUNE

La Planté Aux Charles

En Boeuf

La Chanière

Les Vignots

En Chiveau

En Mareau

La Cornière

La Vache

Les Vaumuriens-Bas

Les Vaumuriens-Hauts

Les Lamboes

Les Chanlins Hauts

Les Chanlins Bas

Rugiens-Hauts

Les Jarolières

Les Rugiens-Bas

Les Chaponnières

Les Croix Noires

Les Fremiers

Les Saussilles

Les Poutures

Les Bertins

Les Combes Dessus

Les Combes Dessous

Clos Micot

Les Cras

Le Pezerolles

La Croix Planet

Rue au Porc

Village

Village

Trois Follots

Clos du Boucher

Clos de Vergy

Clos de la Commaraine

La Refène

Clos Blanc

Les Arvelets

Les Saussiles

Les Petits Noizons

En Brescul

Le Bas des Saussiles

Les Noizons

Les Charmots

En Largillière

Les Pézerolles

Les Grands Epenots

Les Petits Epenots

Les Boucherottes

La Croix Blanche

Les Riottes

La Crois Planet

Le Pezeret

Chanlin

Chaniaud

La Levrière

Les Tavannes

Les Perrières

R.N. 74

LEGEND

❶ Village
❷ Derrière Saint-Jean
❸ En Moigelot

Premier Cru

Village

SCALE

0   1 km

0   .5 mi

Pommard

In fact, the wines of the lesser-known communes, when of equal quality, were sold under the name of a well-known commune. Chassagne and Santenay, for instance, which produce admirable growths, were usually labelled Pommard. The consumer suffered no loss, but he knew nothing about it. . . . . For when the boundaries of Pommard, Volnay and the rest were first laid down, no one dreamed of making them coincide with the limits of the estates which produced the first growths. Administrative considerations prevailed, not those of winegrowing.

—PAUL DE CASSAGNAC, *French Wines* (1930)

It no longer is a revelation, as it was in 1930, that wines labeled "Pommard" were not Pommard. That was no news to shippers. For centuries, they had been selling all sorts of wines labeled "Pommard" that were nothing of the sort. Nor did the practice cease with Appellation Contrôlée. As late as 1969, the great American wine authority Frank Schoonmaker, who imported numerous domaine-bottled Burgundies, wrote of Pommard, "It is a long way from certain, despite strict controls, that everything sold as 'Pommard' is really genuine."

Why was Pommard singled out for such treatment? The usual answer is that Anglo-Saxons could pronounce the name easily. This makes some sense, but it hardly accounts for the persistence of generations of fraudulent wines.

More likely is that Pommard means something to the local Burgundian mind: a dark-hued wine of robust character, substantial tannins, and long life. These were attributes much prized by export markets where red Bordeaux was the benchmark against which all other red wines were judged: the Netherlands, Scandinavia, Germany, the United States, and, above all, Great Britain.

When buyers from these countries demanded marketable red Burgundies, it seemed natural to the ever-obliging *négociants* to label it Pommard, a name that evoked for them the style being sought. The native Pommard wine came closest. This is further buttressed by the fact that the two other communes boasting similar intrinsic qualities—Nuits-Saint-Georges and Gevrey-Chambertin—saw their names usurped as well. The shippers may even have tried to supply the authentic article at first, but demand swelled beyond supply.

This history has been a mixed blessing for Pommard, like a famous opera singer who makes a fortune singing pop tunes. On the one hand, the Pommardois sell everything they make because their name is golden. On the other hand, their wines have lost esteem in the eyes (and palates) of the so-called cognoscenti because, well, everyone knows Pommard. Or thinks he does.

The fact is that some of the most gloriously pure wines of Burgundy today are being produced in Pommard. Only its neighbor Volnay has a comparable collection of upstanding growers.

What can we rightfully expect from Pommard? A wine of longevity, for starters. Although not every Pommard is robust, many of them are structured for long life and demand ten or even fifteen years of age to unfurl. They can be made to mature sooner, but that's not the distinction of Pommard. Rather, Pommard calls to mind an image of peasant wealth. Where Volnay can make one think of a seventeenth-century Parisian dandy, all frippery and handkerchiefs tucked in the wrist, Pommard is one of those thick-muscled farmers whose wealth is proudly displayed in an ever-mounting pile of manure in the farm courtyard. It is Pinot Noir *brut*: chewy, concentrated, forthright.

This may seem faint praise, but it's not so. There are moments at the table when a mature Pommard is the supreme wine. Game often is mentioned, and rightly. Also well-hung beef and lamb, in addition to strong-flavored innards such as kidneys, liver, and the like. Try Pommard with cassoulet or other bean stews. The reason Pommard allies so well with these dishes is that it provides, at its best, an unmistakable tang, a *goût de terroir* delivered in such volume as to be nearly shoveled up. One taste of a mature Pommard "Rugiens," and you will search the Côte d'Or for another like it, only to concede its uniqueness.

THE VINEYARDS

There are 336.8214 ha/832 acres, of which 309 acres are ranked *premier cru*. There are no *grands crus*.

POMMARD PREMIERS CRUS

Of the twenty-six *premiers crus* of Pommard, only a few are noted on the label. This is probably because so much Pommard is purchased by *négociants*, who necessarily are forced to blend multiple lots of both *premier cru* and commune-level Pommard in order to create a wine with the magical Pommard name. Unlike Volnay, which largely is domaine-bottled, one rarely sees a wine labeled "Pommard Premier Cru," as that would be too confining for shippers straining to meet the demand for anything labeled Pommard.

LES EPENOTS—A slightly confusing vineyard name since it seems to crop up in several variations. You have Grands-Epenots, Petits-Epenots, and Clos des Epeneaux—which doesn't even share the same spelling, yet really is a section carved out from both Grands and Petits! And then you have labels such as that from Domaine de Courcel, which declares its Pommard to be "Grand Clos des Epenots." It actually comes from Petits Epenots, as the grower listings reveal.

Nomenclature aside, the distinction of Epenots is that it is one of the two best vineyards in Pommard, exceeded only by Rugiens. The two often are discussed jointly, if only for the contrasts they offer. The key to the distinction of Epenots is its location: Where Rugiens is close to Volnay, Epenots abuts Beaune. It has a silkiness to it and is more early-maturing than Rugiens. Still, it is a wine with unmistakable Pommard stuffings.

Clos des Epeneaux is a 12.9-acre *monopole* of the Domaine Comte Armand. Happily, this is one of the great producers of Pommard and this wine is one of the two or three best bottlings of Pommard in any given vintage. It is Epenots magnified.

LES RUGIENS—Surely the finest *premier cru* of Pommard. A distinction is drawn between Rugiens-Hauts and Rugiens-Bas, with insiders proclaiming Rugiens-Bas to be the superior *climat*. Nevertheless, I cannot recall ever seeing a Pommard "Rugiens" label that draws the distinction. The grower listings below are the first ever to show the major ownerships in each *climat*.

The reason for the distinction between *Hauts* and *Bas* is subsoil and slope. Rugiens-Hauts is sited farther up the slope and is steeper and slightly less well exposed. A geological map of the area shows it to be astride an isolated outcropping of chalky subsoil different from that of Rugiens-Bas, which is more limestone and marl. The result, along with the effect of exposure and elevation, is that Rugiens-Hauts is slightly lighter in weight, with a less forceful, although still substantial, *goût de terroir*.

Whichever *climat*, Rugiens is a remarkable vineyard, an undisputed candidate for *grand cru* status. It has depth, concentration, and enormous flavor impact. It is also intimidatingly long-lived. A well-made Rugiens from a top vintage needs fifteen years to blossom, and it can then skip along for another fifteen in a cool cellar with little diminution of character.

LES BERTINS—One of the most Volnaylike of Pommards, for the reason that it lies close by. It still is Pommard, though not so much by law as by its straightforward forcefulness. Les Bertins seems to mature a little more readily than some other vineyards, which is to say that it needs only seven or eight years, rather than ten or fifteen.

LES JAROLIÈRES—The Siamese-twin vineyard to Volnay "Frémiets," it too matures more rapidly, yet it somehow is coarser and more full-bodied than Frémiets. This may be as much a matter of winemaking as anything. I've never tasted a Frémiets and a Jarolières by the same producer in the same vintage. Still there does seem to be a difference, varibles aside. Jarolières has more "punch."

Les Arvelets—8.4577 ha/20.9 acres

	Hectares	Acres	Cases*
M. Félix Clerget	0.2925	0.7	154
M. Jean-Marc Cyrot	0.2442	0.6	129
M. Alexandre Gaunoux	0.2646	0.7	140
Mme. Veuve Claude Henriot	0.0635	0.2	34
Hospices Civils de Beaune	0.4655	1.2	246
M. Armand Jacquelin	0.2517	0.6	133
M. et Mme. Serge Lahaye	0.2717	0.7	143
M. Pierre Masson	0.3118	0.8	165
M. et Mme. Georges Mure	0.6058	1.5	320
M. et Mme. René Mure	0.5377	1.3	284
SC du Domaine Parent	0.3126	0.8	165
M. Jean Perrin	0.1289	0.3	68
M. Louis Poirier	0.4088	1.0	216
M. Roger Rossignol	0.2907	0.7	153
M. Claude Segaut	0.9740	2.4	514
M. José Tartois	0.1292	0.3	68
M. Jean-Baptiste Virely	0.1609	0.4	85
M. et Mme. Bernard Virely	0.7064	1.7	373
M. François Virely	0.4552	1.1	240
M. et Mme. Louis Virely	0.4034	1.0	213
M. René Virely	0.5251	1.3	277

Les Bertins—3.5412 ha/8.7 acres

GFA du Domaine Billard-Gonnet	0.4065	1.0	215
M. et Mme. Henri Delagrange	0.4529	1.1	239
Mme. Roger Faivre	0.1794	0.4	95
M. Pierre Glantenay	0.1042	0.3	55
Hospices Civils de Beaune	0.2481	0.6	131
Mme. Pierre Huber	0.1812	0.4	96
GFA du Domaine Chantal Lescure	1.9470	4.8	1028

Clos Blanc—4.1760 ha/ 10.3 acres

Mme. Veuve Henri Bardet	0.5888	1.5	311
M. Félix Clerget and M. Pierre Masson	0.2019	0.5	107
M. Mario Garbero	0.0877	0.2	46
M. et Mme. Charles Genot	0.3278	0.8	173
GFA Jules Guillemard	0.1814	0.4	96
M. Ferdinand Launay	0.1690	0.4	89
JC Pidault Père et Fils	1.5482	3.8	817
M. Louis Poirier	0.2002	0.5	106
M. Michel Jaboulet-Vercherre	0.2996	0.7	158

---

*Cases calculated on the *rendement de base* of 40 hl/ha plus 20 percent

	Hectares	Acres	Cases*
Les Boucherottes—1.8483 ha/4.6 acres			
GFA Pommard Clos des Coucherottes	1.8483	4.6	976
La Chanière—2.7832 ha/6.9 acres			
M. Georges Cabaret and M. Jacques Cabaret	0.4701	1.2	248
Mme. Veuve Bernard Chatain and Mme. Jacques Bergeret	0.2493	0.6	132
M. Félix Clerget and M. Pierre Masson	0.6792	1.7	359
M. Jean-Marc Cyrot	0.4546	1.1	240
Mme. Marie Jay	0.1815	0.4	96
M. et Mme. Paul Lecouvreur	0.1090	0.3	58
M. Henri Monthelie and Mme. Veuve Victor Monthelie	0.2792	0.7	147
Mme. Albert Saintemarie and M. Albert Saintemarie	0.0474	0.1	25
M. et Mme. Eugène Vaivrand	0.0480	0.1	25
Les Chanlins-Bas—4.4337 ha/11 acres			
M. et Mme. Jean Allexant	0.1845	0.5	97
M. Christian Bergeret and M. Daniel Bergeret	0.1035	0.3	55
M. Albert Boillot	0.2555	0.6	135
M. Alexandre Boillot and M. Louis Boillot	0.2504	0.6	132
M. Gilbert Caillet and M. Patrick Caillet	0.1307	0.3	69
Mme. François Clerc	0.2871	0.7	152
M. Félix Clerget and M. Pierre Masson	0.1238	0.3	65
M. et Mme. Eugène Cordelier	0.1035	0.3	55
M. et Mme. Charles Delagrange	0.0923	0.2	49
GFA Domaine Delagrange-Battault	0.3738	0.9	197
Mme. Jean Desmazières	0.4552	1.1	240
Mlle. Marie Douhairet	0.2722	0.7	144
Mme. Georges Jacquelin	0.2083	0.5	110
M. Henri Montagny	0.2812	0.7	148

*Cases calculated on the *rendement de base* of 40 hl/ha plus 20 percent

	Hectares	Acres	Cases*
Mme. Suzanne Montagny	0.0950	0.2	50
M. et Mme. Jean Oesch	0.1950	0.5	103
SC du Domaine Parent	0.3495	0.9	185
M. Jean Parent	0.1334	0.3	70
Mme. Veuve François Phillippon	0.1075	0.3	57
M. Pierre Valencia	0.3895	1.0	206

Les Chaponnières—2.8670 ha/7.1 acres

	Hectares	Acres	Cases*
Mme. Pierre André	0.1537	0.4	81
Mme. Pierre André and Mme. Veuve Eugène Boillot and M. Jean Boillot	0.0335	0.1	18
GFA du Domaine Billard-Gonnet	0.7495	1.9	396
Mme. Marie Jay	0.7428	1.8	392
M. et Mme. Ferdinand Launay	0.5903	1.5	312
SC du Domaine Parent	0.5952	1.5	314

Les Charmots—5.8476 ha/14.5 acres

	Hectares	Acres	Cases*
Mme. Veuve Charles Allamagny and M. Charles Allemagny	0.3058	0.8	161
M. et Mme. Michel Arcelain	0.1027	0.3	54
Mme. Philippe Ballot	0.2100	0.5	111
Hospices Civils de Beaune	0.4780	1.2	252
M. et Mme. Gabriel Billard	0.3728	0.9	197
M. et Mme. Prosper Billard	0.0824	0.2	44
GFA du Domaine Billard-Gonnet	0.4335	1.1	229
M. Pierre Billot	0.0510	0.1	27
M. Daniel Bouchard	0.4905	1.2	259
M. Georges Broichot	0.2618	0.6	138
M. Bernard Caillet	0.0421	0.1	22
Mme. Veuve Bernard Chatain and Mme. Jacques Bergeret	0.0625	0.2	33
Domaine du Château de Meursault	0.1513	0.4	80
M. Félix Clerget and M. Pierre Masson	0.3717	0.9	196
M. Joseph Cyrot and M. Olivier Cyrot	0.1295	0.3	68
M. Lucien Dechaume	0.2703	0.7	143
Mme. Veuve Paul Drain	0.2175	0.5	115
Mme. Maurice Fournier	0.1658	0.4	88
M. Alexandre Gaunoux	0.2553	0.6	135
M. et Mme. Henri Girardin	0.1209	0.3	64

*Cases calculated on the *rendement de base* of 40 hl/ha plus 20 percent

	Hectares	Acres	Cases*
M. Armand Jacquelin	0.1270	0.3	67
M. et Mme. Ernest Jacquelin	0.0762	0.2	40
M. Louis Jobard	0.2760	0.7	146
Mme. Maurice Lafouge	0.4598	1.1	243
M. Henri Lamarche and Mme. Joseph Moissenet	0.2075	0.5	110
M. Jean-François Lambert	0.0801	0.2	42
M. Raoul Leneuf	0.1603	0.4	85
M. Bernard Monnot and M. Léon Monnot	0.0480	0.1	25
M. Victor Louis	0.1915	0.5	101
M. Eugène Michelot	0.0300	0.1	16
M. Jean Michelot	0.1303	0.3	69
M. Paul Mignon	0.3105	0.8	164
Mme. Veuve Victor Monthelie	0.0470	0.1	25
M. et Mme. Justin Mouillot	0.0300	0.1	16
M. Georges Parigot and Mme. Jean Demougeot	0.2990	0.7	158
M. Jean Perrin	0.0527	0.1	28
Mme. Veuve Louis Picard	0.3292	0.8	174
M. Louis Poirier	0.1955	0.5	103
GFA Belorgey Pommard	0.2338	0.6	123
GFA du Domaine Pothier-Rieusset	0.3060	0.8	162
Safer	0.1550	0.4	82
M. Joseph Tartois	0.2885	0.7	152
M. Jean de Tremeuge and M. Marcel Clemencet	0.2033	0.5	107
M. et Mme. Pierre Vaudoissey	0.0932	0.2	49

Les Combes-Dessus—2.7882 ha/6.9 acres

	Hectares	Acres	Cases*
GFA Domaine Henri Boillot	0.1345	0.3	71
Bouchard Père et Fils	0.7368	1.8	389
GFA Domaine François Buffet	0.0853	0.2	45
M. Bernard Caillet	0.1887	0.5	100
Mlle. Claude Caillet and M. Gilbert Caillet	0.2433	0.6	128
GFA du Clos des Ducs	0.3784	0.9	200
M. Bernard Delagrange	0.1064	0.3	56

*Cases calculated on the *rendement de base* of 40 hl/ha plus 20 percent

	Hectares	Acres	Cases*
M. Charles Delagrange	0.1066	0.3	56
M. Michel Gaunoux	0.2540	0.6	134
Hospices Civils de Beaune	0.1628	0.4	86
Mme. Veuve Victor Monthelie	0.0798	0.2	42
Mme. Veuve Edmond Pillot and M. Edmond Pillot	0.1198	0.3	63
M. et Mme. Bernard Rossignol	0.1668	0.4	88

Clos de la Commaraine—3.7450 ha/9.2 acres

M. Michel Jaboulet-Vercherre	1.7450	9.3	1977

Les Croix Noires—1.2776 ha/3.2 acres

Mme. Lucien Boillot	0.3700	0.9	195
M. Maurice Chodron de Courcel	0.5807	1.4	307
SC du Domaine Parent	0.2153	0.5	114

Derrière Saint-Jean—0.2759 ha/0.7 acre

M. et Mme. Barthélémy Guillemard	0.1111	0.3	59

Clos des Epeneaux—5.2308 ha/12.9 acres divided between two *climats:* Clos des Epeneaux in Grands Epenots (1.5 acres) and Clos des Epeneaux in Les Petits Epenots (11.4 acres)

Clos des Epeneaux-Les Petits Epenots

SC du Domaine des Epeneaux	4.6215	11.4	2440

Clos des Epeneaux-Les Grands Epenots

SC du Domaine des Epeneaux	0.6093	1.5	322

Les Grands Epenots—10.1478 ha/25.1 acres

M. et Mme. Valéry Carre	0.2283	0.6	121
Mme. Jean Dewailly	0.5241	1.3	277
Mme. Jean Dewailly and Mme. Veuve André Loubet	0.5009	1.2	264
M. et Mme. Bernard Dubreuil	0.2716	0.7	143
M. Alexandre Gaunoux and Mme. Veuve Alexandre Gaunoux	2.9202	7.2	1542

*Cases calculated on the *rendement de base* of 40 hl/ha plus 20 percent

	Hectares	Acres	Cases*
M. et Mme. Henri Girardin	0.2280	0.6	120
M. et Mme. André Loubet	0.9255	2.3	489
M. Jean Monnier and M. Jean-Claude Monnier	2.9177	7.2	1541
M. Hubert Bizouard de Montille and Mme. Veuve Louis Bizouard de Montille	0.2283	0.6	121
SC du Domaine Parent	0.2732	0.7	144
M. Thiérry Poirier	0.8586	2.1	453
M. et Mme. Henri Rebourgeon	0.2714	0.7	143

Les Petits Epenots—15.1428 ha/37.4 acres

	Hectares	Acres	Cases*
M. et Mme. André	0.2085	0.5	110
M. Jean Boillot and Mme. Veuve Eugène Boillot and Mme. Pierre André	0.2118	0.5	112
Domaine du Château de Meursault	3.6372	9.0	1920
M. Gilles Chodron de Courcel	1.2570	3.1	664
M. Maurice Chodron de Courcel	3.6371	9.0	1920
M. Bernard Dubreuil and M. Pierre Dubreuil and Mme. Maurice Maratray	0.1418	0.4	75
Mme. Jean-Baptiste Garreaux	0.1769	0.4	93
M. François Gaunoux	0.7893	2.0	417
GFA Domaine de Corton-Grancey (Louis Latour)	0.4088	1.0	216
M. et Mme. Barthélémy Guillemard	0.0742	0.2	39
GFA Jules Guillemard	0.2464	0.6	130
Hospices Civils de Beaune	1.2303	3.0	650
Mme. Ernest Jacquelin	0.3028	0.7	160
M. Jean-Luc Joillot	0.3685	0.9	195
M. Henri Lamarche and Mme. Joseph Moissenet	0.9013	2.2	476
Mme. Veuve Emile Lambert and M. Jean-François Lambert	0.2154	0.5	114
M. André Mussy and M. Serge Mussy	0.5794	1.4	306
SC du Domaine Parent	0.3060	0.8	162
Mme. et Mlle. Pierre Vaudoisey	0.2643	0.7	140

---

*Cases calculated on the *rendement de base* of 40 hl/ha plus 20 percent

	Hectares	*Acres*	*Cases**
Les Fremiers—5.1292 ha/12.7 acres			
Mme. Maurice Bertrand	0.2184	0.5	115
GFA du Domaine Henri Boillot	0.5697	1.4	301
M. Gilbert Caillet and M. Patrick Caillet	0.0147	0.04	8
Domaine du Château de Meursault	0.3075	0.8	162
M. Gilles Chodron de Courcel	0.4445	1.1	235
M. Maurice Chodron de Courcel	0.3098	0.8	164
M. Charles Delagrange	0.1963	0.5	104
Mlle. Marie Douhairet	0.1940	0.5	102
M. Armand Jacquelin	0.1376	0.3	73
M. Louis Jacquelin	0.1797	0.4	95
M. Jean Monnier and Mlle. Yvette Monnier	0.3815	0.9	201
GFA Pommard Clos des Boucherottes	1.2307	3.0	650
M. et Mme. Jean-Pierre Prunier	0.4922	1.2	260
M. Roger Rossignol	0.1358	0.3	72
M. Jean-Paul Sordet	0.4224	1.0	223
Les Jarolières—3.2369 ha/8 acres			
GFA du Domaine Billard-Gonnet	0.0623	0.2	33
GFA du Domaine Henri Boillot	1.3000	3.2	686
SC d'Exploitation du Domaine de la Pousse d'Or	1.0482	2.6	553
M. Sylvester Harris	0.3965	1.0	209
Mme. Suzanne Montagny	0.1078	0.3	57
M. Daniel Mure	0.1103	0.3	58
Mme. Veuve Edmond Pillot and M. Edmond Pillot	0.2018	0.5	107
En Largillière—3.9932 ha/9.9 acres			
M. Albert Boillot	0.4994	1.2	264
M. Pierre Boillot	0.5034	1.2	266
M. et Mme. Fernand Garaudet	0.0684	0.2	36
M. et Mme. Ernest Jacquelin	0.0862	0.2	46
M. Louis Jacquelin	0.4245	1.0	224
Mlle. Marie-Hélène Jacquelin	0.1386	0.3	73
SCI du Domaine Lejeune	1.3918	3.4	735
M. Jean Monnier and Mlle. Yvette Monnier	0.5853	1.4	309

*Cases calculated on the *rendement de base* of 40 hl/ha plus 20 percent

	Hectares	Acres	Cases*
SC du Domaine Parent	0.2953	0.7	156

Clos Micot—2.8288 ha/7 acres

	Hectares	Acres	Cases*
GFA Domaine François Buffet	0.2371	0.6	125
M. François Jourda de Vaux de Foletier and M. Régis Jourda de Vaux de Foletier	2.1705	5.4	1146
M. et Mme. Georges Mure	0.1483	0.4	78
M. Michel Vaudoisey	0.1331	0.3	70
M. Paul Voillot	0.1398	0.3	74

Les Pézerolles—5.9118 ha/14.6 acres

	Hectares	Acres	Cases*
M. Philippe Bergeret	0.1370	0.3	72
GFA du Domaine Billard-Gonnet	0.6233	1.5	329
M. Marcel Cuinet	0.5990	1.5	316
M. Armand Dancer	0.3008	0.7	159
Mme. Veuve Marc Garaudet and Mme. Michel Dupont	0.1370	0.3	72
Mme. Jean-Baptiste Garreaux	0.3980	1.0	210
M. et Mme. Barthélémy Guillemard	0.2708	0.7	143
M. Henri Lamarche and Mme. Joseph Moissenet	0.2535	0.6	134
M. Bernard Lochardet	0.3144	0.8	166
M. Marie-Charles Lochardet	0.6028	1.5	318
M. Paul Masson	0.0767	0.2	40
Mme. Veuve Louis Michelot and Mlle. Danièle Michelot	0.1102	0.3	58
Mme. Veuve Hubert Bizouard de Montille and Mme. Veuve Louis Bizouard de Montille	0.4943	1.2	261
M. André Mussy and Mme. Michel Meuzard	0.0980	0.2	52
GFA Mussy Frères	0.2507	0.6	132
SC du Domaine Parent	0.3408	0.8	180
M. Jean Perrin	0.0690	0.2	36
M. Jean-Pierre Portheret	0.0915	0.2	48
M. Henri Potinet	0.4740	1.2	250
M. Gilbert Violot	0.0830	0.2	44
M. René Virely	0.1866	0.5	99

*Cases calculated on the *rendement de base* of 40 hl/ha plus 20 percent

	Hectares	*Acres*	*Cases**
La Platière—2.5274 ha/6.2 acres			
M. Julien Coche	0.2187	0.5	115
GFA Domaine Edmond Girardin	0.1831	0.5	97
GFA Jules Guillemard	0.6985	1.7	369
M. Charles de Mérode	0.7980	2.0	421
GFA Domaine Louis Nie Clos Bellefond	0.2903	0.7	153
M. Guy Prieur and Mme. Guy Prieur	0.0900	0.2	48
Mlle. Suzanne Vaivrand	0.0957	0.2	51
Les Poutures—4.1274 ha/10.2 acres			
M. et Mme. René Blanc	0.1953	0.5	103
GFA Domaine François Buffet	0.2745	0.7	145
Mme. Martine Comiti and M. Fernand Granier	0.1953	0.5	103
SCI du Domaine Lejeune	1.0880	2.7	574
Mme. Jay Marie	0.3305	0.8	175
M. Marie-Charles Lochardet	0.6608	1.6	349
M. Pierre Mazilly	0.7811	1.9	412
M. Louis Poirier	0.2346	0.6	124
M. et Mme. Pierre Vaudoisey	0.3905	1.0	206
La Refène—2.3057 ha/5.7 acres			
Mme. Phillippe Ballot	0.5440	1.3	287
GFA Pommard Clos des Boucherottes	0.0647	0.2	34
M. Félix Clerget and M. Pierre Masson	0.0867	0.2	46
M. et Mme. Henri Girardin	0.3976	1.0	210
GFA Jules Guillemard	0.2050	0.5	108
Hospices Civils de Beaune	0.3107	0.8	164
M. Bernard Monnot and M. Léon Monnot	0.0940	0.2	50
M. et Mme. Jean-Pierre Prunier	0.1016	0.3	54

Les Rugiens—12.6645 ha/31.3 acres divided into two *climats*: Les Rugiens-Bas (14.4 acres) and Les Rugiens-Hauts (16.9 acres)

Les Rugiens-Bas

GFA du Domaine Billard-Gonnet	0.3014	0.7	159
GFA du Domaine Henri Boillot	0.1517	0.4	80

*Cases calculated on the *rendement de base* of 40 hl/ha plus 20 percent

	Hectares	Acres	Cases*
M. Daniel Buisson	0.0861	0.2	45
M. Félix Clerget	0.3114	0.8	164
Mme. Clair François	0.0732	0.2	39
GFA du Clos des Gatsulard	0.0838	0.2	44
M. Alexandre Gaunoux and M. Michel Gaunoux	0.6925	1.7	366
Hospices Civils de Beaune	0.5416	1.3	286
M. Armand Jacquelin	0.3644	0.9	192
M. Louis Jacquelin	0.3629	0.9	192
M. Louis Jobard	0.3523	0.9	186
SCI du Domaine Lejeune	0.2651	0.7	140
M. et Mme. André Loubet	0.4542	1.1	240
Mme. Pierre Millot	0.3256	0.8	172
M. Hubert Bizouard de Montille and Mme. Veuve Louis Bizouard de Montille	0.3667	0.9	194
M. Hubert Bizouard de Montille and Mme. Veuve Louis Bizouard de Montille and M. Jacques Arbon	0.6492	1.6	343
GFA du Domaine Pothier-Rieusset	0.2107	0.5	111
M. Paul Voillot	0.2546	0.6	134

Les Rugiens-Hauts

	Hectares	Acres	Cases*
Mlle. Madeleine Boillot	0.4260	1.1	225
Bouchard Père et Fils	0.4179	1.0	221
M. et Mme. Jean-Marc Boulet	0.2803	0.7	148
GFA Domaine François Buffet	0.1758	0.4	93
M. Gilles Chodron de Courcel	1.0722	2.6	566
M. et Mme. Adrien Clement	0.2802	0.7	148
GFA du Domaine Clerget	0.8530	2.1	450
M. Charles Delagrange	0.2160	0.5	114
Mme. Richard Fontaine	0.2159	0.5	114
M. François Gaunoux	0.3800	0.9	201
GFA Glantenay-Midant	0.2159	0.5	114
GFA Louis Glantenet et Ses Enfants	0.2160	0.5	114
Hospices Civils de Beaune	0.1855	0.5	98
GFA Jules Guillemard	0.4200	1.0	222
M. Marie-Charles Lochardet	0.4318	1.1	228
M. Jean Parent	0.4995	1.2	264
M. Michel Rebourgeon	0.1750	0.4	92
GFA du Domaine Pothier-Rieusset	0.3589	0.9	189

*Cases calculated on the *rendement de base* of 40 hl/ha plus 20 percent

	Hectares	Acres	Cases*
Les Saussilles—3.8383 ha/9.5 acres			
M. Félix Clerget	0.5060	1.3	267
M. Bernard Glantenay	0.5001	1.2	264
GFA Louis Glantenay et Ses Enfants	0.6491	1.6	343
M. et Mme. Barthélémy Guillemard	0.8295	2.0	438
M. et Mme. Serge Lahaye	0.1247	0.3	66
Mme. Denise Loget	0.4040	1.0	213
M. André Mussy and Mme. Michel Meuzard	0.5555	1.4	293
M. Gilbert Violot	0.2695	0.7	142
Clos de Verger—2.1111 ha/5.2 acres			
GFA du Domaine Billard-Gonnet	1.4818	3.7	782
GFA du Domaine Pothier-Rieusset	0.6293	1.6	332

Village—0.1534 ha/0.4 acre

PRODUCERS WORTH SEEKING OUT

DOMAINE COMTE ARMAND—The sole owner of Clos des Epeneaux. Spectacularly fine Pommard, an exemplar: intense, concentrated, beefy, and needing years of aging. The off-vintages are worth investigating. The comte himself lives in Paris. There is an occasional *vieilles vignes* (old vines) bottling, which, regrettably, I have never tried.

DOMAINE BILLARD-GONNET—One of the major property owners in Pommard. Well-structured wines, typical Pommard in the best sense. Look for lovely Rugiens-Bas and excellent Chaponnières from old vines.

DOMAINE HENRI BOILLOT—A Volnay producer who is the largest owner of Les Jarolières, who does an outstanding job. It is instructive, as well as rewarding, to compare Boillot's Jarolières with

---

*Cases calculated on the *rendement de base* of 40 hl/ha plus 20 percent

that of the Domaine de la Pousse d'Or, which offers a silkier style. Both are outstanding.

CHÂTEAU DE POMMARD—This enormous property consists of one fifty-acre enclosed vineyard of commune-level vines. It is the largest single contiguous vineyard owned by one family in the Côte d'Or, namely Jean-Louis Laplanche, who is a psychology professor in the Sorbonne in Paris. Château de Pommard is as close to a brand name as Burgundy gets, yet the wine is reliably good, thanks to old vines and conscientious winemaking. It is sturdy, fleshy, and authentically Pommardlike. If there's a problem here, it's that the wines can be a bit oaky, courtesy of the lavish use of 100 percent new oak barrels. You can't accuse them of stinting. You also can't miss the château, which lies just off the road entering Pommard and is announced by several signs. It welcomes visitors and has scheduled tours.

DOMAINE DE COURCEL—Enviable holdings in both Epenots (the largest owner of Petits Epenots) and Rugiens-Hauts. In the past, de Courcel created strong, intense Pommards in need of extended cellaring. But since the 1985 vintage the style has lightened up considerably. Maybe it's just a passing phase.

DOMAINE MICHEL GAUNOUX—One of the brightest stars in the constellation of good Pommard producers. Gaunoux makes Pommard the way its admirers expect: dense, full, even a little forbidding. He owns the largest parcel of Grands Epenots as well as a sizable chunk (1.7 acres) of Rugiens-Bas.

HOSPICES DE BEAUNE—Three *cuvées* are composed from Pommard:

Cuvée Cyrot-Chaudron—The blend is unspecified.

Cuvée Dames de la Charité—Les Epenots (0.4 ha/1 acre); Les Rugiens (0.33 ha/0.8 acre); Les Noizons (commune-level; 0.33 ha/ 0.8 acre); La Refene (0.33 ha/0.8 acre); Les Combes Dessus (0.2 ha/0.5 acre)

Cuvée Billardet—Les Epenots (0.66 ha/1.6 acres); Les Noizons (commune-level; 0.5 ha/ 1.2 acres); Les Arvelets (0.4 ha/ 1 acre); Les Rugiens (0.33 ha/ 0.8 acre)

JABOULET-VERCHERRE—This *négociant* has the *monopole* for the 9.2-acre Clos de la Commaraine. The wine is sturdy, well made but rarely thrilling. There are worse Pommards, but then, there also are better.

DOMAINE LEJEUNE—Another leading estate creating superlative Pommards. The specialty is Les Argillières, where Lejeune is the leading owner. Also a small (0.6-acre) plot in Rugiens-Bas. Young vines in Poutures *premier cru*. Lejeune still sells some of his wines —presumably the lesser ones—to *négociants*, notably Barton and Guestier.

DOMAINE CHANTAL LESCURE—Madame Chantal Lescure is the heir to a French fortune derived from her father, the leading manufacturer of pressure cookers in France. She has allied herself with the Nuits-Saint-George *négociant* Labouré-Roi, which oversees the winemaking. Excellent Les Bertins (she is the largest owner, with almost five acres) with a soft, furry quality. Problems of excessive oakiness in earlier vintages seem to have been resolved.

DOMAINE DE MONTILLE—The fabled Volnay producer issues his best wine (for me) from a choice plot in Rugien-Bas. Stunning stuff, all that Pommard should be with intense *goût de terroir* and brooding color.

DOMAINE MUSSY—Seventy-five-year-old André Mussy is everyone's vision of the classic Burgundian *vigneron*. Would that this vision be realized by others! Mussy makes a not-so-simple commune-level Pommard and a splendid Petits Epenots, as well as a terrific Pommard Premier Cru. Old vines; old methods; lovely young wine that ages beautifully. The Mussy domaine will someday fall into the hands of his nephew Bernard Fèvre of Saint-Romain (q.v.), as André Mussy is the last of his line.

DOMAINE PARENT—Another of the great names of Pommard. It was one of Jacques Parent's ancestors (Étienne Parent) who was Thomas Jefferson's "wine man" in Burgundy. Beautiful Epenots and Chaponnières, sturdy and full-bodied. They are wines of polish and substance.

DOMAINE POTHIER-RIEUSSET—Classic old-style Pommard, meant to be aged for years. Superb Rugiens from both *Bas* and *Haut*, as well as Epenots and Clos de Verger. This is one of the top Pommard domaines.

DOMAINE DE LA POUSSE D'OR—Silky, stylish Jarolières worth seeking out.

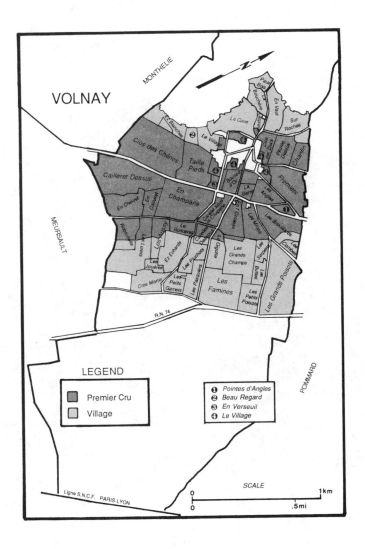

VOLNAY

MONTHELIE

MEURSAULT

POMMARD

Paul Bois
Bouchère
La Cave
En Vaut
Sur Roches
Pitures Dessus
Chanlin
Les Bouches
Le Village
Clos des Chênes
Taille Pieds
Clos Dyc Duc
Cailleret Dessus
En Champans
En Chevret
En Cailleret
Bousse d'Or
La Barre
Les Angles
Fremiets
Les Mitans
Les Brouillards
Robardelle
Taille Lunes
Les Aussy
Le Ronceret
Carelle sous Chapelle
Carelle Dessous
Les Combes
Les Echards
La Gigotte
Les Pluchots
Les Pasquiers
Les Grands Champs
Les Serpens
Les Jouères
Les Petits Gamets
Cros Martin
Les Famines
Les Brnes
Les Grands Poisots
Les Petits Poisots

❶ Pointes d'Angles
❷ Beau Regard
❸ En Verseuil
❹ Le Village

R.N. 74

LEGEND

Premier Cru

Village

❶ Pointes d'Angles
❷ Beau Regard
❸ En Verseuil
❹ Le Village

SCALE
0 _____ 1 km
0 _____ .5 mi

Ligne S.N.C.F. PARIS-LYON

Volnay

Volnay is a little white village, situated charmingly enough on the lower slope of the Côte d'Or. A plain old church, a much plainer new mairie, and 40 or 50 houses, occupied almost exclusively by the propriétaires who grow the wine and the tonneliers who make casks for it—such is Volnay.

—"A Correspondent Writes to Us from Volnay on the Burgundy Vintage," *Pall Mall Budget*, London (1875)

Visitors to Burgundy, especially those who are already smitten by the wines, never fail to comment on the plainness and simplicity of Burgundian villages, as our anonymous correspondent to the London *Pall Mall Budget* evokes in 1875. Volnay is a choice instance, not because the village is so ugly—it isn't—but because its wines are so achingly beautiful.

More than most, the wines of Volnay have enjoyed unrelenting renown. It was the most famous wine of Burgundy in the 1300s, courtesy of the Knights of Malta, which owned vineyards there since 1207. After them was the powerful Burgundian duke Philippe de Valois. He drank Volnay at his coronation in 1328, presumably from his vineyard Caille de Roi, which now is Caillerets. The duke must have had good advisers. Caillerets is considered by many Volnaysiens to be the best vineyard of Volnay. And so it went. Louis

XI liked Volnay so much—perhaps because it symbolized his long sought-after incorporation of the Burgundy duchy into his kingdom after the death of Charles the Bold—that he siphoned the entire 1447 vintage into his personal cellar.

Because of this continuing renown, we have more descriptions of ancient Volnay than almost any other Burgundy. It is through Volnay that one can see the grape-growing and winemaking changes of red Burgundies. For example, prior to the early 1800s, all of the descriptions of Volnay showed it to be very pale in color, what's known as "partridge-eye." This was not only because the Pinot Noir grapes were vinified with very little skin-contact time—the pigments are in the skins—but because many of the vines were Fromenteau, what today is called Pinot Gris, a white wine grape.

These pre-1800 Volnays were exceedingly delicate, not only in color, but weight. They were meant to be drunk within a year or so of the vintage. It is a testament to the penetrating flavor imparted by the Volnay *terroir* that even wines as slight as these could convey such recognizable distinction.

The recognition is no less today. If you knew nothing about Burgundy, neither producer nor vintage nor vineyard, the odds of getting a bottle worth drinking are greater in Volnay than in any other commune of the Côte d'Or. This surely is due to an unusually high standard among the commune's growers, but also because Volnay is relatively small and its site and soils almost uniformly good. For the wine writer—this one, anyway—there is no greater pleasure than to extoll the virtues of Volnay. No other red Burgundy, except Chambolle-Musigny, can convey the perfume and finesse of Pinot Noir as well as Volnay. Few are more seductive.

If Volnay has suffered any injustice it is its lack of a *grand cru*. This is not a matter of *terroir*, but politics. This is strange, if only because Volnay was recognized for so long by so many high-ranking personages. Yet when Appellation Contrôlée was instituted in 1937, only one red wine was designated *grand cru* in the Côte de Beaune: Corton. With the exception of Pommard "Rugiens" (which itself is close to the Volnay boundary), the most deserving candidates were in Volnay. Yet the acknowledgment escaped them.

Two reasons are likely. The first is politics. It is no secret that when the Appellation Contrôlée deliberations were made in the late 1930s, various wine shippers with strong vested interests in certain vineyards lobbied hard and skillfully to get these vineyards anointed *premier* or *grand cru*. Local politicians did the same. It was a matter of proving, or pretending to prove, that a certain vineyard always had been recognized, by price or in contemporary writings, that it was of an elevated stature. Volnay did not put itself forward with sufficient force.

The other reason—the one so often proffered to explain why Nuits-Saint-Georges, Beaune, and Pommard also lack *grands crus*— is that the overall standard of vineyards is so high that no one vineyard was sufficiently and dramatically individual to be crowned *grand cru*. This is less convincing, but still plausible.

THE VINEYARDS

Volnay is one of only seven communes in the Côte d'Or—out of thirty-two—with more *premier* or *grand cru* vineyards than commune-level. (The others are Morey-Saint-Denis, Vougeot, Flagey-Echézeaux, Aloxe-Corton, Beaune, and Puligny-Montrachet.)

There are 213.2676 ha/527 acres, of which 284 acres are ranked *premier cru*. There are no *grands crus*.

Wines labeled as Volnay-Santenots come from six vineyards located in the commune of Meursault.

VOLNAY PREMIERS CRUS

Of the twenty-six *premiers crus* only a few stand out, either by virtue of the size of the vineyard (Champans, Clos des Chênes) or because of unrivaled distinction, such as Clos des Ducs or Caillerets. Volnay seems to issue more bottlings under the general designation *premier cru* than other communes. A close look at the ownership will reveal the same owners spread thinly across a number of small *premier cru* vineyards, with the result that minuscule lots of wine are necessarily fashioned into one commercial quantity sold as "Volnay Premier Cru." This is an honorable practice—as well as practical— and the wines typically are excellent.

CLOS DE LA BOUSSE D'OR—This 4.8-acre vineyard is the *monopole* of Domaine de la Pousse d'Or. The similarity of names is no coincidence. Until 1967, the vineyard was called Clos de la Pousse d'Or, *pousse* meaning a shoot or sprout. Since it was an exceptional vineyard, its owners chose its name as their own. But in 1967 the French government decided that a domaine could not use the name of a vineyard as its own unless it was the only wine it produced. (The Domaine de la Romanée-Conti was exempted, the French always having a weakness for royalty in any form.) So the Domaine de la Pousse d'Or successfully petitioned to change not its own name, but that of its namesake vineyard, to Bousse d'Or. It's wonderful wine: rich, concentrated, and intense. Note that it is contiguous with three of the Le Village *climats* (q.v.), which share a similar concentration and depth.

CAILLERETS—If you took a poll of Volnaysiens, the chances are more than good that they would nominate Caillerets as the *grand cru* of Volnay. It is divided into three *climats*, with no distinction drawn among them that I've heard about. Still, the Volnay *amateur* has the rare opportunity of investigating for himself or herself. One of the *climats* is the six-acre Clos des Soixante Ouvrées, a *monopole* of Domaine de la Pousse d'Or.

An *ouvrée* is an ancient and still commonly used term in Burgundy. To this day, the size of vineyards for sale is expressed in *ouvrées*: .0428 hectares or one tenth of an acre or 428 square meters. Dating to the Middle Ages, an *ouvrée* was the amount of vineyard one man could work in one day. One hectare is twenty-four ouvrées. A vineyard of 60 *ouvrées* would be 2.568 hectares. Actually, the Clos is 2.3925 hectares.

Anyway, the Domaine de la Pousse d'Or also makes a regular Volnay "Caillerets" in addition to its Clos des Soixante Ouvrées. The winemaking is the same; the vintage is identical. Yet the wines are never identical. The Clos is almost always superior, although rarely dramatically so. It usually is more concentrated and has an additional dimension of flavor.

Caillerets is reckoned to be the most long-lived of Volnays, an assertion that I cannot endorse or refute. It certainly requires the best part of a decade to show its breed. It is neither the richest *premier cru* (try Bousse d'Or or Champans) nor the one with the greatest finesse (Clos des Ducs has that honor). Instead, it consolidates both attributes, resulting in a wine different from the other *premiers crus*. Because of this, it is supreme.

CHAMPANS—The second-largest *premier cru*, Champans is one of the most distinctive. It offers a noticeable *goût de terroir*, something vaguely ironlike. More than most, it can be spotted in a blind tasting, an attribute that saved me a few years ago when I was put through my paces when visiting Jacques d'Angerville, who makes a great Champans. He extracted an absolutely grisly-looking bottle from a niche in his tiny private cellar. (Very few Burgundy domaines have any wine libraries of any size, if at all.)

The bottle was engulfed in woolly black fungus and devoid of a label. D'Angerville pulled the cork on this fossil and poured wine into two glasses. The cellar was dim, so you couldn't tell much by appearance, except that it looked awfully fresh. D'Angerville moved in for the kill: "What is it?" Intellectually, I knew which wines he made; I could also figure out which ones were most likely to be reserved for a wine library. Still, you never know with these guys. But after one sniff and one taste I knew: It was Champans. And it was. The vintage was 1964, which I got wrong. (I said '66.) It was one of the few times in my life that I was grateful that a Burgundy grower didn't offer to have me taste yet another old bottle.

CLOS DES CHÊNES—The largest *premier cru* of Volnay, Clos des Chênes is, for me, one of the less satisfying vineyards. It has some of the austerity of neighboring Caillerets, but not its breed. It certainly has depth and some fullness, but not as notably as Champans or Bousse d'Or. It lacks the consolidation that Caillerets manages to achieve. One is tempted to say that it's a very fine Monthelie, which it adjoins. I suspect that elevation keeps it from achieving real distinction. Where Caillerets is smack at the 250-meter "sweet spot," Clos des Chênes is at 300 meters. Nevertheless, it's certainly rewarding wine and worth seeking out.

CLOS DES DUCS—As the name indicates, this 5.3-acre enclosed vineyard was once a ducal property. Today, it is a *monopole* of Domaine Marquis d'Angerville. Sited high up on the steep Volnay slope, the soil is extremely chalky, with a great deal of scree washed from the higher slopes above, resulting in a wine of unusual finesse and tremendous perfume, even by Volnay standards. Many Volnay fans think Clos des Ducs is the finest vineyard of all, original and fine enough to be *grand cru*.

FRÉMIETS—This vineyard, curiously, creates delicate, more early maturing wine than many others. One possible, even likely, reason is geological: A tongue of chalky subsoil called "Oxfordian" extends from the northern edge of the village of Volnay right through most, although not all, of Frémiets. Interestingly, this same subsoil also underlies part of Pommard "Les Jarolières," which happens to be a relatively lighter-weight wine as well. Not to be discounted in both cases is the role of exposure and elevation; both vineyards are at 275 meters with similar exposures. It lacks the pronounced *goût de terroir* of Clos des Ducs or Pitures, which it adjoins. The tongue of Oxfordian subsoil does not extend up the slope to either of those vineyards.

SANTENOTS—As already mentioned, Santenots really is in Meursault, with the red wines from the six *climats* entitled to be called Volnay-Santenots. To be fair, the vineyards really are an extension of Volnay. The best *climat* has long been thought to be Santenots-du-Milieu, which was planted exclusively to Pinot Noir even when other vineyards in Meursault were mixed plantings of red and white grapes. Santenots creates robust Volnays, long-lived with an earthy, vaguely coarse quality—but only when compared to polished Caillerets.

LE VILLAGE—Even by Burgundian measures, this vineyard is Balkanized. It is composed of seven *climats* that ring the town, hence the collective name. Five of them are *monopoles*, as the grower listings reveal, and they are issued under the *climat* name, e.g., Volnay "Clos du Château des Ducs" from Domaine Lafarge. It is therefore more difficult than usual to generalize, except to suggest that the wines seem to have a certain "meaty" quality, rich and chewy. Could their proximity to the town give them slightly warmer microlimates? Or maybe it's just winemaking.

Les Angles—3.3423 ha/8.3 acres

	Hectares	Acres	Cases*
M. Hubert Boillereault	1.7130	4.2	904
M. Lucien Boillot	1.1422	2.8	603
Mme. Veuve Louis Bizouard de Montille and M. Louis Bizouard de Montille	0.1470	0.4	78
M. Régis Rossignol	0.1452	0.4	77
M. Roger Rossignol	0.0766	0.2	40

Les Aussy—1.7019 ha/4.2 acres

	Hectares	Acres	Cases*
M. Jean Bitouzet	0.5089	1.3	269
M. Louis Bouzereau and M. Michel Bouzereau	0.1815	0.5	96
M. Charles Genot	0.4035	1.0	213
GFA Glantenay-Midant	0.4007	1.0	212
M. Vincent Pont	0.2073	0.5	109

Clos de la Barre—1.3160 ha/3.2 acres

	Hectares	Acres	Cases*
M. Julien Charau	1.3160	3.3	695

Bousse d'Or or Clos de la Bousse d'Or—2.1382 ha/5.3 acres divided into two *climats*: Le Village/Clos de la Bousse d'Or (0.5 acre) and Bousse d'Or (4.8 acres)

	Hectares	Acres	Cases*
SCI d'Exploitation du Domaine de al Pousse d'Or	1.9532	4.8	1031

Les Brouillards—5.6314 ha/13.9 acres

	Hectares	Acres	Cases*
GFA du Domaine Delagrange-Battault	0.3744	0.9	198
GFA du Domaine Henri Boillot	0.6182	1.5	326
M. Bernard Dubreuil	0.1696	0.4	90
GFA Louis Glantenay et Ses Enfants	1.1792	2.9	623
GFA Glantenay-Midant	1.1022	2.7	582
M. Bernard Jessiaume	0.2617	0.6	138
Mme. Veuve Louis Bizouard de Montille and M. Louis Bizouard de Montille	0.3700	0.9	195
M. Jean-Claude Pothier	0.1762	0.4	93
M. Michel Rebourgeon	0.1694	0.4	89
M. François Roblet	0.3694	0.9	195

*Cases calculated on the *rendement de base* of 40 hl/ha plus 20 percent

	Hectares	Acres	Cases*
M. François Rossignol and M. Régis Rossignol	0.3881	1.0	205
M. Claude Segaut	0.2408	0.6	127
M. Paul Voillot	0.1928	0.4	102

Caillerets—14.3385 ha/35.4 acres divided into three *climats*: Caillerets-Dessus (22.4 acres); En Cailleret (7.1 acres); and Clos des Soixante Ouvrées in Caillerets-Dessus (5.9 acres)

Caillerets-Dessus (Clos des Soixante Ouvrées)

SC d'Exploitation du Domaine de la Pousse d'Or	2.3925	5.9	1263

Cailleret-Dessus (Les Caillerets)

M. Jacques d'Angerville d'Auvrecher and Mme. Veuve d'Angerville d'Auvrecher	0.4582	1.1	242
GFA Domaine Delagrange-Battault	0.3334	0.8	176
Mme. Veuve Henri Bitouzet and M. Vincent Bitouzet	0.1532	0.4	81
GFA Domaine Henri Boillot	0.3523	0.9	186
M. Jean Boillot	0.7215	1.8	381
Maison Bouchard Père et Fils	3.1156	7.7	1645
M. Christian Bouley	0.1768	0.4	93
M. Félix Clerget and M. Jean-Claude Fontaine	0.1867	0.5	99
M. et Mme. Charles Delagrange	0.3334	0.8	176
GFA Louis Glantenay et Ses Enfants	0.1857	0.5	98
M. Jean-Claude Fontaine	0.1868	0.5	99
Mme. Veuve François Guillaume	0.2272	0.6	120
Hospices Civils de Beaune	0.1773	0.4	94
Établissements Jaboulet-Vercherre	0.2755	0.7	145
M. Georges Mure	0.3187	0.8	168
M. Jean Pascal	0.1833	0.5	97
M. Michel Pont	0.4465	1.1	236
M. Michel Prunier	0.2937	0.7	155
M. Eugène Rossignol	0.1833	0.5	97
Mme. Veuve Michel Sergent and M. Michel Sergent	0.1870	0.5	99

---

*Cases calculated on the *rendement de base* of 40 hl/ha plus 20 percent

	Hectares	*Acres*	*Cases**
M. Serge Thilloux	0.1069	0.3	56
M. Bernard Vaudoisey	0.1068	0.3	56
M. Joseph Voillot	0.1398	0.4	74

En Cailleret

Maison Bouchard Père et Fils	0.6242	1.5	330
SC d'Exploitation du Domaine de la Pousse d'Or	2.2433	5.5	1184

Carelle sous la Chapelle—3.7315 ha/9.2 acres

M. Julien Bidot	0.1395	0.3	74
GFA Domaine Henri Boillot	0.2786	0.7	147
M. Louis Boillot	0.3577	0.9	189
M. Jean-Marc Bouley	0.2650	0.7	140
M. Roger Caillot and Mme. Florian Brochot	0.0607	0.2	32
GFA Domaine Clerget	0.3085	0.7	163
M. Claude Deconclois and M. Jean Deconclois	0.1232	0.3	65
Hospices Civils de Beaune	0.3186	0.8	168
Mme. Veuve Louis Bizouard de Montille and M. Louis Bizouard de Montille	0.1972	0.5	104
GFA Mussy Frères	0.0785	0.2	41
M. Michel Perrin	0.1268	0.3	67
Mme. Veuve Edmond Pillot and M. Edmond Pillot	0.2339	0.6	123
M. Michel Rebourgeon	0.1391	0.3	73
M. Marcel Rossignol	0.2444	0.6	129
M. René Stehly	0.0902	0.2	48

Carelle Dessous—1.4613 ha/3.6 acres

M. Jean-Charles Bouley	0.0448	0.1	24
GFA du Domaine François Buffet	0.4427	1.1	234
GFA du Domaine Clerget	0.2374	0.6	125
M. Charles Delagrange	0.0543	0.1	29
M. Henri Jandot	0.1614	0.4	85

---

*Cases calculated on the *rendement de base* of 40 hl/ha plus 20 percent

	Hectares	Acres	Cases*
M. Michel Vaudoiset	0.1545	0.4	82
M. Henri Vinceneux	0.3151	0.8	166

Champans or En Champans—11.1934 ha/27.7 acres

	Hectares	Acres	Cases*
M. Émile Bouley	0.2612	0.7	138
M. Pierre Bouley	0.2612	0.7	138
M. Pierre Bouzereau	0.2340	0.6	124
GFA Domaine François Buffet	0.4679	1.2	247
GFA Domaine Clerget	0.0683	0.2	36
GFA du Clos des Ducs	3.9822	9.9	2103
M. Bernard Delagrange	0.3925	1.0	207
M. Charles Delagrange and Mme. Charles Delagrange	0.3649	0.9	193
Mlle. Marie Douhairet	0.8967	2.2	473
Mlle. Marie Emonin	0.5346	1.3	282
M. Jacques Gagnard	0.3649	0.9	193
Mme. Veuve Louis Guidot and M. Hubert Guidot	0.5355	1.3	283
Mme. Veuve Louis Guidot and Mme. Raymond Moufle	0.5355	1.3	283
Hospices Civils de Beaune	0.6440	1.6	340
SCI Domaine des Comtes Lafon	0.5240	1.3	277
Mme. Veuve Louis Bizouard de Montille and M. Louis Bizouard de Montille	0.4200	1.0	222
Mme. Veuve Louis Bizouard de Montille and M. Hubert Bizouard de Montille	0.2429	0.6	128
SD d'Exploitation du Domaine de la Pousse d'Or	0.0227	0.1	12
SC Domaine Jacques Prieur	0.3504	0.8	185

Chanlin—2.8598 ha/7 acres

	Hectares	Acres	Cases*
Maison Bouchard Père et Fils	0.4405	1.1	233
M. Claude et Jean Deconclois	0.1722	0.4	91
M. Jean Deconclois and M. Henri Montagny	0.1495	0.4	79

---

*Cases calculated on the *rendement de base* of 40 hl/ha plus 20 percent

	Hectares	Acres	Cases*
M. Jean-Claude Fontaine	0.2897	0.7	153
Mlle. Claudine Gagnard	0.3712	0.9	196
M. Bernard Lafarge	0.1641	0.4	87
Mme. Veuve François Naudin and M. François Naudin	0.1255	0.3	66
Mme. Veuve Edmond Pilot and M. Edmond Pillot	0.2518	0.6	133
M. Michel Pont	0.3772	0.9	199
M. Jean Poulleau	0.1230	0.3	65
M. Michel Poulleau	0.1308	0.3	44

Clos des Chênes—15.4085 ha/38.1 acres

	Hectares	Acres	Cases*
M. Michel Lafarge	0.8953	2.2	473
M. Jean Bitouzet	0.1814	0.5	96
M. Christian Bouley	0.3780	0.9	200
GFA du Domaine François Buffet	0.9572	2.4	505
Mlle. Claude Caillet and M. Gilbert Caillet	0.1384	0.3	73
SC du Domaine du Château de Meursault	2.6313	6.5	1389
M. Georges Coche	0.1613	0.4	85
M. et Mme. Charles Delagrange	0.6492	1.6	343
M. Henri Delagrange	0.6540	1.6	345
M. Louis Deschamps	0.3198	0.8	169
Domaine Joseph Drouhin	0.2713	0.7	143
M. Richard Fontaine	0.3681	0.9	194
M. François Gaunoux	0.5005	1.2	264
M. François Gaunoux and M. Jean-Michel Gaunoux	0.5744	1.4	303
GFA Louis Glantenay et Ses Enfants	0.4906	1.2	259
GFA Domaine René Thévenin-Monthelie	0.0806	0.2	43
M. Hubert Grillot	0.3642	0.9	192
Societe Foncière du Domaine du Village Antonin Guyon	0.8710	2.2	460
SCI du Domaine des Comtes Lafon	0.3852	1.0	203
GFA Pierre Latour et Ses Enfants	0.2460	0.6	130
M. André Loubet	0.3943	1.0	208

*Cases calculated on the *rendement de base* of 40 hl/ha plus 20 percent

	Hectares	Acres	Cases*
Mme. Veuve René Monnier and Mme. Hubert Monnot	0.3610	0.9	191
Mme. Hubert Monnot	0.3860	1.0	204
M. Jean Parent and Mme. Marie-Christine Parent and Mme. Yves Jayet	0.4259	1.1	225
Mme. Veuve Edmond Pilot and M. Edmond Pilot	0.0985	0.2	52
M. Michel Pont	0.1256	0.3	66
SCI Domaine Ropiteau-Mignon	0.8525	2.1	450
Mlle. Yvonne Rossignol	0.0942	0.2	50
M. Roger Sauvestre	0.1213	0.3	64
GFA Domaine René Thévenin-Monthelie			
M. Pierre Verdereau	0.4365	1.1	230

En Chevret—6.3535 ha/15.7 acres

	Hectares	Acres	Cases*
M. René Regnault De Beaucaron	1.8807	4.7	993
M. Jean Boillot	2.0578	5.0	31
Maison Bouchard Père et Fils	0.2513	0.6	133
Mme. Veuve François Guillaume	1.9467	4.8	1028

Clos Des Ducs—2.1457 ha/5.3 acres

	Hectares	Acres	Cases*
GFA du Clos des Ducs	2.1457	5.3	1133

Frémiets—7.9186 ha/19.6 acres divided into three *climats*: Frémiets (14.5 acres); Frémiets-Clos de la Rougeotte (3.8 acres); and Le Village-Clos de la Rougeotte (1.3 acres)

	Hectares	Acres	Cases*
M. Jean Boillot	0.5929	1.5	313
M. Henri Boillot M. Jean Boillot	0.7255	1.8	383
Mlle. Claude Caillet and M. Gilbert Caillet	0.1794	0.4	95
M. François Charles	0.6063	1.5	320
GFA du Clos des Ducs	1.5785	3.9	833
M. Roger Graindorge	0.0308	0.08	16
Hospices Civils de Beaune	0.2291	0.6	121
M. Pierre Hubert	0.1068	0.3	56
M. Armand Jacquelin	0.0729	0.2	38
M. Louis Jacquelin	0.0398	0.1	21

---

*Cases calculated on the *rendement de base* of 40 hl/ha plus 20 percent

	Hectares	Acres	Cases*
Mme. Suzanne Montagny	0.1645	0.4	87
M. Jean Parent	0.7404	1.8	391
M. Paul Voillot	0.5824	1.4	308

La Gigotte—0.5185 ha/1.3 acres

M. Michel Perrin	0.2713	0.7	143
M. Pierre Perrin	0.2712	0.7	143

Les Grands Champs—0.2411 ha/0.6 acre

M. Émile Bouley	0.2411	0.6	127

Lassolle—0.2155 ha/0.5 acre

M. Hubert Grillot	0.2155	0.5	114

Les Lurets—2.0715 ha/5.1 acres

Mlle. Claude Caillet and M. Gilbert Caillet	0.0145	0.03	8
M. Antonin Changarnier	0.0757	0.2	40
M. Pierre Changarnier	0.0800	0.2	42
M. Louis Develey	0.3444	0.9	182
M. Bernard Dubreuil	0.0962	0.2	51
GFA Mussy Frères	0.1896	0.5	100
M. Marc Garot	0.0746	0.2	39
M. François Gerbeault	0.0676	0.2	36
GFA Louis Glantenay et Ses Enfants	0.3164	0.8	167
M. Henri Rebourgeon	0.0963	0.2	51
Mme. Veuve Michel Sergent and M. Michel Sergent	0.1468	0.4	78
M. Michel Sergent	0.1478	0.4	78
M. René Stehly	0.0559	0.1	30
M. Henri Vinceneux	0.3657	0.9	193

Les Mitans—3.9799 ha/9.8 acres

M. Maurice Bertrand	0.1236	0.3	65
M. Bernard Bridot	0.0668	0.2	35
M. Antonin Changarnier	0.3000	0.7	158
Mme. Veuve Pierre Changarnier and M. Pierre Changarnier	0.1345	0.3	71
M. Pierre Changarnier	0.1655	0.4	87
M. Jean-François Delagrange	0.1957	0.4	103

*Cases calculated on the *rendement de base* of 40 hl/ha plus 20 percent

	Hectares	Acres	Cases*
M. Roger Faivre	0.0845	0.2	45
M. Jean-Marc Lafarge	0.1711	0.4	90
Maison Louis Latour	0.2664	0.7	141
Mme. Veuve Hubert Bizouard de Montille and Mme. Veuve Louis Bizouard de Montille	0.7285	1.8	385
M. François Mure	0.1690	0.4	89
M. Georges Mure	0.2212	0.6	117
M. Jean Parent	0.0048	0.01	3
M. Michel Pont	0.3620	0.9	191
M. Robert Richez	0.0880	0.2	46
M. Roger Rossignol	0.2132	0.5	113
M. Serge Thilloux	0.4485	1.1	237
M. Jean Vaudoisey	0.1650	0.4	87

En l'Ormeau—4.3260 ha/10.7 acres

M. Jacques D'Angerville d'Auvrecher	0.6557	1.6	346
M. René Regnault de Beaucaron	0.1330	0.3	70
M. Jean Bitouzet	0.1514	0.4	80
M. Christian Bouley	0.1230	0.3	65
GFA du Clerget Domaine	0.1646	0.4	87
M. Claude Deconclois and Mme. Gilbert Corrand	0.1937	0.5	102
M. Claude Deconclois and Mlle. Marie Deconclois	0.1218	0.3	64
M. Jean-François Delagrange	0.0233	0.06	12
GFA Louis Glantenay et Ses Enfants	0.3326	0.8	176
Hospices Civils de Beaune	0.2517	0.6	133
M. François Mure	0.3978	1.0	210
M. René Mure	0.2289	0.6	121
M. Jean Parent	0.2258	0.6	119
M. Jean-Louis Pont	0.0988	0.2	52
M. Michel Pont	0.1384	0.3	73
M. Henri Rebourgeon	0.0949	0.2	50
M. François Roblet	0.0862	0.2	46
Mlle. Yvonne Rossignol	0.0992	0.3	52
M. Pierre Verdereau	0.0912	0.2	48

Pitures—4.0797 ha/10.1 acres

M. Jacques d'Angerville d'Auvrecher	0.3269	0.8	173

---

*Cases calculated on the *rendement de base* of 40 hl/ha plus 20 percent

	Hectares	*Acres*	*Cases**
GFA du Domaine Delagrange-Battault	0.2000	0.5	106
M. Jean Bitouzet	0.4930	1.2	260
GFA du Domaine Henri Boillot	0.4433	1.1	234
M. Gilbert Caillet and M. Patrick Caillet	0.0628	0.2	33
M. Charles Delagrange	0.3644	0.9	192
SCI de Notre-Dame des Vignes	0.5122	1.3	270
Mme. Veuve Edmond Pillot and M. Edmond Pillot	0.0777	0.2	41
M. François Roblet	0.0615	0.2	32
M. François Rossignol and M. Michel Rossignol	0.6591	1.6	348
M. Serge Thillouy	0.0810	0.2	43

Pointes des Angles—1.2283 ha/3 acres

M. Jacques d'Angerville d'Auvrecher	0.5348	1.3	282
Mlle. Madeleine Boillot	0.5567	1.4	294
M. Marcel Rossignol	0.0740	0.2	39

Robardelle—2.9379 ha/7.3 acres

M. Pierre Bouley	0.1808	0.5	95
M. Ferdinand Carre	0.2611	0.7	138
M. Antonin Changarnier	0.1220	0.3	64
Mme. Veuve Louis Charlier	0.2107	0.5	111
Mme. Gilbert Corrand and M. Claude Deconclois	0.1044	0.3	55
GFA Glantenay-Midant	0.3616	0.9	191
M.Émile Jacquelin	0.1976	0.5	104
M. François Roblet	0.2677	0.7	141
M. Bernard Rossignol	0.4302	1.1	227
M. Marcel Rossignol	0.4302	1.1	227
M. Roger Sauvestre	0.2160	0.5	114
M. René Stehly	0.1556	0.4	82

Le Ronceret—1.9000 ha/4.7 acres

GFA Domaine Henri Boillot	0.3208	0.8	· 169
Mme. Veuve Georges Garaudet and M. Georges Garaudet	0.1880	0.5	99
M. Marc Garot	0.2335	0.6	123

---

*Cases calculated on the *rendement de base* of 40 hl/ha plus 20 percent

	Hectares	Acres	Cases*
Hospices Civils de Beaune	0.3562	0.9	188
GFA Mussy Frères	0.2914	0.7	154
M. Antoine Nardot	0.1298	0.3	69
M. Jean-Claude Pothier	0.0480	0.1	25
M. René Stehly	0.1721	0.4	91
M. Michel Vaudoisey	0.1602	0.4	85

Taille Pieds—7.1698 ha/17.7 acres

	Hectares	Acres	Cases*
GFA du Domaine Delagrange-Battault	0.3135	0.8	166
Mme. Maurice Bertrand	0.1880	0.5	99
M. Roger Boisson	0.2102	0.5	111
Maison Bouchard Père et Fils	1.1040	2.7	583
M. Charles Bousset and M. Eric Bousset	0.0962	0.2	51
M. Charles Boussey and M. Denis Boussey	0.0921	0.2	49
GFA du Domaine François Buffet	0.2953	0.7	156
M. Valéry Carre	0.4727	1.2	250
GFA Clos des Ducs	1.0703	2.6	565
M. Hubert Grillot	0.7125	1.7	376
Hospices Civils de Beaune	0.7427	1.8	392
M. Charles Lochardet de Berthles	0.3750	0.9	198
Mme. Veuve Louis Bizouard de Montille and M. Louis Bizouard de Montille	0.7885	1.9	416
M. Jean Poulleau	0.1184	0.3	63
M. François Roblet	0.1880	0.5	99
M. Eugène Rossignol	0.1183	0.3	62

En Verseuil or Clos de Verseuil—0.6807 ha/1.7 acres

	Hectares	Acres	Cases*
GFA du Domaine Clerget	0.6807	1.7	359

Le Village—6.4219 ha/15.9 acres divided into seven *climats*: Le Village (7 acres); Clos de la Cave des Ducs (1.6 acres); Clos du Château des Ducs (1.4 acres); Clos de l'Audignac (2.7 acres); Clos de la Chapelle (1.4 acres); Clos de la Bousse d'Or (0.5 acre); Le Village-Clos de la Rougeotte (1.3 acres)

Le Village (Clos de la Cave des Ducs)

	Hectares	Acres	Cases*
M. Valéry Carre	0.5394	1.3	285

---

*Cases calculated on the *rendement de base* of 40 hl/ha plus 20 percent.

	Hectares	*Acres*	*Cases**
Le Village (Clos du Château des Ducs)			
M. Bernard Lafarge	0.5692	1.4	301
Le Village (Clos de l'Audignac)			
SCI d'Exploitation du Domaine de la Pousse d'Or	0.8050	2.0	425
Le Village (Clos de la Chapelle)			
M. Louis Boillot	0.5557	1.4	293
Le Village			
GFA du Domaine Henri Boillot	0.1085	0.3	57
M. Jean Boillot	0.2640	0.7	139
M. Bernard Delagrange	0.1485	0.4	78
Hospices Civils de Beaune	0.8063	2.0	426
M. Michel Lafarge	0.0912	0.2	48
Mme. Veuve Louis Bizouard de Montille and M. Louis Bizouard de Montille	0.1340	0.3	71
SCI d'Exploitation du Domaine de la Pousse d'Or	0.1850	0.5	98
SCI de Notre-Dame des Vignes	0.2712	0.7	143
Le Village (Clos de la Rougeotte)			
GFA Domaine François Buffet	0.5185	1.3	274

Volnay-Santenots

LES PLURES OR LES PETURES—10.4501 ha/25.8 acres

LES SANTENOTS BLANCS—2.9203 ha/7.2 acres

LES SANTENOTS DU MILIEU—15.6483 ha/38.7 acres divided into three *climats*: Les Santenots du Milieu (16.8 acres); Clos des Santenots (3 acres); Les Santenots Dessous (18.9 acres)

---

*Cases calculated on the *rendement de base* of 40 hl/ha plus 20 percent

LES VIGNES BLANCHES—0.0544 ha/0.13 acre

VINEYARDS WORTH SEEKING OUT

Any of the famous *premiers crus*, of course. Also, anything labeled "Volnay Premier Cru" is a good bet and, usually, a very good buy.

PRODUCERS WORTH SEEKING OUT
(AND A FEW NOT)

DOMAINE MARQUIS D'ANGERVILLE—In a commune with luminous names, none is brighter than d'Angerville. It was the current Jacques d'Angerville's father—also named Jacques—who in the 1930s was the point man in the nasty war with the *négociants* over fraudulent practices. He also was instrumental in pursuing superior clones of Pinot Noir, isolating one small-berried clone in particular that now colloquially bears his name. Growers refer to "the d'Angerville clone."

Jacques d'Angerville the son, now in his sixties, is no less active, being a member of all sorts of official Burgundian winegrowers' organizations. He is the current president of the Association pour l'Institut de la Vigne et du Vin, which is designed to help create a university research institute on the Dijon-Montmuzard campus. It is just the sort of activity that the d'Angervilles find important. One other telling point: d'Angerville is no weekend winegrower wandering through his vineyards in a sport jacket and ascot. He really is the winemaker.

The wines of d'Angerville are for many Volnay fans, present company included, the epitome of what Volnay is or should be: delicate, fragrant wines of great finesse that are structured for long life. Oddly, his wines have not been lauded in recent years by journalists who descend on the Côte d'Or for exhaustive barrel tastings. Sometimes wines that show well in barrel later turn out to be excessively oaky or just showy wines. The d'Angerville style, which is signature-free, does not serve him well in this situation. The wines are dismissed or marked down for lacking concentration or depth or character. In fact, they emerge from the bottle six or eight or ten years after the vintage as Volnays of immense detail and formidable flavor impact. They remind one of a ninety-pound karate champion who breaks six bricks with one blow.

The great d'Angerville wine surely is Clos des Ducs, followed closely by Champans. His Volnay Premier Cru bottling is a worthy wine, usually very delicate and graceful. His Frémiets, which is not exported to the States, is a pure example of this vineyard. Also notable is d'Angerville's one white wine, a Meursault-Santenots. If d'Angerville has a fault, it is an apparent reluctance to modify his winemaking approach to offset a deficiency in a vintage. In a light vintage, you get a light wine. In this sense, the wines are accurate. Ideally, d'Angerville would engage in more manipulation, but as can be seen with those who do manipulate, the temptation to do so every vintage seems too often to lead to bad judgments.

BOUCHARD PÈRE ET FILS—The only major *négociant* with large vineyard holdings in Volnay. Bouchard has enviable vineyards: Taille Pieds; Caillerets-Dessus (labeled "Ancienne Cuvée Carnot"); Frémiets-Clos de la Rougeotte. Although the wines are acceptable, they are not exemplars of Volnay, lacking definition and character compared to other offerings from the same sites, especially the Caillerets.

DOMAINE JEAN-MARC BOULEY—A producer who has been touted recently, for reasons that escape me. The Bouley style seems to be one of intense grapiness and deep, extracted color. *Extraction* seems to be the operative word here. Rustic wines from vineyards that shouldn't be rustic such as Caillerets and Clos des Chênes.

DOMAINE BERNARD DELAGRANGE—A Meursault-based grower issuing good, workmanlike Volnays from choice vineyards: Caillerets; Champans (labeled "Clos des Champans").

HOSPICES DE BEAUNE—The charity hospital has extensive holdings in Volnay, resulting in four *cuvées*.

Cuvée Blondeau—Champans (0.6 ha/1.5 acres); Taille Pieds (0.6 ha/

1.5 acres); Ronceret (0.33 ha/0.8 acre); and En l'Ormeau (0.2 ha/0.5 acre)

Cuvée General Muteau—Le Village (0.8 ha/2 acres); Carelle sous la Chapelle (0.33 ha/0.8 acre); Caillerets-Dessus (0.2 ha/0.5 acre); Frémiets (0.2 ha/0.5 acre); and Taille Pieds (0.2 ha/0.5 acre)

Cuvée Jehan de Massol—Les Santenots (1.5 ha/3.7 acres)

Cuvée Gauvain—Les Santenots (1.5 ha/3.7 acres) and Santenot-Les Pitures (0.33 ha/0.8 acre)

Since the departure of André Porcheret (to Domaine Leroy), who dramatically improved the Hospices de Beaune reds during his tenure as head winemaker from 1977 to 1987, the red wines of the Hospices have declined. The '89s were appallingly light, including the various Volnay *cuvées*. Given the prices . . .

DOMAINE MICHEL LAFARGE—One of the trinity of supreme Volnay producers, along with d'Angerville and Pousse d'Or. Wonderfully rich, intense wines of a style equal to, but different from, either Pousse d'Or or d'Angerville. Compare Lafarge's Clos du Château des Ducs with d'Angervilles's Clos des Ducs and you'll see it instantly. The structure of one is heavily timbered; the other is spiderweb-gossamer. Both are awe-inspiring. The Lafarge Clos des Chênes is about as good as this vineyard gets; also there is superb commune-level Volnay.

DOMAINE DES COMTES LAFON—The famed Meursault producer is viticulturally ambidextrous: It makes great red wines too, namely Volnay-Santenots du Milieu and Clos des Chênes. Long-lived, beautifully structured wines.

LEROY—Volnay is a specialty with this *négociant*. Madame Bize-Leroy somehow manages to locate superb lots of different Volnay vineyards such as Brouillards, Taille Pieds, Lassolle, and Clos des Chênes, among others. The wines, as always, are very long-lived and very pure expressions of Volnay.

DOMAINE MONCEAU-BOCH—Owned by Madame Louis Guidot, this relatively little-known Meursault domaine issues excellent Champans in a clean, pure style. Worth looking for.

DOMAINE DE MONTILLE—One of the famous names of Volnay and a producer that many consider a leader in all of the Côte d'Or. The de Montille style is for great delicacy and balance, which it has in abundance. The wines seem to lack stuffings, but maybe I just haven't had the right ones. Champans seems to be its best effort. Certainly a producer to look for. I always do.

DOMAINE MICHEL PONT—This producer is perhaps best known for owning a pleasant, unpretentious restaurant in Volnay called Le Cellier Volnaysien. The food is decent, and it sells its considerable array of wines there at very reasonable prices. Its very good Caillerets 1985 or Clos des Chênes 1985 was selling for eighty-five francs a bottle on the list (when it was still available), about fourteen dollars, which hardly is gouging as restaurant wine lists go.

DOMAINE DE LA POUSSE D'OR—The third of the great trio with d'Angerville and Lafarge. The wines of Pousse d'Or are the creation of Gérard Potel, who manages the thirty-two-acre estate for principal owner Jean Ferté and a consortium of seven Australian owners. Potel is rightly regarded as one of the most innovative Burgundian wine-makers. Rarely does his search for improvement lead to excesses or missteps, which says something about him right there. The Pousse d'Or style is one that prizes polish and finesse over bravado.

Prize for the best wine seesaws between the Caillerets-Clos des Soixante Ouvrées and Bousse d'Or. Some years it's Soixante Ouvrées (1985, for example); other years it's Bousse d'Or (1982). All of the wines are standouts. Pousse d'Or has the *monopole* Le Village-Clos d'Audignac, which lies right by the prominent house and cellars of the estate.

DOMAINE MICHEL PRUNIER—This Auxey-Duresses producer owns about three quarters of an acre of Caillerets-Dessus and does an outstanding job with it; pure, signature-free winemaking. A great Caillerets.

Monthelie

$\mathbf{M}$onthelie is one of the least-known (and seen) *appellations* of the Côte de Beaune. Sandwiched between Volnay, Meursault, and Auxey-Duresses, it not only is the smallest of the three, but has the least distinctive wines. Unlike Meursault and Auxey-Duresses, it does not make white wine of any distinction. In fact, it barely makes white wine at all: Two tenths of one percent of Monthelie's total wine production is white. The locals say that it oxidizes readily. The best version is thought to be from the *premier cru* vineyard Le Château Gaillard, which is a *monopole* of Domaine Parent.

The red wine of Monthelie is not easily characterized. It most often is described more by what it is not, usually in relation to neighboring Volnay. In that vein, it lacks the perfuminess and silkiness of Volnay. It is, however, fuller and richer than red Auxey-Duresses. What you can expect from Monthelie is a wine of depth and flavor that is slightly coarse or rustic. It's a sturdy wine. The best vineyards, not surprisingly, are thought to be those adjacent to Volnay: Les Champs Fuillot and Sur la Velle, both *premiers crus*. It is always revealing to taste a Volnay "Clos des Chênes" against a Monthelie to see just what a transitional vineyard Clos des Chênes really is.

The name *Monthelie* often is spelled "Monthélie," with an *accent aigu* over the first *e*. This exceedingly minor nomenclatural matter is mentioned only because it seems to occasion problems for various writers. In December 1989, I received a frantic call from a staffer in *The New Yorker* magazine's fabled fact-checking department. An article by one of their writers was to appear (in the January 1, 1990, issue) about the elderly Monthelie grower Armande Douhairet. What was the proper spelling of Monthelie?

Famous for punctiliousness in such matters, the magazine was desperately trying to establish once and for all whether Monthelie was spelled with or without an *accent aigu*. One thing is certain: It is pronounced as if it lacked one: Mont-lee. Flattered that I was asked, the best I could do was note that while the Dutch writer Hubrecht Duijker in *The Great Wines of Burgundy* went to pains to point out that the proper spelling was without the *accent aigu*, the authoritative *Atlas des Grands Vignobles de Bourgogne* by Sylvain Pitiot and Pierre Poupon includes it. I referred them to several Burgundians who, I felt, were in a position to know. When the article appeared, Monthelie was spelled without an *accent aigu*. That's good enough for me.

THE VINEYARDS

There are 139.9025 ha/345.7 acres of which seventy-seven acres are *premier cru*. There are *no grands crus* in Monthelie.

THE PREMIERS CRUS

Le Cas Rougeot—0.5650 ha/1.4 acres
Les Champs Fuillots—8.1122 ha/20 acres
Le Château Gaillard—0.4857 ha/1.2 acres
Le Clos Gauthey—1.8015 ha/4.5 acres
Les Duresses—6.7234 ha/16.6 acres
Le Meix Bataille—2.2775 ha/5.6 acres
Les Riottes—0.7450 ha/1.8 acres

Sur la Velle—6.0301 ha/14.9 acres
La Taupine—1.4980 ha/3.7 acres
Le Village de Monthelie—0.2240 ha/0.6 acre
Les Vignes Rondes—2.7200 ha/6.7 acres

PRODUCERS WORTH SEEKING OUT (AND SOME NOT)

DOMAINE MONTHELIE-DOUHAIRET—The eighty-three-year-old Mademoiselle Armande Douhairet was the subject of the *New Yorker* profile mentioned previously. Her Monthelie is a classic of its type: robust, substantial, and what the French call *typique*. In other words, if you don't ask it to be Volnay, you won't be disappointed. The Monthelie *premier cru* bottling, not surprisingly, is superior to the commune-level bottling, with greater depth and richness.

CHÂTEAU DE MONTHELIE—The most famous producer in the commune is Robert Suremain, who issues just one wine under the name Château de Monthelie. It is one of the best: unusually concentrated, with a rich, chocolaty quality, and long-lived.

JOSEPH DROUHIN—This *négociant* has long offered a commune-level Monthelie. The Drouhin style is present here: The wine is a little light, but finely flavored, in the soft, easy-down-the-gullet Drouhin red wine style.

HOSPICES DE BEAUNE—One *cuvée* is offered from Monthelie:

Cuvée Lebelin—Les Duresses (0.88 ha/2.2 acres)

LOUIS JADOT—The *négociant* is one of the better sources of good commune-level Monthelie: solid, straightforward Pinot Noir with a mouthful of unsubtle flavor.

DOMAINE ROPITEAU-MIGNON—Producers of a Clos des Champs-Fuillot bottling, it fails to make a case. Too often the wine is light and thin, and tastes overchaptalized.

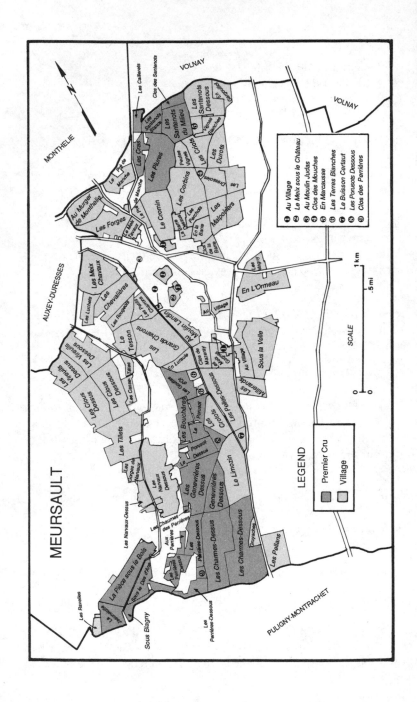

MEURSAULT

VOLNAY

VOLNAY

MONTHELIE

AUXEY-DURESSES

PULIGNY-MONTRACHET

LEGEND

Premier Cru
Village

1. Au Village
2. Le Meix sous le Château
3. Au Moulin Judas
4. Clos des Mouches
5. En Marcausse
6. Les Terres Blanches
7. Le Buisson Certaut
8. Les Porusots Dessous
9. Clos des Perrières

SCALE

0 — .5 mi
0 — 1 km

Les Caillerets
Clos des Santenots
Les Santenots
Les Santenots du Milieu
Vignes Blanches
Les Plures
Les Crâs
Les Suchots Blancs
Petite Vignes
Les Criots
Les Durots
Les Corbins
Les Dressoles
Au Murger de Monthelie
Le Pré de Manche
Le Pré de Manche
La Barre Dessus
Les Forges
Le Meix Tavaux
Le Cromin
Les Pâchots
En la Barre
Les Malpoiriers
Clos de la Barre
Les Magni
En L'Ormeau
Les Meix Chavaux
Les Luchets
Les Chevalières
Les Rougeots
Le Point
Caumes
Au Moulin Landin
Au Village
Les Vireuils Dessous
Les Vireuils Dessus
Les Clous Dessus
Les Tesson
Les Grands Charrons
En Luraule
Les Caves Tétes
Clos de Mazeray
Au Village
Les Millerands
Sous la Velle
Au Village
Les Tillets
Les Clous Dessous
Les Bouchères
Les Gouttes
Le Porusot
Les Gruots-Dessous
Les Petits Dessous
Les Narvaux-Dessus
Les Gorges de Narvaux
Le Porusot Dessus
Les Narvaux Dessous
Les Genevrières Dessus
Le Limozin
Genevrières Dessous
Les Chaumes des Perrières
Les Perrières-Dessus
Les Charmes-Dessus
Les Charmes-Dessous
Les Ravelles
La Pièce sous le Bois
Aux Perrières
Supériéure n°1
Sous le Dos d'Âne
Les Perrières-Dessous
Les Perrières-Dessous
Pruzeilles
Les Poruzots
Les Peilans
Sous Blagny

Meursault

At Pommard and Voulenay I observed them eating good wheat bread; at Meursault, rye. I asked the reason of the difference. They told me that the white wines fail in quality much oftener than the red, and remain on hand. . . . At Meursault only white wines are made, because there is too much stone for the red. On such slight circumstances depends the condition of man!

—THOMAS JEFFERSON (1787),
The Papers of Thomas Jefferson, Volume II

The appeal of Meursault is direct: It is a gush of flavor in the mouth. With a young Puligny- or Chassagne-Montrachet, you have to work a little. They hint at dimensions to come. So too does young Meursault, but it's more of a broad wink. The surprise is that, given its inviting qualities, Meursault transforms as much as it does.

What a mature Meursault offers is a combination of flavors found in few Chardonnays anywhere: honey, coffee, hazelnuts, minerals, butter, and spices such as cinnamon. These are delivered in abundance, yet somehow softly so. Perhaps its rich color is too suggestive, but the luxuriance of a good Meursault can make you think that if gold were a flavor, it would taste like Meursault.

The town itself has several unusual features: a towering church spire unique among the wine villages of the Côte d'Or; the largest number of inhabitants (1,646) outside of Beaune in the Côte de

Beaune; and an improbably large number of grand (for Burgundy) residences. It was once the town of choice for the residences of many *négociants*. And it has long had wealthy growers, such as Domaine Jacques Prieur, which still retains a jewel of a house and landscaped park that can be seen just outside the center of town. All this informs us of the traditional wealth of Meursault.

Today's white wine boom is not Meursault's first brush with prosperity. According to Cyrus Redding in *French Vineyards and the Way to Find Them* (1860), a ten-year average of prices fetched by the Hospices de Beaune wines during the 1840s shows that its Meursault wines—Genevrières and Gouttes d'Or—fetched an average of 450 francs per *queue* (two barrels of 228 liters each), more than any other white wine except Le Montrachet. Common white wines commanded just 75 francs to 90 francs a *queue*.

A stroll through the town reveals one new feature: the number of growers who domaine-bottle their wines. It's a good bet that no other village in Burgundy has as many domaines as Meursault. Partly this is because of the size of the town; largely it is due to the scale of its vineyards (over twelve hundred acres). Above all it is a testament to the lucrativeness of Meursault in the market today.

For the Burgundy enthusiast, this profusion of wines is a delicious agony, like visiting the Louvre. I have stayed in Meursault multiple times, always arriving with optimism and ambition, only to slink away despondent at ever getting a grip on the place. Still, my notebooks bulge with tasting notes, from samples sipped *sur place* as well as at home.

A once-prominent feature of Meursault is all but absent today: red wine. It no longer grows Pinot Noir in quantity. Jefferson's observation notwithstanding, red Meursault was once almost as abundant as white. Now, red wine is just half of one percent of its production.

Dr. Jules Lavalle in his *Histoire et Statistique de la Vigne et des Grands Vins de la Côte d'Or* (1855) makes clear that Pinor Noir was widely planted in Meursault, citing numerous vineyards where Pinot Noir was planted and exclaiming over the price commanded by the Santenots *rouge*, which was "rarely less than 400 or 500 francs the queue, and in the good years, these prices are greatly exceeded." Now, the presence of Pinot Noir is mostly legal nicety. The Appellation Contrôlée philosophy of *loyal, local et constant*—traditional, individual to the area, and demonstrably long-term—explains why virtually every vineyard in Meursault still is allowed to grow Pinot Noir.

The vineyards that offer Meursault at its best—white wine, to be sure—are the *premiers crus*. Here, there is a reassuring consistency. Thomas Jefferson was a great enthusiast for Gouttes d'Or, which today is still among the best *premiers crus*. The vineyard then was thirteen acres. It still is. For centuries, the resonant names have been Perrières, Genevrières, Charmes, Poruzot, Bouchères, and Gouttes d'Or. They still are. These six vineyards—just 204 acres combined—make wines that linger in the mind.

The problem today, especially in Meursault, is that demand is so intense that many growers allow their yields to creep up. The result is diluted wine, especially in abundant vintages such as 1982. Still, the best producers adhere to uncompromising standards, offering wines with the concentration, definition, and, above all, the texture, that distinguishes Meursault. A great, mature Meursault is almost creamy. The wine needs eight to ten years of age for it to be revealed, but no one has yet to suggest that it isn't worth the wait.

THE VINEYARDS

The Meursault *appellation* has its confusing aspects. Its name embraces the hamlet of Blagny, some of the white wines of which can be sold as Meursault. Moreover, the red wines of certain vineyards in Meursault can be sold as Volnay-Santenots, even though the vines are not in Volnay. This is because that's how they once were sold, prior to the installment of Appellation Contrôlée in 1937.

There are 438.8 ha/1,079 acres in 89 named vineyards in Meursault itself, excluding Blagny. There are no *grands crus*.

In the hamlet of Blagny are four *premiers crus* entitled to be sold as Meursault or Meursault-Blagny. All Blagny red—including any red wine produced in the *premiers crus* of Blagny—may only be sold as Blagny.

The *appellation* Volnay-Santenots—which is really six named vineyards in Meursault sailing under one flag—is exclusively *premier cru*: 29.0731 ha/71.8 acres. If the wines are red, they are called Volnay-Santenots. The few white wines from these same six vineyards are labeled Meursault-Santenots.

MEURSAULT PREMIERS CRUS

Sorting through the six major *premiers crus* of Meursault is one of the great games of Burgundy. No sooner do you think that you've got them pinned at last than you sit down to a blind tasting and wind up bungling every guess as to what's what. Still, the challenge is irresistible.

LES PERRIÈRES—The greatest of them all surely is—or should be—Les Perrières. If Meursault had a *grand cru*, Perrières would be it. A great, mature Perrières ranks with Le Montrachet, Chevalier-Montrachet, and Corton-Charlemagne as one of the most profound white wines of Burgundy.

Perrières displays as much depth as the richest Charmes or Genevrières, but with a rigor distinct from these two. It is the most intense Meursault. As the *climat* names suggest, Perrières is broken up into subsections. In this case, "broken up" is a literal description. The vineyard seems nearly a quarry, with gouges and depressions resulting in tufts of vineyard here and there. The finest *climats* are Perrières-Dessous and, above all, Clos des Perrières, a tiny enclosed vineyard in Perrières-Dessous, the distinction of which is thought to be magnesium in the soil. It is owned exclusively by Domaine Albert Grivault. In late 1989 about half of the 2.3-acre vineyard was replanted to what looked to be one-year-old vines.

LES GENEVRIÈRES—Genevrières is close to Perrières, both in fact and esteem. Where Perrières is a matter of stoniness, Genevrières is less insistent and more refined. The site is thought to be slightly warmer than Perrières, likely because of its greater consistency of exposure. It is less austere than Perrières; more inviting. No one draws much distinction between Genevrières *dessus* and *dessous*, at least not that I've heard.

LES CHARMES—The largest of the *premiers crus* and the most variable as a result. At its best, Les Charmes is the most voluptuous, almost pillowy, wine. It can display a stunning amount of mineraliness, especially, I suspect, the closer the vines are to Les Perrières.

A distinction is drawn here between Charmes *dessus* (above) and *dessous* (below). Charmes-Dessus is considered the finer of the two, by reasons of superior exposure and less-rich soil than is found farther down the slope in Charmes-Dessous.

LES PORUZOT—The most delicate of the *premiers crus*. Still, it reveals a surprising strength. The image of a steel cable on a suspension bridge comes to mind. Because of this, it is almost as long-lived as Perrières or Genevrières, although never as meaty or weighty, but very stony-tasting. Indeed, the name derives from "*por*" or "*porée*," referring to a stone pit. In many respects, it is the most accommodating of great Meursaults to many dishes, as the others can be bullying because of their power. It is interesting to compare Poruzot (or "Porusot") with Genevrières, if for no other reason than to see how the two wines have a similarly refined delivery, but of different characters and flavors.

LES BOUCHÈRES—It is revealing that a distinction has always been drawn distinguishing Bouchères from Poruzot, which it abuts. Given that Poruzot is composed of three *climats*, the question occurs: Why wasn't Bouchères called Poruzots-Dessus? The answer, I believe, is found in the glass. They really do not taste at all similar. Bouchères has the superior exposue, at least to judge from the "density" of the wine. Hazelnuts and honey are found, more than the minerally austerity of adjoining Poruzot. According to M. René Manuel, who owns the largest parcel of Boucherès, the name derives either from *bouches chères*—precious mouths—or from the word *bouchon*, which in this case refers not to a cork, but an ancient term for a small patch of woods. He notes that a small path leading to his house, which is located at the base of the slope near Bouchères, there is a "rue du Pied de la Forêt," which suggests that the section was a forest in some earlier time.

LES GOUTTES D'OR—The "golden drops" of this aptly named vineyard represent what might be described as the last stop of the train of great Meursault *premiers crus*. From here the slope moves rapidly upward, already arching its way up at Gouttes d'Or. It demonstrates the critical role of exposure, its slant making up for its elevation. Gouttes d'Or is the least subtle wine of the pack (forgive me, Thomas Jefferson), filled with a strong, direct richness but lacking the subtlety of Charmes (they don't call it "Charmes" for nothing) or the suaveness of Bouchères. It is, however, an enriching wine and worth seeking out.

Les Bouchères—4.4166 ha/10.9 acres

	Hectares	Acres	Cases*
Mme. Odette Battault	0.0945	0.2	56
Mme. Jean Desmazières	0.3546	0.9	211
M. Louis Giroux and Mme. Paul Sadrin	0.3008	0.7	179
M. Yves Latour	0.1358	0.3	81
GFA du Domaine René Manuel	1.5117	3.7	898
M. Guy Mognier	0.1551	0.4	92
M. Edouard Petit	0.2448	0.6	145
Mme. Veuve Camille Pothier and Mme. Camille Pothier	0.3505	0.9	208
Mme. Veuve Antoine Serpin	0.1553	0.4	92
M. Erick Urena	0.7583	1.9	450
M. Franck Urena	0.0310	0.08	18

Les Caillerets—1.0319 ha/2.5 acres

M. Raymond Ballot	0.1310	0.3	78
Mme. Veuve Pierre Boillot and Mlle. Noelle Boillot	0.1221	0.3	73
M. Georges Coche	0.1835	0.5	109
Mme. Veuve Eugène Garaudet and M. Henri Garaudet	0.0524	0.1	31
GFA Pierre Latour	0.1844	0.5	110
GFA du Domaine Pothier-Rieusset	0.2768	0.7	164

Les Cras—3.5504 ha/8.8 acres divided into two *climats*: Les Cras (7.2 acres) and Clos Richmont (1.6 acres)

M. André Brunet and Mme. Veuve Ernest Guillemier	0.2841	0.7	169
M. André Brunet	0.4908	1.2	292

---

*Cases calculated on the *rendement de base* of 45 hl/ha for white Meursault, plus 20 percent. Red Meursault has a lower *rendement de base* of 40 hl/ha.

	Hectares	Acres	Cases*
M. Michel Buisson	0.1913	0.5	114
M. Lucien Chouet	0.4917	1.2	292
GFA Domaine Darnat	0.5735	1.4	341
Mme. François Durand	0.1055	0.3	63
Mlle. Anne Emboulas	0.5972	1.5	355
Hospices Civils de Beaune	0.1755	0.4	104
M. Jean Latour	0.1909	0.5	113
Commune de Meursault	0.0054	0.0	3
M. Robert Richez	0.2172	0.5	129
M. Joseph Voillot	0.1260	0.3	75

Les Charmes—31.1179 ha/76.9 acres divided into Charmes-Dessus (35.3 acres) and Charmes-Dessous (41.6 acres)

Les Charmes-Dessus

	Hectares	Acres	Cases*
M. Michel Ampeau and M. Robert Ampeau	0.2753	0.7	164
M. Raymond Ballot	0.3487	0.9	207
M. Charles Bocard	0.3920	1.0	233
M. Jean-Baptiste Bouzereau	0.6659	1.7	396
M. André Brunet	0.6502	1.6	386
M. Dominique Carrara	0.3231	0.8	192
M. René Chalet	0.0214	0.1	13
SC du Domaine du Château de Meursault	3.0399	7.5	1806
Mme. Veuve Camille Chouet	0.1444	0.4	86
Mme. François Durand	0.2051	0.5	122
SC du Domaine de la Guyonnière	0.6878	1.7	409
Hospices Civils de Beaune	1.0218	2.5	607
Mme. Georges Jackson	0.1784	0.4	106
M. Charles Jobard	0.1677	0.4	100
M. Émile Jobard	0.3258	0.8	194
M. Francois Jobard	0.1678	0.4	100
SCI du Domaine des Comtes Lafon	1.7133	4.2	1018
GFA Pierre Latour	0.2237	0.6	133
Mme. Veuve Jean Loiselet	0.2067	0.5	123
M. Claude Martenot	0.0913	0.2	54
SCI du Domaine Joseph Matrot	0.5388	1.3	320
M. Alfred Michelot and M. Bernard Michelot	0.2822	0.7	168
M. Léon Millot	0.0727	0.2	43

---

*Cases calculated on the *rendement de base* of 45 hl/ha for white Meursault, plus 20 percent. Red Meursault has a lower *rendement de base* of 40 hl/ha.

	Hectares	Acres	Cases*
M. Pierre Millot	0.7233	1.8	430
M. Pierre Moingeon	0.0040	0.009	2
M. Léon Ozga and Mlle. Agnes Bouzereau	0.1574	0.4	93
M. Claude Patriarche	0.0758	0.2	45
M. Justin Patriarche	0.0758	0.2	45
M. Raymond Patriarche	0.0758	0.2	45
M. Pierre Perrin	0.3062	0.8	182
M. Hubert Prieur	0.2311	0.6	137
M. Michel Tessier	0.5948	1.5	353
M. Bernard Virely	0.1568	0.4	93

Les Genevrières—16.4794 ha/40.7 acres divided into four *climats*: Les Chaumes des Perrières (three-fourths acre); Les Genevrières-Dessus (26.3 acres); Les Genevrières Dessous (13.3 acres); and Les Chaumes de Narvaux (one-third acre).

Les Genevrières-Dessus

Mme. Gaston de Masson d'Autume	0.5371	1.3	319
M. Raymond Ballot	0.4350	1.1	258
M. Jean Boillot	0.1560	0.4	93
Mme. André Briotet	0.4006	1.0	238
Hospices Civils de Beaune	0.8473	2.1	503
SCI du Domaine des Comtes Lafon	0.5555	1.4	330
GFA Pierre Latour	1.9177	4.7	1139
Mme. Paul Maillard and Mme. Gérard Dangelzer and M. Emmanuel Monick	0.6302	1.6	374
M. Alfred Michelot	0.3990	1.0	237
Mme. Veuve Alfred Michelot and M. Alfred Michelot	0.3699	0.9	220
M. Bernard Michelot	0.4280	1.1	254
M. Jean-Claude Monnier	0.2895	0.7	172
Mme. Richard Moore	0.1174	0.3	70
M. Henri Passerotte	0.1484	0.4	88
Maison Bouchard Père et Fils	1.3920	3.4	827
M. Edouard Petit	0.4011	1.0	238
SC du Domaine Ropiteau-Mignon	1.0247	2.5	609
M. Michel Tessier	0.3122	0.8	185

---

*Cases calculated on the *rendement de base* of 45 hl/ha for white Meursault, plus 20 percent. Red Meursault has a lower *rendement de base* of 40 hl/ha.

	Hectares	Acres	Cases*
Les Genevrières-Dessous			
M. Charles Bocard	0.1791	0.4	106
Mlle. Madeleine Boillot	0.9935	2.5	590
M. Jean-Baptiste Bouzereau	0.1955	0.5	116
M. Jean-Louis Bouzereau and M. Louis Bouzereau	0.2644	0.7	157
M. Louis Bouzereau and M. Michel Bouzereau	0.2643	0.7	157
M. André Brunet	0.1193	0.3	71
M. Albert Chavy	0.1352	0.3	80
Hospices Civils de Beaune	1.2043	3.0	715
M. Charles Jobard	0.5438	1.3	323
M. François Jobard	0.5386	1.3	320
M. Claude Martenot	0.1910	0.5	113
M. Alfred Michelot and M. Bernard Michelot	0.1363	0.3	81
M. Bernard Michelot	0.1420	0.4	84
M. Georges Pitoiset	0.2869	0.7	170
M. Pierre Porcheray	0.2028	0.5	120
Les Gouttes d'Or—5.3260 ha/13.2 acres			
Mme. Veuve Pierre Boillot and M. Pierre Boillot	0.2027	0.5	120
M. Louis Bouzereau and M. Pierre Bouzereau	0.2072	0.5	123
M. Julien Coche	0.1866	0.5	111
Mme. Jean Desmazières	0.3895	1.0	231
Mme. François Durand	0.1220	0.3	72
M. Rémy Ehret	0.0980	0.2	58
M. Michel Garnier	0.1021	0.3	61
M. François Gaunoux	0.5985	1.5	356
M. Jean Gaunoux and Mme. Veuve Roger Passerotte	0.3108	0.8	185
M. Louis Giroux and Mme. Paul Sadrin	0.2599	0.6	154
Mme. Veuve Louis Guidot and M. Hubert Guidot	0.1031	0.3	61

*Cases calculated on the *rendement de base* of 45 hl/ha for white Meursault, plus 20 percent. Red Meursault has a lower *rendement de base* of 40 hl/ha.

	Hectares	Acres	Cases*
SCI du Domaine des Comtes Lafon	0.3928	1.0	233
Mme. Paul Maillard and Mme. Gerard Dangelzer and M. Emmanuel Monick	1.3867	3.4	824
M. Pierre Millot	0.0976	0.2	58
M. Raymond Millot	0.2525	0.6	150
Mme. Veuve Camille Pothier and M. Camille Pothier	0.2040	0.5	121
SC du Domaine Ropiteau-Mignon	0.1575	0.4	94
M. Phillippe Thévenot	0.2183	0.5	130

Les Perrières—13.7079 ha/33.9 acres divided into four *climats*: Aux Perrières (2 acres); Perrières-Dessus (8.2 acres); Perrières-Dessous (21.4 acres); and Clos des Perrières (2.3 acres)

Les Perrières-Dessus

	Hectares	Acres	Cases*
Mme. Roger Boisson	0.2901	0.7	172
M. André Boyer	0.6093	1.5	362
Mme. Veuve Marcel Boyer and M. Marcel-Émile Boyer	0.6254	1.6	371
SCI Domaine du Château de Meursault	1.6646	4.1	989
M. Joseph Leflaive and M. Patrick Leflaive	0.0276	0.07	16
Commune de Meursault	0.0050	0.01	3
M. Raymond Millot	0.0770	0.2	46
M. Pierre Moingeon	0.1955	0.5	16
Mlle. Berthe Morey	0.5278	1.3	314

Aux Perrières

	Hectares	Acres	Cases*
M. Jean-François Coche	0.2305	0.6	137
Mlle. Ginette Gauffroy	0.1400	0.4	83
M. Pierre Perrin	0.2890	0.7	172
M. Jean-Louis Ropiteau	0.3395	0.8	202

Les Perrières-Dessous

	Hectares	Acres	Cases*
M. Michel Ampeau and M. Robert Ampeau	0.3860	1.0	229
M. Henri Bardet	2.4127	6.0	1433

---

*Cases calculated on the *rendement de base* of 45 hl/ha for white Meursault, plus 20 percent. Red Meursault has a lower *rendement de base* of 40 hl/ha.

	Hectares	Acres	Cases*
Mme. Veuve Henri Bardet and M. Henri Bardet	0.0784	0.2	47
M. Joseph Belicard	0.2388	0.6	142
M. Jean-Marie Boileau	0.1780	0.4	106
Mme. André Briotet	0.1539	0.4	91
Mme. Veuve Camille Chouet	0.1758	0.4	104
M. Armand Dancer and Mme. Charles Dancer	0.2895	0.7	172
Mme. Charles Dancer and Mme. Phillippe Ballot	0.4472	1.1	266
SCI des Domaines Jobard Drain	0.1570	0.4	93
M. Jean Gaunoux and Mme. Veuve Roger Passerotte	0.5924	1.5	352
Mme. Heitz	0.2895	0.7	172
SCI du Domaine des Comtes Lafon	0.7680	1.9	456
GFA Pierre Latour	0.1480	0.4	88
Mlle. Brigitte Lochardet and M. Marie-Charles Lochardet	0.4472	1.1	266
M. Pierre Matrot	0.5313	1.3	316
SC du Domaine du Château de Meursault	0.1058	0.3	63
Mme. Veuve Alfred Michelot and M. Alfred Michelot	0.1988	0.5	118
M. Henri Potinet	0.3040	0.8	181
M. Hubert Prieur	0.2751	0.7	163
SC Domaine Jacques Prieur	0.2792	0.7	166
Domaine Guy Roulot	0.2605	0.6	155
Mme. Bernard Tricot	0.4120	1.0	245
M. Gaston Turlier	0.5205	1.3	309

Porusot or Poruzot—11.4318 ha/28.2 acres divided into three *climats*: Le Porusot-Dessus (13.1 acres); Les Porusot-Dessous (4.4 acres); and Le Porusot (10.7 acres)

Poruzot-Dessus

Mme. Gaston de Masson d'Autume	0.6227	1.5	370

---

*Cases calculated on the *rendement de base* of 45 hl/ha for white Meursault, plus 20 percent. Red Meursault has a lower *rendement de base* of 40 hl/ha.

	Hectares	Acres	Cases*
M. André Buisson	0.2423	0.6	144
Mme. Veuve Camille Chouet	0.2880	0.7	171
M. Gerard Creusefond	0.4328	1.1	257
M. Jean-Paul Gauffroy	0.2212	0.6	131
M. Robert Gauffroy and Mlle. Nicole Gauffroy	0.2627	0.7	156
M. Jean-Pierre Javillier	0.1148	0.3	68
M. Charles Jobard	0.6970	1.7	414
M. François Jobard	0.6499	1.6	386
M. Jean-Pierre Jobard	0.1814	0.5	108
M. Alfred Michelot	0.1040	0.3	62
M. André Ropiteau	0.4130	1.0	245
Mme. Marie-France Ropiteau	0.2190	0.5	130
M. Michel Tessier	0.6303	1.6	374
GFA Roux Verdot	0.2205	0.5	131

Poruzot-Dessous

	Hectares	Acres	Cases
M. André Buisson	0.1688	0.4	100
GFA du Domaine René Manuel	1.1302	2.8	671
Mme. Richard Moore	0.1810	0.5	108
M. Michel Pouhin	0.2322	0.6	138
M. André Ropiteau	0.0811	0.2	48

Le Poruzot

	Hectares	Acres	Cases
Mme. André Briotet	0.1285	0.3	76
Mme. Veuve Camille Chouet	0.5901	1.5	351
Hospices Civils de Beaune	0.7894	2.0	469
M. Émile Jobard	0.4603	1.1	273
Mme. Veuve Émile Jobard and M. Émile Jobard	0.0537	0.1	32
M. Louis Jobard	0.2570	0.6	153
M. Yves Latour	0.1237	0.3	73
M. Georges Pitoiset	0.3906	1.0	232
Mme. Veuve Camille Pothier and M. Camille Pothier	0.7165	1.8	426
SC du Domaine Ropiteau-Mignon	0.4380	1.0	260
Mme. Veuve Thomas Urena	0.3511	0.9	209

Meursault-Blagny Premiers Crus (allowed to produce red or white wines)

---

*Cases calculated on the *rendement de base* of 45 hl/ha for white Meursault, plus 20 percent. Red Meursault has a lower *rendement de base* of 40 hl/ha.

	Hectares	Acres	Cases*
La Jeunelotte—5.0455 ha/12.5 acres			
M. Bernard de Cherisey	1.2519	3.1	744
Mme. Veuve Jacques de Montlivault Guyon and Mme. Jacques de Montlivault Guyon	1.7716	4.4	1052
Mme. Veuve Jacques de Montlivault Guyon and Mme. Bernard de Cherisey	2.2002	5.4	1308
La Pièce Sous le Bois—11.1472 ha/27.5 acres			
M. Michel Ampeau and M. Robert Ampeau	1.4972	3.7	889
GFA Blondeau Danne	1.7642	4.4	1048
M. Maurice Boullin	0.2310	0.6	137
M. François Jobard	0.5033	1.2	299
M. Bernard Lamy	0.2423	0.6	144
Mme. Veuve Robert Langoureau and M. Hubert Langoureau	0.4516	1.1	268
SCI du Domaine Joseph Matrot	4.1325	10.2	2445
M. Jacques de Montlivault Guyon	0.7490	1.9	445
Mme. Veuve Jacques de Montlivault Guyon and M. Jacques de Montlivault Guyon	0.6401	1.6	380
Mme. Richard Moore	0.4403	1.1	262
M. Paul Pernot and M. Paul-Lucien Pernot	0.6513	1.6	387
Sous le Dos d'Âne—5.0344 ha/12.4 acres			
Le Dos d'Âne			
Mme. Jean Dupont	1.3236	3.3	786
Sous le Dos d'Âne			
Mme. Veuve Jacques de Montlivault Guyon and M. Jean de Montlivault Guyon	1.9594	4.8	1164

*Cases calculated on the *rendement de base* of 45 hl/ha for white Meursault, plus 20 percent. Red Meursault has a lower *rendement de base* of 40 hl/ha.

	Hectares	Acres	Cases*
M. Jean de Montlivault Guyon	1.1120	2.8	661
M. Joseph Leflaive	0.8077	2.0	480
M. Patrick Leflaive			
Mlle. Anne Leflaive and M. Vincent Leflaive	0.8173	2.0	485

SOUS BLAGNY—2.2109 ha/5.5 acres

Blagny Premiers Crus (allowed to produce only red wine)
La Garenne or Sur la Garenne—9.8688 ha/24.4 acres
Hameau de Blagny—4.2768 ha/10.6 acres
Sous le Puits—6.7983 ha/16.8 acres

Meursault-Santenots (white) or Volnay-Santenots (red) Premiers Crus
Les Plures or Les Petures—10.4501 ha/25.8 acres
Les Santenots Blancs—2.9203 ha/7.2 acres
Les Santenots du Milieu—15.6483 ha/38.7 acres divided into three *climats*: Les Santenots du Milieu (16.8 acres); Clos des Santenots (3 acres); Les Santenots Dessous (18.9 acres)
Les Vignes Blanches—0.0544 ha/0.13 acre

VINEYARDS WORTH SEEKING OUT

Although the *premiers crus* rightfully get the lion's share of attention, the fact is that a number of commune-level vineyards can offer a depth and dimension not suggested by their official status. Look for: Les Narvaux; Les Tillets; Les Casses-Têtes; Les Chevalières; Les Rougeots; Les Meix Chavaux; Le Tesson; Le Limozin; Le Cromin; and Clos de Cromin. They will often have the stony taste of the *premiers crus*, but not the fleshiness.

---

*Cases calculated on the *rendement de base* of 45 hl/ha for white Meursault, plus 20 percent. Red Meursault has a lower *rendement de base* of 40 hl/ha.

PRODUCERS WORTH SEEKING OUT

DOMAINE ROBERT ET MICHEL AMPEAU—Robert (the father) and Michel (the son) Ampeau are in the top rank in Meursault, and have been for years. Beautifully structured wines. Look particularly for their Meursault-Blagny "La Pièce sous le Bois," Charmes, and, not least, Perrières.

DOMAINE BERNARD BACHELET—At times it seems that the Burgundians lack imagination in surnames: Bachelets pop up in Gevrey-Chambertin (Denis Bachelet), Puligny-Montrachet (Jean-Claude Bachelet), and Chagny, which actually is where Domaine Bernard Bachelet is based. That location notwithstanding, Domaine Bernard Bachelet is one of the better Meursault estates, creating fine, long-lived wines of real breed. Check out their Narvaux and Charmes.

CHÂTEAU DU MEURSAULT/COMTE DE MOUCHERON—If you visit Meursault, be sure to take the self-guided tour of the Château de Meursault cellar. It likely is the most beautiful ancient cellar in Burgundy. This is one of the few real châteaux in the Côte d'Or, originally owned by the comtes de Moucheron. However, the last count was also the last of his line, and he began selling off some of his choice vineyards. (The Domaine de la Romanée-Conti bought his 0.8-acre slice of Le Montrachet in 1963.) In 1973, the giant Burgundy *négociant* Patriarche purchased the property, including the long-uninhabited château, and refurbished the cellars, vineyards, and wines. They sell the wines under the trademarked brand name of Château de Meursault/Comte de Moucheron. The wines are admirable, but not usually first rank.

DOMAINE JEAN-FRANÇOIS COCHE-DURY—One of the newest legends of Meursault. He took over his father's estate called "Coche-Bouillicaut." The Dury name is his wife's. Although still young, born in 1950, Jean-François Coche-Dury has catapulted to the front ranks by virtue of creating austere, beautifully detailed wines. Although the wines are available in this country, they sell for painfully high prices. This is largely due to demand. Jean-François Coche-Dury himself, an extremely modest, self-effacing fellow with the countenance of an intelligent bloodhound, sells his wines for pretty much the going rate for the vineyard in question—or at least he used to. He believes in early harvesting, as compared to Domaine des Comtes Lafon, which advocates late picking. Yet the wines are profound. Go figure. Low yields are the key. Look for Chevalières, Narvaux, Rougeots, and, above all, Charmes and Perrières. Also, if you can find it, Coche-Dury makes an austere, long-lived Meursault *rouge* and an exceptional Bourgogne *blanc*. Because of the austere style of winemaking, Coche-Dury wines, more than most, require extended bottle age.

MAISON JEAN GERMAIN—A *négociant* specializing in various Meursaults of varying quality, of a lighter style but often good. Worth noting is that this house represents Domaine Darnat, which owns the 1.6-acre Clos Richmont subplot of the Les Cras vineyard.

DOMAINE ALBERT GRIVAULT—What should be the most brilliant jewel in Meursault, courtesy of exclusive ownership of the 2.3-acre Clos des Perrières, as well as another parcel in Perrières-Dessous, is instead a continuing frustration. Domaine Albert Grivault is owned by the Bardet family, currently represented by Michel Bardet. In the past, the domaine would bottle the wines from the barrel only when an order was received. I do not know if this practice still continues. Recent vintages have been variable, with 1986 a standout. About half of the Clos des Perrières has been replanted, which means minuscule quantities for the next few years and potentially lesser wines when the young vines start to bear fruit.

HOSPICES DE BEAUNE—Numerous holdings in Meursault sold in different *cuvées* under the following names:

> **Cuvée Baudot**—A blend of Genevrières-Dessus (0.66 ha/1.6 acres) and Genevrières-Dessous (0.75 ha/1.8 acres)
> **Cuvée Philippe le Bon**—A blend of Genevrières-Dessus (0.2 ha/½ acre) and Genevrières-Dessous (0.4 ha/1 acre)

Cuvée de Bahezre de Lanlay—A blend of Charmes-Dessus (0.5 ha/1.2 acres) and Charmes-Dessous (0.4 ha/1 acre)
Cuvée Albert Grivault—Exclusively Charmes-Dessus (0.5 ha/ 1.2 acres)
Cuvée Jehan Humblot—A blend of Premier Cru Le Poruzot (0.6 ha/1.5 acres) and commune-level Grands Charrons (0.1 ha/ 0.25 acre)
Cuvée Loppin—Exclusively commune-level Les Criots (0.6 ha/1.5 acres)
Cuvée Goureau—A blend of Le Poruzot (0.33 ha/0.8 acres), Les Pitures (0.33 ha/0.8 acres) and Les Cras (0.2 ha/0.50 acre)

The overall quality of the Hospices de Beaune Meursaults is very good, but no better than from many other good producers. Moreover, once they leave the Hospices cellars—no later than March following the harvest—they are then subject to dramatically varying treatments in the cellars of the *négociants* who bid for them. In other words, the dice are rolled not once, but twice, to come up with a win. Given the astronomical prices these wines currently fetch, only those who can afford to lose big money with a smile should bet.

DOMAINE PATRICK JAVILLIER—A young producer to watch. Best efforts from this fifteen-acre domaine are two commune-level named vineyards: a Les Narvaux from a 0.50-acre holding and a 1.25-acre holding in Clos du Cromin, a climat of Le Cromin. Also promising is Les Tillets.

DOMAINE FRANÇOIS JOBARD—François Jobard makes Jean-François Coche look like a vaudeville performer, so self-effacing is he. (How do they do it, given the droves of admirers and the ego-inflating prices?) Anyway, Jobard's Meursaults are extraordinary, so much so that they are a little baffling when very young. The intensity is such that they don't taste quite like other versions from the same vineyard, yet give them five years and they blossom where others wilt. Best of all, he owns choice plots: Poruzots; Genevrières; Charmes; his Meursault-Blagny "La Pièce Sous le Bois" is the standard by which the others are judged.

LABOURÉ-ROI—This Nuits-Saint-Georges *négociant* has become a leading source of high-quality Meursault, especially good commune-level Meursault. The effort to find quantities of Meursault of high quality—not an easy task these days—pays off: Labouré-Roi has won several blind tastings performed by wine consultants to airlines, with the result that the company's Meursault bottlings are served on various first-class flights. Labouré-Roi also is responsible for the wines of Domaine René Manuel (q.v.).

DOMAINE DES COMTES LAFON—Does Meursault get any better than the wines of Comtes Lafon? Not likely. One thing is certain: The list of producers whose wines are lesser is far longer than those who are equal or better: maybe Jobard? Coche-Dury? Ampeau? Leroy? What Lafon offers is that unbeatable combination of implacably high standards coupled with low yields applied to some of the best vineyards in Meursault: Perrières; Charmes; Genevrières; Gouttes d'Or.

The Lafon wines make a case for late harvesting, which is their specialty. It doesn't always work. It was their undoing in the hot 1983 vintage, but it's usually a bright idea. When Lafon wines first achieved international acclaim about ten years ago, some observers suggested that, far from being rich and golden in color, the wines were, in fact, simply oxidized. This was a misapprehension, as anyone tasting a fully mature Lafon Meursault can attest. The rich color comes from the late picking; rarely is the faintest whiff of oxidation present.

The only problem with Lafon wines is: a) finding them and b) affording them. As with Coche-Dury, the word has long been out. But if you can, try to taste the Charmes, and especially the Perrières. They are reference-standard. Also very good Volnay-Santenots (q.v.). Quantities should increase, as a significant acreage currently *en mètayage* with Pierre Morey will revert to Lafon over the next few years. Since René Lafon's two sons, Dominique and Bruno, are more than capable, the luster of Lafon can only increase.

LOUIS LATOUR—Good Meursault-Blagny and Genevrières in the characteristic light Latour style.

LEROY—This is the only *négociant* offering Meursaults of the same standard as the greatest domaines. Leroy specializes in Meursault, offering the whole *gamme*, as the French like to say, the full wad of Meursaults. The style here is for old-fashioned wines with a pronounced toastiness. The quality is undeniable, but the style seems somehow more suited for old-fashioned cream-sauce dishes than today's slip of raw salmon down the gullet. They also are wonderfully long-lived. Leroy's 1964 Genevrières was in full bloom in the late eighties, which shows just how long-lived Meursault can be in a great vineyard, vintage, and cellar. Look for sublime Perrières. The commune-level Meursault is often a standout, especially in top vintages.

DOMAINE RENÉ MANUEL/LABOURÉ-ROI—The largest owner in the Poruzot and Bouchères *premiers crus*. René Manuel is now in his nineties, and it will be interesting to see whether this estate will remain in his large family. The French law of equal inheritance coupled with crushing death taxes can make matters difficult unless everyone is in accord. The quality of the wines at Domaine Manuel is very high, although there have been lapses. The wines are distributed by the *négociant* Labouré-Roi, which also assists in the winemaking and bottling. There's also a pleasant, early-maturing commune-level red Meursault (and labeled as such) called Meursault "Clos de la Baronne." It is a six-acre vineyard at the base of the slope in which the Manuel residence is located. Some Chardonnay has been planted there recently. Good Bourgogne *blanc*, as well.

DOMAINE JOSEPH AND PIERRE MATROT—One of the great old-line names in Meursault. The lineage is Joseph (grandfather), Pierre (son); and both wines are made by Thierry, Pierre's son, who is doing great things. Although there are separate labels, the wines are the same. (Seagram Château and Estate handles the "Pierre" label; Robert Haas's Vineyard Brands distributes "Joseph.") For me, this is Meursault as it should be: concentrated, creamy-textured, long-lived, and very pure. The wines have been described as okay, but this is unlikely. Thierry Matrot does buy new barrels, only to loan them out to others for two years in order to avoid excess oakiness. The vines are mostly older, fifteen to forty-five years, and one third of each vineyard is renewed every fifteen years, which keeps the overall standard consistently high. Superb Perrières: Charmes; Meursault-Blagny Premier Cru. Also very good reds from Volnay-Santenots and red Blagny "La Pièce Sous le Bois."

DOMAINE MICHELOT-BUISSON—A large domaine of some fifty acres with a typically complicated collection of owner names. You have Michelot-Buisson, which is the label of Bernard Michelot, the father, who also has another label called Domaine Bernard Michelot. Bernard has three daughters, all of whom have their own piece of the domaine, resulting in other labels: Domaine Geneviève Michelot, the oldest of the three daughters; Domaine Chantal Michelot; and Domaine Mestre-Michelot, which incorporates the name of Bernard's son-in-law. All of these wines, I believe, are actually made by Bernard Michelot. The quality is variable. The Michelot style leans heavily toward oakiness, which in some vintages is literally insupportable. A tasting of '87s left me unimpressed. Still, in good vintages, they can be rewarding. The vineyards owned are mouth-watering: Perrières (very young vines; replanted in the early eighties); Charmes; Genevrières; Narvaux. Worth investigating: the commune-level Le Tillet, Sous la Velle, Les Narvaux, Grands Charrons, Le Limozin, and Clos de Cromin vineyards. Value for the money usually is found with these vineyards.

DOMAINE PIERRE MOREY—One of the great Meursault producers who, unhappily, makes most of his wine from vineyards *en métayage* with Domaine des Comtes Lafon. The long-term contracts are coming to an end in the next few years, with all of the grapes reverting to Lafon, leaving Pierre Morey with far less wine. This is a pity, if only because Morey makes terrific wine from wonderful vineyards. The fact that the grapes will soon go to Domaine Lafon is at least comforting. A few wines also are sold under the name of Auguste Morey, Pierre's father. Rich, intense, beautifully made wines.

DOMAINE JACQUES PRIEUR—Another vast domain that doesn't quite live up to its potential. There's hope, though. The Prieur family sold half of its interest in 1988 to a group headed up by the *négociant* Antonin Rodet, which is run by Bertrand Devillard, who is intent on restoring the luster of the Prieur name. Happily, the latest generation of Prieurs is in full accord. Look for Perrières and "Clos de Mazeray," a commune-level vineyard just outside the village producing both red and white wines.

DOMAINE ROPITEAU-MIGNON—This is the label used for the Ropiteau family vineyard holding. The *négociant* business, Ropiteau Frères, was sold to Chantovent, a big table-wine company in the Midi. The family retained its vineyards which, in the hometown of Meursault, are enviable: Perrières; Genevrières; Gouttes d'Or. Unfortunately, the winemaking is lackluster.

DOMAINE GUY ROULOT—One of the deservedly lustrous names of Meursault, who also runs a distillation business on the side. The label garnered attention in the States when the estate hired a young American named Ted Lemon as the winemaker, following the death of Guy Roulot at the age of fifty-two in 1982. Lemon left for California after the '83 vintage. In the meantime, the wines seem to have held a steady course. Roulot owns parcels in Perrières and Charmes (old vines), but also produces an unusually large number of excellent named-vineyard commune-level Meursaults from the choice vineyards above the *premiers crus*: Les Tillets, Le Tesson, Les Meix Chavaux, Les Vireuils, and Les Luchets. These really are the specialties of Roulet and worth seeking out, especially since they are less expensive than the *premiers crus*.

Blagny

B lagny is the chameleon *appellation* of Burgundy. You can't see it except when the wine is red. Otherwise, its white wines become either Meursault or Puligny-Montrachet, depending upon the vineyard. There is such a place as Blagny. It's a hamlet on the border between Meursault and Puligny-Montrachet, high up on the slope. These white wines are very fine: high-acid with great character and flavor definition.

You occasionally see a label reading "Meursault-Blagny Premier Cru" or just "Meursault Premier Cru." Only four vineyards are so entitled, all *premier cru*: Le Jeunelotte; La Pièce Sous le Bois; Sous le Dos d'Âne; and Sous Blagny.

Then there are the vineyards in the Puligny-Montrachet sphere of influence. Under that protective coloration, they become Puligny-Montrachet: the *premiers crus* of Sous le Puits; La Garenne; Hameau de Blagny; and the commune-level Le Trezin.

So why does Blagny exist as an *appellation*? Because of its red wine. Any red wine grown in Blagny must be called Blagny. There's very little of it, just twenty-four hundred cases a year. It is distinctively flavored: very earthy, almost pungently so, with a hardness that allows it to age well. It also has an unsual delicacy of structure, no doubt due to the limestone soils and the high elevation. Pinot Noir is grown in the same *premier cru* vineyards as the white wines.

If you see a red Blagny on a list somewhere, try it. It is forceful wine, best tasted with food that needs to be cut, such as kidneys or veal in a cream sauce. The few producers who create red Blagny are devoted to it. They'd have to be: They would make a lot more money replanting the plot to Chardonnay, which they are entitled to do. Some outstanding producers are devoted to making red Blagny, all of whom make first-rate wines: Domaine François Jobard, Domaine Leflaive, and Domaine Matrot.

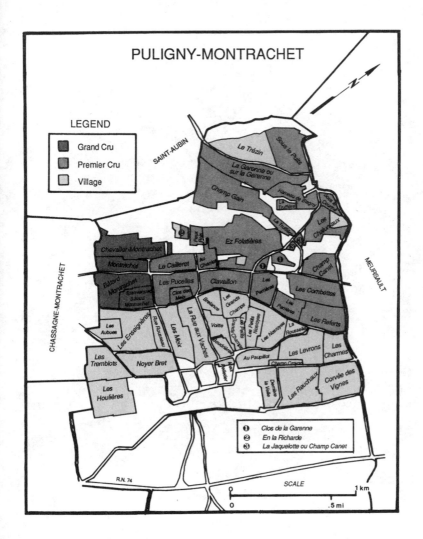

Puligny-Montrachet

This is it. Two of the three great vineyards lie half in Puligny and half in the adjoining township of Chassagne. With these exceptions, Puligny stands alone. Curiously enough, it is nevertheless a town in which it is almost impossible to construct a proper cellar, for an underground river floods any cave that is six feet or better below ground level.

—FRANK SCHOONMAKER, *Gourmet*, June 1949

Frank Schoonmaker's terse assessment of Puligny-Montrachet says it all: This is *it*. In the same way that Cîteaux was the motherhouse of hundreds of Cistercian monasteries, so too is Puligny-Montrachet the motherhouse of Chardonnay. At its best—and not just in its *grands crus*—the white wines of Puligny-Montrachet offer a distinction of originality unmatched in any other locale.

Why this is so is one of the most delicious of wine mysteries. The fact that it remains unanswered is not for lack of trying. The soil of Puligny-Montrachet has been analyzed as exhaustively as a presidential candidate. The rainfall has been measured; the phrenology of its slope traced; its microclimates pinpointed. Still, it comes down to what Colette called "celestial wizardry."

Where Meursault can sometimes flop over from excessive fruitiness or Chassagne-Montrachet succumb to softness, the white wine of Puligny is always taut. Green and gold are its colors. High acidity is its trademark. Long life is its prerogative. Other wines have all of these distinctions, yet none taste quite like Puligny. None have that taut bowstring tension of taste. The *goût de terroir* of Puligny seems somehow more sharply etched than elsewhere. The fruit is defined and powerful yet restrained, like the musculature of a martial artist. Its perfect composition is revealed by its ability to withstand magnification. As you increase the resolution, from commune-level Puligny to a *premier cru* and then zoom to Bâtard-, Chevalier- and Le Montrachet, you find no blemishes, no distortions in taste or balance.

This is Puligny-Montrachet at its best. It is increasingly hard to find. Today, much of what is sold as Puligny-Montrachet fails to deliver the full measure of these attributes. The problem, for a change, is easily pinpointed: high yields. The average yield in Puligny-Montachet today is 60 hectoliters per hectare (4.4 tons per acre)—with the blessing of the authorities. And it has been known to soar to 100 hl/ha (7.3 tons per acre) in vintages such as 1979 and 1982. Although Chardonnay is more forgiving than Pinot Noir in matters of yield, it's not *that* forgiving. The market pressure on the Pulignieusiens (I like to call them, Italian-style, the Pulignese) is relentless. Happily, Puligny-Montrachet also is home to a number of producers whose personal standards are more resolute than those of the government.

A tiny amount of red Puligny-Montrachet is produced, less than half of one percent of Puligny's total wine production. This wasn't always the case. In the nineteenth century, a considerably larger proportion of Puligny's output was red wine, especially from the *premiers crus* of Caillerets, Clavoillon, and Pucelles, than is found today. What little red Puligny I've tasted has been characterful, if a little light. It certainly isn't at all on the same order as the whites. The limestone soil surely doesn't lend itself to red as well as white.

THE VINEYARDS

There are 245.2553 ha/606 acres of vineyards. There are fourteen *premiers crus* (247.4 acres) and four *grands crus* (76.4 acres).

THE PREMIERS CRUS

Le Cailleret—3.9323 ha/9.7 acres divided into two *climats*: Le Cailleret (8.2 acres) and Les Demoiselles (1.5 acres). This Les Demoiselles is different from that of Chevalier-Montrachet "Les Demoiselles" (q.v.).

	Hectares	Acres	Cases*
SCI Saint-Abdon	0.3051	0.8	181
M. Jean-Georges Chartron	3.3302	8.2	1978
M. François Colin	0.1508	0.4	90
M. Louis Colin	0.1462	0.4	87

Les Chalumaux—5.7930 ha/14.3 acres divided into two *climats*: Les Chalumaux (10.3 acres) and Sous le Courthil (4 acres)

Les Chalumaux

M. et Mme. Hubert Langoureau	0.1843	0.5	109
SCI du Domaine Joseph Matrot	0.9422	2.3	560
M. Pierre Matrot	0.3877	1.0	230
Mme. Veuve Jacques de Montlivault Guyon	0.1680	0.4	100
Mme. Veuve Paule de Montlivault Guyon and Mme. Bernard de Cherisey	0.4495	1.1	267
M. Jacques de Montlivault Guyon and M. Jean-Louis de Montlivault Guyon and Mme. Bernard de Cherisey	0.0592	0.2	35
M. Paul Pernot	0.5464	1.4	325
M. Georges Pitoiset	0.2245	0.6	133
M. Roger Poil	0.3337	0.8	198
M. André Ropiteau	0.0159	0.04	9
Mme. Marie Ropiteau	0.4410	1.1	262
Mme. Bernard Tricot	0.4451	1.1	264

Sous Le Courthil

Mme. Veuve René Guerin and Mme. Veuve Paul Giraudet	0.4470	1.1	266
M. et Mme. Jean Pascal	0.3169	0.8	188
Mlle. Anne Rateau	0.1500	0.4	89
M. François Rateau	0.3898	1.0	232

Champ Canet—5.5900 ha/13.8 acres divided into three *climats*: Champ Canet (8 acres); La Jaquelotte (2 acres); and Clos de la Garenne (3.8 acres)

---

*Cases calculated on the *rendement de base* of 45 hl/ha plus 20 percent

	Hectares	Acres	Cases*
Champ Canet			
M. Fernand Baudrand	0.5815	1.4	345
M. et Mme. Alfred Belicard	0.2208	0.6	131
M. et Mme. Robert Carillon	0.0878	0.2	52
Mme. Veuve Henri Dupont	0.3328	0.8	198
GFA Pierre Latour et Ses Enfants	0.3400	0.8	202
M. Leon Ozga and Mme. Michel Bouzereau	0.1293	0.3	77
M. et Mme. Roger Rudnai	0.5403	1.3	321
M. Étienne Sauzet and Mme. Jean Boillot	1.5940	3.9	947
La Jaquelotte			
M. Jacques Carillon	0.1928	0.5	115
M. et Mme. Robert Carillon	0.2690	0.7	160
M. Jean-Marc Pernot	0.0587	0.2	35
M. Paul Pernot and M. Jean-Marc Pernot	0.1985	0.5	118
M. Paul Pernot	0.0821	0.2	49
Clos de la Garenne			
M. Philippe de Mac Mahon	0.8382	2.1	498
M. Paul Pernot	0.6747	1.7	401
Champ Gain—10.6977 ha/26.4 acres			
Mme. André Barolet	0.1057	0.3	63
M. Roger Belland	0.4539	1.1	270
M. et Mme. Michel Bouzereau	0.2406	0.6	143
M. et Mme. Philippe Bouzereau	0.6290	1.6	374
M. et Mme. Robert Carillon	0.2290	0.6	136
M. et Mme. Albert Chavy	0.2542	0.6	151
Mme. Veuve Henry Clerc and M. Henry Clerc	0.3217	0.8	191
M. et Mme. Camille David	0.2448	0.6	145
M. Raymond Dureuil	0.1953	0.5	116
Mme. Charles Eloy	0.3496	0.9	208
M. Gérard Guerin	1.7007	4.2	1010

---

*Cases calculated on the *rendement de base* of 45 hl/ha plus 20 percent

	Hectares	Acres	Cases*
M. Gérard Guerin	0.2607	0.6	155
M. et Mme. Daniel Joly	0.1000	0.3	59
Mme. Jean-Pierre Edouard Joly and Mme. Jean-Pierre Joly and M. Jean-Pierre Joly	0.1472	0.4	87
Mme. Veuve Edouard Joly and M. Edouard Joly	0.5148	1.3	306
M. Pierre Joly	0.1382	0.3	82
M. et Mme. Pierre Lafouge	0.3788	1.0	225
M. et Mme. Roland Maroslavac	0.1205	0.3	72
M. Stéphan Maroslavac	0.3953	1.0	235
M. et Mme. Stéphan Maroslavac	2.7926	6.9	1659
Mlle. Anne Rateau	0.5615	1.4	334
M. François Rateau	0.2550	0.6	151

Clavaillon or Clavoillon—5.5855 ha/13.8 acres

M. Gérard Chavy and M. Jean Chavy	0.7895	2.0	469
Mlle. Anne Leflaive and Mme. Bernard Suremain	1.1865	2.9	705
M. Joseph Leflaive and M. Patrick Leflaive	1.2263	3.0	728
M. Vincent Leflaive and Mlle. Anne Leflaive	1.1868	2.9	705
Mme. Veuve Louis de Noue and M. Bernard de Noue	1.1964	3.0	711

Les Combettes—6.7614 ha/ 16.7 acres

M. Michel Ampeau and M. Robert Ampeau	0.6760	1.7	402
Mme. Veuve Denis Bizot and Mme. Jacques Coudray	0.2633	0.7	156
M. et Mme. Robert Carillon	0.4654	1.2	276
M. Henry Clerc	0.3224	0.8	192
M. et Mme. Henry Clerc	0.2987	0.7	177
Mme. Veuve Henri Jacquin	0.3508	0.9	208
Mlle. Anne Leflaive and Mme. Bernard Suremain	0.7331	1.8	435

*Cases calculated on the *rendement de base* of 45 hl/ha plus 20 percent

	Hectares	Acres	Cases*
M. Pierre Matrot	0.3114	0.8	185
M. Jean Charles Moroni	0.0584	0.1	35
SC Domaine Jacques Prieur	1.4971	3.7	889
M. Etienne Sauzet and Mme. Jean Boillot	1.4337	3.5	852
Mme. Veuve Georges Trémeau and Mme. Stephane Maroslavac	0.1601	0.4	95
M. Erick Urena	0.1440	0.4	86

Les Folatières—17.6376 ha/43.6 acres divided into four *climats:* Ez Folatières (33.7 acres); En la Richarde (1.3 acres); Peux-Bois (3.7 acres) and Au Chaniot (4.9 acres)

Au Chaniot

M. Pierre Bouzereau	0.2882	0.7	171
M. et Mme. Albert Chavy	0.2737	0.7	163
GFA Louis Glantenay et Enfants	0.1715	0.4	102
GFA Domaine Manceron	0.6947	1.7	413
M. et Mme. Bernard Thévenot	0.2193	0.5	130
M. Jacques Thévenot	0.2194	0.5	130
M. Pierre Thomas	0.1395	0.3	83

Ez Folatières

M. Charles Allexant	0.2761	0.7	164
M. Patrice Allexant	0.0797	0.2	47
M. Robert Beeusaert	0.1186	0.3	70
M. Robert Beeusaert	0.1103	0.3	66
M. Fernand Bouzereau and Mme. Jean Poulet	0.4024	1.0	239
M. et Mme. Roger Caillot	0.1723	0.4	102
Mme. Veuve Charles Carillon and M. Charles Carillon	0.0569	0.1	34
M. Jean-Georges Chartron	0.5918	1.5	352
Mme. Veuve Jean Chartron and M. Jean-Georges Chartron	0.9173	2.3	545
M. Alain Chavy	0.2025	0.5	120
M. et Mme. Gérard Chavy	1.8063	4.5	1073
M. et Mme. Albert Chevy	0.2977	0.7	177

---

*Cases calculated on the *rendement de base* of 45 hl/ha plus 20 percent

	Hectares	Acres	Cases*
M. et Mme. Bernard Clerc	0.0647	0.2	38
M. Henry Clerc	0.5650	1.4	336
M. et Mme. Henry Clerc	0.0056	0.013	3
Mme. Veuve Henry Clerc and M. Henry Clerc	0.0833	0.2	49
M. Bernard Courreaux	0.1287	0.3	76
M. André Crepeau and M. Gaston Crepeau	0.1011	0.3	60
GFA Louis Glantenay et Enfants	0.2339	0.6	139
Mme. Claude Gacon	0.1858	0.5	110
Mme. Veuve René Guerin and M. Gérard Guerin	0.5323	1.3	316
M. P. Jaboulet-Vercherre	0.7992	2.0	475
Mlle. Blanche Joly	0.0810	0.2	48
Mme. Veuve René Monnier	0.6161	1.5	366
Mme. Veuve Hubert Monnot and M. Hubert Monnot	0.2112	0.5	125
M. et Mme. Jean-Pierre Monnot	0.4278	1.1	254
M. et Mme. Jean Pascal	0.4917	1.2	292
M. Paul Pernot	2.6911	6.7	1599
Mlle. Anne Rateau	0.0691	0.2	41
M. François Rateau	0.0658	0.2	39

Peux-Bois

	Hectares	Acres	Cases*
M. Louis Bachelet	0.3563	0.9	212
M. et Mme. Henry Clerc	0.4407	1.1	262
Mme. Veuve Henry Clerc and M. Henry Clerc	0.1016	0.3	60
M. André Crepeau and M. Gaston Crepeau	0.1965	0.5	117
M. Joseph Leflaive and M. Patrick Leflaive	0.1774	0.4	105
M. Paul Pernot	0.1929	0.5	115

En la Richarde

	Hectares	Acres	Cases*
M. et Mme. Camille David	0.2710	0.7	161
M. et Mme. Alan Gerson	0.2710	0.7	161

---

*Cases calculated on the *rendement de base* of 45 hl/ha plus 20 percent

	Hectares	Acres	Cases*
La Garenne or Sur la Garenne—9.8688 ha/24.4 acres			
M. et Mme. Jean-Baptiste Barolet	0.4876	1.2	290
M. Louis Baudrand	0.1786	0.4	106
Mme. Veuve Louis Baudrand and M. Louis Baudrand	0.2944	0.7	175
M. Marius Baudrand	0.3376	0.8	201
M. Joseph Blanchet and M. Paul Blanchet	0.1843	0.5	109
M. Lucien Blanchet	0.1121	0.3	67
GFA Danne Blondeau	0.2952	0.7	175
M. et Mme. Maurice Bouillin	0.4269	1.1	254
M. Bernard Bouton	0.0883	0.2	52
M. et Mme. René Changarnier	0.7797	1.9	463
M. Louis Duchemin	0.1004	0.3	60
Mme. Louis Duchemin	0.1904	0.5	113
Mme. Charles Eloy	0.0326	0.1	19
Mlle. Marie-Thérèse Forin	0.1539	0.4	91
Mme. Veuve René Guerin and M. Gérard Guerin	0.1338	0.3	79
M. Jacques de Montlivault Guyon and M. Jean-Louis de Montlivault Guyon and Mme. Bernard de Cherisey	0.0540	0.1	32
Mme. Veuve Jacques de Montlivault Guyon	0.0912	0.2	54
M. Jean Lafouge	0.2500	0.6	149
M. et Mme. Bernard Langoureau	0.2743	0.7	163
M. Gilbert Langoureau	0.1808	0.5	107
M. et Mme. Hubert Langoureau	0.3252	0.8	193
Mme. Veuve Robert Langoureau	0.8091	2.0	481
M. Antoine Larue	0.1267	0.3	75
M. et Mme. Guy Larue	0.2568	0.6	153
M. Philippe de Mac Mahon	1.0628	2.6	631
M. André Moingeon	0.4283	1.1	254
M. Robert Moingeon	0.1111	0.3	66
Mme. Veuve Gaston Peteuil and M. Georges Peteuil and M. Paul Peteuil	0.1729	0.4	103
M. Jacques Ponavoy	0.1438	0.4	85
Mme. Pierre Prunier	0.3731	0.9	222
Mme. Veuve Alfred Roze	0.1400	0.4	83

*Cases calculated on the *rendement de base* of 45 hl/ha plus 20 percent

	Hectares	Acres	Cases*
M. André Thomas	0.3768	0.9	224
M. et Mme. Gérard Thomas	0.0907	0.2	54
M. Paul Truchot	0.1445	0.4	86
Mme. Madeleine Voillery	0.2148	0.5	128

Hameau de Blagny—4.2768 ha/10.6 acres

Mme. Bernard de Cherisey	1.3733	3.4	816
M. Gérard Guerin	0.2715	0.7	161
Mme. Veuve René Guerin and M. Gérard Guerin	0.2588	0.6	154
Mme. Veuve Jacques de Montlivault Guyon	0.2428	0.6	144
Mme. Veuve Jacques de Montlivault Guyon and M. Jean-Louis de Montlivault Guyon	0.7905	2.0	470
M. et Mme. Jean Pascal	0.2782	0.7	165
M. Jean Roze	0.1806	0.5	107
M. Pierre Thomas	0.1842	0.5	109

Les Perrières—8.4082 ha/21 acres divided into two *climats*: Les Perrières (11.1 acres) and Clos de la Mouchère (9.7 acres)

M. et Mme. Bernard Belicard	0.5218	1.3	310
M. Henri Boillot and M. Jean Boillot (Clos de la Mouchère)	3.9198	9.7	2328
M. et Mme. Louis Carillon	0.9396	2.3	558
M. Gérard Chavy and M. Jean Chavy	0.3603	0.9	214
M. Bernard Jacquin	0.2325	0.6	138
Mme. Veuve Henri Jacquin	0.6346	1.6	377
M. Pierre Patin	0.3606	0.9	214
M. Étienne Sauzet and Mme. Jean Boillot	0.4835	1.2	287

Les Pucelles—6.7634 ha/16.7 acres divided into two *climats*: Les Pucelles (12.7 acres) and Clos des Meix (4 acres)

Les Pucelles

M. Louis Bachelet	0.1814	0.5	108

---

*Cases calculated on the *rendement de base* of 45 hl/ha plus 20 percent

	Hectares	Acres	Cases*
M. Jean-Georges Chartron	1.0887	2.7	647
M. et Mme. Albert Chavy	0.2026	0.5	120
M. Gérard Chavy and M. Jean Chavy	0.1534	0.4	91
M. et Mme. Bernard Clerc	0.0828	0.2	49
M. Bernard Delesalle	0.5253	1.3	312
Mlle. Anne Leflaive and Mme. Bernard Suremain	0.3892	1.0	231
M. Joseph Leflaive and M. Patrick Leflaive	0.7601	1.9	451
M. Vincent Leflaive and Mlle. Anne Leflaive	0.0210	0.1	12
M. Marc Morey	0.4007	1.0	238
Mme. Veuve Louis de Noue and M. Bernard de Noue	0.7601	1.9	451
M. Lucien Pernot	0.2027	0.5	120
M. Paul Pernot	0.1836	0.5	109
M. Thierry Poirier	0.1815	0.5	108

Clos des Meix

	Hectares	Acres	Cases*
M. Jean-Georges Chartron	0.0751	0.2	45
Mme. Veuve Henri Jacquin	0.1650	0.4	98
Mlle. Anne Leflaive and Mme. Bernard Suremain	0.3807	0.9	226
M. Vincent Leflaive and Mlle. Anne Leflaive	0.7488	1.9	445
Mme. Veuve Henri Moroni and Mme. Veuve Henri Jacquin	0.2707	0.7	161

Les Referts—5.5247 ha/13.6 acres

	Hectares	Acres	Cases*
M. Fernand Beudrand	0.8090	2.0	481
M. Bernard Bigeard	0.1192	0.3	71
M. André Buisson	0.1136	0.3	67
M. et Mme. Louis Carillon	0.2400	0.6	143
Mme. Veuve André Chavy and M. André Chavy	0.2810	0.7	167

*Cases calculated on the *rendement de base* of 45 hl/ha plus 20 percent

	Hectares	Acres	Cases*
M. Bernard Courreaux	0.0490	0.1	29
M. Edouard Courreaux	0.1392	0.3	83
M. et Mme. Camille David	0.2557	0.6	152
Mme. Veuve Georges Debaumarche and M. Georges Debaumarche	0.4495	1.1	267
M. Pierre Dureuil	0.2016	0.5	120
M. et Mme. Daniel Fichet	0.2220	0.6	132
M. Marc Gauffroy	0.1273	0.3	76
M. Albert Jante	0.2196	0.5	130
M. et Mme. Jean-Pierre Monnot	0.4549	1.1	270
Mme. Veuve Henri Moroni	0.3706	0.9	220
Mme. Veuve Henri Jacquin M. Jean Richez	0.4028	1.0	239
M. Étienne Sauzet and Mme. Jean Boillot	1.3097	3.2	778

Sous le Puits—6.7983 ha/16.8 acres

	Hectares	Acres	Cases*
M. et Mme. Maurice Bouillin	0.1120	0.3	67
M. Bernard Bouton	0.2845	0.7	169
M. Gilles Bouton	0.7959	2.0	473
Mme. Henri Bouton	0.0645	0.2	38
Mme. Henri Bouton	0.2127	0.5	126
M. et Mme. René Changarnier	1.4672	3.6	872
M. Bernard Charreau	0.8455	2.1	502
Mme. Veuve René Guerin and Mme. Veuve Paul Giraudet	0.5857	1.5	348
M. et Mme. Bernard Langoureau	0.2153	0.5	128
M. et Mme. Guy Larue	0.2745	0.7	163
M. et Mme. Jean Pascal	0.1834	0.5	109
Mme. Alfred Skarzynski	0.2936	0.7	174
Mme. Georges Vallot	0.6263	1.6	372

La Truffière—2.4822 ha/6.1 acres

	Hectares	Acres	Cases*
M. et Mme. David Camille	0.9748	2.4	579
M. Gérard Guerin	0.1410	0.4	84
GFA Laurence	0.9939	2.5	590
M. Étienne Sauzet and Mme. Jean Boillot	0.2412	0.6	143

---

*Cases calculated on the *rendement de base* of 45 hl/ha plus 20 percent

LE CAILLERET—One look at the map tells you all you need to know about the distinction of Le Cailleret: It is a continuation of Le Montrachet itself. Should you ever doubt the primacy of Le Montrachet, you need only compare it to Le Cailleret. The latter lacks the resonant depth of the former. It shares more with Chevalier-Montrachet in its stony, metallic flavors. Cailleret is superb *premier cru* and difficult to obtain. It is owned almost exclusively by Jean Chartron. The Les Demoiselles *climat* is the property of the Colin family of Chassagne-Montrachet.

LES CHALUMAUX—Again, location tells us a great deal here. Les Chalumaux is high up on the slope, close to Blagny. All of the vineyards in the Blagny sector share common characteristics: pronounced *goût de terroir*, higher acidity, and great finesse. Chalumaux is noted for its perfuminess, which is outsized relative to the good but not massive scale of the wine.

CHAMP CANET—If you wander through this vineyard, you can see with little effort that almost nothing except a grapevine could love such a spot: It is nearly devoid of topsoil. As might be expected, the wine is stony-tasting, lean, and powerful, with a buttery, honeyed scent. Champ Canet is one of the best of the *premiers crus*. The *climat* Clos de la Garenne was made famous by the Domaine Duc de Magenta (now produced and sold by Louis Jadot). It is superb wine.

CLAVAILLON—You can take your choice of spellings here, what the French call *"facultatif"*: Clavaillon or Clavoillon. As the ownership listing shows, this vineyard is divided between only two owners: the Leflaive and Chavy families. In either case, Clavaillon creates a rounded, softer, fatter Puligny than some others, more early-maturing than, say, Folatières, higher up on the slope. Still, it's lovely wine. The Leflaive holding was replanted in the 1970s, and there is every reason to expect ever-better Clavaillon from them as the years go by.

LES COMBETTES—One of the richer, intensely minerally *premiers crus*. The distinction of Les Combettes is perhaps realized when comparing it to Meursault "Charmes," which adjoins it. The "tension" of Puligny-Montrachet makes itself apparent compared to the lushness of the Meursault. Both are delicious; the Combettes is the more faceted and finely cut.

LES FOLATIÈRES—One of the best-known *premiers crus*, courtesy of its size. Exposure is the source of its distinction. It also has a strong, persistent *goût de terroir*. Part of the vineyard was reclaimed from the rocky summit of the slope after World War II. The best versions ally the richness available to the site with the *goût de terroir*. Lesser bottlings can be either heavy and flat or stony but light. The only red *premier cru* of Puligny-Montrachet comes from Les Folatières.

LES PERRIÈRES—One of those vineyard names that Burgundy abounds in and that usually provide pleasure. Perrières is well situated and creates classic Puligny-Montrachet: rich, perfectly structured, and intense. Regrettably, it is rarely seen. The ownership is dominated by Domaine Boillot in Volnay, which owns the 9.7-acre *monopole* Clos de la Mouchère, which borders the Les Referts vineyard.

LES PUCELLES—Along with Les Folatières, Les Pucelles is the best known of the *premiers crus*. Leflaive dominates both the vineyard holdings and the name. As with Clavaillon next door, Pucelles has a softness to it, with that underlying steeliness that characterizes Puligny-Montrachet. Here, you'll find a scent of honey. Pucelles is one of the early-maturing *premiers crus*.

LES REFERTS—Again, proximity to Meursault shows in this wine. Les Referts has a roundness and richness lacking in the Pulignys higher up on the slope, yet somehow retains a measure of restraint that allows it to age beautifully.

LA TRUFFIÈRE—The only version of this wine that I have tasted comes from Domaine Sauzet. Judging from that, La Truffière reveals what its position high up on the slope would lead one to expect. It is a wine of high acidity, with a steely, minerally taste, but lacking the honeyed unctuosity of the better-situated Folatières below it. It would seem to reward aging, given its structure.

PRODUCERS WORTH SEEKING OUT (AND SOME NOT)

DOMAINE ROBERT ET MICHEL AMPEAU—The Meursault producers create superb Combettes, their only Puligny.

DOMAINE JEAN CHARTRON/CHARTRON ET TRÉBUCHET—Two separate labels, with Jean Chartron keeping some of his vineyard holdings separate from the *négociant* Chartron et Trébuchet label he owns with Louis Trébuchet. The wines under both labels are examples of the so-called "modern style" of white Burgundies: very clean, crisp, and devoid of apparent oak. They are always good, sometimes very good, but rarely are the wines in the top rank. They appear to lack the necessary concentration. The *négociant* label offers a terrific Bourgogne Blanc called "Homage à Victor Hugo" (a relation of one of the partners), which is rumored to be partly declassified Puligny-Montrachet.

DOMAINE GÉRARD CHAVY—I never have cared for the wines of Chavy, finding them excessively oaky and often somehow flat. This is too bad, as Chavy owns some choice vineyards. Folatières seems to be his best wine, but even that is variable.

DOMAINE MADAME FRANÇOIS COLIN/DOMAINE MICHEL COLIN—Should one need a lesson in the Byzantine business arrangements of Burgundian winegrowers, the Colin family offers a prime example. You have Michel Colin; his wife, Mme. Colin-Deleger; his mother, Mme. François Colin (who uses her late husband's name on her label); Marc Colin, his cousin; and the name Colin-St. Abdon. Michel Colin has a sharecropping arrangement with a M. St. Abdon, from whom he receives one third of the crop. And St. Abdon himself is sharecropping the same vineyards for the actual owner (Jean Chartron)! All of these names wind up on labels. In Puligny-Montrachet, the Colin name has resonance simply because they own three quarters of an acre of the Les Demoiselles *climat* in Le Cailleret. The wine is superb.

JOSEPH DROUHIN—The Beaune *négociant* is the source of superb Folatières. The reason is that Drouhin has, since 1961, purchased roughly three quarters of the production of Paul Pernot—who not only owns the largest piece of Les Folatières, but arguably makes the best wine as well. Drouhin's version is a little oakier than Pernot's (who bottles some under his own name). Presumably, it is augmented by barrels of Folatières from other sources.

LOUIS JADOT—Courtesy of a twenty-year contract with Domaine Duc de Magenta, the Jadot label now has the Clos de la Garenne, which is wonderful wine. Also, Jadot has long issued a Les Referts of great distinction.

LOUIS LATOUR—Fine Folatières and Les Referts in the refined, restrained Latour style. It is fascinating to compare Drouhin's Folatières to that of Latour, to see the effects of style. One of the specialty bottlings is excellent Hameau de Blagny.

DOMAINE LEFLAIVE—The most renowned producer in Puligny is Vincent Leflaive, and justly so. Leflaive wines are damnably hard to find, and too often, it seems, they are drunk too young when they are found. Leflaive is best known for his *grands crus*, but more of his Pucelles, Clavaillons, and Combettes are to be seen, along with excellent commune-level Puligny. The Leflaive style is for beautifully defined wine that is almost signature-free. In lighter years, the Pucelles and Clavaillon can be a shade too thin and watery, but the vineyard distinction still is there. Do not confuse this estate with the name Olivier Leflaive (q.v.).

OLIVIER LEFLAIVE—A nephew of Vincent Leflaive who embarked on a *négociant* business in the early eighties. The wines, including several Pulignys, are clean, well made, and in the modern style. Rarely do they ascend to any great heights.

DOMAINE JOSEPH MATROT—This Meursault producer offers wonderful Les Chalumaux, with an intense fragrance and long life.

DOMAINE PAUL PERNOT—This producer probably is the best-kept secret in Puligny-Montrachet. His wines are no secret to the locals. Far from it. But to outsiders, the Pernot name is almost unknown, largely because he sells 60 percent to 80 percent of his production to Maison Joseph Drouhin. Pernot owns wonderful vineyards and is a superb winemaker in his own right. His Folatières is magnificent, as is his Pucelles, which is the finest example I know. His plot in Pucelles is right next to Bienvenues-Bâtard-Montrachet. Should he someday choose to estate-bottle all of his wines, Domaine Pernot could rival Leflaive as the greatest Puligny domaine.

DOMAINE ÉTIENNE SAUZET—The late Étienne Sauzet was surely one of the great winemakers of Puligny. The winemaking style then and now is characterized by a severe austerity. Sauzet wines are not designed to be drunk young, nor should they be. But few producers offer a comparable degree of concentration, definition, and detail as Sauzet does in virtually all of the production. Every wine deserves praise: a superb commune-level Puligny; the rare La Truffière; intensely powerful Les Perrières; and a rich Les Combettes. Sauzet wines are reference-standard.

Montrachet

Sound of inner stone with heart on fire

—W. S. Merwin, *The Rock*

Montrachet holds two temptations for the wine lover: One is to drink it. The other is to debunk it. The temptation is strong in both cases and, strangely enough, almost equally valid. The drinking part is the more worthwhile. Montrachet *is* what everyone has long declared it to be, namely, the finest, richest, most perfect of all white Burgundies.

What Montrachet offers are more attributes of a higher order put together more cohesively. Its fruit is as strong, intense, and detailed as Corton-Charlemagne—but it is delivered with far greater finesse. Its spicy *goût de terroir* is as pronounced and profound as that of neighboring Chevalier-Montrachet—but conveyed by a more resonant fruit. Its fragrance is as forceful as Meursault "Perrierès," but it has dimensions that exhaust the drinker long before one feels that its offerings have been fully explored. It is what the poet suggests: a *taste* of inner stone with heart on fire.

To look at the vineyard is to be disappointed. It rubs up against a rocky eyebrow that is the summit of the slope, a cataract of stony-white soil. Its exposure is ideal, an east-facing supplicant to the sun. Yet this description applies equally well to neighboring Cailleret. In truth, nothing you can see gives away any secrets.

Given its undeniable distinction, why, then, is the temptation to debunk the standing of Montrachet so tempting? The reason is as simple as it is disturbing: Too few Montrachets taste as good as they should. Even a lesser Montrachet is a fascinating experience, but its stature as a wine apart doesn't hold up when faced with first-rank examples of Chevalier-Montrachet or Bienvenues-Bâtard-Montrachet or Bâtard-Montrachet. In fact, a really great Meursault "Perrières" can put to shame a number of lesser Montrachets.

How can such a situation exist? After all, the growers can get virtually any price they ask. The retail price of the Montrachet of the Domaine de la Romanée-Conti—which happens to be one of the finest of them all—is five hundred dollars a bottle. And people clamor for it. It's an incredible price, and only Montrachet could even pretend to justify it.

The problem is that any Montrachet, regardless of its quality, will fetch at least two hundred dollars a bottle and have ten buyers for every bottle. The market offers no incentive. Those who taste a truly great Montrachet and come home to tell the tale aren't lying. But you can't blame the next person who goes out, only to try something called Montrachet that doesn't even remotely resemble the saga of the storyteller, and doubts the greatness of Montrachet.

To be fair, sometimes the problem is one of wine maturity. Montrachet is a wine that requires at least ten years of bottle age. And it will improve for at least ten more. Although the greatest examples from the greatest vintages are self-evident even in the barrel, it's possible for less-than-perfect vintages to need years of bottle age in order for the depth of the wine to surface. Nevertheless, a wine like Montrachet should never be a distant voice, no matter how young.

Why are so many Montrachets less than they should be? One reason is that Montrachet suffers from a vine disease called *court noué*, sometimes known as "leaf roll." A virus that lives in the soil and, like phylloxera, has no known remedy, it affects both the roots of the vine and, an outward manifestation, causes the leaves to turn bright yellow along the veins and roll under, hence the name "leaf roll." Photosynthesis is diminished, the vine is weakened, sugar levels in the grapes are reduced. It is spread and intensified by plowing. The only solution is to pull up the vines.

The affected vines slowly die. The first generation of vines growing in the affected soil may live to forty years. But the second generation won't make it much past fifteen years. The plot then has to be left fallow for years to allow the roots to rot, and then the soil is fumigated. Montrachet is beset by *court noué*. The Burgundian wine writer Jean-François Bazin in his definitive book *Montrachet* wonders whether it is "the AIDS of Montrachet". Other vineyards also are affected.

Other factors include rootstocks that are too vigorous for the vine, resulting in enlarged grapes of little character. Not least is the problem of vines that simply are too young to deliver real character. On the other hand, the old vines are affected by *court noué*.

THE VINEYARD

Montrachet is 7.9980 ha/19.76 acres divided between Puligny-Montrachet (4.0107 ha/9.91 acres) and Chassagne-Montrachet (3.9873 ha/9.85 acres). It is entirely *grand cru*.

Puligny-Montrachet side

	Hectares	Acres	Cases*
Bouchard Père et Fils	0.8894	2.2	470
Héritiers de M. Lazare Boillerault de Chauvigny	0.7998	2.0	422
M. Jean de Laguiche and M. Philibert de Laguiche	2.0625	5.1	1089
M. André Ramonet and M. Pierre Ramonet	0.2590	0.6	137

Chassagne-Montrachet side

M. Pierre Amiot	0.0910	0.2	40
Mme. Claudine Blain-Gagnard	0.0783	0.2	41
M. et Mme. Marc Colin	0.1068	0.3	47

*Cases calculated on the *rendement de base* of 40 hl/ha plus 20 percent

	Hectares	Acres	Cases*
Mme. Laurence Fontaine-Gagnard	0.0780	0.2	41
Mme. Jacques Gaye	0.0821	0.2	43
SCI du Domaine des Comtes Lafon	0.3182	0.8	140
SC du Domaine de la Romanée-Conti	0.6759	1.7	297
M. et Mme. René Fleurot	0.0833	0.2	44
M. Louis Petitjean	0.0542	0.1	24
Domaine Jacques Prieur	0.5863	1.5	258
SC du Domaine Thénard	1.8331	4.5	807

PRODUCERS WORTH SEEKING OUT (AND SOME NOT)

HÉRITIERS DE M. LAZARE BOILLERAULT DE CHAUVIGNY—
Something should be said about this unusual property, if only
because it reveals how vineyards are owned, and wines sold, in
Burgundy. Monsieur Lazare Boillerault, originally from Volnay,
died in 1930. His wife, Geneviève de Chauvigny, died in 1969. As
the listings reveal, their estate is the fourth-largest in Montrachet.
Inevitably, it passed to their children. It is now divided into four
parcels, two of 0.2666 ha/0.66 acre and two of 0.1333 ha/0.33 acre.
All four parcels are administered under the name of Domaine Regnault de Beaucaron, as one of the daughters married Comte René-
Marc Regnault de Beaucaron, who lives in Paris. The vines are
tended by Eugène and Bruno Rossignol of Volnay, and the new
wine sold to various *négociants* with Maison Louis Latour acting as
the *courtier*. (I am indebted to Jean-François Bazin's *Montrachet* for
this information.)

BOUCHARD PÈRE ET FILS—Along with their Chevalier-Montrachet,
this is—as it should be—the best wine made by Bouchard. Nevertheless, it could be better, as too often it lacks sufficient concentration. That aside, it is well made. Bouchard should be considered
only in the best vintages. The wine is sold under Bouchard's domaine
name of Domaines du Château de Beaune.

---

*Cases calculated on the *rendement de base* of 40 hl/ha plus 20 percent

DOMAINE MARC COLIN—I have not tasted Colin's Montrachet, but the reports are encouraging. The vines were planted in 1940, and his other wines are admirable. Given that, I'd certainly look for his Montrachet.

DOMAINE DELAGRANGE-BACHELET—Several vintages of this producer's Montrachets have left me underwhelmed. Light, cleanly made wines of no great profundity. And with Montrachet, you've got a right to get profundity.

DOMAINE RENÉ FLEUROT—The few opportunities I've had to taste Fleurot's Montrachet have failed to leave much of an impression. Perhaps things have improved, but so far the wine has lacked depth. A few barrels of Fleurot's Montrachet are sold to the *négociant* Labouré-Roi, which actually does a better job of cellaring than does Fleurot.

DOMAINE GAGNARD-DELAGRANGE—Good but not great Montrachet, with some character and dimension, but not the full measure. A 1982 showed fine concentration for the vintage, with a piny mushroom-scented bouquet and a metallic aftertaste. Still, this is a good producer for Montrachet and worth watching.

DOMAINE DES COMTES LAFON—Here we have Montrachet as it should be: resonant, powerful, profound. One expects Lafon to create a great Montrachet, and Lafon delivers. This is a producer where even an off-vintage Montrachet is better than many others' good-vintage versions. I still recall the '81 Montrachet—but only because it was excelled by Lafon's Meursault "Perrières." That usually doesn't happen.

MARQUIS DE LAGUICHE/JOSEPH DROUHIN—The largest owner of Le Montrachet, the de Laguiche family has owned a part of Montrachet since 1776. The wine is made and distributed by Maison Joseph Drouhin. Although the de Laguiche Montrachet is arguably the best known—and one of the most frequently seen—it rarely rises to the top. Too often, it has lacked depth. A 1982 was so watery as to be indistinguishable as a *grand cru*, let alone Montrachet. However, in easier vintages the wine is good, although rarely great. It is second-rank Montrachet.

DOMAINE JACQUES PRIEUR—For too many years, this privileged estate has loafed along issuing wines with famous names and high prices, but not delivering on the promise. Nowhere is this more the case than with its Montrachet. The wine lacks concentration, despite yields of only 30 hl/ha. Perhaps it's the winemaking. Or the rootstocks. Or any number of possible reasons. Too bad.

DOMAINE RAMONET—When you taste a Ramonet Montrachet, the failings of other Montrachets become apparent. Here, finally, is what the French call *sève*—sappiness, concentration, unctuosity. Pierre Ramonet, eighty-five, is the most celebrated winemaker in Burgundy, affectionately known in the region as "Père Ramonet." His son André is the winemaker, but Pierre set the standard long ago. The father had no secrets, just immense integrity. For decades, he has labored in his vineyards in Chassagne-Montrachet, dreaming of someday owning a piece of Montrachet itself. Finally, in 1978, he was able to buy 0.2590 ha/0.63 acre—just over half an acre—from the Milan and Mathey families. He had achieved a life's dream.

Should anyone doubt that great Montrachets can be made if the owner so desires, they need only look at Domaine Ramonet, which also sells its wines under the name Ramonet-Prudhon. Virtually overnight, Ramonet's Montrachet emerged as one of the reference standards. There's only one problem: Ramonet makes only about one hundred cases. But if you can find one, you are better advised to buy Ramonet's Montrachet, which usually sells for about twice everybody else's (except the Domaine de la Romanée-Conti), than spend half as much for something likely much lesser. After all, if you're in for 150 bucks, you may as well drop $300—which is what I last saw this Montrachet selling for in the States.

DOMAINE DE LA ROMANÉE-CONTI—There are three reference-standard Montrachets currently being made: Lafon, Ramonet, and the Domaine de la Romanée-Conti. Not surprisingly, that of DRC is by far the most expensive and the hardest to obtain. In order to get one case of the DRC Montrachet, an importer must purchase fifty cases of the same vintage of their various red wines. So when a bottle is offered by a retailer, it usually exacts an eye-opening price: five hundred dollars, at last look. (On the importer's list, the Montrachet usually is priced the same as Romanée-Conti.) There's no sense in debating whether a wine, any wine, is worth that kind of money. The only question is one of quality. How good is the DRC Montrachet? The answer is simple: It's as good as it gets. This is Montrachet in full cry, replete with the array of honey, cinnamon, stony, buttery, smoky scents and flavors coupled with a texture that tells you all you need to know about the yields. You don't make wine like this from just any grapes.

The domaine purchased three parcels of Montrachet at different times, according to Jean-François Bazin in his book *Montrachet*. The first parcel of 0.3419 ha/0.84 acre was bought in 1963 from the comte de Moucheron in Meursault (see Château de Meursault). The second—0.1670 ha/0.4 acre—was bought in 1965. The third—0.1670 ha/0.4 acre—came from Roland Thévenin (who was involved in a divorce at the time) in 1980. Two of the three parcels, according to Bazin, were planted fifty years ago; the third was planted in the 1960s. The domaine makes about 180 cases of Montrachet.

DOMAINE BARON THÉNARD—Along with the Marquis de La-guiche, the Montrachet of Baron Thénard is one of the most widely seen bottlings. Until 1985, virtually all of the wine was sold by the *négociant* Remoissenet, which shared a jointly named label. Remoissenet still handles the Thénard Montrachet, but more now in the office of *courtier* or go-between, as other *négociants* have been able to buy Thénard's wine.

Based on the Remoissenet bottlings, the Thénard Montrachet is certainly one of the better examples, but not quite in the top rank. The wine is made in a cellar in Givry, in the Côte Chalonnaise. It has a good measure of depth and fullness, but lacks the degree of texture, breadth, and detail that distinguish the Montrachets of Lafon, Ramonet, and the Domaine de la Romanée-Conti. Still, it's better than many.

Chevalier-
Montrachet

For all practical purposes, the greatest white Burgundy made today is Chevalier-Montrachet. This is not to say that Chevalier, at its best, is superior to Montrachet at its best. It isn't, although it comes close. Rather, you can find Chevalier-Montrachet at its best more often than you can Montrachet. It is endowed with a stellar collection of owners. It is the *grand cru* white Burgundy I would buy before any other.

As the map shows, Chevalier-Montrachet lies directly above and next to Montrachet. Unlike Montrachet, it lies entirely in Puligny. Yet the vineyard and its wine are distinctively different. The soil of Chevalier-Montrachet is much stonier and chalkier than in Montrachet; the slope is steeper, the elevation higher: Where Montrachet lies between 250 meters and 270 meters, Chevalier-Montrachet is sandwiched between the 265-meter line and 290 meters.

What Chevalier-Montrachet offers is perhaps the most intense, distinctive *goût de terroir* of any white Burgundy. It is spicier than any other. Not as plump as Montrachet, it has as much finesse, which is its supreme attribute. If Montrachet did not exist, what is now a Chevalier would instead be the king.

There exists a separate bottling of Chevalier-Montrachet that is the exclusive province of the *négociants* Louis Jadot and Louis Latour. This is the wine called Chevalier-Montrachet "Les Demoiselles." This scrap of a *climat*—1.0270 hectares or 2.5 acres—originally was part of what is now the *premier cru* vineyard Le Cailleret. Jean-François Bazin in *Montrachet* recounts how the two *négociants*, through their lawyers, lobbied to have this parcel, traditionally called "Demoiselles"—after two sisters, Adele and Julie Voillot, who owned it in the mid-1800s—made part of the *grand cru* Chevalier-Montrachet. They submitted, with abundant documentation, that Demoiselles always was sold as Chevalier-Montrachet. Moreover, when it was sold to them in 1913, the advertisement had it being "*en* Chevalier-Montrachet." They paid for the name, they said.

In 1974, Chevalier-Montrachet again was extended with the addition of yet another piece of Cailleret, a 0.6-acre parcel owned by Jean Chartron, whose family had lobbied for its inclusion since 1955.

THE VINEYARD

Chevalier-Montrachet is 7.3614 ha/18.2 acres. It is entirely *grand cru*.

	Hectares	Acres	Cases*
GFA du Domaine Belgrand-Latour	0.2538	0.6	134
Bouchard Père et Fils	2.0280	5.0	1071
M. Jean-Georges Chartron	0.7111	1.8	375
M. et Mme. Henry Clerc	0.1510	0.4	80
M. Armand Dancer	0.0965	0.2	51
M. Georges Deleger	0.1595	0.4	84
M. Robert Deleger	0.1595	0.4	84
SC du Domaine Louis Jadot	0.5200	1.3	275

*Cases calculated on the *rendement de base* of 40 hl/ha plus 20 percent

	Hectares	Acres	Cases*
Mlle. Anne Leflaive and Mme. Bernard Suremain	0.5072	1.3	268
M. Joseph Leflaive and M. Patrick Leflaive	0.5079	1.3	268
M. Vincent Leflaive and Mlle. Anne Leflaive	0.5074	1.3	268
M. Marie-Charles Armand Lochardet and M. Bernard Lochardet	0.0966	0.2	51
GFA du Domaine Marchal-Latour	0.2537	0.6	134
M. Michel Niellon	0.2273	0.6	120
Mme. Veuve Louis de Noue and M. Bernard de Noue	0.4837	1.2	255
SC Domaine Jacques Prieur	0.1365	0.3	72

PRODUCERS WORTH SEEKING OUT (AND SOME NOT)

BOUCHARD PÈRE ET FILS—As with their Montrachet, Bouchard's Chevalier-Montrachet is well made and certainly enjoyable drinking, but too light to be in the top rank. Nevertheless, the breed shows through, and this, along with their Montrachet, is as good as Bouchard gets.

DOMAINE JEAN CHARTRON—As discussed previously, Chartron's Chevalier-Montrachet comes from a 0.6-acre parcel of the Le Cailleret vineyard that was baptized Chevalier-Montrachet in 1974. It was itself part of a larger *climat* called the Clos du Cailleret, part of which was included in Chevalier-Montrachet in 1939. The fight was to get the rest of it in as well. Chartron's Chevalier is well made in the light, clean modern style preferred by this producer. It is good, but rarely great.

DOMAINE GEORGES DELEGER—One of the great producers of Chevalier-Montrachet, a glance at the ownership listings reveals that

*Cases calculated on the *rendement de base* of 40 hl/ha plus 20 percent

Georges Deleger owns 0.1595 ha/0.4 acre and his brother Robert owns another slice of precisely the same size. (Thanks to Napoleon Bonaparte.) You would think that Robert would go in with Georges to create one wine, but no, this is Burgundy. Robert sells all of his grapes to Maison Louis Jadot.

Georges Deleger creates profound Chevalier-Montrachet, brimming with the intense spiciness that makes this vineyard so distinctive. Ninety percent of his production is exported to the States so, for once, you've got to be here rather than there to sample a great grower's tiny production.

LOUIS JADOT—The *négociant* offers two Chevaliers: a regular bottling labeled Chevalier-Montrachet that is assembled from several sources, and their domaine-bottled Chevalier-Montrachet "Les Demoiselles." The Les Demoiselles version is the superior. It is one of the great examples of Chevalier-Montrachet, made in Jadot's exacting, austere style. If ever a wine demanded ten years of age before it was ready to reveal its authority, it is Jadot's Les Demoiselles. The regular Chevalier-Montrachet, in comparison, is merely very good—which is saying a lot.

LOUIS LATOUR—Along with his Corton-Charlemagne, Latour's Chevalier-Montrachet "Les Demoiselles" is this *négociant*'s best white wine. It always is fascinating to compare the Latour Demoiselles to the Jadot version. The Latour wine is usually a shade lighter, although the detail is fully in force. It is exceptional wine.

DOMAINE LEFLAIVE—This outstanding producer creates the reference-standard Chevalier-Montrachet: pungent, graceful, and long-lived. The wine gleams with the characteristic Leflaive polish. It is the Chevalier-Montrachet against which all others are compared.

DOMAINE MICHEL NIELLON—A superb producer of an array of wines in Chassagne-Montrachet, the Niellon Chevalier-Montrachet is stunning wine: concentrated, signature-free, and almost digital in its definition. This producer rarely, if ever, lets you down.

DOMAINE JACQUES PRIEUR—The strength of Chevalier-Montrachet is evident in this chronically disappointing domaine: Its Chevalier is better than its Montrachet. The tiny one-third-acre plot was replanted in 1967. Given that size, one rarely sees this wine, as only two barrels or fifty cases are made.

Bâtard-
Montrachet

Bâtard-Montrachet, by virtue of the size of the vineyard (29.3 acres), is the most variable of the constellation of *grands crus* surrounding Montrachet. It's worth pointing out that the Agricultural Committee of Beaune's vineyard classification in 1860 gave only the upper third of Bâtard-Montrachet the highest ranking, *première classe*. All of what is now Bienvenues-Bâtard-Montrachet was designated *deuxième*, or second, class. The upper third is that section closest to Montrachet, sharing a similar soil and approximately the same exposure.

Although completely forgotten today, Bâtard-Montrachet used to be even bigger, some fifty-five acres. Prior to Appellation Contrôlée in 1939, what was sold as Bâtard-Montrachet came from six *climats*: Bâtard-Montrachet (23.5 acres); Les Criots (3.7 acres); Bienvenues (14.9 acres); Blanchot Dessous (5 acres); Vide Bourse (3.5

acres); and Les Encegnières (4.8 acres). Of these, Blanchot Dessous and Les Encegnières now are commune-level vineyards in Chassagne-Montrachet; Vide Bourse is a *premier cru* in Chassagne.

The bastard Montrachet, as the name unblushingly declares, should be the fattest, most voluptuous wine of them all, rounder and richer even than Montrachet. What makes it a bastard is, if you will, the lack of the pedigree found in Montrachet and Chevalier: finesse. On the other hand, the virtues of Bâtard-Montrachet are not to be dismissed. Few, if any, white Burgundies offer more intensive scents of honey. Few are more unctuous—at least the good ones are. Only Corton-Charlemagne is as massively fruity, and here Bâtard-Montrachet shows its Puligny heritage: It is more taut than Corton-Charlemagne.

Because of the size of the vineyard, and the number of owners, more Bâtard-Montrachet is seen than any other of the hyphenated Montrachets. Regrettably, too many of the bottlings lack the stuffings that the best versions have. Partly this is due to an overly generous set of boundaries for the *appellation*; partly it is due to *négociants* having to blend multiple lots of often-indifferent wines to create a commercial quantity. One should be very cautious in buying Bâtard-Montrachet for these reasons.

That said, the best bottlings are a delight: rich, suave, mouth-filling, and long-lived. A great Bâtard-Montrachet really deserves ten years of age. Then it is like drinking bottled sunbeams.

THE VINEYARD

Bâtard-Montrachet lies across two communes, almost equally. The total vineyard area is 11.8663 ha/29.3 acres divided 6.0221 ha/14.9 acres in Puligny-Montrachet and 5.8442 ha/14.4 acres in Chassagne-Montrachet. It is entirely *grand cru*.

Puligny-Montrachet side

	Hectares	Acres	Cases*
Mme. Veuve Claude André	0.3968	1.0	210
GFA Domaine Bachelet	0.1675	0.4	88
M. Charles Bavard	0.3385	0.8	179

*Cases calculated on the *rendement de base* of 40 hl/ha plus 20 percent

	Hectares	Acres	Cases*
M. et Mme. Paul Bavard	0.3386	0.8	179
Mlle. Gisèle Bonneau and Mlle. Marguérite Bonneau and Mlle. Sarah Bonneau	0.1184	0.3	63
Mme. Veuve Henri Jacquin (now Hospices de Beaune)	0.3223	0.8	170
Mlle. Anne Leflaive and Mme. Bernard Suremain	0.4491	1.1	237
M. Joseph Leflaive and M. Patrick Leflaive	0.4491	1.1	237
M. Vincent Leflaive and Mlle. Anne Leflaive	0.3512	0.9	185
M. et Mme. Jean-Pierre Monnot	0.4972	1.2	263
M. Lucie Pernot	0.3836	1.0	203
M. Claude Poirier	0.9703	2.4	512
M. Louis Poirier	0.6695	1.7	353
M. André Ramonet and M. Claude Ramonet	0.1674	0.4	88
M. Pierre Ramonet	0.2649	0.7	140
M. Étienne Sauzet and Mme. Jean Boillot	0.1377	0.3	73
Chassagne-Montrachet side			
Mme. Jean Boillot	0.1831	0.5	81
M. André Bouchard and Mme. Veuve Pierre Corne	0.0785	0.2	35
M. Max Brenot	0.3744	1.0	165
Mme. Veuve André Chavy and M. André Chavy	0.1411	0.4	62
M. Henri Clerc	0.1835	0.5	81
M. Henri Coffinet	0.2607	0.6	115
M. Georges Colin	0.0922	0.2	41
SC du Domaine de la Romanée-Conti	0.1746	0.4	77
M. Prosper Delagrange and Mlle. Claudine Gagnard	0.3445	0.9	152
M. et Mme. Prosper Delagrange	0.1413	0.4	62

*Cases calculated on the *rendement de base* of 40 hl/ha plus 20 percent

	Hectares	Acres	Cases*
M. Prosper Delagrange and Mme. Richard Fontaine	0.2025	0.5	89
M. et Mme. Jacques Gagnard	0.1623	0.4	71
M. et Mme. Jacques Gagnard	0.1030	0.3	45
M. et Mme. Joseph Gagnard	0.3607	0.9	159
Mlle. Laurence Gagnard	0.1002	0.3	44
Mme. Paul Gailliot	0.2907	0.7	128
Mme. Jacques Gaye	0.0450	0.1	20
Mme. Roger Graindorge	0.0455	0.1	20
M. et Mme. Gabriel Jouard	0.0370	0.1	16
M. Pierre Jouard	0.1270	0.3	56
M. Vincent Leflaive and Mlle. Anne Leflaive	0.1553	0.4	68
M. Jean Lemonde	0.1304	0.3	57
M. Robert Lemonde	0.1304	0.3	57
Monsiuer Albert Morey	0.1499	0.4	66
M. et Mme. Marc Morey	0.1360	0.3	60
M. Michel Niellon	0.1190	0.3	52
Mme. Veuve Louis de Noue and M. Ludovic de Noue	0.5065	1.3	223
M. Lucien Pernot	0.1017	0.3	45
M. Michel Pernot and M. Paul Pernot	0.2229	0.6	98
M. Georges Prieur and M. Guy Prieur	0.0763	0.2	34
GFA du Domaine Lequin-Roussot	0.2433	0.6	107
Mme. René Roux	0.0886	0.2	39
Maison Joseph Drouhin	0.0945	0.2	42
GFA Picard-Stoeckel	0.0826	0.2	36
M. Erick Urena	0.1557	0.4	69

PRODUCERS WORTH SEEKING OUT (AND SOME NOT)

DOMAINE BACHELET-RAMONET—Despite the aura of having the name Ramonet, this estate should not be confused with Domaine Ramonet. Owner Jean-Claude Bachelet (not to be confused with the small Domaine Jean-Claude Bachelet, which is owned by a different person) is Pierre Ramonet's nephew. This estate was formed when Pierre Ramonet's sister married Georges Bachelet earlier in this cen-

---

*Cases calculated on the *rendement de base* of 40 hl/ha plus 20 percent

tury, hence the hyphenated name. Its wines are not remotely in the same league. The Bachelet-Ramonet version of Bâtard-Montrachet is disappointingly thin and light.

DOMAINE BLAIN-GAGNARD—The family complications of Burgundy are in force with the Gagnard name. You have the owner of the estate, Madame Claudine Blain-Gagnard. She married Jean-Marc Blain. Her father is Jacques Gagnard-Delagrange. Her grandfather is Edmond Delagrange-Bachelet. Her sister is Laurence Fontaine-Gagnard. All of them have his or her own domaine.

The Bâtard-Montrachet of Blain-Gagnard is one of the better examples, although the style of this estate leans toward the lighter, crisper white Burgundies favored by many young producers. (It also lends itself conveniently to higher yields too.) Nevertheless, this is a good estate that seems to get better every vintage. Worth watching.

DOMAINE DELAGRANGE-BACHELET—Although I find the Bâtard-Montrachet from Blain-Gagnard to be admirable, that from Delagrange-Bachelet always seems to me to be lighter and less concentrated. Rarely have I found it to be anything worth the premium commanded by the Bâtard name.

JOSEPH DROUHIN—Very fine, rich, intense Bâtard. Drouhin owns one quarter-acre of Bâtard in Chassagne-Montrachet. This is augmented by the purchase of Bâtard-Montrachet from Paul Pernot, who happens to own one of the finest sections of the vineyard (near Montrachet). That, more than anything, helps explain the singular quality of the Drouhin wine, plus Drouhin's own careful handling, to be sure. It is exemplary Bâtard-Montrachet.

DOMAINE FONTAINE-GAGNARD—Lighter-style Bâtard-Montrachet of good but not exceptional quality. The recurring problem of lack of concentration is present here.

DOMAINE JEAN-NOËL GAGNARD—I've never figured out how this Gagnard is related to the rest of the clan. A large estate with varying quality wines: its Bâtard-Montrachet is first-rate: rich, unctuous, and deep. This is genuine *grand cru*.

HOSPICES DE BEAUNE—In October 1989, the Hospices purchased a 0.2907 ha/0.7-acre plot of Bâtard on the Chassagne side for 4.2 million French francs or about $700,000. This works out to $100,000 an *ouvrée* or one tenth of an acre. It is the highest price ever paid for a Burgundy vineyard. Presumably, the 1990 vintage from this holding will be offered at the Hospices auction.

DOMAINE LEFLAIVE—Once again, Leflaive creates superb wine, this time in Bâtard-Montrachet. Should the opportunity ever present itself, a comparison of Leflaive's Chevalier-Montrachet with his Bâtard-Montrachet will reveal the fundamental superiority of Chevalier as a vineyard. Where the Bâtard has almost ebullient fruit and strength, the Chevalier has a refinement absent in the Bâtard.

DOMAINE MICHEL NIELLON—Superb Bâtard from this outstanding producer: strong, intense, and yet—the comments about the Leflaive wines notwithstanding—wonderfully refined. Niellon makes, along with Leflaive, the most stylish Bâtard, but not at the expense of intensity or depth. A complete wine. Reference-standard.

DOMAINE PAUL PERNOT—I am hard-pressed to recall a better Bâtard-Montrachet than that from Paul Pernot. When I pressed him for a reason, Pernot shrugged. The good ones always do. So I went in for the kill: Show me on a map where your vineyard plots are located. He beamed. There are three *morceaux* (mouthfuls), he said. All of them bordered Montrachet. *Voilà!* Coupled with Pernot's impeccable winemaking, his Bâtard-Montrachet is as good as it gets: an explosive scent, lemony, honeyed, and blessed with a seemingly endless aftertaste. All this from vines planted mostly in 1976, with a few patches of old vines, according to Paul Pernot. Of the ten barrels he makes, eight go to Maison Joseph Drouhin, leaving just fifty cases of wine for the domaine bottling. Reference-standard.

DOMAINE RAMONET—Just what you'd expect: intense, rich wonderfully defined Bâtard-Montrachet. Few Bâtards are as lush as the Ramonet version. Those who scoff at the vineyard distinctions in Burgundy should try Ramonet's Bâtard-Montrachet side by side with his Bienvenues. They are utterly different.

DOMAINE DE LA ROMANÉE-CONTI—Although it is little known, the Domaine de la Romanée-Conti also owns slightly less than one half-acre of Bâtard-Montrachet, from which they make a few barrels. They never bottle the wine, which is very good. Instead, it is sold to various *négociants*. But if you're ever privileged enough to taste wines in the DRC's cellar, make sure to ask for a taste of their Bâtard-Montrachet. It's a pity that they don't estate-bottle it.

DOMAINE ETIENNE SAUZET—The Bâtard-Montrachet of this great producer reminds one of a team of powerful horses pulling madly but kept firmly in control by a tight hand on the reins. The austere Sauzet style results in an elegant, although not especially rich Bâtard. The flavor definition is superb. One wishes for a little more weight though.

Bienvenues-
Bâtard-
Montrachet

Despite the chamber of commerce name—Welcome to Bâtard-Montrachet—this is one of the most subtle white Burgundies. Lighter and more delicate than Bâtard-Montrachet, in the right hands it can deliver more detail with greater finesse than most versions of Bâtard. It also benefits from have a predominance of right-thinking owners: Ramonet, Leflaive, Sauzet, and Pernot.

The problem is finding any Bienvenues. The vineyard is minuscule: 9.1 acres. That's about twelve hundred cases of wine, total. But if you do locate some, you will discover what is, really, the most perfect example of Puligny-Montrachet, an ultra *premier cru*. It is the most elegant of white Burgundies. It also matures sooner than either Montrachet or Chevalier-Montrachet, coming to its fullest expression in eight years, rather than twelve or fifteen years. Still, in a cold cellar it can remain fresh for decades. It is also more accessible sooner. A three-year-old Bienvenues tips you off about its distinction more openly than any of the other *grands crus*.

The French wine writer Michel Bettane reports in *Revue des Vins de France* that because some of the vineyard holdings in Bienvenues are so small, it is almost impossible for a grower to create a separate bottling of Bienvenues. (The grower listings below account for 91 percent of the ownerships, down to holdings as small as one quarter-acre.) The INAO authorities, he says, look the other way, allowing the growers to add the grapes to their vats of Bâtard-Montrachet.

THE VINEYARD

Bienvenues-Bâtard-Montrachet is 3.6860 ha/9.1 acres. It is entirely *grand cru*.

	Hectares	Acres	Cases*
GFA Domaine Bachelet	0.1320	0.3	70
Mme. Veuve Jean Bachelet and M. Jean Bachelet	0.0942	0.2	50
Mlle. Gisèle Bonneau and Mlle. Marguérite Bonneau and Mlle. Sarah Bonneau	0.1947	0.5	103
M. et Mme. Robert Carillon	0.1144	0.3	60
M. et Mme. Henry Clerc	0.6446	1.6	340
Mlle. Anne Leflaive and Mme. Bernard Suremain	0.3217	0.8	170
M. Joseph Leflaive and M. Patrick Leflaive	0.3208	0.8	169
M. Vincent Leflaive and Mlle. Anne Leflaive	0.2583	0.6	136
M. et Mme. Jean-Pierre Monnot	0.1764	0.4	93
Mme. Veuve Louis de Noue and M. Bernard de Noue	0.2572	0.6	136
M. Lucien Pernot	0.1818	0.5	96
M. André Ramonet and M. Claude Ramonet	0.1320	0.3	70

*Cases calculated on the *rendement de base* of 40 hl/ha plus 20 percent

	Hectares	Acres	Cases*
M. Pierre Ramonet	0.3188	0.8	168
Mlle. Anne Rateau	0.0936	0.2	49
M. Étienne Sauzet and Mme. Jean Boillot	0.1162	0.3	61

PRODUCERS WORTH SEEKING OUT

DOMAINE JEAN-CLAUDE BACHELET—I have not tasted this producer's bottling of Bienvenues. It does, however, come recommended by several Burgundian friends. Any Bienvenues is worth trying, as so little of it is available.

DOMAINE LEFLAIVE—Impeccable Bienvenues: light yet with immense flavor impact. The elegant Leflaive style lends itself to Bienvenues as superbly as it does in Chevalier-Montrachet. This may be the most underestimated—if that's possible—of Leflaive's wines.

DOMAINE RAMONET—The master of Bienvenues. Ramonet's Bienvenues is superior to the majority of Montrachets and Bâtard-Montrachets. That's how intense and concentrated is this wine. How does Ramonet do it? The wine has an amazing resinous scent that blossoms early in the wine's life. For once, it's not infanticide to drink a wine when it is, say, just five years old.

DOMAINE ÉTIENNE SAUZET—I have not tasted Sauzet's Bienvenues either, but given the sterling performance of this domaine, it's got to be one of the few safe bets in an otherwise chancy Burgundian world.

---

*Cases calculated on the *rendement de base* of 40 hl/ha plus 20 percent

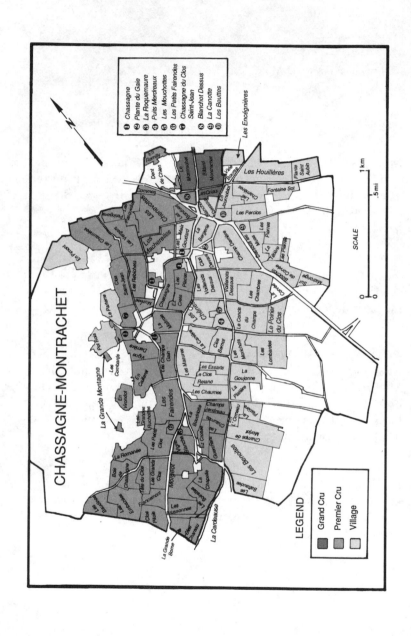

CHASSAGNE-MONTRACHET

1. Chassagne
2. Plante du Gaie
3. La Roquemaure
4. Puits Mardreaux
5. Les Mouchottes
6. Les Petits Fairendes
7. Chassagne du Clos Saint-Jean
8. Blanchot Dessus
9. La Canotte
10. Les Beuttes

Les Encégnières

Les Houillères

SCALE

0   .5 mi
0   1 km

LEGEND

Grand Cru
Premier Cru
Village

Criots-
Bâtard-
Montrachet

T he smallest (3.9 acres) of the *grands crus*, Criots-Bâtard-Montrachet is a triangular patch of vineyard located entirely in Chassagne-Montrachet. Despite that, it still has ten owners, all of whom are accounted for in the grower listings below. The only Criots-Bâtard-Montrachet that I have tasted are two: Domaine Fontaine-Gagnard and Domaine Blaine-Gagnard.

In both cases, Criots seems to be very fine if light, infused with an intense stony/metallic *goût de terroir*, but without the dimension or opulence of Bâtard-Montrachet. It is not faint praise to say that Criots is a lesser (good-quality) Bâtard with a more pronounced *goût de terroir*. It only seems lesser when compared to the other *grands crus*, and is certainly a wonderful wine, worth buying should you ever spot it. Domaine Joseph Belland in Santenay also issues a well-reputed Criots, but I have not tasted it. Presumably, the INAO authorities wink at the inevitable practice of grapes from Criots finding their way into vats of other wines (probably Bâtard-Montrachet), so tiny is the quantity.

THE VINEYARD

Criots-Bâtard-Montrachet is 1.5721 ha/3.9 acres. It is entirely *grand cru*, located entirely in Chassagne-Montrachet.

Criots-Bâtard-Montrachet

	Hectares	Acres	Cases*
M. et Mme. Charles Bonnefoy	0.2627	0.7	116
GFA Blondeau-Danne	0.0504	0.1	22
M. Prosper Delagrange and Mme. Laurence Gagnard	0.3313	0.8	146
M. Prosper Delagrange and Mme. Jean-Marc Blain	0.2055	0.5	90
GFA Saint-Joseph	0.6120	1.5	269
Mme. Veuve André Perrot and M. André Perrot	0.0465	0.1	20
M. René Renner	0.0637	0.2	28

---

*Cases calculated on the *rendement de base* of 40 hl/ha plus 20 percent

Chassagne-
Montrachet

Chassagne-Montrachet seems to lead a dual existence. Its public profile is as a source of lovely white wines rivaling those of neighboring Puligny-Montrachet. Yet like a double agent, it has another, less heralded role: Chassagne-Montrachet makes terrific red wines. In fact, it produces more red than white: roughly seventy thousand cases of red compared to sixty-five thousand cases of white. Yet the image of Chassagne-Montrachet as a white wine commune persists. Partly this is due to the massive interest in white Burgundies and partly to its having appended "Montrachet" to its name.

The great game of Burgundy drinkers is distinguishing between the white wines of Puligny-Montrachet and those from Chassagne-Montrachet. The best I can offer is this: Look for the "tension." Chassagne-Montrachet whites seem somehow more "relaxed," vaguely softer and less edgy than those from Puligny-Montrachet. Such descriptions are anthropomorphic, I grant you, but they work for me. (In wine writing, the Pathetic Fallacy is rivaled only by the abuse of scientific jargon, which is the Pathetic Pretense.)

Distinguishing the best Chassagne reds from those of, say, Nuits-Saint-Georges is not always as easy as might be expected. They have a similar peppery, tannic harshness when young, and can often be as long-lived, although rarely as "finished" or detailed as the best Nuits *premiers crus*. Still, it is a game too rarely played and worth trying, if only to demonstrate how substantial and fine Chassagne-Montrachet *rouge* can be. The best *premiers crus* of Chassagne-Montrachet are not white but red.

It is often said that the white wines of Chassagne-Montrachet are among the most reliable in Burgundy and, according to one guide, "seldom disappointing." In looking at my notes, I confess to being frequently disappointed. Too often, white Chassagne-Montrachets have proved excessively thin and lifeless. There are exceptions, and they are wonderful. The red Chassagnes are another matter. They can be more rewarding, as well as much less expensive.

THE VINEYARDS

There are 349.7081 ha/864 acres of vineyard in Chassagne-Montrachet. Of this, 836 acres are commune-level and *premier cru*. The remaining twenty-eight acres are *grand cru*, as follows:

CRIOTS-BÂTARD-MONTRACHET—1.5721 ha/3.9 acres, of which 100 percent is in Chassagne-Montrachet

MONTRACHET—3.9873 ha/9.85 acres or 50 percent of Montrachet is in Chassagne-Montrachet

BÂTARD-MONTRACHET—5.8442 ha/14.4 acres or 49 percent of Bâtard-Montrachet is in Chassagne-Montrachet

THE PREMIERS CRUS

Abbaye de Morgeot—8.5557 ha/21.1-acre subsection of Morgeot composed of nearly all of the Morgeot *climat* (9.8 acres) and La Chapelle (11.3 acres)

Blanchot Dessus—1.1715 ha/2.9 acres

	Hectares	Acres	Cases*
Mme. Veuve Jean Bachelet and M. Jean Bachelet	0.1242	0.3	55
M. et Mme. Fernand Coffinet	0.0640	0.2	28
M. et Mme. Georges Deleger	0.1335	0.3	59
M. et Mme. Joseph Gagnard	0.1262	0.3	56
Mme. Veuve Aimé Jouve	0.3870	1.0	170
M. et Mme. Jean Milan	0.0428	0.1	19
Mme. Veuve Georges Ponsot	0.2939	0.7	129

Bois de Chassagne—13.5801 ha/33.5 acres divided into three *climats*: Bois de Chassagne (11.8 acres); Les Embazées (12.8 acres); and Les Baudines (8.9 acres)

Les Embazées

M. et Mme. Lucien Belland	2.9266	7.2	1288
M. Claude Gonet	0.2059	0.5	91
M. Albert Morey and M. Bernard Morey	1.0472	2.6	461
M. Georges Prieur	0.1169	0.3	51

Les Baudines

M. et Mme. Lucien Belland	0.6299	1.6	277
M. Charles Blondeau-Danne	0.1240	0.3	55
M. et Mme. Gabriel Jouard	0.9451	2.3	416
M. Bernard Morey	0.2060	0.5	91

La Boudriotte—15.6230 ha/38.6 acres divided into six *climats*, all of which can be called Morgeot as well: La Roquemaure (1.5 acres); Champ Jeandreau (5.2 acres); Les Chaumes (6.6 acres); La Boudriotte (5.5 acres); Les Fairendes (17.7 acres); and Les Petites Fairendes (2 acres)

Les Brusonnes—15.7589 ha/38.9 acres divided into seven *climats*, all of which can be called Morgeot as well: La Grande Borne (4.3 acres); La Cardeuse (2.4 acres); Les Brusonnes (7.1 acres); Les Boirettes (7 acres); Clos Chareau (4.9 acres); Francemont (5.9 acres); Clos Pitois (7.3 acres)

---

*Cases are calculated on the *rendement de base* for white Chassagne-Montrachet: 45 hl/ha plus 20 percent. The *rendement de base* for the red wines is lower, at 40 hl/ha.

See Morgeot	*Hectares*	*Acres*	*Cases**

Caillerets—10.6756 ha/23.4 acres divided into four *climats*: Chassagne (2.8 acres); Les Combards (1.6 acres); En Cailleret (12.6 acres); and Vigne Derrière (9.3 acres)

Chassagne

M. et Mme. Joseph Gagnard	0.0450	0.1	20
M. Albert Morey and M. Bernard Morey	0.2265	0.6	100
M. Marc Morey and M. Michel Morey	0.2003	0.5	88
M. et Mme. Jean-Marc Morey	0.0829	0.2	36
M. et Mme. Fernand Pillot	0.0270	0.1	12
M. Albert Pillot and M. Henri Pillot	0.1047	0.3	46

Les Combards

M. et Mme. Fernand Coffinet	0.2595	0.6	114
M. et Mme. Joseph Gagnard	0.2825	0.7	124

En Cailleret

GFA Domaine Bachelet	0.0720	0.2	32
M. et Mme. Georges Bachelet	0.0622	0.2	27
M. et Mme. Jean-Claude Bernard	0.2129	0.5	94
M. et Mme. Jean-Baptiste Bouzereau	0.0779	0.2	34
M. et Mme. Fernand Chauve	0.5492	1.4	242
M. Pierre Chavance	0.1731	0.4	76
M. François Colin	0.1653	0.4	73
M. et Mme. Marc Colin	0.4673	1.2	206
Mme. Roger Duperrier	0.2985	0.7	131
Mme. Jean-Pierre Dussauge	0.1824	0.5	80
M. et Mme. Joseph Gagnard	0.7267	1.8	320
M. Colin Georges	0.2957	0.7	130
M. Albert Morey and M. Jean-Marc Morey	0.5769	1.4	254
M. Marc Morey and M. Michel Morey	0.4920	1.2	216
M. et Mme. Jean-Marc Morey	0.0588	0.2	26
M. Henri Pillot	0.1365	0.3	60
M. André Ramonet	0.0508	0.1	22
M. et Mme. Pierre Ramonet	0.1001	0.3	44

---

*Cases are calculated on the *rendement de base* for white Chassagne-Montrachet: 45 hl/ha plus 20 percent. The *rendement de base* for the red wines is lower, at 40 hl/ha.

	Hectares	Acres	Cases*
Vigne Derriére			
M. Guy Amiot and M. Pierre Amiot	0.5978	1.5	263
GFA Domaine Bachelet	0.4030	1.0	177
Mme. Prosper Delagrange	1.1200	0.8	493
Mme. Roger Duperrier	0.9862	2.4	434
M. Pierre Lacroix	0.0307	0.1	14
M. et Mme. Pierre Lacroix	0.4051	1.0	178
M. André Ramonet	0.1964	0.5	86

Les Champs Gain—4.6206 ha/11.4 acres

	Hectares	Acres	Cases*
M. Pierre Amiot and Mme. Jean Monnot	0.3180	0.8	140
M. Guy Amiot and M. Pierre Amiot	0.1116	0.3	49
Mme. Veuve Paul Bouley and M. Paul Bouley	0.2262	0.6	100
M. et Mme. Fernand Chauve	0.1130	0.3	50
M. Pierre Chavance	0.4675	1.2	206
M. et Mme. Fernand Coffinet	0.1050	0.3	46
M. Georges Colin	0.4778	1.2	210
Mlle. Claudine Gagnard	0.1163	0.3	51
M. Pierre Jouard	0.5412	1.3	238
M. et Mme. Bernard Moreau	0.0708	0.2	31
M. Albert Morey and M. Jean-Marc Morey	1.0210	2.5	449
M. Michel Niellon	0.4407	1.1	194
M. et Mme. Fernand Pillot	0.0117	0.03	5
M. Henri Pillot and Mme. André Perriau	0.1635	0.4	72
M. Fernand Pillot and M. Louis Pillot	0.3163	0.8	139

Les Chaumées—7.4336 ha/18.4 acres

	Hectares	Acres	Cases*
M. Jacques Baudrand	0.3727	0.9	164
M. et Mme. Hubert Bouzereau	0.5000	1.2	220
Mlle. Marie Noëlle Bresson	0.0856	0.2	38
M. Maurice Clerget	0.0711	0.2	31
M. et Mme. Bernard Colin	0.0787	0.2	35
Mme. Veuve François Colin and M. François Colin	0.1424	0.4	63

*Cases are calculated on the *rendement de base* for white Chassagne-Montrachet: 45 hl/ha plus 20 percent. The *rendement de base* for the red wines is lower, at 40 hl/ha.

	Hectares	Acres	Cases*
Mme. Veuve Paul Jouard and Mlle. Denise Jouard	0.7975	2.0	351
M. Pierre Jouard	0.6282	1.6	276
Mme. René Lochet	0.3727	0.9	164
Mme. Yves Metier and M. Gabriel Launay	0.0470	0.1	21
M. Albert Morey and M. Jean-Marc Morey	0.2870	0.7	126
GFA Picard-Stoeckel	0.1454	0.4	64
SCI du Domaine du Pimont	0.3410	0.8	150
M. Georges Pouleau	0.5385	1.3	237
M. André Ramonet	0.0700	0.2	31
SCI Saint-Abdon	1.3097	3.2	576
M. Jean Villard	0.1960	0.5	86

Les Chenevottes 10.9901—ha/27.2 acres divided into three *climats*: Les Chenevottes (20.3 acres); Les Commes (2.6 acres); Les Bondues (4.3 acres)

Les Commes

M. Robert Deleger	0.4904	1.2	216
M. et Mme. Pierre Lacroix	0.0965	0.2	42
Mme. Veuve Louis Maurice and Mme. Maurice Blondeau and Mme. Gilbert Regazzoni	0.0852	0.2	37
Mlle. Rolande Moingeon and Mme. Marc Thevenin	0.2470	0.6	109
Mme. Henri Prudhon	0.1188	0.3	52

Les Chenevottes

M. et Mme. Bernard Bachelet	0.0757	0.2	33
Mme. Veuve Charles Biot	0.0769	0.2	34
M. et Mme. Charles Bonnefoy	0.2223	0.6	98
M. et Mme. Pierre Bonnefoy	0.0629	0.2	28
M. Louis Carillon	0.0716	0.2	32
M. et Mme. Bernard Colin	0.1111	0.3	49
Mme. Veuve François Colin and M. François Colin	0.0924	0.2	41

---

*Cases are calculated on the *rendement de base* for white Chassagne-Montrachet: 45 hl/ha plus 20 percent. The *rendement de base* for the red wines is lower, at 40 hl/ha.

	Hectares	Acres	Cases*
Mme. Veuve Louis Colin and M. Louis Colin	0.0660	0.2	29
M. Louis Colin	0.1484	0.4	65
M. Andre Crépeau	0.0827	0.2	36
M. André Crépeau and M. Gaston Crépeau	0.0967	0.2	43
M. Gaston Crépeau	1.4838	3.7	653
GFA Blondeau-Danne	0.0616	0.2	27
M. et Mme. Georges Deleger	0.3187	0.8	140
Mme. Veuve Raymond Desbrosses and M. Raymond Desbrosses	0.6388	1.6	281
M. et Mme. Joseph Gagnard	0.3807	1.0	168
M. et Mme. Charles Genot	0.2480	0.6	109
M. Théodore Jacob	0.0807	0.2	36
M. Pierre Jouard	0.2156	0.5	95
Mlle. Laurel de Laguiche	0.2242	0.6	99
M. et Mme. Michel Masson	0.6256	1.6	275
Mme. Veuve Louis Maurice and M. Gérard Maurice	0.0745	0.2	33
Mme. Veuve Louis Maurice	0.2500	0.6	110
Mme. Veuve Louis Maurice and M. Gérard Maurice	0.1132	0.3	50
Mme. Veuve Louis Maurice and M. Gérard Maurice	0.3337	0.8	147
M. et Mme. Albert Merle	0.2152	0.5	95
Mlle. Rolande Moingeon and Mme. Marc Thévenin	0.0697	0.2	31
Mme. Veuve Lucien Moreau and M. Lucien Moreau	0.1067	0.3	47
M. Jacky Moreau and M. Marcel Moreau	0.1990	0.5	88
M. Michel Niellon	0.0812	0.2	36
Mme. Salvator Peredda	0.0888	0.2	39
M. Marcel Picard	0.2304	0.6	101
Mlle. Marie Picard and M. Paul Picard	0.0962	0.2	42

---

*Cases are calculated on the *rendement de base* for white Chassagne-Montrachet: 45 hl/ha plus 20 percent. The *rendement de base* for the red wines is lower, at 40 hl/ha.

	Hectares	Acres	Cases*
M. et Mme. Jean Pillot	0.1295	0.3	57
Mme. René Roux	0.2880	0.7	127
GFA Picard-Stoeckel	0.2595	0.6	114
Mme. Hervé Courlet de Vregille	0.1643	0.4	72

Les Bondues

M. André Crepeau	0.2827	0.7	124
M. Marc Morey and Mlle. Catherine Morey	0.6856	1.7	302
Mme. Veuve Georges Ponsot	0.3108	0.8	140
Mme. Ernest Raffard	0.1271	0.3	56
Mme. René Roux	0.2010	0.5	88

Clos Saint-Jean 14.1601—ha/35 acres divided into four *climats*: Clos Saint-Jean (12.5 acres); Les Reichets (13.5 acres); Les Murées (4 acres); and Chassagne du Clos Saint-Jean (5 acres)

Clos Saint-Jean

GFA Domaine Bachelet	0.6055	1.5	266
M. Bernard Baudrand	0.4484	1.1	197
Mme. Fernand Baudrand	0.3951	1.0	174
M. Fernand Baudrand	0.3951	1.0	174
M. Guy Baudrand	0.4484	1.1	197
Mme. Veuve Maurice Boschung	0.1716	0.4	76
Mme. Veuve Paul Bouley and M. Paul Bouley	0.3294	0.8	145
M. et Mme. Jacques Gagnard	0.2950	0.7	130
M. Pierre Jouard	0.1826	0.5	80
M. Michel Niellon	0.1900	0.5	84
Mme. Veuve André Perrot and M. André Perrot	0.1657	0.4	73
M. et Mme. Fernand Pillot	0.1011	0.3	44
M. Georges Pouleau	0.1705	0.4	75
M. André Ramonet	0.4175	1.0	184
M. André Ramonet and M. Claude Ramonet	0.2021	0.5	89
M. et Mme. René Roux	0.5580	1.4	246

---

*Cases are calculated on the *rendement de base* for white Chassagne-Montrachet: 45 hl/ha plus 20 percent. The *rendement de base* for the red wines is lower, at 40 hl/ha.

	Hectares	Acres	Cases*
Les Rebichets			
M. Guy Amiot and M. Pierre Amiot	0.3072	0.8	135
GFA Domaine Bachelet	0.5994	1.5	264
M. Fernand Baudrand	0.1962	0.5	86
M. et Mme. Fernand Coffinet	0.1535	0.4	68
M. Louis Colin	0.4200	1.0	185
M. et Mme. Jean-Baptiste Couson	0.0536	0.1	24
Mme. Veuve François Gacon	0.0765	0.2	34
Mme. Charles Genot	0.0588	0.2	26
M. Pierre Jouard	0.0577	0.1	25
M. et Mme. Bernard Moreau	0.0258	0.1	11
Mme. Veuve Lucien Moreau and M. Lucien Moreau	0.1860	0.5	82
GFA Picard-Stoeckel	0.3919	1.0	172
Mme. Veuve Georges Ponsot	0.0885	0.2	39
Mme. René Roux	0.3900	1.0	172
Safer	0.7773	1.9	342
SCI Saint-Abdon	0.1442	0.4	63
SC du Domaine Thénard	0.1748	0.4	77
M. Jean Villard	0.1755	0.4	77
Les Murées			
M. et Mme. Michel Masson	0.0197	0.1	9
M. et Mme. Jean Milan	0.3446	0.9	152
M. Henri Pillot and M. Paul Pillot	0.3298	0.8	145
M. Louis Pillot and Mme. Pierre Paillard	0.2974	0.7	131
Mme. Veuve Georges Vadot and M. Georges Vadot	0.0396	0.1	17
M. Jean Villard	0.0988	0.2	43
M. Jacques Villien	0.3430	0.9	151
Chassagne du Clos St. Jean			
M. et Mme. Georges Cayon	0.0051	0.012	2
M. Michel Morey	0.2053	0.5	90
M. Paul Pillot	1.8117	4.5	797

Dent de Chien—0.6376 ha/1.6 acres

---

*Cases are calculated on the *rendement de base* for white Chassagne-Montrachet: 45 hl/ha plus 20 percent. The *rendement de base* for the red wines is lower, at 40 hl/ha.

	Hectares	Acres	Cases*
Mme. Veuve Aimé Jouve	0.1265	0.3	56
GFA Picard-Stoeckel	0.2015	0.5	89
Mme. Veuve Georges Vadot and M. Georges Vadot	0.0765	0.2	34

La Grande Montagne—8.2625 ha/20.4 acres divided into four *climats*: La Romanée (8.3 acres); En Virondot (5.6 acres); Les Grandes Ruchottes (5.3 acres); La Grande Montagne (also called Tonton Marcel) (1.2 acres)

La Romanée

GFA Domaine Bachelet	0.3018	0.8	133
M. et Mme. Fernand Chauve	0.2242	0.6	99
M. et Mme. Fernand Coffinet	0.8180	2.0	360
M. et Mme. Charles Dancer	0.3303	0.8	145
Mlle. Marie Picard and M. Paul Picard	0.3585	0.9	158
M. Henri Pillot and M. Paul Pillot	0.4077	1.0	179
GFA Picard-Stoeckel	0.1325	0.3	58

La Grande Montagne

M. et Mme. René Lamy	0.1440	0.4	63
M. Philippe Mestre	0.2460	0.6	108
M. Paul Pilot	0.1050	0.3	46

En Virondot

M. Marc Morey and Mme. Bernard Mollard	0.6273	1.6	276

Les Grandes Ruchottes

GFA Domaine Bachelet	0.1213	0.3	53
M. André Colombo and M. Lucien Colombo	0.2641	0.7	116
Madame Veuve Lucien Moreau and M. Lucien Moreau	0.3668	0.9	161
M. Bernard Moreau and M. Marcel Moreau	0.3455	0.9	152
M. André Ramonet and M. Claude Ramonet	0.1212	0.3	53

---

*Cases are calculated on the *rendement de base* for white Chassagne-Montrachet: 45 hl/ha plus 20 percent. The *rendement de base* for the red wines is lower, at 40 hl/ha.

	Hectares	Acres	Cases*
M. et Mme. Pierre Ramonet	0.3800	0.9	167
GFA Picard-Stoeckel	0.2883	0.7	127

Les Macherelles—5.1896 ha/12.8 acres

M. Guy Amiot and M. Pierre Amiot	0.4866	1.2	214
Mme. Veuve Jean Bachelet and M. Jean Bachelet	0.5382	1.3	237
Mme. Veuve Adonis Barolet and M. Jean-Baptiste Couson	0.2665	0.7	117
M. et Mme. Charles Bonnefoy	0.1118	0.3	49
M. et Mme. Pierre Bonnefoy	0.1574	0.4	69
M. et Mme. Jean-Baptiste Bouzereau	0.0670	0.2	29
Mlle. Monique Bresson	0.1490	0.4	66
M. et Mme. Bernard Colin	0.3275	0.8	144
M. Louis Colin	0.0284	0.1	12
Mme. Veuve Louis Colin and M. Louis Colin	0.1900	0.5	84
M. et Mme. Jean-Baptiste Couson	0.2101	0.5	92
M. Gaston Crépeau	0.1654	0.4	73
M. et Mme. Pierre Lacroix	0.1212	0.3	53
M. Marc Morey and Mlle. Catherine Morey	0.4334	1.1	191
M. Marc Morey and Mme. Bernard Mollard	0.1576	0.4	69
Mme. Veuve André Perrot and M. André Perrot	0.5888	1.5	259
M. et Mme. Fernand Pillot	0.0372	0.1	16
M. et Mme. Jean Pillot	0.6858	1.7	302
Mme. René Roux	0.3204	0.8	141
GFA Picard-Stoeckel	0.0858	0.2	38

La Maltroie or Maltroye—11.6101 ha/28.7 acres divided into four *climats*: La Maltroie (9.9 acres ; Les Places (5.9 acres); Ez Crets (5.7 acres) and Chassagne (7.2 acres)

Chassagne

M. Ferdinand Bonnardot	0.1718	0.4	76
M. et Mme. Bernard Colin	0.0553	0.1	24

---

*Cases are calculated on the *rendement de base* for white Chassagne-Montrachet: 45 hl/ha plus 20 percent. The *rendement de base* for the red wines is lower, at 40 hl/ha.

	Hectares	Acres	Cases*
M. et Mme. Georges Deleger	0.0600	0.2	26
M. Prosper Delagrange and Mlle. Laurence Gagnard	0.1047	0.3	46
M. et Mme. Jacques Gagnard	0.0814	0.2	36
M. Pierre Jouard	0.4071	1.0	179
M. et Mme. Jean Milan	0.0941	0.2	41
M. Moreau	0.2115	0.5	93
Mlle. Marie Picard and M. Paul Picard	0.1771	0.4	78
M. René Renner	0.0888	0.2	39

Les Places

M. et Mme. Pierre Bonnefoy	0.0757	0.2	33
Mme. Veuve Maurice Boschung	0.0555	0.1	24
M. et Mme. Fernand Coffinet	0.2790	0.7	123
Mme. Pierre Gailliot and Mme. Veuve Edgard Bruchon	0.1665	0.4	73
Mme. Veuve Adonis Gonet and M. Albert Gonet	0.2858	0.7	126
M. Jean Lemonde	0.2313	0.6	102
M. et Mme. Marie-Charles Lochardet	0.2997	0.7	132
M. et Mme. Bernard Moreau	0.2632	0.7	116
M. Bernard Moreau and M. Marcel Moreau	0.1026	0.3	45
M. Georges Pouleau	0.1399	0.4	62

La Maltroie

M. Pierre Amiot and Mme. Jean Monnot	0.1806	0.5	79
M. et Mme. Joseph Gagnard	0.3365	0.8	148
GFA Picard-Stoeckel	2.5522	6.3	1123
M. Jean Villard	0.9325	2.3	410

Les Cretz

GFA Domaine Bachelet	0.0337	0.1	15
M. et Mme. Georges Deleger	0.4209	1.0	185
M. Prosper Delagrange and Mlle. Laurence Gagnard	0.4730	1.2	208

---

*Cases are calculated on the *rendement de base* for white Chassagne-Montrachet: 45 hl/ha plus 20 percent. The *rendement de base* for the red wines is lower, at 40 hl/ha.

	Hectares	Acres	Cases*
Mme. Roger Duperrier	0.2025	0.5	89
M. Marie-Charles Lochardet and Mme. Hervé Courlet de Vregille	0.2257	0.6	99
Mme. Veuve Pierre Niellon and Mme. Georges Deleger	0.0290	0.1	13
GFA Picard-Stoeckel	0.4890	1.2	215
M. Jean Villard	0.0947	0.2	42

Morgeot—58.1608 ha/143.7 acres divided into 21 *climats:* La Grande Borne (4.3 acres); La Cardeuse (2.4 acres); Les Brusonnes (7.1 acres); Les Boirettes (7 acres); Clos Chareau (4.9 acres); Francemont (5.9 acres); Clos Pitois (7.3 acres); La Grande Borne (4.3 acres); La Cardeuse (2.4 acres); Les Brusonnes (7.1 acres); Les Boirettes (7 acres); Clos Chareau (4.9 acres); Francemont (5.9 acres); Clos Pitois (7.3 acres); Morgeot (10.6 acres); La Chapelle (11.3 acres); Vigne Blanche (5.5 acres); Ez Crottes (5.8 acres); Guerchère (5.4 acres); Tête du Clos (5.2 acres); Les Petits Clos (12.6 acres); Les Grands Clos (9.7 acres); La Roquemaure (1.5 acres); Champ Jeandreau (5.2 acres); Les Chaumes (6.6 acres); La Boudriotte (5.5 acres); Les Fairendes (17.7 acres); and Les Petites Fairendes (2 acres)

La Grande Borne

M. Armand Dancer and Mme. Charles Dancer	0.3268	0.8	144
Mme. Veuve Louis Demaizière and Commune de Santenay	0.3157	0.8	139
M. et Mme. Jacques Gagnard	0.4707	1.2	207
Mlle. Laurence Gagnard	0.2337	0.6	103
GFA Clair-Popille	0.3101	0.8	136

La Cardeuse

M. Bernard Moreau and M. Marcel Moreau	0.8113	2.0	357

Les Brussonnes

M. Armand Dancer and Mme. Charles Dancer	0.0585	0.1	26
M. et Mme. Georges Deleger	0.2370	0.6	104
M. et Mme. Jacques Gagnard	0.2885	0.7	127

---

*Cases are calculated on the *rendement de base* for white Chassagne-Montrachet: 45 hl/ha plus 20 percent. The *rendement de base* for the red wines is lower, at 40 hl/ha.

	Hectares	Acres	Cases*
SCI du Domaine des Hautes Cornières Phillippe Chapelle et Fils	1.4402	3.6	634
GFA Domaine Louis Nie Clos Bellefond	0.6977	1.7	307

Les Boirettes

	Hectares	Acres	Cases*
M. André Borgeot and M. Gaston Borgeot	0.1066	0.3	47
M. Paul Bouley	0.2297	0.6	101
M. Raymond Candiard	0.1295	0.3	57
SCI du Domaine des Hautes Cornières Phillippe Chapelle et Fils	0.3308	0.8	146
M. Armand Dancer and Mme. Charles Dancer	0.0470	0.1	21
M. Prosper Delagrange and Mlle. Claudine Gagnard	0.8577	2.1	377
M. et Mme. Jacques Gagnard	0.1434	0.4	63
M. Marcel Mestre	0.1806	0.5	79
M. Albert Morey and M. Bernard Morey	0.3340	0.8	147
GFA Domaine Louis Nie Clos Bellefond	0.3780	0.9	166

Clos Chareau

	Hectares	Acres	Cases*
M. et Mme. Adrien Belland	0.4833	1.2	213
M. et Mme. Joseph Gagnard	0.1360	0.3	60
Mlle. Anne-Marie Girardin	0.4927	1.2	217
M. Jacques Girardin and M. Vincent Girardin	0.7237	1.8	318
M. Jean Lemonde	0.1374	0.3	60

Francemont

	Hectares	Acres	Cases*
M. et Mme. Bernard Bachelet	0.1130	0.3	50
M. Joseph Belland and Mlle. Marie Belland	0.2280	0.6	100

---

*Cases are calculated on the *rendement de base* for white Chassagne-Montrachet: 45 hl/ha plus 20 percent. The *rendement de base* for the red wines is lower, at 40 hl/ha.

	Hectares	Acres	Cases*
M. Armand Dancer and Mme. Charles Dancer	0.0615	0.2	27
Mme. Georges Deleger	0.4172	1.0	184
Mme. Veuve Louis Demaizière and Commune de Santenay	0.2598	0.6	114
M. et Mme. Marc Morey	0.2023	0.5	89
Mlle. Marie Picard and M. Paul Picard	0.2382	0.6	105
Mlle. Alice Prieur	0.2362	0.6	104
M. Georges Prieur	0.3140	0.8	138
Mme. Hervé Courlet de Vregille	0.2984	0.7	131

Clos Pitois

M. Joseph Belland and Mlle. Marie Belland and M. Roger Belland	2.8398	7.0	1250

Morgeot or Abbaye de Morgeot

M. et Mme. René Fleurot	1.6188	4.0	712
Mme. Jacques Gaye	1.0457	2.6	460
Mme. Roger Graindorge	0.9188	2.3	404

La Chapelle or Abbaye de Morgeot

M. Philippe de Mac Mahon	4.5735	11.3	2012

Vigne Blanche

M. Georges de Laguiche and M. Philibert de Laguiche	1.1772	2.9	518
GFA Picard-Stoeckel	1.0600	2.6	466

Les Crottes

GFA Domaine Bachelet	0.6322	1.6	278
Mme. Jean Bernard and Mme. Veuve Max Chauve and Mme. Jean Dussauge	0.0261	0.1	11
M. Roger Brazey	0.1498	0.4	66
M. et Mme. Fernand Chauve	0.3781	1.0	166
Mme. Veuve Max Chauve and M. Max Chauve	0.2495	0.6	110

*Cases are calculated on the *rendement de base* for white Chassagne-Montrachet: 45 hl/ha plus 20 percent. The *rendement de base* for the red wines is lower, at 40 hl/ha.

	Hectares	Acres	Cases*
M. Bernard Mollard	0.2440	0.6	107
M. André Ramonet and M. Claude Ramonet	0.6323	1.6	278
Guechère			
M. Roger Brazey	0.5483	1.4	241
M. et Mme. Fernand Chauve	0.5237	1.3	230
Mme. Veuve Max Chauve and M. Max Chauve	0.7308	1.8	322
M. Bernard Mollard	0.3750	0.9	165
Tête du Clos			
Mme. Charles Dancer and Mme. Philippe Ballot	0.5712	1.4	251
M. Armand Dancer and Mme. Charles Dancer	0.3440	0.9	151
GFA Domaine Louis Nie Clos Bellefond	0.5632	1.4	248
GFA du Domaine Roussot-Lequin	0.4880	1.2	215
Mme. Hervé Courlet de Vregille	0.1500	0.4	66
Les Petits Clos			
GFA Domaine Bachelet	0.2710	0.7	119
M. Marcel Bachey	2.1040	5.2	926
GFA Domaine Louis Nie Clos Bellefond	0.2876	0.7	127
Mme. Christian Bergeret	0.2471	0.6	109
Mme. Veuve Charles Biot	0.1735	0.4	76
M. et Mme. Joseph Gagnard	0.3007	0.7	132
M. et Mme. René Lamy Mme. René Lamy	0.2298	0.6	101
M. Marie-Charles Lochardet and Mme. Hervé Courlet de Vregille	0.4364	1.1	192
M. et Mme. Fernand Pillot	0.2469	0.6	109
M. Louis Pillot	0.1277	0.3	56
M. et Mme. Pierre Ramonet	0.4812	1.2	212
Mme. René Roux	0.1580	0.4	70

---

*Cases are calculated on the *rendement de base* for white Chassagne-Montrachet: 45 hl/ha plus 20 percent. The *rendement de base* for the red wines is lower, at 40 hl/ha.

	Hectares	Acres	Cases*
Les Grands Clos			
M. et Mme. Fernand Coffinet	0.3627	0.9	160
Mme. Charles Dancer and Mme.			
Philippe Ballot	0.3254	0.8	143
M. Georges de Laguiche	1.5205	3.8	669
M. Jean Lemonde	0.1645	0.4	72
M. Robert Lemonde	0.1606	0.4	71
GFA Domaine Louis Nie Clos			
Bellefond	0.6730	1.7	296
GFA du Domaine Roussot-Lequin	0.7215	1.8	317
Morgeot			
M. et Mme. René Lamy	0.3110	0.8	137
La Roquemaure			
M. et Mme. René Fleurot	0.5780	1.4	254
Champ Jendreau			
M. et Mme. Jacques Gagnard	0.4982	1.2	219
M. Louis Pillot and Mme. René Lamy	0.1140	0.3	50
M. André Ramonet	0.4928	1.2	217
M. André Ramonet	0.7594	1.9	334
La Boudriotte			
GFA Domaine Bachelet	1.0350	2.6	455
M. et Mme. Pierre Lacroix	0.1800	0.4	79
M. André Ramonet and M. Claude			
Ramonet	0.3470	0.9	153
M. et Mme. Pierre Ramonet	0.6700	1.7	295
Les Fairendes			
GFA Domaine Bachelet	0.1068	0.3	47
M. Georges Bachelet and Mlle. Marie			
Bachelet	0.1711	0.4	75
M. et Mme. Jean-Claude Bernard	0.1161	0.3	51
M. Max Chauve	0.0693	0.2	30

*Cases are calculated on the *rendement de base* for white Chassagne-Montrachet: 45 hl/ha plus 20 percent. The *rendement de base* for the red wines is lower, at 40 hl/ha.

	Hectares	Acres	Cases*
M. Prosper Delagrange and Mlle. Claudine Gagnard	0.4614	1.1	203
Mme. Jean-Pierre Dussauge	0.1466	0.4	65
M. et Mme. Jacques Gagnard	1.1500	2.8	506
M. et Mme. Gabriel Jouard	0.2837	0.7	125
M. Pierre Jouard	1.1519	2.9	507
M. et Mme. René Lamy	0.0473	0.1	21
M. Albert Morey and M. Bernard Morey	0.3038	0.8	134
M. Henri Pillot and Mme. Fernand Coffinet	1.0312	2.6	454
M. Louis Pillot and Mme. Henri Germain	0.5746	1.4	253
M. Jean Pillot and M. Louis Pillot	0.4994	1.2	220
M. André Ramonet	0.8210	2.0	361
M. et Mme. Pierre Ramonet	0.1943	0.5	85

Les Chaumes

	Hectares	Acres	Cases*
Mme. Veuve Jean Bachelet and M. Jean Bachelet	0.1120	0.3	49
M. Bernard Charreau and Mme. Louis Charreau	0.1930	0.5	85
M. Prosper Delagrange and Mme. Laurence Gagnard	0.3149	0.8	139
M. et Mme. Joseph Gagnard	0.4830	1.2	213
M. Pierre Jouard	0.1938	0.5	85
M. Robert Lemonde	0.1895	0.5	83
SC d'Exploitation du Château de la Maltroye	0.1908	0.5	84
Mlle. Marie Picard and M. Paul Picard	0.2184	0.5	96
M. Jean-Pierre Pillot and M. Louis Pillot	0.2610	0.6	115
M. Noël Ramonet	0.5355	1.3	236

---

*Cases are calculated on the *rendement de base* for white Chassagne-Montrachet: 45 hl/ha plus 20 percent. The *rendement de base* for the red wines is lower, at 40 hl/ha.

	Hectares	Acres	Cases*
Les Petites Fairendes			
M. et Mme. Bernard Moreau	0.1757	0.4	77
GFA Picard-Stoeckel	0.6007	1.5	264
En Remilly—1.5642 ha/3.9 acres			
M. Henri Bonnefoy	0.1035	0.3	46
M. et Mme. Fernand Coffinet	0.3523	0.9	155
Mme. Veuve François Colin and			
M. François Colin	0.1890	0.5	83
M. Louis Petitjean	0.1699	0.4	75

Les Vergers—9.4122 ha/23.3 acres divided into three *climats*: Les Vergers (12.9 acres); Les Pasquelles (6.1 acres) and Petingeret (4.3 acres)

	Hectares	Acres	Cases*
Petingeret			
M. Fernand Baudrand	1.7557	4.34	773
Les Pasquelles			
M. Philippe Bouzereau	0.1475	0.4	65
M. André Crépeau	0.0693	0.2	30
M. Gaston Crépeau	0.0475	0.1	21
M. et Mme. Georges Deleger	0.4855	1.2	214
M. et Mme. Charles Genot	0.0445	0.1	20
Mme. Charles Genot	0.2160	0.5	95
M. et Mme. Fernand Pillot	0.4919	1.2	216
M. Fernand Pillot and M. Louis Pillot	0.3391	0.8	149
M. André Ramonet	0.1654	0.4	73
M. André Ramonet and M. Claude			
Ramonet	0.0911	0.2	40
M. et Mme. Pierre Ramonet	0.2790	0.7	123
Les Vergers			
M. Guy Amiot	0.0998	0.3	44
M. Guy Amiot and M. Pierre Amiot	0.5461	1.4	240
GFA Domaine Bachelet	0.0552	0.1	24
M. Marc Baudrand	0.3755	0.9	165

---

*Cases are calculated on the *rendement de base* for white Chassagne-Montrachet: 45 hl/ha plus 20 percent. The *rendement de base* for the red wines is lower, at 40 hl/ha.

	Hectares	Acres	Cases*
M. et Mme. Charles Bonnefoy	0.3056	0.8	134
M. et Mme. Pierre Bonnefoy	0.0712	0.2	31
M. et Mme. Bernard Colin	0.1404	0.4	62
M. François Colin	0.4535	1.1	200
Mme. Veuve Louis Colin and M. Louis Colin	0.0386	0.1	17
M. et Mme. Michel Colin	0.5000	1.2	220
M. Louis Desbois	0.2935	0.7	129
Mme. Veuve François Gacon	0.1416	0.4	62
Mlle. Laurence Gagnard	0.3418	0.8	150
M. Pierre Jouard	0.0517	0.1	23
M. et Mme. Jean Lamanthe	0.0575	0.1	25
M. Michel Lamanthe	0.0585	0.1	26
M. et Mme. René Lamy	0.1377	0.3	61
M. et Mme. Albert Merle	0.0477	0.1	21
M. Marc Morey and Mme. Bernard Mollard	0.8703	2.2	383
M. Michel Niellon	0.3930	1.0	173
M. et Mme. Fernand Pillot	0.0409	0.1	18
M. Marcel Robe	0.0404	0.1	18

Vide Bourse—1.3243 ha/3.3 acres

	Hectares	Acres	Cases*
M. et Mme. Marc Colin	0.2346	0.6	103
M. et Mme. Gabriel Jouard	0.4462	1.1	196
Mme. Veuve Georges Perrin	0.1890	0.5	83
M. et Mme. Fernand Pillot	0.4545	1.1	200

PRODUCERS WORTH SEEKING OUT (AND SOME NOT)

DOMAINE PIERRE AMIOT-BONFILS—The few wines I've tasted from this producer give me reason to think that Guy Amiot is one of the unheralded top-rank winemakers in Chassagne-Montrachet. Lovely white Caillerets and Vergers. Supposedly, he makes a great Montrachet from seventy-year-old vines, but that, alas, has never

---

*Cases are calculated on the *rendement de base* for white Chassagne-Montrachet: 45 hl/ha plus 20 percent. The *rendement de base* for the red wines is lower, at 40 hl/ha.

come my way. Wonderful red Clos Saint-Jean and Maltroie. Wines also are sold as Domaine Amiot-Ponsot.

DOMAINE BACHELET-RAMONET—A major source of Chassagne-Montrachet, both white and red. Regrettably, the white wines are frequently thin, watery productions despite an impressive array of *premiers crus*: Caillerets, Morgeot, La Romanée, Grandes Montagnes, and Grandes Ruchottes. A tasting of '85s and '86s—which between them should offer something of quality—resulted in one bland, listless wine after another. On the other hand, they excelled in the difficult 1983 vintage. A red Clos Saint-Jean seem to be the strongest, along with a red Clos de la Boudriotte, both worth seeking out.

DOMAINE BLAIN-GAGNARD—Good red and white Morgeot and outstanding white Caillerets.

DOMAINE MARC COLIN—A good producer. Colin makes the wine for SCI Saint-Abdon, which issues a very good Les Chaumées. The wines are generally austere and severe, which is good; they display considerable *goût de terroir*. A producer worth watching. One wishes for a little more concentration, though. Another label is Domaine Colin-Deleger.

DOMAINE JEAN-NOEL GAGNARD—Generally, very strong in the whites, but surprisingly weak in red wines. Where the whites usually are rich, if a little too oaky, the reds seem light and designed for early consumption. The '87s were unusually thin for this producer.

MARQUIS DE LAGUICHE/JOSEPH DROUHIN—An excellent source of far better-than-average commune-level Chassagne-Montrachet. The Drouhin style of slightly oaky freshness coupled with real depth and concentration make this an outstanding wine given its commune-level status. Drouhin vinifies and distributes the Laguiche wines exclusively.

DUC DE MAGENTA/LOUIS JADOT—The source of some of the best white and red Chassagne. After a few rough spots in recent years, the wines are back in top form with Maison Louis Jadot at the helm with a twenty-year contract signed in 1987. Magenta's best wine is the 11.3-acre *monopole* of Clos de la Chapelle, one of the most luscious white Chassagnes made. Some very good red Chassagne also is produced from the same vineyard.

CHÂTEAU DE LA MALTROYE—This is one of those domaines that people either love or leave. The style is opulent, almost blowsy, and is laced with a strong vanillin oakiness. The wine underneath all of these stylistic flourishes is very good, but it's tough to get past a signature that makes John Hancock look shy. The namesake wine is a white Clos de la Maltroye (an oaky, almost soupy red is made as well); also there's a Morgeot from the Vigne Blanche vineyard.

DOMAINE BERNARD MOREY—Rich, intense, rather oaky wines from an array of small vineyards: Les Baudines; Les Embrazées and Cailleret. The wines often seem flashy and overdone, but in more restrained vintages such as 1986, some restraint is present. A producer worth watching. Good red Chassagne too. Wines are sold under the Domaine Albert Morey label as well, notably a Bâtard-Montrachet.

DOMAINE MARC MOREY—One of the innumerable Moreys of Chassagne. The style of this producer is admirably austere. The signature wine is a high-acid, beautifully defined Virondot that is brimming with a stony *goût de terroir*.

DOMAINE MICHEL NIELLON—A personal favorite. I am hard put to recall a Niellon wine that was not an exemplar of its type. His white Vergers is the biggest, richest version of this vineyard that I know, more than hinting at its proximity to Puligny. Also terrific Chenevottes, contiguous to Vergers yet indisputably different. Tasting Niellon wines (and Ramonet) reminds one of how good white Chassagne can be—and so rarely is. Most others look washed-out or flashy in comparison.

DOMAINE RAMONET—The undisputed master of Chassagne-Montrachet. Although Ramonet is best known for white wines—and rightly so—this producer's red Clos Saint-Jean is superb wine with eye-opening depth and character, as is the red Clos de la Boudriotte. Among the whites, the commune-level Chassagne puts to shame most *premier cru* bottlings. The Ramonet whites seem to have an almost resinous character, so intense is the fruit. The white Morgeot is an exercise in sophisticated excess. Who says that you can't have too much of a good thing? Also, elegant, graceful Ruchottes and Caillerets. This producer's Chassagnes are the wines against which the others are judged.

If there's a flaw it's that Ramonet was famously reluctant to bottle his wines, with the result that the American importer (Seagram Château & Estate) had to haul off barrels to a *négociant* (Maison Noirot-Carrière) to get some of them bottled, while Ramonet waited until he gets around to do his own bottling. The domaine-bottled versions are considered superior. This problem seems to have ended, perhaps because André Ramonet (son of Pierre, who is in fading health at eighty-five) has turned over more of the winemaking responsibilities to his sons Jean-Claude and Noël.

ROUX PÈRE ET FILS—Based in Saint-Aubin, this is one of the most successful sources of modern-style Chassagne-Montrachet. Too often, winemakers in pursuit of the freshness and light touch that characterize the so-called modern style do so at the expense of flavor definition and depth, but Roux Père is an exception.

Auxey-Duresses

In those days, before table wines were bottled, the great wines could never come into their own, and no doubt those of Auxey could hold their own with most of those available. But today they seem quite humble things—though by no means as humble as the complete obscurity of their name might suggest; for the best of them are usually sold as Volnay or Pommard.

—JULIAN JEFFS, *The Wines of Europe* (1970)

It was the fate of many communes of the Côte d'Or to be sold as something else. As Julian Jeffs asserts as recently as 1970, the red wines of Auxey-Duresses were passed off as Volnay or Pommard. He might also have mentioned that the white wines were baptized as Meursault. It's no wonder that the name of Auxey-Duresses is so obscure.

Yet this once-commonplace fraudulence tells us something important: that red Auxey-Duresses is good enough to masquerade as Volnay or Pommard. The comparison goes only so far. Auxey-Duresses *rouge* is too hard and coarse to be a true Volnay; as for Pommard, it lacks the necessary upholstery. Actually, red Auxey more resembles red Pernand-Vergelesses, as well as neighboring Monthelie. White Auxey has some of the hazelnut whiff of Meursault, but not the breed.

The reputation—or lack of such—of Auxey-Duresses was the handiwork of *négociants*. Today, all responsibility lies with the Ax-eldien growers who bottle their own production. Now there is a new reputation: Auxey-Duresses is the most underrated commune of the Côte d'Or.

This is so for several reasons. Its wines, red and white, are austere and lean. The whites are not as opulent and immediately accessible as neighboring Meursault; the reds are lean and initially unbending. They are not wines suited to the modern world, which calls for approachability and ease of absolute pronouncement on quality as soon as wines are released, if not before.

Part of the difficulty lies in the geography. Unlike the convenient swaths of Meursault, Vosne-Romanée, or Volnay, the vineyards of Auxey-Duresses cling to a variety of hillsides. The two best sections are cleft by a valley—the Combe de Saint-Romain—with the southern flank (Coteaux du Mont Melian) really being an extension of the Meursault *premier cru* alignment and, across the breach, the northern flank (the Montagne du Bourdon) an opposite extension of Monthelie. The soils are largely chalky, with marl in some vineyards such as Les Duresses and Clos du Val.

Added to this is an isolated huddle of thirteen vineyards higher up the slope abutting Saint-Romain. It doesn't take a wine genius to figure out that Chardonnay grown near Saint-Romain is destined to be different from Chardonnay produced along the more promising Meursault axis.

Yet another element intrudes: Three times as much red wine is produced as white. In a world that clamors for white Burgundy, a commune that produces far more red, let alone a lean, hard style of red, is destined for market difficulties. This helps explain why so much Auxey-Duresses *rouge* gets blended and sold by *négociants* as Côte de Beaune-Villages; the white is often a constituent in many shippers' Bourgogne *blanc*.

So why is Auxey-Duresses underrated? Simply because the wines, style aside, are far superior to the prices asked. It's a matter of unusually good value, a phrase not often heard in Burgundy today. With the right producer and vintage, the canny Burgundy buyer can scoop up red and white Burgundies of uncommon goodness. Patience, however, is required to see a hedonistic return on this investment. The reds need at least five years from the vintage, preferably seven or eight years. The whites are more accommodating:

They are enjoyable drinking after four years, but will continue improving for ten years, vintage permitting.

THE VINEYARDS

Auxey-Duresses has 169.6 ha/419.1 acres of commune-level and *premier cru* vineyards. There are no *grands crus* among the forty-five named vineyards in Auxey-Duresses. There are seven *premiers crus*:

Climat du Val—9.3012 ha/23 acres (including the 2.3-acres Clos du Val *climat*)
Les Bréterins—1.9265 ha/4.8 acres
Reugne—3.0184 ha/7.5 acres
Les Duresses—7.9183 ha/19.6 acres
Bas des Duresses—2.3903 ha/6 acres
Les Grands-Champs—4.0314 ha/10 acres
Les Écussaux—3.1752 ha/7.8 acres

VINEYARDS WORTH SEEKING OUT—Any of the *premiers crus*, especially Les Duresses (after which the former Auxey-le-Grand renamed itself in 1924); Clos du Val; Climat du Val (also called Le Val) and the vineyard called La Chapelle, which actually is a 3.2-acre *climat* or subplot almost entirely in the *premier cru* Reugne vineyard. If you see a label for Les Écussaux, look to make sure that it is *premier cru*, as only half of this vineyard, the upper slope, is so designated.

PRODUCERS WORTH SEEKING OUT

DOMAINE ROBERT AMPEAU—A top Meursault producer who, like a number of other Murisaltiens, also produces a good white Auxey-Duresses.

DOMAINE JEAN-FRANÇOIS COCHE-DURY—This famous Meursault (q.v.) producer also makes, since 1985, a lean, concentrated Auxey-Duresses red.

DOMAINE GÉRARD CREUSEFOND—A former cellarmaster for Leroy, Creusefond has his own holdings in Auxey, including a five-acre piece of Climat du Val. The wines are austere, long-lived, and worth looking for.

DOMAINE JEAN-PIERRE DICONNE—One of the stars of Auxey-Duresses, with a good white and an excellent *premier cru* from Les Duresses.

DOMAINE DUC DE MAGENTA/LOUIS JADOT—One of the great names for Auxey-Duresses is Philippe de Magenta. For years, his white Auxey-Duresses was the reference standard. A 1978 tasted in the States in late '89 was stunning in its depth, freshness, and breed; a 1983 was a triumph, concentrated yet beautifully balanced. The wines seemed to take a brief turn for the worse as the owner's health began to decline from a serious and long-term ailment. Now, however, the domaine has entered into a twenty-year contract with the *négociant* Louis Jadot, with the wines from the Duc de Magenta properties so-named on the Louis Jadot label. The wines are returning to glorious form.

DOMAINE BERNARD FÈVRE—Very good red Auxey-Duresses from old vines. A young producer to watch.

DOMAINE ALAIN GRAS—The Saint-Romain producer also issues a good red Auxey-Duresses from a half-acre plot.

HOSPICES DE BEAUNE—One *cuvée* of red Auxey-Duresses is offered.

Cuvée Boillot—Les Duresses (0.75 ha/1.8 acres)

DOMAINE FRANÇOIS JOBARD—This great Meursault grower also offers a red Auxey from the Les Écussaux vineyard. I had it once, at the La Paulée bash in Meursault, and I never did get to see whether it was from the *premier cru* part of Les Écussaux or not. Whatever, it was classic red Auxey: firm, concentrated, obviously long-lived.

LEROY—Red and white Auxey-Duresses are a particular pride for Leroy, partly because it owns vineyards in Auxey, but mostly because Leroy is headquartered in the town. *Noblesse oblige.* If you want to see just how long-lived—and characterful—Auxey red and white can be, look for a Leroy bottling from a great vintage. A red 1937, although drying out, still was vibrant and agreeable.

DOMAINE MICHEL PRUNIER—One of the best in Auxey-Duresses. The town boasts multiple Pruniers, just as Volnay has its Clergets and Vosne-Romanée its Mugnerets. What Michel Prunier has is superb white Auxey, rich, intense, even somehow oily in a good sense. But the star is his red *premier cru* Clos du Val produced from very old vines: concentrated, intense, profound. I believe he owns the entire 2.3-acre Clos du Val subplot.

DOMAINE PASCAL PRUNIER—Another Prunier producing outstanding red Auxey from a 1.2-acre holding in the great Les Duresses *premier cru*.

DOMAINE ROY FRÈRES—A major Auxey producer—also sold under the name Bernard Roy—which has been making Auxey wines since 1682. The Roy specialties are the *premiers crus* Climat du Val (labeled Le Val) and Les Duresses. Roy is the largest owner of Climat du Val, with about twelve acres. Good wine, especially in the top vintages.

DOMAINE THÉVENIN-MONTHELIE—The Saint-Romain producer also makes good red and white Auxey-Duresses from a 2.5-acre holding.

Saint-
Romain

*When they strive only to "understand the high" without "study-
ing the low," how can their understanding of the high be right?*

—Chhêng Ming-Tao (eleventh century), *Science and
Civilization in China*

Of all the communes on the slope of the Côte d'Or, Saint-
Romain is the least recognized. One might almost say that it is
abused. It's not even mapped in Hugh Johnson's *The World Atlas of
Wines*, let alone mentioned in discussions of the great wines of Burgundy. This is because the red and white wines of Saint-Romain
are not great. However, in the best vintages—1978, 1983, 1985,
1986, 1988, and 1989—they offer unusual character, as well as value
for the money.

Saint-Romain whites lack the roundness and richness of Meursault, above which it is sited. Its elevation forbids that. The red
wines do not deliver the suaveness of Volnay or the punch of Corton.
But as the philosopher observes, how can you understand the high
without the invaluable perspective of the low?

Two elements contribute to the character of Saint-Romain: very chalky soil and high elevation. The vineyards lie between 300 meters and 400 meters (984 to 1,312 feet), well above the 250- to 300-meter "sweet spot" where nearly all of the *premiers* and *grands crus* are found.

The critical equation about elevation and temperature applies here: For every 250 feet (76 meters) you go up, the temperature drops one degree Fahrenheit. With grapevines, even a one-degree difference in temperature can be meaningful.

Exposure—how the sun hits the slope and for how long—is critical, especially for vineyards at a higher elevation. This is the salvation for the best Saint-Romain vineyards, such as Sous le Châ-teau, which are steep and easterly, catching the morning sun like a hand held palm-up in front of a fire.

The chalky soil adds its own dimension. It gives delicacy to the red wines, which already are less forceful due to the higher elevation. But it also adds character. What results is red wine of pungency, as well as a certain rusticity. It is accessible at a young age, although the characteristic high acidity—the elevation makes itself known again—allows it to age gracefully. That said, most Saint-Romain reds transform within five years of the vintage, although they will keep for at least another five years after that in a cool cellar. The flavor frequently (and rightly) is described as cherries—from wild, slightly bitter cherries to fat, sweet black-hued Bings.

It is the white Saint-Romain, however, that can make you sit up and take notice. Slightly more white wine than red is produced every year. Here the chalky soil and high acidity make the best Saint-Romain whites reminiscent of old-style Chablis. A strong, minerally *goût de terroir* is present, along with a piercing acidity—too much so in unfavorable vintages.

Saint-Romain shines in the warmer years. In vintages such as 1976 and 1983, where better-situated vineyards suffered from too much heat, the cooler vineyards higher up on the slope—Auxey-Duresses, Monthelie, Saint-Romain—escaped the raisining and bak-ing of the grapes that afflicted Pinot Noirs and, especially, Char-donnays, in the better neighborhoods. Red and white Saint-Romains retained their acidity where others did not, yet were richer and more concentrated than usual. Vintages where the wines were good everywhere—1978, 1985, 1986 (for the whites), 1988 and likely 1989—are equally rewarding for Saint-Romain.

THE VINEYARDS

There are 135 ha/334 acres of vineyard in Saint-Romain. There are no *grand crus* among the sixteen named vineyards. Moreover, there are no *premiers crus*. This makes Saint-Romain one of only two communes in the Côte de Beaune to lack a *premier cru* classification. (The other is Chorey-lès-Beaune, which isn't even on the slope.)

Le Dos d'Âne—0.6220 ha/1.5 acres
Sous Roche—15.7796 ha/39 acres
L'Argillat—2.6496 ha/6.5 acres
La Croix Neuve—4.2066 ha/10.4 acres
En Chevrot—8.6654 ha/21.4 acres
En Gollot—3.2515 ha/8 acres
Combe Bazin—13.5562 ha/33.5 acres
Le Jarron—12.0910 ha/30 acres
Sous le Château—23.8548 ha/59 acres
Sous la Velle—11.9757 ha/29.6 acres
Le Village Bas—0.8292 ha/2 acres
Le Village Haut—2.0412 ha/5 acres
La Périère—14.1139 ha/35 acres
Au Bas de Poillange—10.3620 ha/25.6 acres
En Poillange—6.5609 ha/16 acres
Le Marsain—4.4410 ha/11 acres

VINEYARDS WORTH SEEKING OUT

Sous le Château; Sous la Velle; and Le Jarron

PRODUCERS WORTH SEEKING OUT

DOMAINE HENRI ET GILLES BUISSON—Producers of notable red and white wines. The red is especially good, with an unusual density and concentration. Look for their white Sous la Velle, from a 3.3-acre holding.

DOMAINE DU CHÂTEAU DE PULIGNY-MONTRACHET—Good white wines from owner, and former mayor, Roland Thévenin, who for years was the leading propagandist for Saint-Romain wines. I haven't tasted the wines recently though.

DOMAINE DENIS CARRÉ—Rich reds from a small (1.2 acre) holding in the Le Jarron vineyard.

DOMAINE BERNARD FÈVRE—An up-and-coming producer who owns about eight acres of vines and works an additional ten acres on a sharecropping basis (called *métayage*) in Beaune, Auxey-Duresses, and Saint-Romain. His red Saint-Romain, from a two-acre holding, is good, solid red wine, typical of the village. He is the nephew of André Mussy of Pommard (q.v.), and vinifies his wines with Mussy. Worth watching.

MAISON JEAN GERMAIN—A *négociant* of importance for Saint-Romain, even though located in Meursault. For me, Germain produces the best white Saint-Romain of all, from a two-acre holding in a *climat* called Clos Sous le Château. The wine is brimming with minerally character and a depth that can stand up to many meager commune-level Meursaults.

DOMAINE ALAIN GRAS—A top grower of both red and white. Memories of his 1985 red Saint-Romain still linger. Unlike many, his red wine is more supple and less apparently rustic in style. Seek him out.

LOUIS LATOUR—One of the few major *négociants* to bother with Saint-Romain. Good white wine. Worth looking for on restaurant lists in good vintages.

LEROY—The other major *négociant* who occasionally buys Saint-Romain wines. One of the better buys from this notoriously pricey producer.

DOMAINE THÉVENIN-MONTHELIE—Top producer of white Saint-Romain. No relation to Roland Thévenin. A large domaine of forty acres sprinkled throughout the Côte de Beaune, it owns 7.4 acres in the Sous le Château vineyard, which creates reference-standard white Saint-Romain.

Saint-Aubin

High up on the slope, really the beginning of what's called the *arrière-côte*, or the back slope, is the village of Saint-Aubin. Only now, with Burgundy prices soaring, has there emerged an international market for Saint-Aubin reds and whites. Another reason is the wines are excellent in a light, pure fashion. Location is everything in winegrowing, and Saint-Aubin, by virtue of its elevation, is destined always to create lighter-weight wines. Many drinkers could do worse than to hone their palates on the better Saint-Aubins.

The INAO authorities have been lavish in handing out *premier cru* designations for Saint-Aubin. After all, two thirds of all the vines are *premiers crus*, which seems a bit much for this *appellation*. Saint-Aubin also appears to have taken its cue from Chassagne-Montrachet, with numerous *premier cru climats* authorized to be sold under an alternative vineyard name.

Saint-Aubin white wines are superior to the reds, at least for this taster. The word that comes most readily to mind to describe them is "refined." What they lack in power, they compensate for in grace. The reds often lack weight, but are appealingly stony, with forceful whiffs of strawberry and cherry. *Goût de terroir* is a strong suit in this commune, for both red and white.

The best white wines come from the vineyards located on the steep slopes in the stretch between Saint-Aubin and the neighboring village of Gamay. Here, the soil is nearly pure limestone, and vineyards such as Les Frionnes, Les Perrières, and Les Castets issue white wines of probing *goût de terroir* and pronounced almond scents. Farther down the slope, below the village of Gamay, the soil is richer, with more marl, creating fruitier white wines—a scent of hazelnut here—especially from vineyards such as En Remilly and the delightfully named Les Murgers des Dents de Chien (roughly, the big dog-tooth-shaped rocks) that abut Puligny-Montrachet.

THE VINEYARDS

Saint-Aubin has 236.6190 ha/584.7 acres, of which 387 acres are *premier cru.*

THE PREMIERS CRUS

BAS DE VERMARAIN À L'EST—3.4373 ha/8.5 acres

LES CASTETS—5.4750 ha/13.5 acres

LES CHAMPLOTS—10.9188 ha/27 acres divided into two *climats*: Les Champlots (18.5 acres) and En Montceau (8.5 acres)

LA CHATENIÈRE—8.4468 ha/21 acres divided into two *climats*: La Chatenière (17.7 acres) and Le Bas de Gamay à l'Est (3.2 acres)

LES COMBES AU SUD—24.8880 ha/61.5 acres divided into three *climats*: Les Combes au Sud (19.3 acres); Pitangeret (5.9 acres); and Le Charmois (36.3 acres)

EN CRÉOT—2.1790 ha/5.4 acres

DERRIÈRE CHEZ EDOUARD—3.9643 ha/ 9.8 acres

DERRIÈRE LA TOUR—1.9406 ha/4.8 acres

LES FRIONNES—12.5789 ha/31.1 acres divided into three *climats*: Les Frionnes (7.4 acres); Les Perrierès (12.9 acres); and Les Champs (10.7 acres)

LES MURGERS DES DENTS DE CHIEN—16.0819 ha/39.7 acres

LE PUITS—0.6037 ha/1.5 acres

EN REMILLY—29.7248 ha/73.4 acres divided into two *climats*: En Remilly (54.2 acres) and Les Cortons (19.2 acres)

SUR GAMAY—14.9390 ha/37 acres divided into two *climats*: Sur Gamay (31.4 acres) and Sous Roche Dumay (5.6 acres)

SUR LE SENTIER DU CLOU—18.0204 ha/44.5 acres divided into six *climats*: Sur le Sentier du Clou (5.3 acres); Les Travers de Marinot (9.8 acres); Vignes Moingeon (11.9 acres); En la Ranché (9.9 acres); Marinot (4.5 acres); and Échaille (3.2 acres)

LE VILLAGE—2.8544 ha/7 acres

EN VOLLON À L'EST—0.4080 ha/1 acre (can be sold as Le Charmois)

PRODUCERS WORTH SEEKING OUT

MAISON RAOUL CLERGET/DOMAINE CLERGET/DOMAINE DU PIMONT—No name stands out more in Saint-Aubin than Raoul Clerget, if for no other reason than he sells more Saint-Aubin than anyone else. This is accomplished through two businesses: Domaine Clerget and the *négociant* business Maison Clerget.

The Domaine du Pimont is yet another label, reserved exclusively for the thirty-acre vineyard called "En Pimont" that Clerget literally restored in the mid-1970s from a long-fallow rocky outcropping near the Chenevotte vineyard of Chassagne-Montrachet. About seventeen acres of it is in Chassagne-Montrachet, where it is commune-level wine. The rest is in the Saint-Aubin vineyard of Le Charmois. It is planted to both Chardonnay and Pinot Noir.

The wines of Clerget, no matter which label, project a noticeable oakiness, although not excessively so. The white wines, especially the Les Frionnes and 13.2-acre white Le Charmois (En Pimont), are the strongest contenders.

DOMAINE MARC COLIN—Excellent, precisely defined La Chatenierè from a three-quarter-acre plot. Also a good, characterful red commune-level Saint-Aubin.

ROUX PÈRE ET FILS—Excellent white Saint-Aubin, notably that from a 1.7-acre holding in La Chatenière. Also a good, well-defined commune-level white from the La Pucelle vineyard. The style of this ever-expanding domaine (they're up to fifty-seven acres now, from next to nothing twenty-five years ago) is admirably polished yet concentrated.

Other producers with good reputations (which I have not tried) include: Domaine Michel Lamanthe; Domaine Hubert Lamy; Domaine Henri Prudhon; and Domaine Gérard Thomas.

Santenay

I t is tempting to say that Santenay is the forgotten wine of Burgundy. At least among American fanciers of red Burgundy you almost never hear much about Santenay. This is odd, if only because it is the source of some exceedingly good red wines. Almost no white wine worth mentioning is produced, as less than two tenths of one percent of Santenay's total wine production is white.

Part of its lack of popular acclaim may be traced to the fact that Santenay issues a red wine with an especially earthy *goût de terroir*. When tasters talk about certain red Burgundies being "barnyardy," they could well be discussing Santenay. This quality—and it *is* a quality—tends not to show well when wines are tasted in isolation from the dinner table. Santenay, more than most red Burgundies, should be judged only with food alongside.

Producers' styles notwithstanding, it's fair to say that Santenay is a rough-hewn wine: forceful, slightly coarse, tannic, and persistent. It is a bit *sauvage*, as the French put it—wild. When young, Santenay is closed, with little of the teasing perfume that Volnay can offer or the hint at dimensions to come as in Vosne-Romanée or Corton. But with cellaring, Santenay emerges as a generous wine, with that earthy savor in both scent and taste. The good bottlings can reward up to fifteen years of age, improving with the years.

Santenay sees a fair number of tourists, although one gets the impression that it is more for its thermal springs—for which it is famous—and for its casino—the only one in the region—than for its wines. For the wine tourist, it is far afield from the epicenter of Beaune. If you've never seen Santenay, you should, because it reminds one of how wild the Côte d'Or must once have looked. Despite substantial vineyard cultivation, Santenay still has an air of rusticity that was long ago buffed smooth in Beaune and Meursault. It's also fun to wind through the hills on which part of the town, Santenay-le-Haut, is perched.

THE VINEYARD

Santenay has 378.1810 ha/935 acres, of which 307 acres are *premier cru*. There are no *grands crus* in Santenay.

THE PREMIERS CRUS

BEAUREGARD—17.9147 ha/44.3 acres

LA COMME—22.0667 ha/54.5 acres

CLOS FAUBARD—5.1368 ha/12.7 acres divided into two *climats*: Clos Faubard (9.7 acres) and a section of Clos des Mouches (3 acres)

GRAND CLOS ROUSSEAU—7.9279 ha/19.6 acres

LES GRAVIÈRES (excluding Clos de Tavannes)—23.3959 ha/57.8 acres

LA MALADIÈRE—13.5808 ha/33.6 acres

CLOS DES MOUCHES—1.5758 ha/3.9 acres divided into two *climats*: Clos des Mouches (2.5 acres, excluding the parcel also entitled to be called Clos Faubard) and a section of Beauregard (1.4 acres)

PASSETEMPS—11.4680 ha/28.3 acres

PETIT CLOS ROUSSEAU OR CLOS ROUSSEAU—15.9059 ha/39.3 acres divided into two *climats*: Petit Clos Rousseau (24.3 acres) and Les Fourneaux (15 acres)

CLOS DE TAVANNES—5.3185 ha/13.1 acres. This is a subsection of Les Gravières.

PRODUCERS WORTH SEEKING OUT

DOMAINE ADRIEN BELLAND—One of the leading sources of excellent Santenay, with a constellation of commune-level holdings in Clos Genet, Les Hâtes, Commes Dessus, and others. The specialty is a vibrant, deeply flavored *premier cru* La Comme from a 2.1-acre holding in this *premier cru* bordering Chassagne-Montrachet. Also, a very good, slightly lighter and less fine Clos des Gravières from a three-acre plot.

DOMAINE JOSEPH BELLAND—Yet another Belland, of which Santenay has several, all related of course. Joseph Belland (listed in the records as "G.F.A. Saint-Joseph") has an enviable estate: a plot in Criots-Bâtard-Montrachet; Chassagne-Montrachet "Champ Gain" and "Clos Pitois." But he really is a specialist in Santenay, with holdings in Les Gravières, La Comme, Beauregard, Passetemps, and Clos Rousseau. Of the few that I have sampled, the winemaking in every case was bright, fresh, fruity, and well concentrated. Worth looking for. Domaine Roger Belland is associated with this estate.

DOMAINE DE LA BUISSIÈRE—One of the best estates in Santenay. Lovely, intense Clos Rosseau from a one-acre holding. Also excellent Clos des Mouches from a 2.5-acre plot. The wines always are solid and well structured, requiring several years cellaring to blossom.

JESSIAUME PÈRE ET FILS—Very old-fashioned winemaking with a dominant holding of some twelve acres in Les Gravières, its signature wine. It always is deeply colored, tannic (all the stalks are tossed into the vat), and unpersuasive when young. This is the sort of wine for those who submit that red Burgundies are too light. One could wish for a touch more polish though.

MESTRE PÈRE ET FILS—One of the leading names of Santenay, Philippe Mestre is a major vineyard owner in Santenay with almost twenty-seven acres of vines, most of them *premier cru*. The domaine also has holdings in Chassagne-Montrachet, where it owns outright the 1.2-acre *climat* of La Grande Montagne called "Tonton Marcel." Mestre's specialties are a superb Passetemps from a 1.5-acre plot and a reliable Clos Faubard from a 4-acre holding. Also very good, slightly light Les Gravières from a 5.4-acre plot. If the wines have a drawback, it is that they are a bit too oaky for some tastes. Mestre also makes a rare white Santenay from the *premier cru* Passetemps, which I have not tasted.

DOMAINE PRIEUR-BRUNET—Famous for its bottling of the unappetizingly named vineyard La Maladière (the sick one), this domaine is the dominant owner with 12.8 acres. Despite the name, the wine is, if anything, restorative. Located in the heart of Santenay just above the town, it is not as robust as La Comme or as subtle as Les Gravières, but it's still a mouthful. It also is more early-maturing than some. If ever there was a Burgundy made for sausages—very good ones, mind you—it's this.

DOMAINE DE LA POUSSE D'OR—The famous Volnay producer issues what surely are the most polished, refined Santenays available from a 5.2-acre holding in Clos des Tavannes and a 4.5-acre plot in

Les Gravières. (Pousse d'Or wines are like Chinese puzzle boxes, with plots within plots. Clos des Tavanne is an enclave of Les Gravières, just as Volnay "Clos des Soixante Ouvrées" is an enclave of Caillerets, all four of which Pousse d'Or produces.) The Volnay influence is present in these wines, with winemaker Gérard Potel clearly striving to sandpaper down some of Santenay's inherent roughness. He succeeds admirably. The Clos des Tavanne is magnificent, perhaps the single best Santenay around.

Bibliography

Arlott, John and Christopher Fielden. *Burgundy Vines and Wines.* London: Davis-Poynter, 1976.

Asher, Gerald. *On Wine*, rev. New York: Vintage, 1986.

Bazin, Jean-François. *Le Clos de Vougeot.* Paris: Jacques Legrand, 1987.

Bazin, Jean-François. *Montrachet.* Paris: Jacques Legrand, 1988.

Berry, Charles Walter. *In Search of Wine—A Tour of the Vineyards of France.* London: Constable, 1935.

Blanchet, Suzanne. *Les Vins de Bourgogne.* Paris: Éditions Jema, 1985.

Bloch, Marc. *Feudal Society*, trans. L. A. Manyon. Chicago: University of Chicago Press, 1964.

Braudel, Fernand. *Civilization and Capitalism, 15th–18th Century*; Vols. I, II, III, trans. and revised, Sian Reynolds. New York: Harper and Row, 1982–1984.

Busby, James. *Journal of a Tour*. Australia: 1833; facsimile reprint, Hunter's Hill, NSW: David Ell Press, 1979.

Busby, James. *A Treatise on the Culture of the Vine and the Art of Making Wine*. Australia: 1825; facsimile reprint, Hunter's Hill, NSW: David Ell Press, 1979.

Carter, Youngman. *Drinking Burgundy*. New York: Hastings House, 1966.

Cassagnac, Paul de. *French Wines*, trans., Guy Knowles. London: Chatto and Windus, 1930.

Chalmandrier, J.-E. *Histoire du Village de Gilly-lès-Vougeot*. Dijon: Felix Rey, 1894; facsimile reprint, Marseille: Laffitte Reprints, 1982.

Chaptal, Jean-Antoine. *L'Art de Faire le Vin*. Paris, 1819; facsimile reprint, Marseille: Jeanne Laffitte, 1981.

Chapuis, Claude. *Corton*. Paris: Jacques Legrand, 1989.

Colette. *Prisons et Paradis*. Paris: J. Ferenczi, 1932.

Duijker, Hubrecht. *The Great Wines of Burgundy*. New York: Crescent, 1983.

Engel, René. *Vosne-Romanée*. Nuits-Saint-Georges: Bibliothèque de la Confrérie des Chevaliers du Tastevin, 1980.

Fried, Eunice. *Burgundy: The Country, the Wines, the People*. New York: Harper and Row, 1986.

Gadille, Rolande. *Le Vignoble de la Côte Bourguigonne—Fondements, Physiques et Humains d'une Viticulture de Haute Qualité*. Paris: Les Belles Lettres, 1967.

Hanson, Anthony. *Burgundy*. London: Faber and Faber, 1982.

Haraszthy, Agoston. *Grape Culture, Wines, and Wine-Making*. New York: Harper and Brothers, 1862; facsimile reprint, Hopewell, N.J.: Booknoll Reprints, 1971.

Jeffs, Julian. *The Wines of Europe*. New York: Taplinger, 1971.

Johnson, Hugh. *Vintage: The Story of Wine.* New York: Simon and Schuster, 1989.

Johnson, Hugh. *The World Atlas of Wine*, 3rd ed. New York: Simon and Schuster, 1985.

Jullien, André. *Topographie de Tous les Vignobles Connus*, 3rd. ed., 1832. Facsimile reprint, Paris: Champion-Slatkine, 1985.

Landrieu-Lussigny, Marie-Hélène. *Les Lieux-Dits dans le Vignoble Bourguignon.* Marseille: Jeanne Laffitte, 1983.

Lavalle, Dr. Jules. *Histoire et Statistique de la Vigne et des Grands Vins de la Côte d'Or.* Paris: Dusacq, 1855.

Lefebvre, Lucien. *Life in Renaissance France*, ed. and trans., Marian Rothstein. Cambridge, Mass.: Harvard University Press, 1977.

Loubere, Leo A. *The Red and the White—The History of Wine in France and Italy in the Nineteenth Century.* Albany, N.Y.: State University of New York Press, 1978.

Merwin, W. S. *Selected Translations 1968–1978.* New York: Atheneum, 1979.

Nicolson, Adam. *Long Walks in France.* New York: Harmony, 1983.

Olney, Richard. *Yquem.* Boston: David R. Godine, 1986.

Pitiot, Sylvain and Pierre Poupon. *Atlas des Grands Vignobles de Bourgogne, I et II.* Beaune: J. Michot-Sepia, and Paris: Jacques Legrand, 1985.

Redding, Cyrus. *Every Man His Own Butler.* London: Whittaker, Treacher and Arnot, 1852.

Redding, Cyrus. *French Wines and Vineyards; And the Way to Find Them.* London: Houlston and Wright, 1860.

Redding, Cyrus. *A History and Description of Modern Wines.* London: Whittaker, Treacher and Arnot, 1833.

Robinson, Jancis. *The Great Wine Book.* London: Sidgwick and Jackson, 1982.

Rodier, Camille. *Le Vin de Bourgogne*, 3rd ed. Dijon: Louis Damidot, 1948; facsimile reprint, Marseille: Jeanne Laffitte, and Dijon: Damidot, 1981.

Rouff, Marcel. *La Vie et la Passion de Dodin-Bouffant, Gourmet.* Paris: Delemain, Boutelleau, 1924.

Seward, Desmond. *Monks and Wine.* New York: Crown, 1979.

Shand, P. Morton. *A Book of French Wines.* New York: Alfred A. Knopf, 1928.

Shand, P. Morton. *A Book of French Wines,* rev. and ed., Cyril Ray. Middlesex, England: Penguin, 1964.

Shand, P. Morton. *A Book of Wine.* London: Guy Chapman, 1926.

Shepherd, William R. *Historical Atlas,* 9th ed. New York: Barnes and Noble, 1964.

Sutcliffe, Serena, consulting ed., *Great Vineyards and Winemakers.* New York: Rutledge Press, 1981.

Sutcliffe, Serena. *The Simon and Schuster Pocket Guide to the Wines of Burgundy.* New York: Simon and Schuster, 1986.

Treville Lawrence, Sr., Robert de (ed.). *Jefferson and Wine.* The Plains, Virginia: Vinifera Wine Growers Association, 1976.

Vaughn, Richard. *Valois Burgundy.* Hamden, Conn.: Archon, 1975.

Weber, Eugen. *Peasants into Frenchmen—The Modernization of Rural France 1870–1914.* Palo Alto, Calif.: Stanford University Press, 1976

Young, Arthur. *Travels in France During the Years 1787, 1788, and 1789.* Cambridge, Mass.: Harvard University Press, 1929.

Younger, William. *Gods, Men and Wine.* Cleveland: Wine and Food Society/World, 1966.

Zeldin, Theodore. *France 1848–1945,* Vol I and II. London: Oxford University Press, 1977.

Table of Conversions

One hectare is 2.471 acres.

One hectare is 10,000 square meters. It is composed of 100 ares (100 square meters) or 10,000 centiares (one square meter).

One hectare is planted to between 8,000 vines and 10,000 vines (one-meter by one-meter planting). One vine at 40 hl/ha produces approximately one half bottle of wine at 10,000 vines per hectare. Twenty-four vines are needed to create one case of wine.

One hectoliter is 100 liters or 26.42 U.S. gallons. One hectoliter is 11.1 cases of wine (9 liters of wine per twelve bottles). One hectare at 40 hl/ha equals 440 cases or 4.4 cases per are.

One ton of grapes is about 5.45 hectoliters of wine.

One ton of grapes per acre is about 13.5 hectoliters of wine per hectare (hl/ha).

One hectoliter = 0.0735 ton of grapes per acre
30 hl/ha = 2.2 tons of grapes per acre
35 hl/ha = 2.6 tons of grapes per acre
40 hl/ha = 2.9 tons of grapes per acre
45 hl/ha = 3.3 tons of grapes per acre
50 hl/ha = 3.7 tons of grapes per acre
60 hl/ha = 4.4 tons of grapes per acre
75 hl/ha = 5.5 tons of grapes per acre
100 hl/ha = 7.35 tons of grapes per acre

Index